Microaggressions and Social Work
Research, Practice and Education

While blatant forms of racism and discrimination have largely been condemned in our society, systematic oppression and racism can be manifested in a less obvious form, as 'microaggressions'. The term, originally developed in the 1970s by Chester Peirce to describe the ways in which Black people were "put down" by their White counterparts, has since been expanded to describe both conscious and unconscious acts that reflect superiority, hostility, and racially inflicted insults and demeanors to marginalized groups of people.

This book provides a platform for social work researchers, scholars, and practitioners to present their research, ideas, and practices pertaining to ways in which microaggressions and other subtle, but lethal forms of discrimination impact marginalized populations within social work and human services. Contributors discuss the impact of microaggressions in social work as they relate to race; gender and gender expression; sexual orientation; class; and spirituality. The book also examines curriculum, pedagogy, and the academic climate as targets for intervention in social work education.

This book was originally published as a series of special issues of the *Journal of Ethnic & Cultural Diversity in Social Work*.

Michael S. Spencer is the Presidential Term Professor of Social Work at the University of Washington, USA and the Director of Native Hawaiian, Pacific Islander, and Oceanic Affairs at the Indigenous Wellness Research Institute (IWRI). His research examines inequities in physical and mental health among low-income, populations of color, including the impact of discrimination on the well-being of African Americans, Latinos, and Asian Pacific Islander populations.

Microaggressions and Social Work Research, Practice and Education

Edited by
Michael S. Spencer

Routledge
Taylor & Francis Group

LONDON AND NEW YORK

First published 2019 by Routledge

2 Park Square, Milton Park, Abingdon, Oxon, OX14 4RN
605 Third Avenue, New York, NY 10017

Routledge is an imprint of the Taylor & Francis Group, an informa business

First issued in paperback 2020

British Library Cataloguing in Publication Data
A catalogue record for this book is available from the British Library

ISBN 13: 978-1-138-62471-9 (hbk)
ISBN 13: 978-0-367-73007-9 (pbk)

Typeset in Minion Pro
by RefineCatch Limited, Bungay, Suffolk

Publisher's Note
The publisher accepts responsibility for any inconsistencies that may have arisen during the conversion of this book from journal articles to book chapters, namely the possible inclusion of journal terminology.

Disclaimer
Every effort has been made to contact copyright holders for their permission to reprint material in this book. The publishers would be grateful to hear from any copyright holder who is not here acknowledged and will undertake to rectify any errors or omissions in future editions of this book.

Contents

Citation Information

The following chapters were originally published in the *Journal of Ethnic & Cultural Diversity in Social Work*. When citing this material, please use the original page numbering for each article, as follows:

Chapter 1
The Injurious Relationship Between Racial Microaggressions and Physical Health: Implications for Social Work
Kevin L. Nadal, Katie E. Griffin, Yinglee Wong, Kristin C. Davidoff, and Lindsey S. Davis
Journal of Ethnic & Cultural Diversity in Social Work, volume 26, issues 1–2 (February 2017), pp. 6–17

Chapter 2
Is Ethnic Identity a Buffer? Exploring the Relations Between Racial Microaggressions and Depressive Symptoms Among Asian-American Individuals
Shinwoo Choi, Jioni A. Lewis, Stacy Harwood, Ruby Mendenhall, and Margaret Browne Huntt
Journal of Ethnic & Cultural Diversity in Social Work, volume 26, issues 1–2 (February 2017), pp. 18–29

Chapter 3
"Our Kids Aren't Dropping Out; They're Being Pushed Out": Native American Students and Racial Microaggressions in Schools
Katie Johnston-Goodstar and Ross VeLure Roholt
Journal of Ethnic & Cultural Diversity in Social Work, volume 26, issues 1–2 (February 2017), pp. 30–47

Chapter 4
Correlates of Interpersonal Ethnoracial Discrimination Among Latino Adults with Diabetes: Findings from the REACH Detroit Study
Alana M. W. LeBrón, Michael Spencer, Edith Kieffer, Brandy Sinco, Gretchen Piatt, and Gloria Palmisano
Journal of Ethnic & Cultural Diversity in Social Work, volume 26, issues 1–2 (February 2017), pp. 48–67

Chapter 5

Everyday Racial Discrimination, Everyday Non-Racial Discrimination, and Physical Health Among African-Americans
Dawne M. Mouzon, Robert Joseph Taylor, Amanda Toler Woodward, and Linda M. Chatters
Journal of Ethnic & Cultural Diversity in Social Work, volume 26, issues 1–2 (February 2017), pp. 68–80

Chapter 6

Sexual Orientation, Gender, and Gender Identity Microaggressions: Toward an Intersectional Framework for Social Work Research
Paul R. Sterzing, Rachel E. Gartner, Michael R. Woodford, and Colleen M. Fisher
Journal of Ethnic & Cultural Diversity in Social Work, volume 26, issues 1–2 (February 2017), pp. 81–94

Chapter 7

A Mixed-Methods Inquiry Into Trans Environmental Microaggressions on College Campuses: Experiences and Outcomes*
Michael R. Woodford, Jessica Y. Joslin, Erich N. Pitcher, and Kristen A. Renn
Journal of Ethnic & Cultural Diversity in Social Work, volume 26, issues 1–2 (February 2017), pp. 95–111

Chapter 8

Victimization and Microaggressions Targeting LGBTQ College Students: Gender Identity As a Moderator of Psychological Distress
Kristie L. Seelman, Michael R. Woodford, and Z Nicolazzo
Journal of Ethnic & Cultural Diversity in Social Work, volume 26, issues 1–2 (February 2017), pp. 112–125

Chapter 9

"You are a Besya": Microaggressions Experienced by Trafficking Survivors Exploited in the Sex Trade
Rita Dhungel
Journal of Ethnic & Cultural Diversity in Social Work, volume 26, issues 1–2 (February 2017), pp. 126–138

Chapter 10

Religious Microaggressions: A Case Study of Muslim Americans
Altaf Husain and Stephenie Howard
Journal of Ethnic & Cultural Diversity in Social Work, volume 26, issues 1–2 (February 2017), pp. 139–152

Chapter 11

Homeless Microaggressions: Implications for Education, Research, and Practice
Gina C. Torino and Amanda G. Sisselman-Borgia
Journal of Ethnic & Cultural Diversity in Social Work, volume 26, issues 1–2 (February 2017), pp. 153–165

Chapter 12

Microaggressions in social work classrooms: strategies for pedagogical intervention
Hye-Kyung Kang and Ann Marie Garran
Journal of Ethnic & Cultural Diversity in Social Work, volume 27, issue 1 (February 2018), pp. 4–16

Chapter 13

The impacts of processing the use of derogatory language in a social work classroom

Laurie A. Walker, Deborah K. Davis, and Melissa Lopez

Journal of Ethnic & Cultural Diversity in Social Work, volume 27, issue 1 (February 2018), pp. 41–53

Chapter 14

Microaggressions: Intervening in three acts

Amie Thurber and Robin DiAngelo

Journal of Ethnic & Cultural Diversity in Social Work, volume 27, issue 1 (February 2018), pp. 17–27

Chapter 15

Teaching racial microaggressions: implications of critical race hypos for social work praxis

Lindsay Pérez Huber and Daniel G. Solorzano

Journal of Ethnic & Cultural Diversity in Social Work, volume 27, issue 1 (February 2018), pp. 54–71

Chapter 16

Examining racial microaggressions as a tool for transforming social work education: the case for critical race pedagogy

Susan Nakaoka and Larry Ortiz

Journal of Ethnic & Cultural Diversity in Social Work, volume 27, issue 1 (February 2018), pp. 72–85

Chapter 17

Addressing microaggressions and acts of oppression within online classrooms by utilizing principles of transformative learning and liberatory education

Amelia Ortega, Malwina Andruczyk, and Matthea Marquart

Journal of Ethnic & Cultural Diversity in Social Work, volume 27, issue 1 (February 2018), pp. 28–40

Chapter 18

Multiracial Microaggressions: Implications for Social Work Education and Practice

Babe Kawaii-Bogue, Sreten Franovic, and Andrew Jolivette

Journal of Ethnic & Cultural Diversity in Social Work, volume 27, issue 1 (February 2018), pp. 86–94

Chapter 19

Racial microaggressions in social work education: Black students' encounters in a predominantly White institution

Leslie D. Hollingsworth, Desmond U. Patton, Phylicia C. Allen, and Kimson E. Johnson

Journal of Ethnic & Cultural Diversity in Social Work, volume 27, issue 1 (February 2018), pp. 95–105

For any permission-related enquiries please visit:
http://www.tandfonline.com/page/help/permissions

Notes on Contributors

Phylicia C. Allen is a Doctoral Candidate in Social Work at Brown School at Washington University in St. Louis, USA.

Malwina Andruczyk achieved a Masters from the School of Social Work at Columbia University, USA, and is currently a Trauma Therapist at Safe Horizon, USA.

Margaret Browne Huntt is Senior Research Development Manager and Associate Director of the Cancer Center at the University of Illinois at Urbana-Champaign, USA.

Linda M. Chatters is the Paula Allen-Meares Collegiate Professor of Social Work in the School of Social Work, and Professor of Health Behavior and Health Education in the School of Public Health, at the University of Michigan, USA.

Shinwoo Choi is an Assistant Professor of Sociology, Anthropology, and Social Work in the College of Arts and Sciences at North Florida University, USA.

Kristin C. Davidoff is a member of the Adjunct Faculty at John Jay College of Criminal Justice at the City University of New York, USA.

Deborah K. Davis has been affiliated with the School of Social Work at Arizona State University, USA.

Lindsey S. Davis is a member of the Adjunct Faculty at John Jay College of Criminal Justice at the City University of New York, USA.

Rita Dhungel is a Sessional Instructor in the Faculty of Social Work at the University of Calgary, Canada.

Robin DiAngelo is the Director of Equity and Inclusion at Seattle Senior Services, USA.

Colleen M. Fisher is an Associate Professor in the School of Social Work at the University of Minnesota-Twin Cities, USA.

Sreten Franovic has been affiliated with the Department of Psychology at the University of Michigan, USA.

Ann Marie Garran is an Assistant Professor in the School of Social Work at the University of Connecticut, USA.

Rachel E. Gartner is a PhD Candidate and a Predoctoral Fellow in the School of Social Welfare at the University of California Berkeley, USA.

Katie E. Griffin is an Adjunct Professor at John Jay College of Criminal Justice at the City University of New York, USA.

Stacy Harwood is the Chair and a Professor in the Department of City and Metropolitan Planning at the University of Utah, USA.

Leslie D. Hollingsworth is an Associate Professor Emerita in the School of Social Work at the University of Michigan, USA.

Stephenie Howard is a Research Assistant and Teaching Assistant in the Department of Social Work at Howard University, USA, and an Adjunct Professor at the Chicago School of Professional Psychology in Washington DC, USA.

Altaf Husain is an Assistant Professor in the Department of Social Work at Howard University, USA.

Kimson E. Johnson has been affiliated with the School of Social Work at the University of Michigan, USA.

Katie Johnston-Goodstar is an Associate Professor in the School of Social Work at the University of Minnesota School of Social Work, USA.

Andrew Jolivette is a Professor and former Chair (2010–2016) of the American Indian Studies Department at San Francisco State University, USA.

Jessica Y. Joslin is a PhD Candidate in the School of Education at the University of Michigan, USA.

Hye-Kyung Kang is an Associate Professor in the Department of Sociology at Seattle University, USA.

Babe Kawaii-Bogue achieved a PhD from the Departments of Psychology and Social Work at the University of Michigan, USA, and is a Trauma/Grief and Loss Counsellor at Richmond Area Multi Services.

Edith Kieffer is a Professor in the School of Social Work at the University of Michigan, USA.

Alana M. W. LeBrón is an Assistant Professor in the program in Public Health, and the Department of Chicano/Latino Studies, at the University of California, USA.

Jioni A. Lewis is an Assistant Professor in the Department of Psychology at the University of Tennessee, Knoxville, USA.

Melissa Lopez studied at the School of Social Work at Arizona State University, USA, and is currently working as a therapist.

Matthea Marquart is the Director of Administration for the Online Campus at the School of Social Work at Columbia University, USA.

Ruby Mendenhall is an Associate Professor in the Departments of Sociology, African American Studies, Urban and Regional Planning, and Social Work at the University of Illinois at Urbana-Champaign, USA.

Dawne M. Mouzon is an Associate Professor at the Edward J. Bloustein School of Planning and Public Policy at Rutgers, The State University of New Jersey, USA.

Kevin L. Nadal is a Professor at the John Jay College of Criminal Justice at the City University of New York, USA.

Susan Nakaoka is an Assistant Professor with the Myron B. Thompson School of Social Work, USA.

Z Nicolazzo is an Assistant Professor in the Department of Counseling, Adult, and Higher Education at Northern Illinois University, USA.

Amelia Ortega is a member of the Faculty in the School of Social Work at Columbia University, USA. She is a clinician at Aldea Counseling Services, USA.

Larry Ortiz is a Professor in Social Work and Social Ecology at Loma Linda University, USA.

Gloria Palmisano is the Project Manager at REACH Detroit Partnership, USA.

Desmond U. Patton is an Assistant Professor at the Columbia School of Social Work, USA.

Lindsay Pérez Huber is an Associate Professor in the College of Education at California State University, Long Beach, USA.

Gretchen Piatt is an Assistant Professor in the School of Public Health, and the School of Medicine, at the University of Michigan, USA.

Erich N. Pitcher is the Associate Director of Research and Communication with Diversity and Cultural Engagement, at Oregon State University, USA.

Kristen A. Renn is a Professor of Higher, Adult, and Lifelong Education in the Department of Educational Administration at Michigan State University, USA.

Kristie L. Seelman is an Assistant Professor in the School of Social Work at Georgia State University, USA.

Brandy Sinco is a Healthy Lifestyles Research Associate in the School of Social Work at the University of Michigan, USA.

Amanda G. Sisselman-Borgia is an Assistant Professor in the Department of Social Work at CUNY Lehman College, USA.

Daniel G. Solorzano is a Professor in the Graduate School of Education and Information Studies at the University of California, Los Angeles, USA.

Michael S. Spencer is the Presidential Term Professor of Social Work at the University of Washington, USA and the Director of Native Hawaiian, Pacific Islander, and Oceanic Affairs at the Indigenous Wellness Research Institute (IWRI).

Paul R. Sterzing is an Associate Professor in the School of Social Welfare at the University of California Berkeley, USA.

Robert Joseph Taylor is the Harold R. Johnson Professor of Social Work and the Sheila Feld Collegiate Professor of Social Work in the School of Social Work at the University of Michigan, USA.

Amie Thurber is a Doctoral Candidate in the Department of Human and Organizational Development at Vanderbilt University, USA.

Amanda Toler Woodward is an Associate Professor in the School of Social Work at Michigan State University, USA.

Gina C. Torino is an Associate Professor in the Department of Psychology at SUNY Empire State College, USA.

Ross VeLure Roholt is an Associate Professor, and Director of the Youth Development Leadership Program, in the School of Social Work at the University of Minnesota, USA.

Laurie A. Walker is an Associate Professor in the School of Social Work at the University of Montana, USA.

Yinglee Wong has a Masters Degree from John Jay College of Criminal Justice at the City University of New York, USA, and is currently a Waiver Service Provider Supervisor at SCO Family of Services, USA.

Michael R. Woodford is an Associate Professor in the Lyle S. Hallman Faculty of Social Work at Wilfrid Laurier University, Canada.

Introduction

Michael S. Spencer

While blatant forms of racism and discrimination have largely been "condemned" in our society, systematic oppression and racism can be manifested in the less obvious forms as microaggressions. The term "microaggressions" was originally coined by Chester Pierce in the 1970s (Pierce, 1970, 1974) to describe ways that Black people were put down by their White counterparts. Pierce (1974) stated "one must not look for the gross and obvious. The subtle, cumulative mini-assault is the substance of today's racism" (p. 516). Derald Wing Sue and colleagues (2007) define microaggressions as "brief and commonplace daily verbal, behavioral, or environmental indignities, whether intentional or unintentional, that communicate hostile, derogatory, or negative racial slights and insults toward persons of color." Current definitions have expanded the scope of microaggressions to describe both conscious and unconscious acts that reflect superiority, hostility, discrimination, and racially inflicted insults and demeanors to various marginalized groups of people based on such identities as race/ethnicity, gender and gender identity, sexual orientation, ability, religion, class, and age (Nadal, 2008; Sue, 2010). Although the literature on microaggressions has proliferated over the past decade, the social work literature has been relatively quiet. This book, which came about as a result of three special issues published in the *Journal of Ethnic & Cultural Diversity in Social Work* (*JECDSW*), provides a platform for social work researchers, educators, and practitioners to exchange their research, ideas, and practices pertaining to ways in which microaggressions and other subtle, but powerful forms of discrimination impact marginalized populations within social work and human services.

This book is timely for a number of reasons. We need to look no further than the current political landscape to observe how microaggressions play themselves out in our everyday lives. Certainly, gains have been made and we must thank our ancestors who have always demonstrated various forms of resistance against what Iris Marion Young (2004) notes as the five faces of oppression: violence, exploitation, marginalization, powerlessness, and cultural imperialism. In fact, today, we have greater equity and opportunity, more representation in leadership, and just laws and policies in place to protect underrepresented individuals from discrimination then ever before. Yet, we still see evidence of interpersonal and structural inequality as discrimination has evolved from overt to implicit forms. Disparities continue to exist in health and access to resources and underrepresentation persists with our institutions, including the academy.

From the case of 17 year old Trayvon Martin and 18 year old Mike Brown in Ferguson, Missouri which spurred the #BlackLivesMatter movement to flyers circulated around the University of Michigan campus titled "Why White Women Shouldn't Date Black Men," we see the work that is ahead of us. From a presidential candidate that tweets, "If Hillary Clinton can't satisfy her husband what makes her think can she satisfy America" to a skeleton hanging from a noose wearing a dashiki on a college campus, we see the work that is ahead of us. However, as heinous as these events may be, they do not represent the numerous microinsults (i.e., verbal or nonverbal behaviors that send denigrating messages) and microinvalidations (i.e., unconscious verbal statements in which the perpetrator may be well intentioned but convey negative messages) that marginalized people face on an everyday basis (Sue, 2010). These microaggressions are often most harmful when they are perpetrated by loved ones, trusted friends, and progressive minded people like many in the social work profession. They occur in our research, our practice, and in our classrooms.

In my own life and practice as a Native Hawaiian researcher, I am also keenly aware of the microaggressions that I encounter on a daily basis that seem so innocent to others, but remind me of the oppression that my people face.

What? There are poor people in Hawaii. I never saw them when I visited.

Aren't you afraid of island fever? I could never live on an island!

You're Hawaiian? Do you surf (haha)?

Oh I love Hawaii! My family has a timeshare on Kauai and we visit every year!

What language do you speak there? Can you say something in your native tongue?

On bad days, I usually smile and answer in the most courteous way I know how. On better days, I try to educate. But as much as I feel the sting of their comments, I must understand that as a light-skinned, highly educated, middle class, able bodied, male Native Hawaiian, my story is different, and I can have bad days because in the grand scheme of things I am protected by a shroud of privilege. I do not have to confront or challenge these individuals, because oppression does not require me to actively discriminate to perpetuate it; it just requires that I do nothing to stop it. And this is how microaggressions flourish.

Although microaggressions can occur out of pure ignorance and misunderstanding, ironically, the insidious nature of these microaggressions often originate in what we are taught. They are the conversations that happen at our dinner table, college parties, and workrooms among our family members, friends, and co-workers. They are represented in the memes on the internet, the mascots for the teams we root for, television and movies, classrooms, and billboards. Microaggressions are learned through the dominant culture, which subtly teaches us to suspect, distrust, fear, and claim superiority in morals, behaviors, values, beliefs, and rationale over others. It is what some call "common sense" which is validated by their shared worldview with other members of the dominant group. As social workers, when we intervene, we often assume that we are doing so with good intentions and in the best interest of clients. We use our worldview in making this assumption. However, what we may not understand is that there are costs and benefits for making this assumption. As a Native Hawaiian, my ancestors were colonized and acculturated into the dominant culture. The intention of the colonizer was to tame the savage beast and make the native more like them, perhaps even with good intention, to integrate us into their new society or perhaps for our own salvation. Today, most Native Hawaiian people do not speak their language or practice their culture, but are still not fully integrated into society and instead witness their culture appropriated for profit by the same dominant group that hoped to extinguish it.

Thus, even in the year 2018, we are still in need of education and research in the area of microaggressions and discrimination. I am proud to serve on the Editorial Board of the *Journal of Ethnic & Cultural Diversity in Social Work* and as Guest Editor-in-Chief for the three special issues on microaggressions. I would like to thank Dr. Mo-Yee Lee (*JECDSW* Editor-in-Chief), Nancy Yates, Taylor & Francis, and the Editorial Board of *JECDSW* for their support and assistance in creating the space for these special issues and this subsequent book. The goal of the *JECDSW* is to develop knowledge and promote understanding of the impact of culture, ethnicity, and class on the individual, group, organization, and community on the delivery of human services". Published since 1990, it is one of the only major journals dedicated to examining diversity issues in social work and human services. Since our call for papers, we received an overwhelming number of manuscripts that were outstanding. To accommodate as many of the papers as possible, we divided the special issue into two issues: a double issue published in 2017, which focused on conceptual, theoretical, and research studies, and a second issue published in 2018 that focused on social work education. All three special issues were combined to make up the chapters in this book. The chapters cover a range of social identities and examine various physical, psychological, and social consequences of microaggressions. The first section, organized by chapters focused on physical and mental health, is led by a study by Kevin Nadal and colleagues, which focuses on the relationship between microaggressions and various physical health conditions. The study uses the Racial and Ethnic Microaggressions Scale (REMS), developed by Nadal (2011), one of the most prolific and influential scholars in the microaggression literature. The second chapter by Shinwoo Choi and colleagues demonstrates the moderating role of ethnic identity as a buffer for the relationship between microaggressions and depressive symptoms among Asian Americans. The next chapter by Katie Johnston-Goodstar, a rising indigenous scholar, presents a community-based, mixed method study, which documents microaggressions against Native students in schools and its impact on school climate and "push-out." Alana LeBrón and members of the REACH Detroit partnership co-author the next chapter, which uses data from my REACH Detroit Family Intervention to examine correlates of discrimination among Latinos with type 2 diabetes. The final chapter in this section is led by Dawne Mouzon and members of the National Survey of American Life team from the University of Michigan Institute for Social Research. The study found that among African Americans, everyday racial discrimination had an adverse impact on physical health outcomes while non-racial discrimination did not.

The second section of this book focuses on gender, gender identity, and sexual orientation and microaggressions. The first chapter by Paul Sterzing and colleagues emphasizes an intersectional lens when examining microaggressions across social identities, including gender, gender identity, and sexual orientation. Michael Woodford and colleagues examines environmental microaggressions in a mixed method study of trans* collegians using data from the National Study of LGBTQ Student Success. The authors found that trans* environmental microaggressions had a negative impact on academic outcomes and that systemic microaggressions exist for advancing trans* inclusion in the university. The next chapter by Kristie Seelman and colleagues draws from a survey of 497 LGBTQ college students and demonstrates that microaggressions can lead to lower self-esteem and greater anxiety and stress among LGBTQ students. The study also explores the moderating role of gender identity on this relationship.

The third section of the book examines emerging research on social identities less common in the literature, but growing in their relative importance. The first chapter by Rita Dhungel provides an important qualitative case study of female sex trafficking survivors in Nepal. She documents how these women were called terms like beysa (e.g. whore), treated as other, rejected, and objectified and how this impacted their daily lives. The second chapter by Altaf Husain and Stephenie Howard builds off the literature on religious microaggressions (e.g., Nadal et al., 2012) and offers implications for social work practice, policy, and education. Finally, this section concludes with a chapter by Gina Torino and Amanda Sisselman-Borgia on homeless microaggressions and posit several themes including: sub-human status; aesthetically unappealing; criminal status/dangerous; assumption of mental illness; assumption of substance abuse; laziness and intellectual inferiority.

The next section of the book focuses on social work education, which informs future social workers of the theories, methods, and approaches that guide their practice. Although social work educators have emphasized the role of culture, oppression, power and privilege, students continue to seek guidance and meaningful dialogue about the forms of oppression they observe in society and that they often experience themselves. Within schools of social work, we are not immune to the debilitating effects of microaggressions within our classrooms and our hallways. As a former Associate Dean for Educational Programs, there was not a semester that went by when students were not outraged by microaggressions that took place in class among students and even among instructors. Even in this current year, I have seen student sit-ins, protests, email wars, and angry posts on social media in response to microaggressions that may have occurred in the school or on campus. Schools respond to this through Diversity, Equity, and Inclusion (DEI) strategic plans, healing circles, dialogue, and reaffirmations that their commitment to social justice is sound. Yet, even in this 21st century, we still seek effective responses and solutions that will make these problems go away.

I contend, however, that these problems are not likely to go away anytime soon. Not because I am a pessimist but because I am in search of truth: honest truth about the role of social work in promoting a paternalistic and imperialistic approach to practice that seeks to make disenfranchised people conform to our oppressive society; honest truth about how we cannot have a higher level of discourse if our educators have not engaged in self-reflection around their privileged status; honest truth about how microaggressions on campuses of higher education will likely continue when they are dominated by white, cis-gender, able-bodied students from multiple privileged backgrounds who enter these institutions with little to no previous experience or instruction in power and privilege or microaggressions. Meanwhile, students from subordinate social identities are subjected to "innocent" comments and are often left to process this pain among their peers.

Thus, a major goal of this book on microaggressions is to begin with truth. According to Archbishop Desmond Tutu, "Truth and confession leads to mercy and repentance, mercy leads to forgiveness, and forgiveness leads to justice and restitution." We are a long way from restitution because we are still wrestling with truth. Therefore, it is critical for social work educators to serve as facilitators for both truth-seeking and reconciling, but we need cutting-edge tools and strategies to be successful. This section on microaggressions and social work education makes a significant contribution toward delivering these tools to the classroom.

In this section, we present chapters that address pedagogical approaches to intervening in microaggressions when they occur, ways to teach students about microaggressions, and experiences of students, and notably faculty, who experience microaggressions in schools of social work. The first four chapters attend to perhaps the most urgent matter for social work educators, addressing microaggressions when they occur in the classroom. In the first chapter, Kang and Garran present a case from a faculty development and peer consultation seminar to illustrate strategies for intervening in microaggressions and transforming the incident into a learning opportunity for both facilitators and participants. The second chapter by Walker, Davis, and Lopez presents a critical reflection from the perspective of white instructor, white student, and student of Mexican American heritage around an incident when racially derogatory language was used in the classroom. Thurber and DiAngelo also examine skills for intervening in microaggressions, and go beyond the bystander position that is often portrayed in social work to address three social locations: perpetrator, witness, and target. The next chapter focuses on teaching about microaggressions in social work classrooms. Pérez Huber and Solorzano use a Critical Race Theoretical (CRT) perspective and provide critical race hypos or hypothetical pedagogical tools for teaching about microaggressions and promoting dialogue in social work training.

Nakaoka and Ortiz use critical race pedagogy in their analysis of testimonios by two faculty of color in a university setting. This chapter goes beyond the classroom to examine the structure of the academy and how it privileges those most in line with the dominant cultural narrative. Ortega, Andruczyk, and Marquart address theoretical and pedagogical issues in the classroom, but in their case study, they address microaggression in online classrooms.

Kawaii-Bogue, Franovic, and Jolivette discuss a less commonly talked about microaggression: monoracism experienced by multiracial populations. Besides documenting examples, they propose considerations for the inclusion of multiracial populations in social work education around microaggressions. Finally, Hollingsworth, Patton, Allen, and Johnson present case examples from Black MSW students around their experiences with microaggressions and present a Racial Microaggressions Interaction Framework for understanding how students define racial microaggressions and the socioemotional continuum they follow as a result of their experience.

Taken as a whole, this section provides an excellent resource for faculty who are in need of strategies for intervening in and teaching about microaggressions as they occur in social work education. Through the words of faculty and students found in this issue, we reveal truths that may not have been heard, invalidated, or ignored. If we truly seek restitution and reconciliation, we need to take the next step toward acknowledgement to action. In combination with the previous sections focusing on research, we hope to provide a major contribution to the social work literature on microaggressions and a point of departure for future research, education, and practice.

While I had hoped that a wide range of social identities could be represented in this book, those included are not meant to be inclusive of all possible groups that experience microaggressions. This book also does not cover all possible forms of microaggressions or forms of implicit discrimination that may exist including colorblindness and post-racial attitudes. Although focused on the negative outcomes of microaggressions, the book does not amplify the strengths, instinct for survival, resistance, and resilience of oppressed groups to the extent that it perhaps should. Rather, I hope it is a starting point for dialogue and discussion among social work researchers, educators, practitioners, and students as to how social power and privilege continue to perpetuate inequity within our society. Perhaps it will lead to further reflection on how we too perpetuate microaggressions in our daily lives through our thoughts and actions. I close with a quote from the Chinese philosopher Lao Tzu who said:

Watch your thoughts, they become words.
Watch your words, they become actions.
Watch your actions, they become habits.
Watch your habits, they become character.
Watch your character, it becomes your destiny.

References

Nadal, K. L. (2008). Preventing racial, ethnic, gender, sexual minority, disability, and religious microaggressions: Recommendations for promoting positive mental health. *Prevention in Counseling Psychology: Theory, Research, Practice and Training, 2,* 22–27.

Nadal, K. L. (2011). The Racial and Ethnic Microaggressions Scale (REMS): Construction, reliability, and validity. *Journal of Counseling Psychology, 58*(4), 470.

Nadal, K. L., Griffin, K. E., Hamit, S., Leon, J., Tobio, M., & Rivera, D. P. (2012). Subtle and overt forms of islamophobia: Microaggressions toward Muslim Americans. *Journal of Muslim Mental Health, 6*(2), 15–37.

Pierce, C. (1970). Offensive mechanisms. In F. B. Barbour (Ed.), *The Black seventies* (pp. 265–282) Boston, MA: Porter Sargent.

Pierce, C. (1974). Psychiatric problems of the Black minority. *American Handbook of Psychiatry*, *2*, 512–523.

Sue, D. W., Capodilupo, C. M., Torino, G. C., Bucceri, J. M., Holder, A., Nadal, K. L., & Esquilin, M. (2007). Racial microaggressions in everyday life: Implications for clinical practice. *American Psychologist*, *62*(4), 271.

Sue, D. W. (2010). *Microaggressions in everyday life: Race, gender, and sexual orientation*. Hoboken, NJ: John Wiley & Sons.

Young, Iris Marion (2004). "Five Faces of Oppression". In L. Maree Heldke & P. O'Conor (Eds), *Oppression, Privilege, and Resistance: Theoretical Perspectives on Racism, Sexism, and Heterosexism* (pp. 37–63). New York, NY: McGraw-Hill.

The Injurious Relationship Between Racial Microaggressions and Physical Health: Implications for Social Work

Kevin L. Nadal, Katie E. Griffin, Yinglee Wong, Kristin C. Davidoff, and Lindsey S. Davis

ABSTRACT

In recent years, the study of racial microaggressions (or subtle forms of racial discrimination) has increased significantly in the social sciences, particularly highlighting the negative impact of racial microaggressions on individuals' mental health. Despite this, there is a dearth of literature that has examined the relationship between racial microaggressions and physical and psychological health. Using two self-reported measures—the Racial and Ethnic Microaggressions Scale (REMS) and the RAND 36-Item Short Form Health Survey—with a diverse group of participants ($N = 277$), results suggest that racial microaggressions are significantly correlated with poorer health conditions. Furthermore, racial microaggressions were found to predict various types of physical health conditions, such as general health problems, pain, lower energy levels, and fatigue. Finally, different types of microaggressions (e.g., microaggressions in school or the workplace, environmental microaggressions) were found to be predictors of specific health issues. Implications for social work are discussed.

Introduction

Over the past decade, there have been hundreds of articles that have examined the construct of racial microaggressions, or subtle forms of discrimination (often unconscious) that target people due to their racial background (Sue, 2010; Wong, Derthick, David, Saw, & Okazaki, 2014). Previous scholars have examined how the accumulation of racial microaggressions can negatively influence the psychological well-being of people of color; specifically, researchers have found that microaggressions negatively impact depression(Nadal, Griffin, Wong, Hamit, & Rasmus, 2014), alcohol use (Blume, Lovato, Thyken, & Denny, 2012), low self-esteem (Nadal, Wong, Griffin, Davidoff, & Sriken, 2014), and emotional intensity (Wang, Leu, & Shoda, 2011)

While there is a dearth of literature examining the negative influence of microaggressions on physical health, previous research supports that racial discrimination in general is detrimental to the physical health of various marginalized groups (Pascoe & Richman, 2009; Williams & Mohammed, 2009). Specifically, Williams, Neighbors, and Jackson (2003) conducted a review of articles discussing the relationship between racial and ethnic discrimination and health, ultimately concluding that racism is likely an overlooked contributor to racial disparities in health. Grollman (2012) discussed how individuals with multiple marginalized identities (e.g., people of color from lower socioeconomic statuses) tend to report poorer health outcomes than their more privileged counterparts. Several studies have also revealed that racism is a psychosocial stressor that engenders a stress response in individuals that may result in a physiological reaction (e.g., elevated heart rate and blood pressure) which, when sustained, can lead to serious health complications (Pascoe & Richman, 2009; Williams & Mohammed, 2009). Some scholars have also suggested that experiencing discrimination engenders a stress response that leads to unhealthy coping behaviors, such as cigarette smoking or substance use, which tend to negatively impact physical health (Pascoe & Richman, 2009; Williams & Mohammed, 2009). Perceived racial discrimination has also been found to be a predictor of ambulatory blood pressure (Smart Richman, Pek, Pascoe, & Bauer, 2010), systolic blood pressure (Clark, 2006), and sleep problems (Beatty et al., 2011). Moreover, it has been suggested that those individuals who have internalized racism and have accepted the societal view of their race as inferior suffer psychological distress and chronic health problems (Williams, Yu, Jackson, & Anderson, 1997). Finally, some scholars revealed that individuals who observed subtle discrimination scenarios had higher cardiovascular responses than those who observed scenarios that were blatantly racist, suggesting the possibility that subtle discrimination may actually be much more harmful than overt, more obvious discrimination (Merritt, Bennett, Williams, Edwards, & Sollers, 2006).

Many authors have asserted that everyday stressors, in addition to major life events, are capable of causing stress that interferes with physical functioning. For example, earlier researchers have found that the repeated hassles of everyday life were more strongly associated with somatic complaints than major life events (DeLongis, Folkman, & Lazarus, 1988), while more recent studies have found that daily stress processes have contributed to physical and mental health problems (Almeida, Neupert, Banks, & Serido, 2005; Almeida, Wethington, & Kessler, 2002; Costanzo, Stawski, Ryff, Coe, & Almeida, 2012; Neupert, Almeida, & Charles, 2007). Thus, while the previous literature has supported that overt and hostile racist events may cause life stress and poorer health for people of color, perhaps experiences with racial microaggressions, or experiences of subtle, everyday racial discrimination, may also have a significant impact on physical health outcomes.

Aims of the current study

While discrimination has been described as a life stress that has a negative impact on an individual's physical health, there is a dearth of research regarding whether microaggressions may lead to physical health problems. Similarly, research on microaggressions has established that there are negative consequences with respect to mental health, but has not adequately addressed the outcomes based on physical health. The current study seeks to elucidate the relationship between racial microaggressions and physical health problems by answering the following research questions:

(1) Is there a significant correlation between experiences with racial microaggressions and physical health problems?

(2) Does the cumulative nature of racial microaggressions predict physical health and quality-of-life problems?

(3) Do specific types of racial microaggressions predict physical health and quality-of-life problems?

Method

Participants

Two hundred seventy-seven participants were recruited, comprising 207 females (75.5%) and 67 males (24.5%). Participants' ages ranged from 17 to 63 years ($M = 24.8$, $SD = 8.44$). Eighty-nine participants were Latina/o (32.4%); 69 were Asian-American or Pacific Islander (25.1%); 54 were Black/African-American (19.6%); 32 were multiracial (11.6%); and 3 were "other" (1.1%). Twenty-eight White/European-American participants (10.2%) were also included in the sample, as previous scholars have indicated that they, too, may experience microaggressions in certain settings, such as those situations in which the dominant majority group is not White (Nadal et al., 2010; Sue et al., 2007). The majority of participants (72.7%) were born in the United States ($N = 100$), with others (27.3%) born elsewhere ($N = 75$). Most participants (85.6%) identified as heterosexual ($N = 220$); 17 identified as gay or lesbian (6.6%), 11 as bisexual (4.3%), and 9 as "other" (3.5%). Most participants ($N = 132$) had a high school diploma (47.7%); 71 had a bachelor's degree (25.6%), 47 had a graduate degree (17.0%), and 27 had an associate's degree (9.7%).

Recruitment

Following approval from the Institutional Review Board at the researchers' home institution, participants were primarily recruited (a) through a

Psychology 101 undergraduate research participant pool at a large New York City public college, (b) through electronic mailing lists of college and community organizations, and (c) through online advertisements on public forums (such as craigslist.org). A snowball-sampling method was also used, in that participants were encouraged to advertise the study to their peers and family and community members who met eligibility criteria. Those participants enrolled in the introductory psychology course were awarded points toward their final grade in the course; non-student participants were not compensated for their participation in any way. Approximately half of the participants in this sample were Psychology 101 students and the rest were recruited from community samples.

Measures

Demographic questionnaire

Because being forced to choose specific boxes of identities may be considered a microaggression in itself (Nadal, 2011), participants completed an open-ended demographic form asking them to identify their gender, age, race, ethnicity, sexual orientation, religion, occupation, level of education, place of birth, and years lived in the United States. Using an inter-rater agreement method, researchers then coded participants' information into appropriate categories.

Racial and Ethnic Microaggressions Scale (REMS)

The REMS comprises 45 statements describing commonly identified experiences of racial and ethnic microaggressions; it has been found to be a reliable measure (Cronbach's $\alpha = 0.912$) for African-Americans, Asian-Americans, Latina/o Americans, multiracial people, and White Americans (Nadal, 2011). The REMS is composed of six subscales: Assumptions of Inferiority, Second-Class Citizen and Assumptions of Criminality, Microinvalidations, Exoticization and Assumptions of Similarity, Environmental Microaggressions, and Workplace/School Microaggressions(Nadal, 2011). Cronbach's alphas for the subscales of the REMS range from .783 to .837. Sample items include "Someone did not believe me when I told them I was born in the United States" (Exoticization) and "My opinion was overlooked in a group discussion because of my race" (Workplace/School Microaggressions). Participants are asked to reflect on the previous six months and report whether they had experienced each microaggression during that time (0 = no, 1 = yes). Certain items are reverse-scored such that overall higher scores indicate a greater number of experiences with microaggressions (for example, "I observed people of my race portrayed positively in movies"). The REMS has been reported to have a moderate positive correlation ($r = .464$) with the Racism and Life Experiences Scale—Brief

Version (Utsey, 1998) and a large positive correlation ($r = .698$) with the Daily Life Experiences—Frequency scale (Harrell, 2000). For the current sample, the Cronbach's alpha of the REMS-Total was .898, and subscales ranged from .778 to .823.

RAND 36-Item Short Form Health Survey—Version 1.0 (SF-36)

The RAND 36-Item Short Form Health Survey—Version 1.0 (Brazier et al., 1992) is a quality-of-life measure comprising 36 multiple-choice questions regarding physical and mental health. The SF-36 may be administered in a self-report fashion and results in eight subscale scores: physical functioning, social functioning, role limitations (physical problems), role limitations (emotional problems), pain, mental health, vitality, and general health perception. This measure has been found to have good reliability (Brazier et al., 1992), internal consistency (VanderZee, Sanderman, Heyink, & De Haes, 1996), and convergent validity with related health measures (Brazier et al., 1992; VanderZee et al., 1996). The SF-36 is an appropriate measure for community samples, as it is brief, yet sensitive enough to detect low levels of poor health in patients who received a score of "good health" on the Nottingham Health Profile (Brazier et al., 1992). For the current sample, the Cronbach's alpha of the RAND-36 was .905 and subscales ranged from .878 to .895.

Procedure

All measures were administered online using a survey hosted by the website www.SurveyMonkey.com. First, participants were presented with a statement of informed consent and indicated their understanding of the form and consent to participate by continuing on to the first page of the survey. Participants then filled out a demographic questionnaire, the Racial and Ethnic Microaggressions Scale (REMS), and the RAND 36-item Health Survey (SF-36). Participation consisted of a single session of approximately 20 to 30 minutes, and participants were presented with a debriefing statement at the completion of the survey.

Results

To examine the relationship between racial microaggressions and quality of life, a Pearson's correlation was run with the REMS average score and each RAND SF-36 scale. To control for Type I Error, we used a Bonferroni correction with an alpha of .01; all correlations are presented in Table 1. Results indicate a significant negative correlation between REMS average and seven of the eight RAND SF-36 average scale scores. These include a significant negative correlation between REMS average and Scale 2: Role

Table 1. Correlation matrix of predictor and dependent variables.

	1	2	3	4	5	6	7	8	9
1. REMS Total	1	−0.06	−.25**	−.29**	−.22**	−.19**	−.31**	−.21**	−.18**
2. Physical Functioning		1	.36**	0.09	0.08	.13*	.28**	.18**	.18**
3. Role Limitations Due to Physical Problems			1	.31**	.21**	.16*	.40**	.41**	.26**
4. Role Limitations Due to Emotional Problems				1	.46**	.49**	.55**	.25**	.24**
5. Energy and Fatigue					1	.69**	.51**	.34**	.40**
6. Emotional Well-being						1	.57**	.28**	.34**
7. Social Functioning							1	.46**	.35**
8. Pain								1	.40**
9. General Health									1

* Correlation is significant at the 0.05 level (two-tailed). ** Correlation is significant at the 0.01 level (two-tailed).

Limitations Due to Physical Health ($r = -.253$, $N = 256$, $p = .01$, two-tailed), Scale 3: Role Limitations Due to Emotional Problems ($r = -.286$, $N = 256$, $p = .01$, two-tailed), Scale 4: Energy/Fatigue ($r = -.216$, $N = 255$, $p = .01$, two-tailed), Scale 5: Emotional Well-being ($r = -.190$, $N = 255$, $p = .01$, two-tailed), Scale 6: Social Functioning ($r = -.314$, $N = 255$, $p = .01$, two-tailed), Scale 7: Pain ($r = -.212$, $N = 256$, $p = .01$, two-tailed), and Scale 8: General Health ($r = -.178$, $N = 258$, $p = .01$, two-tailed).

To examine whether the cumulative experience of racial microaggressions predicts specific types of physical health problems, we conducted a regression with REMS average scores as the independent variable and each RAND SF-36 scale as a dependent variable. To control for Type I error, we used a Bonferroni correction of .006; results indicate that REMS average is a predictor of seven of eight RAND SF-36 scales; these include Scale 2: Role Limitations Due to Physical Health, $F(1, 254) = 17.39$, $p < .001$, Scale 3: Role Limitations Due to Emotional Problems, $F(1, 254) = 22.63$, $p < .001$, Scale 4: Energy/Fatigue, $F(1, 253) = 12.38$, $p = .001$, Scale 5: Emotional Well-being, $F(1, 253) = 943$, $p = .002$, Scale 6: Social Functioning, $F(1, 253) = 27.65$, $p = .001$, Scale 7: Pain, $F(1, 254) = 12.01$, $p = .001$, and Scale 8: General Health, $F(1, 256) = 8.36$, $p = .004$. Significant findings accounted for 2.8% to 9.5% of the variance.

To explore whether specific types of microaggressions predicted specific types of physical health and quality-of-life problems, a stepwise method of regression was utilized examining all six REMS subscales as predictor variables and each RAND SF-36 scale as an outcome variable. For Scale 2: Role Limitations Due to Physical Health, a significant model emerged for Workplace and School Microaggressions, $F(6, 249) = 3.71$, $p = .002$, accounting for 6.0% of the variance. For Scale 3: Role Limitations Due to Emotional Problems, a significant model emerged for Environmental Microaggressions and Workplace and School Microaggressions, $F(6, 249) = 5.01$, $p < .001$, accounting for 8.7% of the variance. For Scale 4: Energy/Fatigue, a significant model emerged for Environmental Microaggressions, $F(6, 248) = 3.15$, $p = .005$, accounting for 4.8% of the variance. For Scale 5: Emotional Well-being, a significant model emerged for Workplace and School Microaggressions, $F(6, 248) = 2.98$, $p = .008$, accounting for 4.5% of the variance. For Scale 6: Social Functioning, a significant model emerged for Assumptions of Inferiority and Workplace and School Microaggressions, $F(6, 248) = 6.32$, $p < .001$, accounting for 11.2% of the variance. For Scale 7: Pain, a significant model emerged for Assumptions of Inferiority Microaggressions, $F(1, 254) = 11.41$, $p = .001$, which accounted for 3.9% of the variance. None of the REMS subscales were significant predictors of RAND SF-36 Scale 1: Physical Functioning and Scale 8: General Health ($p > .008$).

Discussion

The results of the present, exploratory study suggest that being a repeated target of racial microaggressions is connected to poorer physical health. First, the current study found a significant negative correlation between the cumulative experience of racial microaggressions and seven of the eight scales of the health measure. While these effect sizes are small (i.e., r-scores ranged from .178 to .286), these results provide some preliminary support that there is a significant, negative relationship between racial microaggressions and health. First, the overall experience of microaggressions was significantly negatively correlated with role limitations due to physical health, as well as role limitations due to emotional problems. This finding suggests that the more microaggressions experienced by an individual, the less able they would be to fulfill various roles and obligations due to increased physical and emotional difficulties. Second, one's energy levels, emotional well-being, social functioning, and pain were also significantly negatively correlated with one's overall experience of microaggressions; thus, an individual who experiences more microaggressions may also tend to have lower energy levels, poorer emotional well-being, more inferior social functioning, and higher levels of pain. Moreover, the experience of microaggressions was negatively correlated with general health, indicating that consistently perceiving experiences of microaggressions can be connected to poorer overall health.

Regression analyses support that experiences with racial microaggressions may predict several types of health issues including (a) role limitations due to physical health, (b) role limitations due to emotional problems, (c) energy and fatigue, (d) emotional well-being, (e) social functioning, (f) pain, and (g) general health problems. Results also indicate that specific types of microaggressions were predictors of almost all of the measured physical health outcomes. First, microaggressions experienced in school and workplace settings were indicative of role limitations due to physical health, role limitations due to emotional problems, emotional well-being, and social functioning. Second, environmental microaggressions were predictors of role limitations due to emotional problems, as well as energy and fatigue. Finally, being treated like an inferior predicted increased pain and lower social functioning. Despite these findings, only a small amount of variance was accounted for in all of these regressions (ranging from 2.8 to 11.4%), suggesting that there are other mediating variables that may contribute to the relationship. Despite this, these preliminary findings provide initial support that the cumulative nature of microaggressions may indeed be harmful to individuals' physical health.

Implications for social work

The current study has many implications for social work—particularly for research and clinical practice. First, because it is one of the only known studies to quantitatively describe the relationship between racial microaggressions and physical health, it provides support that the study of microaggressions is valid, particularly in advocating for the health needs of people of color and other marginalized groups. Accordingly, it is crucial to further study and address microaggressions, particularly since such experiences are likely to negatively influence people of color's physical health. Second, aligned with previous research on physical health and racial discrimination (e.g., Pascoe & Richman, 2009; Williams & Mohammed, 2009; Williams et al., 2003), this study supports that there is also a connection between subtle forms of discrimination with physical health problems. Likewise, in addition to the previous research regarding the relationship between racial microaggressions and mental health (e.g., Nadal, Griffin, et al., 2014; Wang et al., 2011) and health behaviors (e.g., Blume et al., 2012), this study adds to the current literature by supporting that racial microaggressions also influence physical health. Furthermore, given that the field of social work emphasizes the importance of understanding individuals' development from an ecological systems perspective (Siporin, 1980; Ungar, 2002), the findings from this study can be used to further understand how systemic discrimination may influence microaggressions, while also further promoting the notion that both subtle and overt discrimination may impact individuals' physical and psychological health.

Future social work and public health researchers can examine the influence of racial microaggressions on more specific health issues (e.g., cardiovascular health, diabetes, etc.), particularly since these disparities have been known to be prevalent within communities of color (see Williams & Mohammed, 2009). In addition, perhaps future research can focus on other moderating and mediating variables to physical health (e.g., mental health, social support, racial and ethnic identity, etc.) as a way of discovering protective factors and risk factors that may positively or negatively influence the relationship between microaggressions and physical health. One final area for future research is to examine how multiple demographic identities may influence individuals' experiences with microaggressions. Given that intersectional identities are important to understanding individuals' experiences and worldviews, it is necessary to explore how multiple identities may also influence individuals' experiences with microaggressions. For instance, Balsam, Molina, Beadnell, Simoni, and Walters (2011) have found that lesbian, gay, and bisexual (LGB) people of color may experience microaggressions differently as a result of their sexual orientations, genders, and racial/ethnic groups; for instance, their findings include that gay and bisexual men of color reported higher frequencies of racial and heterosexist microaggressions than LGB women, while LGB Asian-Americans reported higher frequencies of microaggressions than their LGB Black and Latina/o counterparts. Similarly, another study that examined microaggressions among Latina/os found that gender, ethnicity, age, and educational level all influenced the types of microaggressions that people experience (Nadal, Mazzula, Rivera, & Fujii-Doe, 2014). Future researchers can continue to investigate these differences, as well as how microaggressions may affect these subgroups' health and health behaviors.

For clinical social workers (and other practitioners), results from this study can be applied to work with clients in a number of ways. First, practitioners can educate their patients and others about microaggressions, so that patients are aware of how subtle discrimination may negatively influence their physical and mental health. If clients were knowledgeable of the definition and examples of microaggressions, perhaps they could develop better ways of coping with such instances, instead of internalizing their negative emotional reactions. In addition, it may be helpful for social workers and other clinicians specifically to discuss clients' experiences with microaggressions in psychotherapy sessions as a way of validating their experiences, while also ensuring that their clients are coping with such experiences in healthy ways. Finally, social workers and other educators may be particularly interested in teaching others about the negative influences of microaggressions on physical health, as a way of preventing such future behavior. If individuals were aware that their discriminatory behaviors, whether intentional or unintentional, had a significant influence on the health of victims, perhaps the frequency of microaggressions would decrease, which could potentially result in a decrease in physical health problems for people of color and other marginalized groups.

Limitations

Although the study was one of the first to substantiate the link between racial microaggressions and physical health outcomes, it is critical to recognize its limitations. First, as aforementioned, because effect sizes were small for both the correlations and regressions, it can be inferred that there are other mediating variables that influence the relationship between racial microaggressions and health. Second, convenient sampling was employed, as many of the participants were recruited at a specific college in the Northeast; thus, results may not be generalizable to other populations. Similarly, there were a greater number of female participants and the sample was younger in age; thus, results may not accurately represent experiences of men or of older populations. Finally, we used a general measure of physical health, which may limit our knowledge of the impact of microaggressions on specific types of physical health.

Despite these limitations, the current study further contributes to our understanding of the negative impacts of microaggressions on people's physical and psychological health. Results support that racial microaggressions are highly injurious in people's lives and indicate the need for further research on the study. Furthermore, given that racial microaggressions were found to be highly correlated with physical health issues like energy levels and pain, as well as psychological health issues like emotional well-being and social functioning, the study supports that microaggressions need to be validated as a legitimate problem in our society. In recognizing this, perhaps we can better address the many health disparities of people of color in the United States.

References

Almeida, D. M., Neupert, S. D., Banks, S. R., & Serido, J. (2005). Do daily stress processes account for socioeconomic health disparities? *The Journals of Gerontology Series B: Psychological Sciences and Social Sciences*, *60*, S34–S39. doi:10.1093/geronb/60. Special_Issue_2.S34

Almeida, D. M., Wethington, E., & Kessler, R. C. (2002). The daily inventory of stressful events: An interview-based approach for measuring daily stressors. *Assessment*, *9*(1), 41–55. doi:10.1177/1073191102009001006

Balsam, K., Molina, Y., Beadnell, B., Simoni, J., & Walters, K. (2011). Measuring multiple minority stress: The LGBT people of color microaggressions scale. *Cultural Diversity and Ethnic Minority Psychology*, *17*(2), 163–174. doi:10.1037/a0023244

Beatty, D. L., Hall, M. H., Kamarck, T. A., Buysse, D. J., Owens, J. F., Reis, S. E.,... Matthews, K. A. (2011). Unfair treatment is associated with poor sleep in African American and Caucasian adults: Pittsburgh SleepSCORE project. *Health Psychology*, *30*(3), 351–359. doi:10.1037/a0022976

Blume, A. W., Lovato, L. V., Thyken, B. N., & Denny, N. (2012). The relationship of microaggressions with alcohol use and anxiety among ethnic minority college students in a historically White institution. *Cultural Diversity and Ethnic Minority Psychology*, *18*(1), 45–54. doi:10.1037/a0025457

Brazier, J. E., Harper, R., Jones, N. M. B., O-Cathain, A., Thomas, K. J., Usherwood, T., & Westlake, L. (1992). Validating the SF-36 Health Survey Questionnaire: New outcome measure for primary care. *British Medical Journal*, *305*, 160–164. doi:10.1136/bmj.305.6846.160

Clark, R. (2006). Perceived racism and vascular reactivity in Black college women: Moderating effects of seeking social support. *Health Psychology*, *25*(1), 20–25. doi:10.1037/0278-6133.25.1.20

Costanzo, E. S., Stawski, R. S., Ryff, C. D., Coe, C. L., & Almeida, D. M. (2012). Cancer survivors' responses to daily stressors: Implications for quality of life. *Health Psychology*, *31*, 360–370. Advance online publication. doi:10.1037/a0027018

DeLongis, A., Folkman, S., & Lazarus, R. S. (1988). The impact of daily stress on health and mood: Psychological and social resources as mediators. *Journal of Personality and Social Psychology*, *54*(3), 486–495. doi:10.1037/0022-3514.54.3.486

Grollman, E. A. (2012). Multiple forms of perceived discrimination and health among adolescents and young adults. *Journal of Health and Social Behavior*, *53*(2), 199–214.

Harrell, S. P. (2000). A multidimensional conceptualization of racism-related stress: Implications for the well-being of people of color. *American Journal of Orthopsychiatry*, *70*, 42–57. doi:10.1037/h0087722

Merritt, M. M., Bennett, G. G., Williams, R. B., Edwards, C. L., & Sollers, J. J. (2006). Perceived racism and cardiovascular reactivity and recovery to personally relevant stress. *Health Psychology*, *25*(3), 364–369. doi:10.1037/0278-6133.25.3.364

Nadal, K. L. (2011). The Racial and Ethnic Microaggressions Scale (REMS): Construction, reliability, and validity. *Journal of Counseling Psychology*, *58*(4), 470–480. doi:10.1037/a0025193

Nadal, K. L., Griffin, K., Vargas, V., Issa, M., Lyons, O., & Tobio, M. (2010). Processes and struggles with racial microaggressions from the White American perspective: Recommendations for workplace settings. In M. Paludi, E. DeSouza, & C. Paludi Jr. (Eds.), *The Praeger handbook on understanding and preventing workplace discrimination: Legal, management, and social science perspectives* (pp. 155–180). Santa Barbara, CA: Praeger.

Nadal, K. L., Griffin, K. E., Wong, Y., Hamit, S., & Rasmus, M. (2014). The impact of racial microaggressions on mental health: Counseling implications for clients of color. *Journal of Counseling & Development*, *92*(1), 57–66. doi:10.1002/j.1556-6676.2014.00130.x

Nadal, K. L., Mazzula, S. L., Rivera, D. P., & Fujii-Doe, W. (2014). Microaggressions and Latina/o Americans: An analysis of nativity, gender, and ethnicity. *Journal of Latina/o Psychology*, *2*(2), 67–78. doi:10.1037/lat0000013

Nadal, K. L., Wong, Y., Griffin, K. E., Davidoff, K., & Sriken, J. (2014). The adverse impact of racial microaggressions on college students' self-esteem. *Journal of College Student Development*, *55*(5), 461–474. doi:10.1353/csd.2014.0051

Neupert, S. D., Almeida, D. M., & Charles, S. T. (2007). Age differences in reactivity to daily stressors: The role of personal control. *The Journals of Gerontology Series B: Psychological Sciences and Social Sciences*, *62*, P216–P225. doi:10.1093/geronb/62.4.P216

Pascoe, E. A., & Richman, L. S. (2009). Perceived discrimination and health: A meta-analytic review. *Psychological Bulletin*, *135*(4), 531–554. doi:10.1037/a0016059

Siporin, M. (1980). Ecological systems theory in social work. *Journal of Sociology & Social Welfare*, *7*, 507.

Smart Richman, L., Pek, J., Pascoe, E., & Bauer, D. J. (2010). The effects of perceived discrimination on ambulatory blood pressure and affective responses to interpersonal stress modeled over 24 hours. *Health Psychology*, *29*(4), 403–411. doi:10.1037/a0019045

Sue, D. W. (2010). *Microaggressions in everyday life: Race, gender, and sexual orientation*. New York, NY: Wiley & Sons.

Sue, D. W., Capodilupo, C. M., Torino, G. C., Bucceri, J. M., Holder, A. M. B., Nadal, K. L., & Esquilin, M. (2007). Racial microaggressions in everyday life: Implications for clinical practice. *American Psychologist, 62*(4), 271–286. doi:10.1037/0003-066X.62.4.271

Ungar, M. (2002). A deeper, more social ecological social work practice. *Social Service Review, 76*(3), 480–497. doi:10.1086/341185

Utsey, S. O. (1998). Assessing the stressful effects of racism: A review of instrumentation. *Journal of Black Psychology, 24,* 269–288. doi:10.1177/00957984980243001

VanderZee, K. I., Sanderman, R., Heyink, J. W., & De Haes, H. (1996). Psychometric qualities of the RAND 36-Item Health Survey 1.0: A multidimensional measure of general health status. *International Journal of Behavioral Medicine, 3*(2), 104–122. doi:10.1207/s15327558ijbm0302_2

Wang, J., Leu, J., & Shoda, Y. (2011). When the seemingly innocuous "stings": Racial microaggressions and their emotional consequences. *Personality and Social Psychology Bulletin, 37*(12), 1666–1678. doi:10.1177/0146167211416130

Williams, D. R., & Mohammed, S. A. (2009). Discrimination and racial disparities in health: Evidence and needed research. *Journal of Behavioral Medicine, 32*(1), 20–47. doi:10.1007/s10865-008-9185-0

Williams, D. R., Neighbors, H. W., & Jackson, J. S. (2003). Racial/ethnic discrimination and health: Findings from community studies. *American Journal of Public Health, 93*(2), 200–208. doi:10.2105/AJPH.93.2.200

Williams, D. R., Yu, Y., Jackson, J. S., & Anderson, N. B. (1997). Racial differences in physical and mental health: Socio-economic status, stress and discrimination. *Journal of Health Psychology, 2*(3), 335–351. doi:10.1177/135910539700200305

Wong, G., Derthick, A. O., David, E. J. R., Saw, A., & Okazaki, S. (2014). The what, the why, and the how: A review of racial microaggressions research in psychology. *Race and Social Problems, 6,* 181–200. doi:10.1007/s12552-013-9107-9

Is Ethnic Identity a Buffer? Exploring the Relations Between Racial Microaggressions and Depressive Symptoms Among Asian-American Individuals

Shinwoo Choi, Jioni A. Lewis, Stacy Harwood, Ruby Mendenhall, and Margaret Browne Huntt

ABSTRACT

This study explores the moderating role of ethnic identity in the relations between racial microaggressions and depressive symptoms. Using survey data from 353 Asian-American college students, we found that racial microaggressions significantly predicted depressive symptoms and accounted for 24% of the variance in a hierarchical multiple regression analysis. In addition, ethnic identity moderated the relations between racial microaggressions and depressive symptoms. Thus, ethnic identity buffers Asian-Americans against the negative mental health effects of racial microaggressions. Implications for research and practice in the field of social work are discussed.

The Asian-American population is a fast-growing population in the United States, and is the third largest racial/ethnic minority group in the country following Latinos and African-Americans (United States Census Bureau, 2010). By 2050, there will be 33.4 million Asian-Americans in the United States (Hoeffel, Rastogi, Kim, & Shahid, 2012). Asian-Americans have been perceived as a "model minority" (Kim & Aquino, 2015) due to their relatively high socioeconomic status. However, much of this research overlooks the difficulties and challenges faced by Asian-Americans, particularly their unique experiences of discrimination and racial microaggressions. The limited research that does exist has found that Asian-Americans have experienced discrimination based on their race, English-language proficiency, and socioeconomic status (SES) since the beginning of their immigration to the United States (Gee, Spencer, Chen, & Takeuchi, 2007; Hing, 1993). In addition, Asian-Americans experience unique forms of racial discrimination based on the stereotypes that exist about their group, such as assumptions of being perpetual foreigners (Alvarez, Juang, & Liang, 2006). Furthermore, Asian-Americans are exposed to various risk factors to their mental health, which are compounded by immigration status and acculturation stress (Yeung et al., 2004). Asian-Americans also tend to underutilize mental health services compared to other racial groups (Abe-Kim, Takeuchi, Hong, Zane, Sue, Spencer, & Algeria, 2007). Thus, it is important to explore the impact of racial microaggressions on the mental health of Asian-American individuals to better understand their unique experiences and develop culturally responsive social work interventions for this population. A secondary aim of this article is to explore a potential resiliency factor—namely, ethnic identity— that might buffer individuals against the negative mental health effects of racial microaggressions.

Literature review

Racial microaggressions

Although much of the empirical research on racial microaggressions has focused on African-American and Latino individuals (Harwood, Huntt, Mendenhall, & Lewis, 2012; Solorzano, Ceja, & Yosso, 2000; Sue, Lin, Torino, Capodilupo, & Rivera, 2009), recently there has been an increase in research exploring the unique racial microaggression experiences of Asian-American populations (Hyunh, 2012; Nadal, Wong, Griffin, Davidoff, & Sriken, 2014; Nadal, Wong, Sriken, Griffin, & Fujii-Doe, 2014; Wang, Leu, & Shoda, 2011). Several qualitative studies have found that Asian-Americans tend to be perceived as perpetual foreigners, have their cultural values and communication styles pathologized by others, and experience an ascription of intelligence (Sue, Bucceri, Lin, Nadal, & Torino (2007). In addition, several recent quantitative studies using Asian-American samples have found racial microaggressions to be associated with greater depression, anxiety, anger, stress, somatic symptoms, and negative affect (Hyunh, 2012; Nadal, Wong, Sriken, et al., 2014; Ong, Burrow, Fuller-Rowell, Ja, & Sue, 2013), Taken together, these findings provide some initial evidence that Asian-Americans experience unique forms of racial microaggressions based on the stereotypes that exist about their group and that these microaggressions are related to negative mental health outcomes for this population. However, very few studies have explored which factors might buffer individuals against the negative effects of racial microaggressions.

Ethnic identity as a buffer?

Although much of the extant literature shows an association between racial microaggressions and mental health, we know less about why racial microaggressions impact individuals differently. One important moderating factor might be ethnic identity (Umana-Taylor, Quintana, Lee, Cross Jr, Rivas-Drake, Scwartz, Syed, Yip, & Seaton, 2014). Ethnic identity refers to the degree to which one develops a sense of affiliation and identification with one's ethnic group (Phinney, 1996). Using Phinney's (1992) conceptualization, ethnic identity includes two dimensions: ethnic exploration (i.e., the extent to which one actively explores one's ethnicity, traditions, and cultural history) and ethnic belonging (i.e., ethnic affiliation and pride). Ethnic exploration refers to the act of searching for one's ethnic identity and/or ethnic background. Ethnic belonging refers to the affective aspects of ethnic identity development by referring to how an individual feels about their ethnicity. Research indicates that greater ethnic identity achievement is positively associated with greater self-esteem and psychological well-being (Kim, 1981; Phinney, 1992).

Despite the growing body of empirical research on racial microaggressions experienced by people of color, there is a dearth of research on the unique experiences of Asian-American individuals. More research is needed to examine the effects of racial microaggressions on Asian-Americans' mental health. In addition, very few studies have examined which resiliency factors might serve a buffering role in the association between racial microaggressions and mental health outcomes. Hence, examining the role of ethnic identity on the relations between racial microaggression experiences and mental health outcomes among Asian-Americans can fill this gap in the literature. Thus, the purpose of the current study is twofold: (a) to explore the impact of racial microaggressions on the mental health of Asian-Americans and (b) to explore whether ethnic identity serves as a buffer against the negative effects of racial microaggressions. Our research questions are as follow: (a) Do racial microaggressions predict depressive symptoms for Asian-American individuals? (b) Does ethnic identity predict depressive symptoms for Asian-American individuals? (c) Does ethnic identity moderate the relations between racial microaggressions and depressive symptoms?

Method

Sample

Undergraduate and graduate students were recruited from a large predominantly White public university in the Midwest. Using stratified random sampling, a total of 3,850 who self-identified as African-American, Asian-American, Latina/o American, or Native American were invited to participate as part of a larger racial microaggressions study. Among them, 1,710 domestic students of color completed the survey during the 2011–2012 academic year. For the purposes of this study, we focused on the responses from all domestic students who self-identified as Asian/Asian-American ($N = 353$). We did not include international students or students who self-identified as biracial/multiracial since research shows that these groups have differential experiences with racial microaggressions (Johnston & Nadal, 2010). Of the total sample (N = 353), there were 54% men and 46% women who ranged in age from 18 to 41 years with a mean age of 21 (SD = 3.15). Eighty-one percent were U.S. citizens and 18% were permanent residents. On average, participants had lived in the United States for 17 years. In terms of the students' academic status, 83% were undergraduate and 17% were graduate or professional students. Forty-nine percent of the students had majors in Science, Technology, Engineering, Mathematics (STEM) and the other 51% were in non-STEM with majors in the social sciences or humanities. In addition, 89.5% of the sample went to a public high school and the rest attended a private high school before attending college.

Procedure

Participants were recruited via an online survey and their responses were sent to a password-protected server operated by SurveyGizmo. Personalized e-mail invitations were sent by using a list obtained from the university administration inviting students to participate in the online survey. Reminder e-mails were sent out over a six-month period to ensure we received a high response rate.

Measures

Racial microaggressions

Racial microaggressions were assessed using a scale that was developed by the research team based on qualitative findings from a series of focus groups with students of color. The team also reviewed the research literature on racial microaggressions, perceived racism, and race-related stress in order to develop their items. The Racial Microaggressions in Higher Education Scale (Lewis, Mekawi, Harwood, Mendenhall, & Huntt, 2017) is a 14-item scale that assesses the frequency of racial microaggressions experienced in higher education settings. Five items reflect micro-insults (e.g., "I have experienced someone making offensive jokes to me on this campus because of my race"), five items reflect intellectual inferiority microaggressions (e.g., "I have experienced discouragement in pursuing my academic or educational goals because of my race"), and four items reflect invisibility microaggressions, (e.g., "I have felt excluded on this campus because of my race"). Participants responded to items based on how often they had experienced a racial microaggression in the past year on a 6-point Likert-type scale, ranging from 0 (never) to 5 (once a week or more). For the purposes of this study, we calculated a total mean score by adding the total score and dividing by the total number of items. The Cronbach's alpha for the total scale was .92.

Ethnic identity

Ethnic identity was measured using six items from the Multigroup Ethnic Identity Measure (MEIM; Phinney, 1992). The original MEIM includes 12 items that assess two components of ethnic identity: exploration/search (e.g., "I have spent time trying to find out more about my ethnic group, such as its history, traditions, and customs") and commitment (e.g., "I feel a strong attachment toward my own ethnic group"). For the current study, a shortened version of the MEIM was used. It included three items for exploration and three items for commitment. Participants responded to items on a 4-point Likert-type scale ranging from 1 (strongly disagree) to 4 (strongly agree), such that higher scores represented a greater exploration, affirmation, belonging, and commitment to one's ethnic group. For the purposes of this study, we used a total mean score. The Cronbach's alpha for this scale was .90.

Depressive symptoms

Depressive symptoms were measured using an adapted version of the Center for Epidemiologic Studies Depression Scale-Revised (Eaton, Muntaner, Smith, Tien, & Ybarra, 2004). Participants were asked to indicate how often they experienced depressive symptoms during their time at the university. Items include depressed mood and physical and cognitive symptoms of depression. A sample item includes, "Felt lacking of energy and strength." Participants responded to 12 items using a 6-point Likert-type scale ranging from 0 (none of the time) to 5 (all of the time). Some items were adapted to measure college students' depressive symptoms as it related to their performance in academic settings. For instance, items such as "lost interest in your coursework" or "felt that this was not the right institution for you" were included. This 12-item scale showed a high reliability with a Cronbach's alpha of .95. We used a total mean score, with higher scores reflecting greater depressive symptoms.

Demographic variables

Participants' demographic variables, including gender, age, academic status, number of years in the United States, and major, were controlled.

Data analysis

In order to explore the three research questions related to the role of racial microaggressions and ethnic identity on Asian-Americans' mental health, hierarchical multiple regression analysis was conducted using SPSS 22.0. The first model examined the relations between racial microaggressions and depressive symptoms while controlling for demographic variables. The second model analyzed the relations between racial microaggressions and depressive symptoms while controlling for demographic variables with ethnic identity added to the model. The third model examined the moderating role of ethnic identity in the relations between racial microaggressions and depressive symptoms by using an interaction term.

Findings

Descriptive statistics

We provide means, standard deviations, and correlations for all of the variables included in this study (see Table 1). There was a significant positive correlation between frequency of racial microaggressions and depressive symptoms ($r = .439$, $p < .001$), suggesting that greater experiences of racial microaggressions were related to greater depressive symptoms. There was also a significant negative correlation between age and depressive symptoms ($r = -.107$, $p < .05$), suggesting that younger individuals reported fewer depressive symptoms. Ethnic identity was not significantly correlated with any of the study variables.

Hierarchical multiple regression analysis

To handle the missing data, we used the estimation maximization (EM) multiple imputation method using SPSS. According to the regression analysis, the full regression model for depressive symptoms achieved significance $R^2 = .209$, $F = 12.694$, $p < .001$ (see Table 2). In the second model, when ethnic identity was also included in the regression model for depressive symptoms, the model itself yielded a significant result ($R^2 = .206$, $F = 13.365$, $p < .001$). However, ethnic identity did not show a significant contribution to the model. In the last model, the interaction term between racial microaggressions and ethnic identity yielded a significant result. The full regression model achieved significance ($R^2 = .219$, $F = 12.694$, $p < .001$). Among the five different control variables (gender, age, academic status, years spent in the United States, and citizenship status), only academic status yielded a significant controlling effect in all three models. Students' gender,

Table 1. Intercorrelations, means, and standard deviations among study variables.

Measure	1	2	3	4	5	6	7	8	9
1. Depression	–								
2. RMA	.439***	–							
3. Ethnic identity	.035	.078	–						
4. Interaction	.396***	.962***	.278***	–					
5. Age	−.107*	−.058	−.023	−.055	–				
6. Academic status	−.167**	−.092	.003	−.084	.714***	–			
7. U.S. years	−.045	−.011	.028	−.008	.167**	.127*	–		
8. Gender	.020	.072	−.078	.066	.041	.068	−.005	–	
9. Citizenship	.067	−.048	.000	−.065	.122*	.149**	−.535***	−.036	–
M	.67	1.26	3.03	3.86	21.96	–	17.66	–	–
SD	.046	.061	.036	.196	.169	–	1.19	–	–

Note. RMA = Racial microaggressions.
*$p \leq .05$. **$p \leq .01$. ***$p \leq .001$.

Table 2. Hierarchical multiple regression analysis of racial microaggressions and ethnic identity predicting depressive symptoms.

Variable	B	SE B	β	$R^2\Delta$
Depressive symptoms				
Step 1				.209
Gender	−.003	.086	−.002	
Age	−.001	.019	−.005	
Academic status	−.304	.145	−.147*	
Time in U.S.	.010	.009	.068	
Citizenship	.298	.134	.133	
Step 2				.206
Gender	−.002	.086	−−.001	
Age	−.001	.019	−.005	
Academic status	−.305	.145	−.148*	
Time in U.S.	.010	.009	.068	
Citizenship	.297	.134	.133	
Ethnic identity	.011	.063	.008	
Step 3				.219
Gender	.016	.086	.238	
Age	.001	.019	.003	
Academic status	−.302	.144	−.146*	
Time in U.S.	.007	.009	.052	
Citizenship	.246	.135	.110	
Ethnic identity	.194	.095	.152*	
Ethnic identity * RMA	−.222	.088	−.688*	

Note. RMA = Racial microaggressions.
* $p \leq .05$. ** $p \leq .01$. *** $p \leq .001$.

citizenship status, and years spent in the United States had no effect on the relationship between racial microaggressions and depressive symptoms.

Discussion

This study makes several important contributions to the current literature on racial microaggressions among Asian-American individuals. It is one of the first studies to explore the effects of racial microaggressions on Asian-American college students' mental health outcomes. This study also took an innovative step by exploring the moderating role of ethnic identity in the relations between racial microaggressions and depressive symptoms. Overall, we found that racial microaggressions were a significant predictor of depressive symptoms and that ethnic identity also served as a buffer against the negative effects of these experiences. Next, we highlight each of the significant findings and discuss the research and clinical implications of this study.

Our first research question explored whether racial microaggressions significantly predicted depressive symptoms. Our findings indicated that racial microaggressions were found to significantly predict depressive symptoms, such that a greater frequency of racial microaggressions was related to greater depressive symptoms. Thus, consistent with previous studies (Nadal, Wong, Griffin, et al., 2014; Ong et al., 2013), we found that racial microaggressions negatively impacted mental health. Our findings indicate that racial microaggressions have a detrimental effect on the psychological well-being of racial/ethnic minority individuals. Despite the model-minority myth that Asian-Americans do not experience hardships, the Asian-American students in our study reported experiencing negative effects of racial microaggressions by exhibiting depressive symptoms.

To answer our second research question, we explored whether ethnic identity significantly predicted depressive symptoms and we found that ethnic identity did not. Our third research question explored whether ethnic identity buffered the association between racial microaggressions and depressive symptoms. We found a significant moderating effect of ethnic identity in the relations between racial microaggressions and depressive symptoms. This indicates that having an achieved ethnic identity works as a protective factor against the detrimental effects of racial microaggressions. This finding supports previous research with other racial/ethnic minority populations. Specifically, previous research on the buffering effects of ethnic identity on the relations between perceived discrimination and depressive symptoms has been found among Latino adolescents (Umana-Taylor & Updegraff, 2007). In addition, our study extends a recent study by Nadal, Wong, Sriken, and colleagues (2014), which found that racial microaggressions were significantly and positively associated with depressive symptoms in a sample of Asian-American individuals. However, our study further extends previous research by exploring the relations among racial microaggressions, ethnic identity, and depressive symptoms among Asian-Americans. Our findings significantly add to our understanding of the factors that might buffer Asian-American individuals against the negative effects of racial microaggressions.

Limitations and future research directions

Despite this study's strengths, there were a few noteworthy limitations. First, since the data were collected from Asian-American students at a large Midwestern university, the findings may not be generalizable to other settings or populations. Respondents in the sample were highly educated and grew up in the United States. Therefore, their English-language proficiency and familiarity with U.S. culture may be different from that of Asian individuals who are international students or more recent immigrants; thus they may experience different types of racial microaggressions. In addition, although the response rate was high for a stratified random sample of students of color, the study design was still cross-sectional. Therefore, the results provide a snapshot of the participants' experiences but do not provide any longitudinal information to make any causal inferences from the findings. For instance, to better capture the cumulative and chronic nature of racial microaggressions, a longitudinal study would be helpful to explore the cumulative negative effect of racial microaggressions on participants. According to Arnett (2000), the college years—emerging adulthood of ages 18 to 25 years— are a critical time for identity development. Therefore, longitudinal data might be especially helpful to understand the effects of ethnic identity because it might be more salient after being at a university for four years.

Another noteworthy limitation was related to the types of demographic information collected from participants. We did not collect information on students' academic status such as their grade point average (GPA). We also did not assess socioeconomic status, which might also be related to students' experiences of racial microaggressions. Individuals with different education levels, household incomes, and immigrants' generational statuses might have differential experiences and reactions to racial microaggressions. Another limitation was related to the heterogeneity of the Asian-American population. Despite the diversity of Asian ethnicities, the current study used the larger category of "Asian-American," which does not allow for the exploration of within-group diversity among Asian ethnic groups. Future research should consider the within-group differences among Asian populations when conducting this type of research (Nadal, Wong, Sriken, et al., 2014).

In terms of future directions, researchers might consider exploring the racial microaggression experiences of Asian international students and the impact on mental health and well-being. Given that the number of Asian international students is growing rapidly in the United States, it is important for researchers to begin to explore their unique experiences and how they may be similar or different from the experiences of domestic Asian-American students (Houshmand, Spanierman, & Tafarodi, 2014).

Implications for practice

According to the National Association of Social Workers (NASW)'s code of ethics, social workers are expected to help people in need, address social problems, and "pursue social change, particularly with and on behalf of vulnerable and oppressed individuals and groups of people" (NASW, 2008). In addition, social workers are expected to focus their efforts primarily on issues of "poverty, unemployment, discrimination, and other forms of social injustice." Therefore, racial microaggressions, which are a form of discrimination and social injustice, should be a focus of social workers' attention. Although college students are often considered a non-vulnerable population in the field of social work, many racial minority and low-income college students are less likely to succeed compared to their White and higher SES students (Chen & Carroll, 2005). Furthermore, generally college students are under an increased amount of stress (Roberti, Harrington, & Storch, 2006). Therefore, studying the well-being of college students in higher education settings should be included as an important area of focus for social work researchers and practitioners.

There is a dearth of research on Asian-American college students due to both the model-minority myth (Lee, 2003) and the fact that they are not often considered as the target population of social work interventions. However, research shows that Asian-Americans experience racial microaggressions and these experiences negatively affect their mental health in terms of lowered self-esteem (Nadal, Wong, Griffin, et al., 2014), negative affect (Ong et al., 2013), and overall poor mental health status (Nadal, Wong, Sriken, et al., 2014). Our findings add support to these previous studies. Given the growing body of research to suggest that Asian-American students' mental health is negatively affected by racial microaggressions, social workers should focus on this issue. Many Asian American students in our study reported that they felt excluded by others on the campus or felt invisible because of their race. It is important for predominantly White institutions to cultivate supportive spaces for Asian American students, such as an Asian-American cultural centers, student coun-seling centers, and Asian student organizations to help students to feel welcomed and included in the campus community. The creation of these spaces can be a macro- or mezzo-level of social work practice. One of the significant findings of the current study was the protective role of ethnic identity. Events that cultivate or promote the ethnic identity of Asian-American college students' ethnic identity would be an important resource on college campuses.

Social workers should be able to understand the nature of cultural social diversity and obtain a knowledge base of their clients' cultures. The current study's findings are highly relevant to the code of ethics for cultural compe-tence, which highlights the need to understand participants' experiences and challenges of diverse individuals. It is important for social workers to increase their knowledge of the unique challenges that Asian American college student's experience, such as racial microaggressions, to be able to provide appropriate services for this population.

References

Abe-Kim, J., Takeuchi, D. T., Hong, S., Zane, N., Sue, S., Spencer, M. S.,... Alegría, M. (2007). Use of mental health-related services among immigrant and U.S.-born Asian Americans: Results from the National Latino and Asian American study. *American Journal of Public Health, 97*(1), 91–98. doi:10.2105/AJPH.2006.098541

Alvarez, A. N., Juang, L., & Liang, C. T. (2006). Asian Americans and racism: When bad things happen to "model minorities". *Cultural Diversity and Ethnic Minority Psychology, 12*, 477–492. doi:10.1037/1099-9809.12.3.477

Arnett, J. J. (2000). Emerging adulthood: A theory of development from the late teens through the early twenties. *American Psychologist, 55*, 469–480. doi:10.1037/0003-066X.55.5.469

Chen, X., & Carroll, C. (2005). *First-generation students in postsecondary education: A look at their college transcripts* (NCES No. 2005-171). U.S. Department of Education, National Center for Education Statistics. Retrieved from http://nces.ed.gov/pubs2005/2005171.pdf

Eaton, W. W., Muntaner, C., Smith, C., Tien, A., & Ybarra, M. (2004). Center for epidemio-logic studies depression scale: Review and revision (CESD and CESD-R). In Maruish M.E. (ed.), *The Use of Psychological Testing for Treatment Planning and Outcomes Assessment* (3rd ed; pp. 363–377). Mahwah, NJ: Lawrence Erlbaum.

Gee, G. C., Spencer, M. S., Chen, J., & Takeuchi, D. (2007). A nationwide study of discrimination and chronic health conditions among Asian Americans. *American Journal of Public Health, 97,* 1275–1282. doi:10.2105/AJPH.2006.091827

Harwood, S., Huntt, M. B., Mendenhall, R., & Lewis, J. A. (2012). Racial microaggressions in the residence halls: Experiences of students of color at a predominantly White university. *Journal of Diversity in Higher Education, 5*(3), 159–173. doi:10.1037/a0028956

Hing, B. O. (1993). Beyond the rhetoric of assimilation and cultural pluralism: Addressing the tension of separatism and conflict in an immigration-driven multiracial society. *California Law Review, 81,* 863–925. doi:10.2307/3480889

Hoeffel, E. M., Rastogi, S., Kim, M. O., & Shahid, H. (2012). *The Asian population: 2010.* Retrieved from http://www.census.gov/prod/cen2010/briefs/c2010br-11.pdf

Houshmand, S., Spanierman, L. S., & Tafarodi, R. W. (2014). Excluded and avoided: Racial microaggressions targeting Asian international students in Canada. *Cultural Diversity and Ethnic Minority Psychology, 20*(3), 377–388. doi:10.1037/a0035404

Hyunh, V. W. (2012). Ethnic microaggressions and the depressive and somatic symptoms of Latino and Asian American adolescents. *Journal of Youth Adolescence, 41,* 831–846. doi:10.1007/s10964-012-9756-9

Johnston, M. P., & Nadal, K. L. (2010). Microaggressions experienced by international students attending U.S. institutions of higher education. In D. W. Sue (Ed.), *Microaggressions and Marginality: Manifestation, Dynamics, and Impact* (pp. 171–192). Hoboken, NJ: John Wiley & Sons.

Kim, E., & Aquino, K. C. (2015). Thwarting or embodying model minority stereotypes: An alternative look at adjustment. In N. D. Hartlet (Ed.), *Modern societal impacts of the model minority stereotypes* (pp. 155–184). Normal, IL: IG Global.

Kim, J. (1981). Processes of Asian American identity development: A study of Janapense American women's perceptions of their struggle to achieve positive identities as Amercians of Asian ancestry. Retrieved from ProQuest Digital Dissertation. (Paper AAI8118010)

Lee, R. M. (2003). Do ethnic identity and other-group orientation protect against discrimination for Asian Americans? *Journal of Counseling Psychology, 2,* 133–141. doi:10.1037/0022-0167.50.2.133

Lewis, J. A., Mekawi, Y., Harwood, S., Mendenhall, R., & Browne-Huntt, M. (2017). *Construction and initial validation of the racial microaggressions in higher education scale.* Unpublished manuscript.

Nadal, K. L., Wong, Y., Griffin, K. E., Davidoff, K., & Sriken, J. (2014a). The adverse impact of racial microaggressions on college students' self-esteem. *Journal of College Student Development, 55*(5), 461–474. doi:10.1353/csd.2014.0051

Nadal, K. L., Wong, Y., Sriken, J., Griffin, K., & Fujii-Doe, W. (2014b). Racial microaggressions and Asian Americans: An exploratory study on within-group differences and mental health. *Asian American Journal of Psychology.* Advance online publication. doi:10.1037/a0038057

National Association of Social Workers. NASW. (1996). *Code of ethics of the National Association of Social Workers.* Retrieved from http://www.socialworkers.org/pubs/code/code.asp

Ong, A. D., Burrow, A. L., Fuller-Rowell, T. E., Ja, N. J., & Sue, D. W. (2013). Racial microaggressions and daily well-being among Asian Americans. *Journal of Counseling Psychology, 60*(2), 188–199. doi:10.1037/a0031736

Phinney, J. S. (1992). The Multigroup Ethnic Identity Measure: A new scale for use with diverse groups. *Journal of Adolescent Research, 7*(2), 156–176. doi:10.1177/074355489272003

Phinney, J. S. (1996). When we talk about American ethnic groups, what do we mean? *American Psychologist, 51*(9), 918–927.

Roberti, J. W., Harrington, L. N., & Storch, E. A. (2006). Further psychometric support for the 10-item version of the Perceived Stress Scale. *Journal of College Counseling, 9*, 135–147. doi:10.1002/(ISSN)2161-1882

Solorzano, D., Ceja, M., & Yosso, T. (2000). Critical race theory, racial microaggressions, and campus racial climate: The experiences of African American college students. *Journal of Negro Education, 69*(1/2), 60–73.

Sue, D. W., Bucceri, J., Lin, A. I., Nadal, K. L., & Torino, G. C. (2007). Racial microaggressions and the Asian American experience. *Cultural Diversity and Ethnic Minority Psychology, 13*(1), 72–81. doi:10.1037/1099-9809.13.1.72

Sue, D. W., Lin, A. I., Torino, G. C., Capodilupo, C. M., & Rivera, D. P. (2009). Racial microaggressions and difficult dialogues on race in the classroom. *Cultural Diversity and Ethnic Minority Psychology, 15*(2), 183–190. doi:10.1037/a0014191

Umana-Taylor, A. J., & Updegraff, K. A. (2007). Latino adolescents' mental health: Exploring the interrelations among discrimination, ethnic identity, cultural orientation, self-esteem, and depressive symptoms. *Journal of Adolescence, 30*, 549–567. doi:10.1016/j.adolescence.2006.08.002

Umana-Taylor, A. J., Quintana, S. M., Lee, R. M., Cross Jr., W. E., Rivas-Drake, D., Schwartz, S. J., Syed, M., Yip, T., & Seaton, E. (2014). Ethnic and racial identity during adolescence into young adulthood: An integrated conceptualization. *Child Development, 85*(1), 21–39.

United States Census Bureau. (2010). *The Asian population: 2010.* Retrieved from https://www.census.gov/prod/cen2010/briefs/c2010br-11.pdf

Wang, J., Leu, J., & Shoda, Y. (2011). When the seemingly innocuous "strings": Racial microaggressions and their emotional consequences. *Personality and Social Psychology Bulletin, 37*(12), 1666–1678.

Yeung, A., Chan, R., Mischoulon, D., Sonawalla, S., Wong, E., Nierenberg, A. A., & Fava, M. (2004). Prevalence of major depressive disorder among Chinese-Americans in primary care. *General Hospital Psychiatry, 26*(1), 24–30. doi:10.1016/j.genhosppsych.2003.08.006

"Our Kids Aren't Dropping Out; They're Being Pushed Out": Native American Students and Racial Microaggressions in Schools

Katie Johnston-Goodstar and Ross VeLure Roholt

ABSTRACT

Poor graduation rates, truancy rates, and standardized tests results have been presented as indicators of a school crisis among Native American youths. This crisis, however, relies on ahistoric and deficit models of intervention, which imagine academic success as an individual- or family-level phenomenon. Responding to Reyhner's (1991) suggestion to assess the role of schools and teachers in working to push students out of school, we explored the experiences of Native American youths in schools. This article documents findings from a community-based mixed-methods study. It establishes not only the significant prevalence of microaggressions for Native American youths in schools but it also presents the unique discriminatory experiences and aspects of those microaggressions. We suggest that these microaggressions play a role in school climate and push-out and provide suggestions for research, professional development, and social action.

Introduction: Still killing the Indian?

Learning and education are often used interchangeably with the term schooling. In the case of Indigenous education, it is important to acknowledge that these words are not always synonymous. This article focuses on formal, settler government-authorized institutions of education that we have come to call "school" and the dominant modes of education that occur in these spaces. Although we take up the subject of "schooling" for Native Americans in the United States, it is important to acknowledge that Indigenous education does not start with colonization, nor does it emerge in the conflict with the colonizer. Indigenous knowledge paradigms and pedagogies have always already been defined by and maintained in tribal communities (Barnhardt & Kawagley, 2005; Cajete, 1994; Deloria & Wildcat, 2001; Meyer, 2003; Smith, 1999).

This acknowledged, Native people also have a collective experience with school because the education of Indigenous children was taken up as a colonial

---

Color versions of one or more of the figures in the article can be found online at www.tandfonline.com/wecd.

strategy. Educational policy was administered via public/private collaboration and with an explicit focus on assimilation. As early as 1819, the United States government authorized the Civilization Fund Act, which directed reform and missionary societies in their efforts to establish schools for Indians and to introduce "the habits and arts of civilization" (Prucha, 2000, p. 33). These efforts took a more ominous turn in the 1870s when Captain Richard H. Pratt (who famously stated, "kill the Indian in him, and save the man") established Carlisle, the first federally funded, off-reservation Indian boarding school. Boarding schools quickly became a widespread strategy. These schools supported the destruction of tribal culture, spirituality, and language, and facilitated the breakup of Indigenous families and community structures.

Attendance at boarding school was far from voluntary. It was part of an explicit attempt at "civilizing" Indian children, and families were expected to comply. The 1906 statute on Indian Reform School (U.S.C. 302) stated "that the consent of parents, guardians, or next of kin shall not be required to place Indian youth in said school." Enrollment increased as Indian agents sought to meet school enrollment quotas (Trafzer, Keller, & Sisquoc, 2006) and they were granted the legal right to withhold "rations, clothing and other annuities" from parents who refused to consent (U.S.C. 283). Parental arrest was also pursued as a strategy to force participation. Seizures of children were common; in December 1890 U.S. soldiers secured 104 Hopi children through coercion and force. This practice continued for years, resulting in the infamous arrest of 19 "hostile" Hopi men who refused to let children in their community be taken (Holiday, n.d.).

Although in some cases the consent of Native parents was sought, notions of consent cannot be separated from the political realities of the time. Some parents believed boarding schools could teach Native American youths to read and write in English and acquire knowledge that might be useful in a colonized world. As a Cherokee elder urged, "unless you can speak their language, read and write as they do, they will be able to cheat you and trample on your rights" (The Missionary Herald, 1827). Still others believed that boarding schools might simply provide solace from the "desperate economic and social conditions in their home communities" (Trafzer et al., 2006, p. 39). Regardless of how Native American young people arrived at boarding school, they were certain to encounter challenging situations while there.

While corporal punishment and crowded conditions are considered hallmarks of early public education in the United States (Mintz, 2004), conditions in boarding schools were beyond dismal. Boarding school attendance resulted in a loss of identity, trauma, and even death (Addams, 1995; Piccard, 2013). School staff sheared children's hair, changed their names, banned traditional clothing and customs, and forced them to worship as Christians. Eliminating Native languages—considered an obstacle to the "acculturation" process—was a top priority, and teachers devised an extensive repertoire of punishments for uncooperative children. "I was forced to eat an entire bar of soap for speaking my language," says Amnesty International USA (AIUSA) activist Byron Wesley (in Smith, 2007). Native children endured sexual and physical abuse at the hands of boarding school teachers and administrators (Braveheart & DeBruyn, 1998; CrowDog, 1990) and were forced to serve as a source of "manual labor" (Grande, 2004, p. 15), a practice that was ironically and discursively presented as in their best interest in order to domesticate, civilize, and prevent them from a life of savagery.

The mortality rate at Indian boarding schools was incredibly high. In some Canadian boarding schools, due to overcrowding and disease, it is estimated that 50% of new students died in the first year (Dawson, 2012). The Truth and Reconciliation Commission on Canadian Residential Schools has used the term *cultural genocide* when describing the consequences of residential schools and has documented the deaths of more than 6,000 students (the report adds that there are probably more). For comparative purposes, it was more likely for a Native child to die in residential schools than for a Canadian soldier to perish in World War II (Schwartz, 2015). We have found no similar accounting for the number of student deaths within boarding schools in the United States. Regardless of a full accounting, the damages caused by the U.S. boarding schools are unmistakable. As Ojibwe historian and writer Anton Treuer states,

> The long-term effects of the residential boarding school system were profound. People learn how to parent by how they are parented, but with as many as three generations of Ojibwe people going through BIA boarding schools, a critical piece of the social fabric was severely damaged. Many Ojibwe families have rebounded from the effects of boarding schools, but their blessings are derived in spite of the system rather than because of it. (Treuer, 2010, p. 26)

Duran, Duran, Yellow Horse Brave Heart, & Yellow Horse-Davis refer to these enduring intergenerational effects as a "soul wound" (1998, p. 361). Given the expansive reach of boarding schools, the depth of their impact, and the fact that many were not closed until the early 1970s, scholars argue that the "boarding school experience should be viewed as a context for work with *all* American Indian/Alaskan Natives" (Evans-Campbell, Walters, Pearson, & Campbell, 2012, p. 426).

As government policies changed, schooling became less physically perilous for Native children, but it is by no means above suspicion. Overtly assimilationist and abusive practices are now largely considered unacceptable but negative student experiences, attacks on tribal identity, and serious academic disparities remain commonplace. Schools continue to serve the educational and economic objectives of mainstream society and they do so at the peril of Indigenous students. In 2011, while most students improved on the National Assessment of Educational Progress in both reading and math, Native American students' progress remained flat and "the gaps separating these students from their white peers has actually widened" (The Education Trust, 2013, p. 3). In 2005, Native American students outperformed both Black and Latino students in both fourth-grade reading and eighth-grade math, but by 2011, this lead had vanished. In 2011, only 18% of Native American students in fourth grade scored proficient or above in reading compared to 42% of their White peers (The Education Trust, 2013). The situation in eighth grade is not much better. In 2011, only 17% were proficient or advanced in math and nearly half were below the basic level (The Education Trust, 2013). These disparities are further documented in Native American student college readiness, with only 1 in 4 Native graduates scoring college-ready level in ACT math, and about one-third scoring college-ready level in ACT reading (The Education Trust, 2013).

Native American students also face disparities in graduation rates. Native American youths have higher educational "dropout" rates than their peers. Approximately 43% to 50% of Native youths do not graduate high school (Engle, 2010; Greene & Winters, 2002). In some areas, disparities are even more pronounced. For example, Faircloth and Tippeconnic III (2010) found that while North Dakota has the highest average graduation rate in the country at 79.2%, only 37.9% of their Native American students graduate. According to the report *Diplomas Count 2014*, Native American students have one of the worst graduation rates of any racialized community, and despite sporadic increases in graduate rates from 2007 to 2010, Native graduation rates actually plateaued and, since that time, have decreased (Swanson, 2014). Following a decade of explicit efforts to improve graduation rates for U.S. students, it appears many efforts have modest to null benefit for Native American students.

More than two decades ago, education scholar Jon Reyhner (1991) called for a shift away from deficit models that placed the blame for dropping out on students and their families, calling instead for studies that assessed the role of schools and teachers in working to push students out of school. We know that "Native American students experience difficulty maintaining rapport with teachers and establishing relationships with other students; feelings of isolation; racist threats; and frequent suspension" (U.S. Commission on Civil Rights, 2003, p. 84). They report demographically disproportionate rates of school bullying (Campbell & Smalling, 2013; Carlyle & Steinman, 2007) and feeling unsafe at school (Minnesota Department of Health, 2012), and are 207% more likely to be expelled than White students (National Caucus of Native American State Legislatures, 2008). Yet much of our research and interventions submerge these important social and political contexts and replace them with a discourse of ahistoric pathology (Tuck, 2009). Our study sought to challenge this individualized deficit analysis of school success by asking questions such as how are Native youths experiencing schools, what messages are they receiving in school and in society, and how do these experiences and messages impact their school success?

Methodology and methods

In 2011, we began a community-based participatory research (CBPR) collaboration with a Midwestern tribal community (Wallerstein & Duran, 2006). Formal and binding requirements around data collection, analysis, publication, and ownership were agreed to with the intent to prevent typical ways that universities have conducted research in Indian country (Cochran et al., 2008; Walters et al., 2009), and to limit the production of damage-centered research (Tuck, 2009). The research team was approved by the Institutional Research Board at our university. This article reports on study data relevant to education and schools, including field observations, interviews conducted with youthworkers, educators, elders, and community members from our tribal partners and statewide Native American community ($N = 42$), an independent analysis of the 2010 Minnesota Student Survey ($N = 130,908$; Native American $N = 6,840$; typically completed by students in all schools across the state, targeted surveying of statewide school policy and discipline records ($N = 12$), youth focus group participants ($N = 53$), and a review of secondary qualitative data held by the Minnesota Historical Society ($N = 3$).

Interview and focus group participants were recruited statewide using targeted and purposeful sampling procedures. Eligibility criteria included (a) self-identifying as Native American or as having a professional capacity with Native American young people and (b) residing, working, or going to school within the geographical area of the study. Young people who participated in the study were not contacted until both parents and elders consented to interviews with young people. All participants were provided with detailed information about the study prior to and at the start of the interview process, and verbal consent and assent was obtained prior to and throughout the interview process. Participants were provided with a $20 gift card in gratitude for their participation. In some instances, to acknowledge the distance traveled to be interviewed, an additional gift card for gas was allowed. The interviewer also provided the interviewee with either a meal or a beverage.

Interviews were conducted in teams, with a lead interviewer and a note taker. Interviewers included the authors and a team of graduate students. Team members varied in age, gender, race/ethnicity, and Indian status. In almost all instances, interview teams included at least one member (if not both) who identified as Native American and/or as having extensive experience with local tribal cultures and histories. A semi-structured interview format was utilized. Interviews often started with the interviewers asking the interviewee to tell us about themselves and allowing them to ask questions and acquaint themselves with the interviewers. Interviews lasted between 90 and 180 minutes. Notes were shared with interviewees to check accuracy and ensure we captured the story and comments as intended.

All data from field observations, interviews, youth focus groups, and second-ary qualitative data were entered into an electronic qualitative data analysis platform. Qualitative analysis followed a whole, part, whole process (van Manen, 1990). Each individual interview was first read by members of the research team individually, and analyzed independently from the other inter-views. This was done as the data were collected. Theoretical thematic analysis technique (Braun & Clarke, 2006) including a search "across a data set to find repeated patterns of meaning" (p. 86) was then conducted. Emergent themes were noted by the individual research team members and then compared with other team members to begin to build codes for the data. Codes were generated and refined. Member checks were conducted with community members and a tribal consultant for narrative accuracy and feedback in the interpretation (Fossey, Harvey, McDermott, & Davidson, 2002). Codes were recorded in the data platform and cohesive presentations of the whole were created.

Findings: Native American youths narrate microaggressions in schools

> I'm really worried about the school system. We focus on attendance issues, how can we get Indian kids to school more. You should ask, are we killing them inside...? Our kids aren't dropping out; they're being pushed out.
> (Native American youthworker)

Microaggressions are the "brief and commonplace daily verbal, behavioral or environmental indignities, whether intentional or unintentional, that communicate hostile, derogatory, or negative racial slights and insults toward people of color" (Sue et al., 2007, p. 273). They appear in three specific categories (microassault, microinsult, and microinvalidation); when these three categories are collectively manifested on systematic or macro levels, this fourth category is referred to as an environmental microaggression. Over the course of our study, we heard stories and analyzed secondary data, which demonstrated the everyday, persistent, and anticipated presence of microag-gressions in schools. Elders, teachers, community members, and youth themselves narrated these experiences and their impact on young people as part of their concerns about schools. Next we present evidence under the three categories (assault, insult, invalidation).

Microassault

Microassaults are "explicit racial derogation characterized primarily by a verbal or nonverbal attack meant to hurt the intended victim" (Sue et al., 2007, p. 274) through name-calling (racial epithets), avoidant behavior (ser-ving a White patron before a person of color), or purposeful discriminatory actions (displaying a swastika, discouraging interracial interaction, etc.).

Microassaults are most likely to be conscious and more public than other microaggressions and thus, are occasionally referenced as "old-fashioned" racism. We observed microassaults on social media, at sporting events, during interpersonal interactions, and in disciplinary patterns.

Discrimination at school sporting events

Public opinion aside, the empirical evidence on mascots, although limited, has consistently shown negative impact on Native Americans. Mascots decrease self-esteem, community worth, and academic aspiration among Native respondents (Fryberg, Markus, Osyerman, & Stone, 2008). They also increase stereotype tendency (Kim-Prieto, Goldstein, Okazaki, & Kirschner, 2010) and implicit stereotype bias and behaviors against American Indians (Chaney, Burke, & Burkley, 2011).

Our project documented multiple discriminatory incidents connected to school sports, including some involving mascots. Some of these were in our region and others were not but evoked memories of similar past events. Because of the empirical evidence and the widespread debate about mascots, we chose to categorize these incidents as explicit and purposeful, and as such, we report them here as microassaults. For example, in November 2013 in Alabama, in an effort to taunt their opponents (the Pinson Valley Indians), McAdory High School cheerleaders displayed a 20-foot sign that read, "Hey Indians, get ready to leave in a Trail of Tears" (see Figure 1).[1] Less than one week later, students supporting the Dyersburg Trojans of Tennessee would display a similar sign against their opponent (a team with a Native mascot).[2] In February 2015 in Minnesota, a barrage of racist tweets targeted a prep athlete of Native American heritage. These tweets evoked similar historical events (e.g., "it was the squaw creek massacre [sic] in the OHS gymnasium" and "[student] recreated the trail of tears tonight."[3]

Discrimination in the school

Racially discriminatory microassaults were not limited to extracurricular hours or events; they continued within the walls of the schools. We heard multiple stories of racial discrimination from teachers, counselors, coaches, and school administrators. One elder told us of Native students being asked to leave the varsity team because they missed practice for ceremonial reasons. While other student-athletes missed practice for religious reasons, the coach told them they just weren't "committed" enough. One youthworker expressed concern about his school counselor's treatment of Native students, saying, "our kids aren't being told they have the opportunity to go to college," and another youthworker stated, "they [teachers] are failing *our* kids 99% of the time." A third youthworker shared a detailed account of attending a conference with a Native family:

Figure 1. Microassaults: Hey Indians.

These schools treat the kids bad and they see the racism. Their education is representative of society.... The dad and I sat in the office looking at each other as we all got "yelled at".... "Why are you skipping class?"... "You're never going to make it to college."... "What are you thinking?" Well it turns out it was ONE class the student was skipping, never once did the counselor say, "Why aren't you going to that class?" The student finally said the "teacher treats me bad," "I came here and tried to transfer out of the class multiple times but the counselor wouldn't do it," "I don't want to skip class; I don't want to be in that class!"

In addition to discriminatory behaviors, the Native youths we interviewed reported experiencing overt racial slurs in school. Seventy-seven percent of our youth focus group participants reported being "called a racial slur at school," with 37% reporting this slur came from a "non-Native student," 29% reporting the slur came from a "teacher or school staff," and 8% reporting the slur came from a "non-Native adult in the community."

Discrimination in discipline

Racialized disciplinary patterns were also observed. While White students and Native American students often have similar behavior, Native American students are disciplined more often and more severely (Gregory, Skiba, & Noguera, 2010). In Minnesota where Native American students are 2% of the total enrollment of students, they account for 7% of out-of-school suspension, expulsions, and exclusions (Minnesota Minority Education Partnership [MMEP], 2013). School discipline patterns were not only observed by community members but described as reinforcing negative stereotypes and creating difficult learning environments for the Native community's young people. Furthermore, although not reported with high frequency, there were reports of conscious efforts to avoid documentation of racial disparities in discipline. Two youthworkers and a community member reported knowledge of "under the table" school discipline procedures in which school administrators negotiated school transfer as a form of discipline. These transfers would occur with coercion and a lack of transparency; a child is told they are transferring to another school and the parent convinced this is the best option so that the discipline will not go on the child's "record."

Microinsult

> The power of racial microaggressions lies in their invisibility.
>
> (Sue et al., 2007, p. 275)

Microinsults are often unconscious and characterized by communications that convey rudeness and insensitivity and demean a person's racial heritage or identity (e.g., a teacher fails to acknowledge a student of color). For Native students, this was reported as a generalized invisibility, patterns of tracking and labeling students, and assumptions of deficiency or pathology.

Invisibility

A prominent theme that emerged from our study included how schools don't include materials, pedagogical strategies, and curricular content that reflect the history and culture of Native American young people. Native Americans are made invisible or, if talked about, are overwhelmingly presented in inaccurate ways that demean the student's identity. A recent review of textbooks finds that "the history of White racism and oppression is muted, and the complexities within groups or involving interaction among groups is virtually ignored" (Sleeter & Grant, 2011, p. 89). K–12 history standards across all 50 states overwhelmingly presented Indigenous peoples in an archaic pre-1900 context and illuminated "a Euro-American narrative that reinstitutes the marginalization of Indigenous cultures and knowledge" (Shear, Knowles, Soden, & Castro, 2015, p. 90). This invisibility and misrepresentation creates a troubling learning environment. In the interviews we conducted, members of the community repeatedly called for a more relevant curriculum for Native American young people (and for non-Indian students). As one youthworker advocated, the curriculum needed to be "related to young people lives." Multiple participants claimed that schools "don't represent" and "don't reflect" who they are or their community's histories and knowledges, with one elder commenting that the current curriculum is an example of how the outside community views Native young people as "inconsequential."

Tracking and labeling

School practices create a challenging learning environment for Native American students—an environment in which insults appear to have immediate and compound effects. We heard stories of how school staff "label" and "track" Native American students based on their success in Eurocentric curriculum and pedagogical styles. One teacher argued the following:

> We MUST fix the relationship with schools... school isn't providing for the youth. School is tracking them by tests. They [students] are red zone, yellow zone, green zone. I have a LOT of smart [Native] kids but I have ONE green zone kid. Get it?

Still other teachers worried about how, and to whom, this tracking happens. One teacher said, "I've got some naturally gifted [Native] kids but they're a little 'naughty' sometimes... then they get labeled special ed." A youthworker added, "Where is the accountability for the schools that produced this? For the schools who just label kids ADD/EBD [attention deficit disorder/emotional and behavioral disorder] and kick them out?"

We found culturally relevant schools where Native youths felt safer and freer from daily insults and "labeling." Some students seek out these schools as spaces of safety but bring with them years of negative experiences that have impacted their academic success, and subsequently the schools become labeled. One youthworker noted, "[these schools are] measured on their final outcomes—how does this make sense... some of these schools are getting kids that come in with a third-grade reading level and they are expected to have them test out [of a standardized test]?"

For one student who just "couldn't listen to that bullshit no more," the daily onslaught of microinsults led to outright anger, but it could also lead to conformity or quiet disengagement that isn't necessarily "labeled" but results in negative outcomes like truancy or "dropout." Regardless, teachers and administrators often deem these responses as individual or family dysfunction (a lack of effort, a chaotic home, indicators of low intelligence) rather than curricular and pedagogical issues. These interpretations leave an indelible mark on each Native child.

Assumptions of deficiency and pathology

Another microinsult experienced by Native youths is the assumption of deficiency. People from across the community told us stories of how Native American young people are put down and assumed to be less-than. Ninety-four percent of the youths in our focus groups reported experiencing something stereotypical or offensive to Native Americans in the media. These experiences didn't occur solely "in schools" but they were common and rarely countered in schools. In other words, schools served as a mirror for Native youth experiences in society. Quijada Cerecer said that teachers' "preconceived notion[s] of Native youth as disinterested in academics and disengaged from the learning process is a result of the dominant discourse perpetuating stereotypes" (2013, p. 603). These stereotypes can be taken up by both teacher and student but ultimately form a type of "benign neglect"—neglect that students become accustomed to in their interactions with teachers (p. 603). While we found young people who yearned to connect to tribal culture and to embody representations of leadership, strength, and power, they were overwhelmingly met with assumptions of deficiency at school. For example, a father told us a story of attending his son's parent-teacher conferences only to have the teacher make a comment about how his son didn't have a father. He said, "I am right here." The teacher responded with "but you don't even look like him," and refused to believe that the child had a father. A social service worker provided another example about the current perceptions of Native youths in her local schools: "that they can't succeed, that they don't want to succeed." According to our independent analysis of the 2010 Minnesota Student Survey, only 36% of Native American youths report that school personnel (teachers, coaches, and other staff) care about them "very much" or "quite a bit," a full 10% lower than the rates reported by their White peers and 4% lower than any other racial/ethnic group.

Microinvalidation

Microinvalidations, also often unconscious, relate to communications that exclude, negate, or nullify the psychological thoughts, feelings, or experiential reality of a person of color. Youths in our study experienced multiple invalidations in schools.

Invalidating historical trauma

Our analysis revealed a generalized ignorance of Native American historical experiences with schools and the impact of this history on contemporary Indian life. Many in the community believed that knowledge about historical trauma and boarding school experience was an essential prerequisite to teaching in school; one teacher lamented, "[t]ypical teachers don't even acknowledge the history; how can they teach Native youth?" Yet another said, "it [trauma] travels through the family; there is a loss of culture... boarding schools and similar experiences make it difficult for families to really trust schools, for parents to participate... the kids get this message." One community member stated, "[t]hink about boarding schools. Several of our grandparents grew up in boarding schools, where they never saw parenting, only beatings, crying themselves self to sleep, disease, etc. My grandma only got to come home three times in her whole life!" Knowledge of this history, historical trauma, and/or skills for engaging trauma are not required for teacher licensure and rarely included in professional development for school staff. Furthermore, school staff often dismissed any attention to historical trauma because it is "in the past." Community members felt strongly that this position was at best invalidating and, at worst, willfully extending the trauma.

Invalidating native voices

Schools have also historically been places, as one community member noted, where American Indian young people have "no voice and are not so much included with things." Native community and youth interpretations of their experiences in school have been and often remain invalidated. Despite the passing of half a century, many community members still resonated with the story of an elder from the 1960s:

> I said, "You know, you really need to do something here.... The lid is coming off of this place." He says, "What do you mean?" I said, "Well, you got kids out there carrying knives and clubs under their coats." And I said, "Somebody's going to get hurt if we don't get this resolved." He got up—it was between classes... [he] looked out his door, and he says, "Looks fine to me." [And then] shuts his door again.... We weren't prepared to, you know, deal with those kinds of levels of racism and ignorance. And so we tried a couple of those meetings, and they just were too volatile to deal with. I was worried some kid was going to get caught in the middle of it and get hurt... so then [we] decided, "Well, we'll just keep the kids out here."' (Minnesota Historical Society, 1992).

Invalidating sovereignty

Our study found evidence of ignorance and resentment toward tribal sovereignty. This appeared in both school and community relations and via non-Native students, parents of non-Native students, and school personnel. In schools, Native American youths were labeled largely as racial minorities as opposed to members of politically distinct and sovereign territories protected under treaty rights. Individuals in the community have resisted the label of "minority," articulating how it discounts their complicated status and dually marginalized experience (as racial minorities in the United States and as citizens of sovereign tribal nations). Schools have not been responsive to these distinctions. Resentment toward sovereignty and tribal rights is also pervasive. One community member recounted having a nice conversation with a local non-Native person at a gas station when the individual glanced down and noticed the tribal license plates on her car. This person had apparently not realized the community member was Native American, and immediately changed his behavior toward the Native. Another shared how schools failed to educate on sovereignty during treaty rights disputes and yet another expressed concern that they'd purchased "Native Pride" sweatshirts for their children only to learn later that individuals at school treated their children poorly (eye-rolling and facial expressions) when they wore them.

Discussion: Research and practice innovations to counter microaggressions

> The war for Indian children will be won in the classroom.

> —Wilma Mankiller, Chief of the Cherokee Nation

A growing body of epidemiological evidence reveals a strong association between racial discrimination and health status among both adults and young people (Krieger, 1999, 2000; Paradies, 2006) even after controlling for economic status (Geronimus, Hicken, Keene, & Bound, 2006). Persistent and ongoing racism has been shown to result in serious health and mental health consequences (Okazaki, 2009; Priest et al., 2013). American Indians' experience of microaggressions has been connected to depression (Walls et al., 2015) and suicidal ideation (O'Keefe et al., 2014). Whitbeck, Hoyt, McMorris, Chen, and Stubben (2001) further linked perceived discrimination with anger and delinquent behavior among Native American youths. In fact, 98% of Native young adults report experiencing daily microaggressions(Jones & Galliher, 2015) and our study confirms that many of these microaggressions occur in schools or school-sponsored/related spaces. Further research is needed to document the prevalence, frequency, and severity of microaggressions experienced in schools and their connection to health and mental health status of Native American students.

Second, it is imperative to explore how microaggressions are connected to academic achievement. Too often we consider schools to be neutral and supportive spaces, leaving much of the debate around academic achievement centered on individual- and familial-level problems/analysis. Research is needed to explore the connection between the experience of microaggressions and indicators of student success (truancy, grades, graduation rates). Recent scholarship demonstrates that school climate can impact student achievement, mental health, and safety (Thapa, Cohen, Guffey, & Higgins-D'Alessandro, 2013), and how many students are "pushed out" rather than drop out of school (Tuck, 2012). Our findings confirm this. Native youths are experiencing overt and covert racism on a daily basis and these experiences are contributing to their feelings of lack of safety, discomfort, and invisibility. Furthermore, our preliminary analysis of the Minnesota Student Survey data suggest that school climate (safety perceptions, teacher relationships, and bullying) is related to perpetration of violence (Johnston-Goodstar, VeLure Roholt, Zieffler, & Fink, in preparation). When so much of our social and economic success depends on our completion of education, we must ensure that the systems of education are not producing inequitable conditions or experiences for students. Our research illustrates how schools continue to be a source of trauma for many Native American students.

In addition, we argue that research on professional self-awareness is a critical step forward. Agreeing that professionals reinforce and support aversive racism (Gaertner & Dovidio, 2005), which by definition is often done unconsciously and unintentionally, is a necessary first step, but this cannot be where practice ends. It is necessary for school administrators, social workers, and teachers to be aware of microaggressive thoughts and actions, particularly in their interactions with Native American students. Sue and colleagues (2007) raised the issue of microaggressions as a way to address "therapy underutilization and premature termination of therapy" by racialized communities. Walls, Gonzalez, Gladney, and Onello (2015) confirmed the necessity of self-awareness among health providers. We also recognize this is not easy to do, as many of these thoughts and actions are unconscious or unintentional. To counteract these tendencies requires a concerted and committed effort.

Finally, collaborations among schools, communities, and scholars must develop and test interventions that can limit exposure to and impact of microaggressions. One promising approach in the field of education has been the development and testing of critical and ethnic studies in public schools (Dee & Penner, 2016). Expanded curricular offerings, especially the portrayal and narration of the historical and contemporary Native Americans, should be a primary focus for both teachers and social workers in schools. Much needs to be done to address the negative and damaging narratives and images of racialized communities that continue to be found in textbooks across the country (Journell, 2008; Loewen, 2008). Social workers and teachers can and should conduct textbook and standards reviews to improve the ways Native Americans are represented in school curriculum. With the continual barrage of negative images and narratives about Native American and other racialized communities, social workers and teachers need to provide pathways and possibilities for the promotion of positive identity among Native American young people, and supporting ongoing efforts in communities and families.

> *Studies suggest that dimensions of racial group identity may be protective and may buffer the influence of discrimination on health. Research has shown that greater racial group identification and racial centrality (the degree to which race is salient to self-identification) moderated the effect of discrimination on mental health among Black and Mexican American youth.* (Chae & Walters, 2009, p. S144)

Supporting interventions such as these have been found to support healthy ethnic identity. "Fostering ethnic identity in all youth serves to enhance mental health functioning, but is especially important for American Indian youth due to the collective nature of their culture" (Smokowski, Evans, Cotter, & Webber, 2014). While Clark and colleagues (2011) indicate, and we agree, that efforts to assist Native American students to cope with racial microaggressions should be supported, we also advocate that Native American communities develop and encourage resistance to these negative attitudes, beliefs, and images.

Notes

1. http://www.cbsatlanta.com/story/24039650/metro-atlanta-native-american-reacts-to-al-trail-of-tears-sign
2. http://indiancountrytodaymedianetwork.com/2013/11/21/second-trail-tears-banner-displayed-tennessee-high-school-football-game-152365
3. http://www.postbulletin.com/news/local/owatonna-students-might-be-suspended-for-racist-tweets/article_0f9c152d-6bbd-5495-9fa8-49cb78d278f7.html

References

Addams, D.W. (1995). *Education for extinction: American Indians and the boarding school experience.* Lawrence, KS: University Press of Kansas.

Barnhardt, R., & Kawagley, A. O. (2005). Indigenous knowledge systems and Alaska Native ways of knowing. *Anthropology and Education Quarterly, 36*(1), 8–23. doi:10.1525/aeq.2005.36.1.008

Braun, V., & Clarke, V. (2006). Using thematic analysis in psychology. *Qualitative Research in Psychology, 3,* 77–101.

Braveheart, M. & DeBruyn, L. (1998). The American Indian holocaust: Healing historic unresolved grief. *American Indian and Alaska Native Mental Heath Research, 8*(2), 60–82.

Cajete, G. (1994). *Look to the mountain: An ecology of Indigenous education.* Durango, CO: Kivaki Press.

Campbell, E. M., & Smalling, S. E. (2013). American Indians and bullying in schools. *Journal of Indigenous Social Development, 2*(1), 1–15.

Carlyle, K. E., & Steinman, K. J. (2007). Demographic differences in the prevalence, co-occurrence, and correlates of adolescent bullying at school. *Journal of School Health, 77*(9), 623–629. doi:10.1111/josh.2007.77.issue-9

Chae, D., & Walters, K. A. (2009). Racial discrimination and racial identity attitudes in relation to self-rated health and physical pain and impairment among two-spirit American Indians/Alaska Natives. *American Journal of Public Health, 99*(S1), S144–S151. doi:10.2105/AJPH.2007.126003

Chaney, J., Burke, A., & Burkley, E. (2011). Do American Indian mascots = American Indian people? Examining implicit bias towards American Indian people and American Indian mascots. *American Indian and Alaska Native Mental Health Research, 18*(1), 42–62.

Clark, D. A., Spanierman, L. B., Reed, T. D., Soble, J. R., & Cabana, S. (2011). Documenting weblog expressions of racial microaggressions that target American Indians. *Journal of Diversity in Higher Education, 4*(1), 39–50.

Cochran, P., Marshall, C., Garcia-Downing, C., Kendell, E., Cook, D., McCubbin, L., & Gover, R. M. (2008). Indigenous ways of knowing: Implications for participatory research and community. *American Journal of Public Health, 98*(1), 22–27. doi:10.2105/AJPH.2006.093641

CrowDog, M. (1990). *Lakota woman.* New York, NY: Grove Press.

Dawson, A. (2012). Histories and memories of the Indian boarding schools in Mexico, Canada, and the United States. *Latin American Perspectives, 39*(5), 80–99. doi:10.1177/0094582X12447274

Dee, T., & Penner, E. (2016). *The causal effects of cultural relevance: Evidence from an ethnic studies curriculum* (Working Paper No. 21865). Retrieved from http://www.nber.org/papers/w21865

Deloria, V., Jr., & Wildcat, D. (2001). *Power and place: Indian education in America.* Golden, CO: Fulcrum Resources.

Duran, E., Duran, B., Yellow Horse Brave Heart, M., & Yellow Horse-Davis, S. (1998). Healing the American soul wound. In Y. Danieli (Ed.), *International handbook on multigenerational legacies of trauma* (pp. 341–354). New York, NY: Plenum Press.

Engle, S. (2010). *Report examines graduation rates among American Indian and Alaska Native students in twelve states.* Retrieved from https://civilrightsproject.ucla.edu/news/press-releases/2010/new-report-examines-graduation-rates-among-american-indian-and-alaska-native-students-in-twelve-states/

Evans-Campbell, T., Walters, K., Pearson, C., & Campbell, C. (2012). Indian boarding school experience, substance abuse, and mental health among two-spirit American Indian/Alaska Natives. *The American Journal of Drug and Alcohol Abuse, 38*(5), 421–427. doi:10.3109/00952990.2012.701358

Faircloth, S. C., & Tippeconnic, J. W., III (2010). *The dropout/graduation crisis among American Indian and Alaska Native students.* Los Angeles, CA: Civil Rights Project, University of California.

Fossey, E., Harvey, C., McDermott, F., & Davidson, L. (2002). Understanding and evaluating qualitative research. *Australian and New Zealand Journal of Psychiatry, 36*(6), 717–732. doi:10.1046/j.1440-1614.2002.01100.x

Fryberg, S., Markus, H., Osyerman, D., & Stone, J. (2008). Of warrior chiefs and Indian princesses: The psychological consequences of American Indian mascots. *Basic and Applied Social Psychology, 30*(3), 208–218. doi:10.1080/01973530802375003

Gaertner, S., & Dovidio, J. (2005). Understanding and addressing contemporary racism: From aversive racism to the common ingroup identity model. *Journal of Social Issues, 61*(3), 615–639. doi:10.1111/josi.2005.61.issue-3

Geronimus, A. T., Hicken, M., Keene, D., & Bound, J. (2006). "Weathering" and age patterns of allostatic load scores among Blacks and Whites in the United States. *American Journal of Public Health, 96*(5), 826–833. doi:10.2105/AJPH.2004.060749

Grande, S. (2004). *Red pedagogy: Native American social and political thought.* Lanham, MD: Rowman & Littlefield.

Greene, J., & Winters, M. (2002). *Public school graduation rates in the United States. Civic report.* New York, NY: Center for Civic Innovation at the Manhattan Institute.

Gregory, A., Skiba, R., & Noguera, P. (2010). The achievement gap and the discipline gap: Two sides of the same coin? *Educational Researcher, 39*(1), 59–68.

Holiday, W. (n.d.) *Hopi Prisoners on the Rock.* Retrieved from https://www.nps.gov/alca/learn/historyculture/hopi-prisoners-on-the-rock.htm

Jones, M. L., & Galliher, R. V. (2015). Daily racial microaggressions and ethnic identification among Native American young adults. *Cultural Diversity and Ethnic Minority Psychology, 21*(1), 1–9. doi:10.1037/a0037537

Journell, W. (2008). When oppression and liberation are the only choices: The representation of African Americans within state social studies standards. *Journal of Social Studies Research, 32*(1), 40–50.

Kim-Prieto, C., Goldstein, L., Okazaki, S., & Kirschner, B. (2010). Effect of exposure to an American Indian mascot on the tendency to stereotype a different minority group. *Journal of Applied Social Psychology, 40,* 534–553. doi:10.1111/jasp.2010.40.issue-3

Krieger, N. (1999). Embodying inequality: A review of concepts, measures, and methods for studying health consequences of discrimination. *International Journal of Health Services,29* (2), 295–352. doi:10.2190/M11W-VWXE-KQM9-G97Q

Krieger, N. (2000). Discrimination and health. *Social Epidemiology, 1,* 36–75.

Loewen, J. (2008). *Lies my teacher told me: Everything your American history textbook got wrong.* New York, NY: The New Press.

Meyer, M. A. (2003). *Ho'oulu our time of becoming: Hawaiian epistemology and early writings.* Honolulu, HI: ʻAi Pōhaku Press, Hawaiʻi.

Minnesota Department of Health. (2012). *Health and wellbeing of Minnesota's adolescents of color and American Indians: A data book.* St. Paul, MN: Minnesota Department of Health.

Minnesota Historical Society. (1992). *Mille Lacs Ojibwe Social History Project* [AV1993.251.10]. Retrieved from http://collections.mnhs.org/cms/display.php?irn= 11127035

Minnesota Minority Education Partnership (MMEP). (2013). *MMEP brief: Solutions not suspensions.* Retrieved from http://mneep.org/wp-content/uploads/2015/02/official_sns_ research-policy_brief.pdf

Mintz, S. (2004). *Huck's raft: A history of American childhood.* Cambridge, MA: Harvard University Press.

National Caucus of Native American State Legislatures (2008). *Striving to achieve: Helping Native American students succeed.* Retrieved from http://www.ncsl.org/research/state-tri bal-institute/striving-to-achieve-helping-native-american-stude.aspx

Okazaki, S. (2009). Impact of racism on ethnic minority mental health. *Perspectives on Psychological Science, 4*(1), 103–107. doi:10.1111/ppsc.2009.4.issue-1

O'Keefe, V. M., Wingate, L. R., Cole, A. B., Hollingsworth, D. W., & Tucker, R. P. (2014). Seemingly harmless racial communications are not so harmless: Racial microaggressions lead to suicidal ideation by way of depression symptoms. *Suicide and Life-Threatening Behavior.*

Paradies, Y. (2006). A systematic review of empirical research on self-reported racism and health. *International Journal of Epidemiology, 35*(4), 888–901. doi:10.1093/ije/dyl056

Piccard, A. (2013). Death by boarding schools: "The last acceptable racism" and the United States genocide of Native Americans. *Gonzaga Law Review, 49*(1), 137–185.

Priest, N., Paradies, Y., Trenerry, B., Truong, M., Karlsen, S., & Kelly, Y. (2013). A systematic review studying the relationship between reported racism and the health and well-being for children and young people. *Social Science & Medicine, 95,* 115–127. doi:10.1016/j. socscimed.2012.11.031

Prucha, F. P. (Ed.). (2000). *Documents of United States Indian policy.* Lincoln, NE: University of Nebraska Press.

Quijada Cerecer, P. (2013). The policing of native bodies and minds: Perspectives on school-ing from American Indian youth. *American Journal of Education, 119*(4), 591–616. doi:10.1086/670967

Reyhner, J. (1991). *Plans for dropout prevention and special school support services for American Indian and Alaska Native students.* Washington, DC: U.S. Department of Education.

Schwartz, D. (2015, June 2). Truth and reconciliation commission: By the numbers. *CBC News.* Retrieved from http://www.cbc.ca/news/indigenous/truth-and-reconciliation-com mission-by-the-numbers-1.3096185

Shear, S. B., Knowles, R. T., Soden, G. J., & Castro, A. J. (2015). Manifesting destiny: Re/presentations of Indigenous peoples in K–12 U.S. history standards. *Theory & Research in Social Education, 43*(1), 68–101. doi:10.1080/00933104.2014.999849

Sleeter, C., & Grant, C. (2011). Race, class, gender, and disability in current textbooks. In E. Porvenzo & A. Shaver (Eds.), *The textbook as discourse: Sociocultural dimensions of American schoolbooks* (pp. 183–215). New York, NY: Routledge.

Smith, A. (2007). *Soul wound: The legacy of Native American schools.* Amnesty International. Retrieved from http://www.amnestyusa.org/node/87342

Smith, L. T. (1999). *Decolonizing methodologies: Research and indigenous peoples.* London, UK: Zed books.

Smokowski, P., Evans, C., Cotter, K., & Webber, K. (2014). Ethnic identity and mental health in American Indian youth: Examining meditation pathways through self-esteem, and future optimism. *Journal of Youth and Adolescence, 43*(3), 343–355. doi:10.1007/s10964-013-9992-7

Sue, D. W., Capodilupo, C. M., Torino, G. C., Bucceri, J. M., Holder, A., Nadal, K. L., & Esquilin, M. (2007). Racial microaggressions in everyday life: Implications for clinical practice. *American Psychologist, 62*(4), 271–286. doi:10.1037/0003-066X.62.4.271

Swanson, C. (2014, June 2). U.S. graduation rates break 80%: 2014 report used different calculation methods. Retrieved from http://www.edweek.org/ew/articles/2014/06/05/34research.h33.html?qs=diplomas±count±Native±American±Students

Thapa, A., Cohen, J., Guffey, S., & Higgins-D'Alessandro, A. (2013). A review of the school climate research. *Review of Educational Research, 83*(3), 357–385. doi:10.3102/0034654313483907

The Education Trust. (2013, August). *The state of education for Native students.* Retrieved from http://edtrust.org/wp-content/uploads/2013/10/NativeStudentBrief_0.pdf

The Missionary Herald. (December, 1827). *Addresses of Indian Chiefs,* Vol. 23 (12)p. 381.

Trafzer, C. E., Keller, J. A., & Sisquoc, L. (Eds.). (2006). *Boarding school blues: Revisiting American Indian educational experiences.* Lincoln, NE: University of Nebraska Press.

Treuer, A. (2010). *Ojibwe in Minnesota.* St. Paul, MN: Minnesota Historical Society.

Tuck, E. (2009). Suspending damage: A letter to communities. *Harvard Educational Review, 79*(3), 409–428. doi:10.17763/haer.79.3.n0016675661t3n15

Tuck, E. (2012). *Urban youth and school pushout: Gateways, get-aways, and the GED.* New York, NY: Routledge.

U.S. Commission on Civil Rights. (2003). *A quiet crisis: Federal funding and unmet needs in Indian country.* Washington, DC: U.S. Commission on Civil Rights.

van Manen, M. (1990). *Researching lived experience: Human science for action sensitive pedagogy.* New York, NY: SUNY Press.

Wallerstein, N., & Duran, B. (2006). Using community-based participatory research to address health disparities. *Health Promotion Practice, 7*(3), 312–323. doi:10.1177/1524839906289376

Walls, M. L., Gonzalez, J., Gladney, T., & Onello, E. (2015). Unconscious biases: Racial microaggressions in American Indian health care. *The Journal of the American Board of Family Medicine, 28*(2), 231–239. doi:10.3122/jabfm.2015.02.140194

Walters, K. A., Evans-Campbell, S. T., Simoni, J., Duran, B., Schultz, K., Stanley, E.,... Guerrero, D. (2009). "Indigenist" collaborative research efforts in Native American communities. In A. R. Stiffman (Ed.), *The field research survival guide* (p. 148). New York, NY: Oxford University Press.

Whitbeck, L. B., Hoyt, D. R., McMorris, B. J., Chen, X., & Stubben, J. D. (2001). Perceived discrimination and early substance abuse among American Indian children. *Journal of Health and Social Behavior, 42*, 405–424. doi:10.2307/3090187

Correlates of Interpersonal Ethnoracial Discrimination Among Latino Adults with Diabetes: Findings from the REACH Detroit Study

Alana M. W. LeBrón, Michael Spencer, Edith Kieffer, Brandy Sinco, Gretchen Piatt, and Gloria Palmisano

ABSTRACT

The purpose of this study is to identify the social and economic correlates of reported experiences of interpersonal ethnoracial discrimination among Latino adults in Detroit. We examine whether the correlates of interpersonal ethnoracial discrimination vary according to the domain of discrimination and compare findings for individual domains of discrimination to a composite measure of experiences of discrimination. This study suggests that the frequency of reported discrimination is moderately high, and relatively common among Latinos with diabetes who live in Detroit. The findings demonstrate that immigration and ethnicity-related factors, such as greater comfort speaking Spanish and being born in the United States, were persistent correlates of more frequent encounters of interpersonal ethnoracial discrimination. Implications for social work research and practice are presented.

Introduction

Discrimination is associated with poor mental, general, and cardiovascular health for Latinos (Williams & Mohammed, 2009). As 17% of the U.S. population (U.S. Census Bureau, 2014), Latinos are the youngest, largest, and fastest-growing ethnoracial minority group in the United States (Passel, Cohn, & Lopez, 2011; U.S. Census Bureau, 2014). Decades of migration from Latin American countries or territories to the continental United States, as well as births, contribute to this growth of the Latino population (Passel & Cohn, 2008). This growth of the Latino population coincides with increases in anti-immigrant and anti-Latino sentiments that are reflected in policies such as increases in immigration enforcement concentrated in Latino communities (Cox & Miles, 2013; Golash-Boza, 2012; Golash-Boza & Hondagneu-Sotelo, 2013) and the exclusion of many immigrants from health insurance expansions under the Affordable Care Act (ACA). These policies may reinforce marginalizing sentiments and treatment towards Latino and immigrants (Chavez, 2013). Anti-immigrant and, by extension, anti-Latino sentiments and policies may both reflect and reinforce experiences of discrimination that Latinos encounter in their day-to-day lives. Indeed, several studies report a moderately high prevalence of discrimination reported by Latinos (Borrell et al., 2010; Gee, Ryan, Laflamme, & Holt, 2006; LeBrón et al., 2014; Perez, Fortuna, & Alegria, 2008).

Previous studies have found that older age, stronger ethnic identity, higher educational attainment, and higher income, as well as migration to the United States at younger age and longer length of U.S. residence (for immigrants) are correlated with greater frequency or prevalence of discrimination in studies involving national samples of Latinos (Borrell et al., 2010; Perez et al., 2008) and one study of discrimination among Latinos in Detroit, Michigan (LeBrón et al., 2014). The majority of these studies are based on national samples of Latinos, precluding an assessment of patterns that may be specific to the contexts in which participants live. In addition, few studies (LeBrón et al., 2014) have reported the correlates of discrimination, particularly after accounting for social and economic factors such as age and educational attainment. Furthermore, limited research (LeBrón et al., 2014; Perez et al., 2008) has considered the correlates of discrimination in a sample of Latino adults while accounting for social characteristics unique to Latinos relative to other groups that do not experience significant growth through immigration, such as immigrant generation, length of U.S. residence (for immigrants), and language use. We consider these associations for a sample of Latino adults with diabetes who live in Southwest Detroit, a predominantly Latino community within the largely African-American city of Detroit.

The interpersonal ethnoracial discrimination scale used in this study (Williams, Yu, & Jackson, 1997) assesses microaggressions (e.g., receiving poor service, being treated with less respect, treated as if not smart), as well as more overt experiences of discrimination (e.g., harassment, threats, or unfair treatment) that participants attributed to their ethnoracial identity. Sue and colleagues (2007) defines racial microaggressions as "brief and commonplace verbal, behavioral, or environmental indignities, whether intentional or unintentional, that communicate hostile, derogatory, or negative racial slights and insults toward people of color" (p. 271). This study aims to extend the microaggressions literature by examining the patterning of reported experiences of subtle and overt forms of discrimination in the day-to-day lives of Latinos.

The purpose of this study is to identify the social and economic correlates of reported experiences of interpersonal ethnoracial discrimination among Latino adults in Southwest Detroit, Michigan, who completed baseline interviews between 2009 and 2013. In addition, we examine whether the correlates of interpersonal ethnoracial discrimination vary according to the domain of discrimination and compare findings for individual domains of discrimination to a composite measure of experiences of discrimination. Participants' experiences of receiving poor service, being treated with less respect, or being treated as if they are not smart, and encounters in which persons act afraid of the participant are conceptualized as facets of interpersonal discrimination that may be conceptualized as microaggressions. In contrast, being threatened or harassed and receiving unfair treatment may better capture overt experiences of discrimination. Thus, we query the patterning of these experiences of interpersonal ethnoracial discrimination by social and economic factors. First, in separate models, we examined correlates of discrimination for each of the six items that assessed different domains of experiences of interpersonal ethnoracial discrimination in routine experiences. Second, we examined the association of social and economic factors with interpersonal ethnoracial discrimination, using a composite scale that included all six discrimination items.

Methods

Sample

Data for this analysis are drawn from the third cohort of the REACH Detroit Partnership diabetes self-management intervention study. Participants in this study were recruited from a Latino-centered federally qualified health center (FQHC) from which they received health care and related services. Patients of the FQHC who had physician-diagnosed type 2 diabetes; did not have severe conditions that might limit their participation in the intervention, including blindness, deafness, treatment for cancer, or a terminal illness; were age 18 or older; lived in Southwest Detroit; and received medical care from the FQHC were recruited to participate in this diabetes intervention. Data for this analysis were from baseline interviews with REACH Detroit participants that were completed between 2009 and 2013, prior to the implementation of the intervention. The University of Michigan Institutional Review Board approved all study protocols prior to data collection.

Measures

Interpersonal ethnoracial discrimination

Interpersonal ethnoracial discrimination, the outcome variable, was adapted from the Everyday Unfair Treatment Scale developed by Williams and colleagues (1997), which assesses the occurrence and frequency of discrimination in routine encounters. These questions were edited to assess experiences of discrimination that participants attributed to their ethnicity. Specifically, participants were asked how often they experienced any of five discriminatory situations that were linked to their Hispanic or Latino ethnicity (i.e., "because you are Hispanic or Latino"). These items included being treated with less courtesy or respect than other people, receiving poorer service than other people at restaurants or stores, people acting as if they think that you are not smart, being threatened or harassed, and being treated unfairly or badly. In addition, participants were asked about the frequency with which they were treated unfairly or badly because of the language that they speak or their accent. Responses to these items ranged from never (1) to always (5). Each of these items was included in separate models as the outcome variable. In addition, we constructed an interpersonal ethnoracial discrimination scale that is the mean of these six items. The Cronbach's alpha for this scale was 0.87. We also conducted tests of sensitivity using a five-item measure of interpersonal ethnoracial discrimination, which only included items that attributed the experience of discrimination to Hispanic or Latino identity.

Participant social and economic characteristics

Social and economic characteristics that were included as independent variables were age, assessed in years; gender (woman or man); marital status (married/partnered or another status); educational attainment (high school graduate or less than high school education); employment status (employed or not employed); country of origin or descent (Mexican, Mexican-American, or Chicano or another Latino subgroup); a combined measure of nativity and length of U.S. residence (for immigrants: less than 10 years, 10 to 19 years, 20 years or more; referent group was U.S.-born participants); language preference; and health literacy. Spanish-language comfort was assessed by a question that asked participants the language in which they felt most comfortable speaking. Response options were Spanish, English, Spanish and English about the same, and neither English nor Spanish. We then created a binary variable: persons who are more comfortable speaking Spanish and those comfortable speaking English, either, or neither (referent group). Health literacy was assessed by participants' response to the question of how often they have someone like a family member, hospital worker, clinic worker, or caregiver help them to read health care materials. We then created a binary variable, categorizing those who reported that they sometimes, often, or always received assistance and those indicating never or rarely received assistance (referent group).

Analysis

Exploratory data analysis techniques were used to assess the distribution of the independent variables. Correlations of predictors were used to investigate possible multicollinearity. Means and frequencies were calculated to determine how to include predictors in the models. Multiple linear regression was used to assess the associations among interpersonal ethnoracial discrimination and age, gender, marital status, educational attainment, employment status, country of origin or descent, nativity, length of U.S. residence, Spanish-language comfort, and health literacy. To address the first research question, regarding the correlates of each domain of interpersonal ethnoracial discrimination with participants' social and economic background, each individual item within the discrimination scale was entered separately into the regression model and the association with participant social and economic characteristics was assessed. In tests of the second research question, regarding the correlates of interpersonal ethnoracial discrimination when the domains of discrimination were in a combined scale, the outcome variable was the mean scale. Analyses were conducted using Stata 13.0.

Findings

Participant characteristics

Summarized in Table 1 are participant characteristics. The average age was 48.9 years (SD = 10.6 years). Approximately one-third of participants were men (39.2%), employed (38.5%), or had a high school education or higher (32.7%). The majority of participants were married or partnered (70.6%) or were more comfortable speaking Spanish (81.0%). All participants identified

Table 1. Participant characteristics, REACH Detroit Cohort 3 (N = 222).

	N	Percentage	Mean	SD
Age (years)			48.85	10.58
Men	87	39.2		
Employed	85	38.5		
High school graduate	70	32.7		
Married or partnered	156	70.6		
Latino subgroup				
Mexican, Mexican-American, or Chicano	178	80.2		
Other Latino origin or descent	44	19.8		
Immigrant	181	82.3		
Length of U.S. residence				
Less than 10 years	40	18.1		
10 to 19 years	79	35.8		
20 years or more	68	30.8		
Lifetime	34	15.4		
Most comfortable speaking Spanish	179	81.0		
Health literacy: Sometimes, often, or always get assistance reading health care materials	106	48.0		
Interpersonal Ethnoracial Discrimination[a]				
Treated with less respect (because Latino)			2.08	1.05
Receive poorer service (because Latino)			1.70	0.92
Think you are not smart (because Latino)			1.90	1.06
Threatened or harassed (because Latino)			1.33	0.77
Treated unfairly (because Latino)			1.62	0.96
Treated unfairly (because of language/accent)			1.95	1.17
Interpersonal Ethnoracial Discrimination Scale			1.76	0.77

[a]For each discrimination item, 1 = never, 2 = hardly ever, 3 = sometimes, 4 = often, and 5 = always.

as Hispanic or Latino. Eighty percent (80.2%) of participants identified as Mexican, Mexican-American, or Chicano and 19.8% identified with another Latin American territory or country of origin or descent. Puerto Rico and Central American countries were among the other most-common Latin American territories or countries with which participants identified. The majority of participants were immigrants (82.3%). Among immigrants, 18.1% had resided in the United States for less than 10 years, 35.8% had lived in the United States for 10 to 19 years, and 30.8% reported living in the United States for 20 years or longer. Approximately half (48.0%) of participants reported that they received support in reading health care-related materials.

The mean frequency of discrimination ranged from 2.08 (SD = 1.05) for participants' experiences of being treated with less respect because the participant was Hispanic or Latino to 1.33 (SD = 0.77) for experiences of being threatened or harassed because of Hispanic or Latino ethnicity. The mean interpersonal ethnoracial discrimination score for the six-item measure was 1.76 (SD = 0.77). Two-thirds (68.5%) of Latinos in this sample reported that they had encountered interpersonal ethnoracial discrimination.

Treated with less respect

Tests of the first research question, regarding the association of participants' social and economic characteristics with specific domains of interpersonal ethnoracial discrimination, are presented in Table 2. We first assessed the association of participants' social and economic characteristics with the frequency with which participants reported that they were treated with less respect than others (Table 2, Model 1). Trends suggest that compared to U.S.-born Latinos in this sample, immigrants reported less frequent encounters with being treated with less respect. However, these differences only reach statistical significance for Latino immigrants who had lived in the United States for 10 to 19 years (b = –0.79, SE = 0.34, p = 0.02). Relative to those who did not report a preference for speaking Spanish, those who were most comfortable speaking Spanish (b = 0.80, SE = 0.30, p = 0.01) reported significantly more frequent experiences of being treated with less respect than others. Age, gender, marital status, educational attainment, employment status, country of origin or descent, and the engagement of others in health literacy encounters were not significantly associated with reports of being treated with less respect.

Received poorer service

Table 2, Model 2, presents tests of the association between social and economic factors and the reported frequency of receiving poorer service than others. Relative to counterparts with lower levels of educational attainment, having at

Table 2. Interpersonal ethnoracial discrimination items regressed on participant social and economic characteristics, REACH Detroit Cohort 3 (N = 222).

| | Treated With Less Respect | | | Received Poorer Service Than Others | | | Treated As If Not Smart | | | Threatened or Harassed | | | Treated Unfairly | | | Treated Unfairly—Accent or Language | | |
| | Model 1 | | | Model 2 | | | Model 3 | | | Model 4 | | | Model 5 | | | Model 6 | | |
	b	SE	p-value	b	SE	p-value	b	SE	p-value	b	SE	p-value	b	SE	p-value	b	SE	p-value
Intercept	2.24	0.46	<0.01	1.93	0.40	<0.01	2.20	0.46	<0.01	1.74	0.33	<0.01	2.19	0.41	<0.01	2.37	0.50	<0.01
Age (years)	-0.01	0.01	0.18	-0.01	0.01	0.06	-0.01	0.01	0.07	**-0.01**	**0.01**	**0.02**	-0.01	0.01	0.05	-0.02	0.01	0.06
Man	-0.16	0.16	0.31	0.04	0.14	0.77	-0.12	0.16	0.46	0.01	0.12	0.95	-0.22	0.14	0.12	-0.14	0.17	0.43
Married or partnered	0.08	0.16	0.63	0.14	0.14	0.32	0.10	0.16	0.53	0.05	0.12	0.67	-0.08	0.15	0.56	<0.01	0.18	0.99
High school education or higher	0.17	0.17	0.31	0.25	0.15	0.09	0.34	0.17	0.05	0.10	0.12	0.41	0.05	0.15	0.73	-0.10	0.19	0.58
Employed	0.20	0.16	0.21	-0.17	0.14	0.21	0.20	0.16	0.20	0.06	0.11	0.62	0.08	0.14	0.56	0.21	0.17	0.24
Mexican	-0.03	0.18	0.88	0.24	0.16	0.14	-0.02	0.18	0.91	-0.04	0.13	0.79	0.15	0.16	0.37	-0.10	0.20	0.62
Lived in U.S. for less than 10 years	-0.50	0.36	0.17	-0.58	0.31	0.07	-0.51	0.36	0.16	-0.35	0.26	0.19	**-0.70**	**0.33**	**0.03**	-0.30	0.40	0.46
Lived in U.S. for 10 to 19 years	**-0.79**	**0.34**	**0.02**	**-0.76**	**0.30**	**0.01**	**-0.80**	**0.35**	**0.02**	**-0.60**	**0.25**	**0.02**	**-0.98**	**0.31**	**<0.01**	-0.50	0.38	0.19
Lived in U.S. for 20 years or longer; less than lifetime	-0.52	0.33	0.12	-0.57	0.29	0.05	-0.63	0.33	0.06	-0.40	0.24	0.10	**-0.73**	**0.30**	**0.02**	-0.39	0.36	0.28
Most comfortable speaking Spanish	**0.80**	**0.30**	**0.01**	**0.67**	**0.26**	**0.01**	**0.78**	**0.30**	**0.01**	**0.61**	**0.22**	**0.01**	**0.84**	**0.27**	**<0.01**	**0.91**	**0.33**	**0.01**
Health literacy assistance	0.24	0.16	0.12	0.11	0.14	0.43	0.24	0.16	0.13	0.11	0.11	0.33	0.16	0.14	0.27	0.10	0.17	0.55
R-Square	0.07			0.09			0.08			0.07			0.09			0.08		

Notes. SE = standard error. Men referenced to women; high school graduate referenced to less than high school education; employed referenced to unemployed; Mexican, Mexican-American, and Chicano participants referenced to participants who did not identify as Mexican, Mexican-American, or Chicano; length of residence for immigrants (<10 years, 10 to 19 years, 20 or more years) referenced to U.S.-born participants; most comfortable speaking Spanish referenced to Spanish language not preferred; health literacy assistance referenced to never or rarely receiving assistance. Bolded estimates indicate estimates that are statistically significant at the p = 0.05 level.

least a high school education (b = 0.25, SE = 0.15, p = 0.09) was marginally associated with reporting more frequent encounters of receiving poorer service. Immigrants who had lived in the United States for less than 10 years (b = –0.58, SE = 0.31, p = 0.07), 10 to 19 years (b = –0.76, SE = 0.30, p = 0.01), and 20 years or more (b = –0.57, SE = 0.29, p = 0.05) reported less frequent experiences of receiving poorer service than others, when compared to their U.S.-born counterparts. These differences between U.S.-born Latinos and Latino immigrants reached statistical significance for immigrants residing in the United States for 10 to 19 years and were marginally significant for immigrants residing in the United States for less than 10 years or 20 years or more. Compared to participants who did not express a preference for speaking Spanish, greater comfort speaking Spanish (b = 0.67, SE = 0.26, p = 0.01) was associated with significantly more frequent reported encounters of receiving poorer service than others. In addition, older age (b = –0.01, SE = 0.01, p = 0.06) was marginally significantly associated with less frequent reports of receiving poorer service than others. There was no significant association of gender, marital status, employment status, country of origin or descent, and engaging the assistance of others in health literacy encounters.

People act as if they think you are not smart

Table 2, Model 3, presents tests of the association of participants' social and economic characteristics with reports of being treated as if they are not smart. Relative to participants with lower levels of educational attainment, participants with at least a high school education (b = 0.34, SE = 0.17, p = 0.05) reported marginally significantly more frequent experiences of being treated as if they were not smart. Immigrants who lived in the United States for 10 to 19 years (b = –0.80, SE = 0.35, p = 0.02) reported significantly less frequent encounters of being treated as if they are not smart, relative to U.S.-born participants. Similarly, immigrants who lived in the United States for at least 20 years (b = –0.63, SE = 0.33, p = 0.06) were marginally significantly less likely than U.S.-born participants to report such treatment. Findings were in a similar direction for participants who lived in the United States for less than 10 years (b = –0.51, SE = 0.36, p = 0.16), although these differences were not statistically significant. Compared to their counterparts, participants who were most comfortable speaking Spanish (b = 0.78, SE = 0.30, p = 0.01) reported more frequent experiences of being treated as if they are not smart. Older age (b = –0.01, SE = 0.01, p = 0.07) was marginally associated with less frequent reports of being treated as if they are not smart. Gender, marital status, employment status, and country of origin or descent, and engagement of reading assistance in health contexts were not associated with participants' reports of being treated as if they are not smart.

Threatened or harassed

Summarized in Table 2, Model 4 are findings from tests of the association of participants' social and economic characteristics with reported frequency of being threatened or harassed. Older age (b = –0.01, SE = 0.01, p = 0.02) was significantly associated with less frequent reports of being threatened or harassed. Relative to U.S.-born Latinos, Latino immigrants who lived in the United States for 10 to 19 years (b = –0.60, SE = 0.25, p = 0.02) reported significantly less frequent accounts of being threatened or harassed. In contrast, there was no difference in these associations for immigrants living in the United States for less than 10 years (b = –0.35, SE = 0.26, p = 0.19) or for 20 years or more (b = –0.40, SE = 0.24, p = 0.10) relative to U.S.-born Latinos. As with other domains of discrimination, participants who were more comfortable speaking Spanish (b = 0.61, SE = 0.22, p = 0.01) were more likely to report being threatened or harassed relative to participants who did not prefer to speak Spanish. Gender, marital status, educational attainment, employment status, country of origin or descent, and utilizing assistance reading health-related items were not associated with reports of being threatened or harassed.

Treated unfairly or badly due to Hispanic/Latino ethnicity

Results from tests of the correlates of being treated unfairly or badly due to Hispanic or Latino ethnicity are presented in Table 2, Model 5. Relative to their U.S.-born counterparts, immigrants reported significantly less frequent experiences of being treated unfairly across each classification of length of U.S. residence (less than 10 years: b = –0.70, SE = 0.33, p = 0.03; 10 to 19 years: b = –0.98, SE = 0.31, $p < 0.01$; 20 or more years: b = –0.73, SE = 0.30, p = 0.02). In addition, those most comfortable speaking Spanish (b = 0.84, SE = 0.27, $p < 0.01$) were more likely to report being treated unfairly relative to those who did not indicate a preference for speaking Spanish. Older age (b = –0.01, 0.01, p = 0.05) was marginally significantly associated with less frequent reports of unfair treatment. Gender, marital status, educational attainment, employment status, country of origin or descent, and engaging health literacy assistance were not associated with reports of unfair or bad treatment due to their ethnicity.

Treated unfairly or badly due to language spoken or accent

Tests of the association of social and economic characteristics with unfair treatment due to language use are presented in Table 2, Model 6. Relative to those who did not prefer to speak Spanish, those who indicated that they were more comfortable speaking Spanish (b = 0.91, SE = 0.33, p = 0.01) reported significantly more frequent experiences of being treated unfairly or badly due to their language use or having an accent. Older age ($b = -0.02$, SE $= 0.01$, $p = 0.06$) was marginally significantly associated with reports of unfair treatment due to language use or having an accent. In contrast to findings for other domains of interpersonal ethnoracial discrimination, there was no difference in frequency of reports of unfair treatment due to language use or having an accent for those who were born in the United States relative to immigrants. These findings were consistent across years of U.S. residence for immigrants. Gender, marital status, educational attainment, employment status, country of origin or descent, and health literacy were not associated with reports of being treated unfairly due to language use or having an accent.

Interpersonal ethnoracial discrimination scale

Finally, tests of the correlates of interpersonal ethnoracial discrimination, as assessed by a six-item scale, are presented in Table 3. Increased age ($b = -0.01$, SE $= 0.01$, $p = 0.02$) was associated with significantly less frequent reports of interpersonal ethnoracial discrimination. These patterns also differed for immigrants relative to U.S.-born participants, although the strength of the association varied according to length of U.S. residence for immigrants. Specifically, immigrants who resided in the United States for 10 to 19 years ($b = -0.74$, SE $= 0.25$, $p < 0.01$) and those who lived in the United States for 20 or more years ($b = -0.54$, SE $= 0.24$, $p = 0.02$) reported significantly less frequent encounters of interpersonal ethnoracial discrimination than their U.S.-born counterparts. Immigrants who lived in the United States for less than 10 years ($b = -0.49$,

Table 3. Interpersonal ethnoracial discrimination scale regressed on participant social and economic characteristics, REACH Detroit Cohort 3 ($N = 222$).

	b	SE	p-value
Intercept	2.11	0.33	<0.01
Age	−0.01	0.01	**0.02**
Man	−0.10	0.11	0.39
Married or partnered	0.05	0.12	0.68
High school education or higher	0.14	0.12	0.27
Employed	0.10	0.11	0.40
Mexican	0.03	0.13	0.80
Lived in U.S. for less than 10 years	−0.49	0.26	0.06
Lived in U.S. for 10 to 19 years	**−0.74**	**0.25**	**<0.01**
Lived in U.S. for 20 years or longer	**−0.54**	**0.24**	**0.02**
Most comfortable speaking Spanish	**0.77**	**0.22**	**<0.01**
Reading assistance	0.16	0.11	0.16
R-Square	0.10		

Notes. SE = standard error. Men referenced to women; high school graduate referenced to less than high school education; employed referenced to unemployed; Mexican, Mexican-American, and Chicano participants referenced to participants who did not identify as Mexican, Mexican-American, or Chicano; length of residence for immigrants (<10 years, 10 to 19 years, 20 or more years) referenced to U.S.-born participants; most comfortable speaking Spanish referenced to Spanish language not preferred; health literacy assistance referenced to never or rarely receiving assistance. Bolded estimates indicate estimates that are statistically significant at the $p = 0.05$ level.

SE = 0.26, p = 0.06) also reported less frequent experiences of interpersonal ethnoracial discrimination than U.S.-born participants, and these associations were marginally significant. Furthermore, participants who reported that they were most comfortable speaking Spanish (b = 0.77, SE = 0.22, p < 0.01) reported significantly more frequent interpersonal ethnoracial discrimination than their counterparts. Results presented here suggest that gender, marital status, educational attainment, employment status, country of origin or descent, and health literacy assistance were not significantly associated with interpersonal ethnoracial discrimination. Findings were similar in tests of sensitivity using a five-item scale.

Discussion

Contribution to the literature

These findings suggest that at least two-thirds of Detroit-based Latinos in this diabetes intervention study experienced interpersonal ethnoracial discrimination. This study indicates that the correlates of interpersonal ethnoracial discrimination in a sample of adult Latinos with diabetes vary according to social characteristics linked with immigration-related factors and language use. Specifically, U.S. nativity and greater comfort speaking Spanish were associated with more frequent reports of interpersonal ethnoracial discrimination across each domain. These findings are consistent with other literature (Borrell et al., 2010; LeBrón et al., 2014; Perez et al., 2008). However, in this study, the strength of these differences was contingent upon the length of U.S. residence of Latino immigrants when compared to their U.S.-born counterparts. Specifically, immigrants who lived in the United States for 10 to 19 years at the time of the survey generally reported less frequent discrimination than their US-born counterparts and immigrants who had lived in the United States for less than 10 years or at least 20 years. To our knowledge, this U-shaped association in the frequency of reported discrimination by length of U.S. residence has not been documented in the literature. In addition, as found in other studies (Borrell et al., 2010; LeBrón et al., 2014; Perez et al., 2008), reports of interpersonal ethnoracial discrimination were less frequent with older age. Trends also suggest that higher educational attainment was associated with more frequent accounts of receiving poorer service than others and being treated as if one is not smart. However, the strength of this association did not hold for other domains of interpersonal ethnoracial discrimination, nor when considering the association of educational attainment with discrimination when assessed as a scale. With the exception of this variation in the association of educational attainment with specific domains of discrimination, the social and economic correlates of each domain of discrimination, as well as the interpersonal ethnoracial discrimination scale, were consistent. In the paragraphs that follow, we discuss the implications of these findings regarding the persistent association of nativity and language use with more frequent discrimination, trends suggesting that older age is correlated with less frequent accounts of discrimination, findings that suggest that certain domains of interpersonal ethnoracial discrimination are patterned by educational attainment, and considerations for using the discrimination scale relative to specific domains of discrimination when evaluating the patterning of interpersonal ethnoracial discrimination.

Nativity and length of U.S. residence

Findings indicate a differential pattern of discrimination based upon whether Latino participants were born in the United States or were immigrants. The strength of these associations was contingent upon the length of U.S. residence of Latino immigrants. Specifically, consistent with findings from Perez and colleagues (2008), U.S.-born Latinos in this sample reported more frequent encounters of interpersonal ethnoracial discrimination than Latino immigrants. In this study, for each domain of discrimination attributed to Hispanic or Latino ethnicity, immigrants who lived in the United States for 10 to 19 years were significantly less likely to report discrimination than U.S.-born Latinos. Findings were in a similar direction, although attenuated, when U.S.-born Latinos were compared to immigrants living in the United States for nine years or less, or for 20 years or more. More frequent experiences of interpersonal ethnoracial discrimination among U.S.-born Latinos relative to Latino immigrants may reflect differential exposure to processes of constructing, navigating, and resisting ethnoracial meanings and inequalities associated with these processes and/or familiarity with frameworks for processing and coping with these experiences (Almaguer, 2009; Omi & Winant, 2015). For example, based on interviews with Mexican and Mexican-American women who lived in Detroit, Viruell-Fuentes (2007) found that U.S.-born and immigrant women described their encounters with discrimination differently. In addition, immigrant women in that study tended to have more insular interactions within their ethnic enclave, and with familiar others, whereas U.S.-born women's lives were embedded in their ethnic enclave, and also in institutions outside of their ethnic enclave. Thus, these findings may be attributed to different opportunities for interaction with people outside of their ethnic enclaves and/or different ways of understanding and coping with discriminatory experiences.

Among immigrants, there was a U-shaped relationship between length of U.S. residence and interpersonal ethnoracial discrimination. Specifically, findings indicate lower reported interpersonal ethnoracial discrimination for immigrants who had resided in the United States for 10 to 19 years relative to U.S.-born Latinos, but not immigrants who lived in the United

States for less than 10 years or more than 20 years. These patterns may be attributed to cohort effects of immigration policies or contexts of reception when participants migrated to the United States. For example, immigrants who had lived in the United States for 10 to 19 years at the time of the study would have arrived in the United States between 1990 and 2003. This period was characterized by increasingly restrictive sentiments and policies toward Latino immigrants leading up to and following the passage of the 1996 Illegal Immigration Reform and Immigrant Responsibility Act (IIRIRA) and 1996 Personal Responsibility and Work Opportunity Reconciliation Act (PRWORA). Each of these policies reinforced anti-Latino and anti-immigrant sentiments, set in motion restricted access to social and economic resources, and restricted opportunities to establish residency or citizenship. However, the 1990–2003 period was less hostile toward Latino immigrants than more recent years (Chavez, 2013). Indeed, in 2005 and 2006, the newly created Department of Homeland Security began to implement new, restrictive immigration enforcement activities within the United States, and anti-immigrant sentiments, which have often been conflated with anti-Latino sentiments, have continued to rise (Chavez, 2013; DeGenova, 2004, 2007; Golash-Boza, 2012). Given these policy shifts, some immigrants who migrated to the United States from 1990 to 2003 may have had better opportunities for improving their immigration status than those who migrated to the United States after 2004.

This U-shaped relationship suggests that further research is needed to disentangle these patterns. Indeed, Perez and colleagues (2008) report that relative to Latino immigrants who lived in the United States for a shorter period, Latino immigrants who lived in the United States for the majority of their lives were more likely to report discrimination. Several factors may contribute to the differences in results presented here relative to findings by Perez and colleagues (2008). First, the present study engaged a different measure, namely length of U.S. residence, whereas Perez and colleagues (2008) examined the age of migration among Latino immigrants. Thus, in this study, the U-shaped association of length of U.S. residence with discrimination may reflect cohort-specific differences in immigration policies and sentiments toward immigrants. Second, this study adjusts for age and educational attainment, factors that may affect both the reporting of discrimination as well as the frequency or domain of discrimination that Latinos may experience and report (LeBrón et al., 2014; Viruell-Fuentes, 2007, 2011). Third, the study by Perez and colleagues (2008) engaged data from a national sample of Latinos. In contrast, this study drew on reports from Latinos in Detroit who have diabetes. It is possible that there are important contextual differences in experiences of discrimination, as well as resources on which Latinos can draw to process and/or address their experiences. For example, participants' residence in an ethnic enclave within Detroit and/or receipt services from a Latino-focused FQHC with bilingual staff may contribute to the findings reported in this study. Future studies are warranted that involve a sizable sample of U.S.-born and immigrant Latinos and that go beyond measuring immigrant generation to include more sophisticated measures of length of U.S. residence and context of reception and residence in the U.S. Additionally, studies are warranted that examine the association of reported discrimination with immigration-related policies and ideologies and other features of the social, economic, and political context of the U.S. and communities in which participants live.

Language use

The results of this study also indicated that Latinos who were more comfortable speaking Spanish reported more frequent interpersonal ethnic discrimination than their counterparts who did not indicate a preference for speaking Spanish. Comfort speaking Spanish may reflect strength of ethnic identity, nativity, and knowledge of Spanish, English, or other languages. Accordingly, these findings may reflect encounters of discrimination based on ethnicity and/or language use. We conceptualized language preferences as assessing the language that participants may be more likely to engage in day-to-day experiences in which they may encounter discrimination, which may be linked with each of the aforementioned factors.

If comfort speaking Spanish is strongly correlated with nativity or length of U.S. residence for immigrants, then it would be anticipated that the association of comfort speaking Spanish with interpersonal ethnoracial discrimination would be similar to patterns for nativity and length of U.S. residence. That is, given the negative association of being born outside of the United States with the frequency of interpersonal ethnoracial discrimination, we would expect Spanish-language use to follow a similar pattern. However, greater comfort speaking Spanish was associated with more frequent discrimination, and U.S.-born Latinos reported more frequent discrimination than immigrants, particularly immigrants who had resided in the United States for 10 to 19 years. There are several plausible explanations for divergent patterns between the association of greater comfort speaking Spanish and nativity and length of U.S. residence with interpersonal ethnoracial discrimination. Although conceptually possible, there was a small ($r = 0.15$ to 0.28) correlation between Spanish-language preference and length of U.S. residence for Latino immigrants and a moderate correlation between Spanish-language preference and U.S. nativity ($r = -0.78$). Although evidence indicates that Spanish-language use declines with length of U.S. residence for Latino immigrants, and with immigrant generation (Rumbaut, Massey, & Bean, 2006; Taylor, Lopez, Martínez, & Velasco, 2012), these low to moderate correlations may reflect participants' residence in an ethnic enclave, which may contribute to the vibrancy of and support for speaking Spanish in this sample. Second, this positive association of Spanish-language comfort with frequency of discrimination may reflect discrimination in which the perpetrator may engage based on the participants' language use. Indeed, language use is observable and easier to discern, and therefore to discriminate against in routine encounters, compared to other identities and statuses, such as length of U.S. residence or nativity.

Age

Consistent with the literature (Borrell et al., 2010; LeBrón et al., 2014; Perez et al., 2008), we also found that frequency of reports of discrimination declined with increasing age, after accounting for social and economic factors. The persistence of these findings in this study and across the literature suggests a need for further research regarding the association of age, immigrant generation, and length of U.S. residence with interpersonal ethnoracial discrimination in samples that involve a sizable number of Latinos. The consistency of this finding, even after accounting for nativity and length of U.S. residence, suggests that social factors associated with age may pattern the risk of discrimination and/or participants' reporting of discrimination. For example, it is plausible that younger Latinos may have more frequent encounters of discrimination either based on their age or based on the structure of their lives, such as their greater likelihood to conduct activities outside of the home (e.g., occupational- or caregiving-related activities) in which they may experience discrimination. In contrast, older participants may engage with others outside of their network or conduct activities outside of their home on a less frequent basis. In addition, this study queried about the frequency of these experiences in participants' day-to-day lives. As this question was not bound by a particular time, the question may have prompted participants to reflect on a more recent time period in their life, rather than their experiences over multiple months, years, or decades. As such, younger participants—who may have more frequent encounters with others—may draw upon their more recent experiences when responding to these questions. In contrast, older participants may also telescope to their more recent encounters—rather than experiences beyond the period to which they are reflecting—which may be patterned on their occupational and caregiving statuses.

Educational attainment

While marginally significant, trends suggested that higher educational attainment was patterned with more frequent encounters of receiving poorer service than others or being treated as if participants were not smart. This finding that educational attainment was patterned with these domains of discrimination, but not other domains, suggests that these encounters may occur in contexts in which educational attainment is salient, such as schools, workplaces, or encounters that may infer ascribed intelligence or knowledge. For example, participants with a high school education or more may be drawing on their experiences in the workplace. In addition, the patterning of high school education with receipt of poorer service may reflect dynamics of socioeconomic status. For example, these experiences may occur in settings in which persons with higher income or educational attainment may engage. Alternatively, these findings may reflect participants' anticipation of respect or good treatment on the basis of their educational achievements, which may not have been met in these settings (James, 1994; James & Thomas, 2000; Sellers & Neighbors, 2008). In addition, the positive association of educational attainment with reports of discrimination may be attributed to differential exposure to frameworks for understanding processes and experiences of discrimination. Exposure to such frameworks may be gained through educational institutions or the engagement in dialogues, activities, and social movements to understand and address discrimination.

Domains of interpersonal ethnoracial discrimination and interpersonal ethnoracial discrimination scale

This study sought to disentangle whether the correlates of discrimination varied according to the domain. Given that some of the discrimination items capture microaggressions and others capture overt forms of discrimination, it was important to assess for variation in the correlates of these domains of discrimination. We found that, in general, the correlates of interpersonal ethnoracial discrimination were consistent across each domain that constitutes the interpersonal ethnoracial discrimination scale, with the exception of the strength of the association of educational attainment. These findings suggest that scales that assess multiple dimensions of experiences of discrimination in routine encounters generally capture the correlates of discrimination, although they may obscure important differences depending on the context.

Limitations and strengths

As with all studies, this investigation is characterized by several limitations. First, the sizable, although moderate, sample size in this study precluded the use of more sophisticated assessments of social characteristics. For example, in this sample the limited variation in educational attainment, combined with a small sample size, prevented the use of a more nuanced measure of educational attainment. In addition, it was important to account for country of origin or descent in these analyses, as there are important differences in immigration policies and contexts of reception based on country of origin or descent. In this study, 80% of participants identified as Mexican, Mexican-American, or Chicano. Therefore, we compared persons who cited Mexico as their country of origin or descent to other Latino subgroups. We acknowledge that there are important differences between groups that were categorized together as non-Mexican. For example, Puerto Ricans (5.4% of this sample) have U.S. citizenship, whereas some participants with ties to other Latin American countries or their family members may lack citizenship or residency status and experience different contexts of reception and opportunity than other Latinos with whom they are classified in this analysis. Second, although this study measures interpersonal ethnoracial discrimination, it does not assess the context of discrimination that participants report, such as where the encounter(s) occurred and the perpetrator(s). This limitation prevents assessments of the implications of these experiences of discrimination for social and economic mobility or ethnic identity. In addition, this limitation precludes opportunities to consider policy and other structural interventions to reduce discrimination. Third, in each regression model, the R-square is modest, suggesting that this study does not account for all of the factors that need to be accounted for in understanding the patterning of discrimination. Future studies that account for other or more specific correlates of discrimination, and that have an adequate sample size to test for interactions, are warranted.

Despite these limitations, there are also several strengths of this study. First, this study extends the small literature (Borrell et al., 2010; Gee et al., 2006; LeBrón et al., 2014; Perez et al., 2008) regarding correlates of discrimination among Latinos. This is the first study of which we are aware that examines the correlates of discrimination by domain of discrimination. The results presented here extend the discrimination and microaggressions literature by disentangling the correlates of interpersonal ethnoracial discrimination and evaluating the possibility of variations in these patterns according to the domain of discrimination. Second, this study considers interpersonal ethnoracial discrimination attributed to ethnicity-related factors such as Hispanic or Latino identity and language use. Third, this study enhances understanding of patterns of discrimination among a sample of Latinos from a Midwestern urban community, from which few such studies (LeBrón et al., 2014) have originated. Fourth, given that Latinos in this sample were burdened by one of the leading chronic diseases among this population (Vega, Rodriguez, & Gruskin, 2009) and received health care from an FQHC in a post-ACA environment, these findings may be generalizable to other populations of Latinos similarly affected by chronic disease and challenges to accessing health care, for whom FQHCs help to mitigate these challenges. Indeed, more than half of participants identified as immigrants, for whom there may be wide variation in their immigration status. At the time of this intervention, health insurance expansions under the ACA were unfolding. While this policy expanded access to health insurance for many individuals and populations, immigrants lacking particular immigration statuses (e.g., citizen, legal permanent resident for at least five years) were the only group that was explicitly excluded from opportunities to gain health insurance through new markets. Despite this exclusionary aspect of this health insurance policy, participants in this study had access to needed health care and other services through their connections with the FQHC. Thus, their affiliation with the FQHC may affect participants' experiences and reporting of discrimination in day-to-day encounters, such as when trying to access medical and social services.

Conclusions

This study suggests that the frequency of reported discrimination is moderately high, and relatively common among Latinos with diabetes who live in Detroit. A central conclusion from this analysis is that immigration and ethnicity-related factors, such as greater comfort speaking Spanish and being born in the United States, were persistent correlates of more frequent encounters of interpersonal ethnoracial discrimination. These findings are particularly important given the association of discrimination with health outcomes generally (Williams & Mohammed, 2009), and with factors associated with diabetes management and progression (LeBrón et al., 2014; March et al., 2015). Findings presented here suggest that discrimination is a critical stressor in the day-to-day lives of Latinos with diabetes. The prevalence and patterns of discrimination reported here illustrate the processes of marginalization that some Latinos navigate on a day-to-day basis.

This study has implications for social work research and practice, as findings provide insight into the patterning of experiences of microaggressions, discrimination, and ultimately marginalization among Latinos with a chronic condition for which service providers may assist Latino individuals and communities to navigate, cope with, and/or respond. In addition, these findings point to strategies that systems such as health care and social service institutions can engage to ensure that their institutions support equity and inclusion through their policies and practices. These findings indicate the need for interventions to foster more inclusive discourses and communities to promote the health and well-being of the youngest, largest, and fastest-growing ethnic minority population in the country (Passel et al., 2011; U.S. Census Bureau, 2014). Policies to support a more inclusive society are urgently needed to reduce the prevalence and frequency of discrimination on the basis of ethnicity and other marginalized identities. In addition, attention to and support of social movements to foster more inclusive dialogues and communities (McAdam & Snow, 1997), as well as interventions such as intergroup dialogues to foster better understanding of differences (Schoem & Hurtado, 2001), and mental health services to process experiences of difference and discrimination are urgently needed.

Funding

This research was supported by the National Institute of Diabetes and Digestive and Kidney Disease (R18DK0785501A1: Spencer, P.I.), the Michigan Center for Diabetes Translational Research (MCDTR), the National Institute of Diabetes and Digestive and Kidney Diseases (P30DK092926), and the National Center for Institutional Diversity.

Acknowledgments

We thank the Community Health and Social Services (CHASS) and REACH Detroit Partnership staff, the REACH Detroit Partnership Steering Committee (www.reachdetroit.org), and the REACH Detroit Family Intervention participants for their involvement in this study. The REACH Detroit Partnership is affiliated with the Detroit Community-Academic Urban Research Center (www.sph.umich.edu/URC).

References

Almaguer, T. (2009). *Racial fault lines: The historical origins of White supremacy in California*. Berkeley, CA: University of California Press.

Borrell, L. N., Roux, A. V. D., David, R., Jacobs, J., Shea, S., Jackson, S. A., ... Blumenthal, R. S. (2010). Perceived racial/ethnic discrimination, smoking and alcohol consumption in the Multi-ethnic Study of Atherosclerosis (MESA). *Preventative Medicine, 51*, 307–312. doi:10.1016/j.ypmed.2010.05.017

Chavez, L. R. (2013). *The Latino threat: Constructing immigrants, citizens, and the nation* (2nd ed.). Stanford, CA: Stanford University Press.

Cox, A. B., & Miles, T. J. (2013). Policing immigration. *The University of Chicago Law Review, 80*(1), 87–136.

DeGenova, N. (2004). The legal production of Mexican/migrant "illegality." *Latino Studies, 2*, 160–185. doi:10.1057/palgrave.lst.8600085

DeGenova, N. (2007). The production of culprits: From deportability to detainability in the aftermath of "Homeland Security." *Citizenship Studies, 11*(5), 421–448. doi:10.1080/13621020701605735

Gee, G. C., Ryan, A., Laflamme, D. J., & Holt, J. (2006). Self-reported discrimination and mental health status among African descendents, Mexican Americans, and other Latinos in the New Hampshire REACH 2010 initiative: The added dimension of immigration. *American Journal of Public Healthx, 96*, 1821–1828. doi:10.2105/AJPH.2005.080085

Golash-Boza, T. M. (2012). *Immigration nation: Raids, detentions, and deportations in post-9/11 America*. Boulder, CO: Paradigm Publishers.

Golash-Boza, T. M., & Hondagneu-Sotelo, P. (2013). Latino immigrant men and the deportation crisis: A gendered racial removal program. *Latino Studies, 11*, 271–292. doi:10.1057/lst.2013.14

James, S. A. (1994). John Henryism and the health of African Americans. *Culture, Medicine, and Psychiatry, 18*, 163–182. doi:10.1007/BF01379448

James, S. A., & Thomas, P. E. (2000). John Henryism and blood pressure in Black populations: A review of the evidence. *African American Research Perspectives, 6*(3), 1–10.

LeBrón, A. M. W., Valerio, M. A., Kieffer, E., Sinco, B., Rosland, A.-M., Hawkins, J., ... Spencer, M. (2014). Everyday discrimination, diabetes-related distress, and depressive symptoms among African Americans and Latinos with diabetes. *Journal of Immigrant and Minority Health, 16*(6), 1208–1216. doi:10.1007/s10903-013-9843-3

March, D., Williams, J., Wells, S., Eimicke, J. P., Teresi, J. A., Almonte, C.,.... Luchsinger, J. A. (2015). Discrimination and depression among urban Hispanics with poorly controlled diabetes. *Ethnicity & Disease*, *25*, 130–137.

McAdam, D., & Snow, D. A. (1997). *Social movements: Readings on their emergence, mobilization, and dynamics.* Los Angeles, CA: Roxbury Publishing Company.

Omi, M., & Winant, H. (2015). *Racial formation in the United States* (3rd ed.). New York, NY: Routledge.

Passel, J., & Cohn, D. (2008). *U.S. population projections: 2005–2050.* Washington, DC: Pew Hispanic Center.

Passel, J., Cohn, D. V., & Lopez, M. H. (2011). *Census 2010: 50 million Latinos: Hispanics account for more than half of the nation's growth in past decade.* Washington, DC: Pew Hispanic Center.

Perez, D. J., Fortuna, L., & Alegria, M. (2008). Prevalence and correlates of everyday discrimination among Latinos. *Journal of Community Psychology*, *36*(4), 421–433. doi:10.1002/jcop.20221

Rumbaut, R. G., Massey, D. S., & Bean, F. D. (2006). Linguistic life expectancies: Immigrant language retention in Southern California. *Population and Development Review*, *32*(3), 447–460. doi:10.1111/padr.2006.32.issue-3

Schoem, D., & Hurtado, S. (Eds.). (2001). *Intergroup dialogue: Deliberative democracy in school, college, community, and workplace.* Ann Arbor, MI: The University of Michigan Press.

Sellers, S. L., & Neighbors, H. W. (2008). Effects of goal-striving stress on the mental health of Black Americans. *Journal of Health and Social Behavior*, *49*, 92–103. doi:10.1177/002214650804900107

Sue, D. W., Capodilupo, C. M., Torino, G. C., Bucceri, J. M., Holder, A. M., Nadal, K. L., & Esquilin, M. (2007). Racial microaggressions in everyday life: Implications for clinical practice. *American Psychologist*, *62*(4), 271–286. doi:10.1037/0003-066X.62.4.271

Taylor, P., Lopez, M. H., Martínez, J. H., & Velasco, G. (2012). *When labels don't fit: Hispanics and their views of identity.* Washington, DC: Pew Hispanic Center. Retrieved from http://www.pewhispanic.org/files/2012/04/PHC-Hispanic-Identity.pdf

U.S. Census Bureau. (2014). *ACS demographic and housing estimates.* Washington, DC: U.S. Census Bureau.

Vega, W. A., Rodriguez, M. A., & Gruskin, E. (2009). Health disparities in the Latino population. *Epidemiologic Reviews*, *31*, 99–112. doi:10.1093/epirev/mxp008

Viruell-Fuentes, E. A. (2007). Beyond acculturation: Immigration, discrimination, and health research among Mexicans in the United States. *Social Science & Medicine*, *65*, 1524–1535. doi:10.1016/j.socscimed.2007.05.010

Viruell-Fuentes, E. A. (2011). "It's a lot of work": Racialization processes, ethnic identity formations, and their health implications. *Du Bois Review*, *8*(1), 37–52. doi:10.1017/S1742058X11000117

Viruell-Fuentes, E. A., Miranda, P. Y., & Abdulrahim, S. (2012). More than culture: Structural racism, intersectionality theory, and immigrant health. *Social Science & Medicine*, *75*, 2099–2106. doi:10.1016/j.socscimed.2011.12.037

Williams, D. R., & Mohammed, S. A. (2009). Discrimination and racial disparities in health: Evidence and needed research. *Journal of Behavioral Medicine*, *32*, 20–47. doi:10.1007/s10865-008-9185-0

Williams, D. R., Yu, Y., & Jackson, J. S. (1997). Racial differences in physical and mental health: Socioeconomic status, stress, and discrimination. *Journal of Health Psychology*, *2*(3), 335–351. doi:10.1177/135910539700200305

Everyday Racial Discrimination, Everyday Non-Racial Discrimination, and Physical Health Among African-Americans

Dawne M. Mouzon, Robert Joseph Taylor, Amanda Toler Woodward, and Linda M. Chatters

ABSTRACT
Past research has identified a link between discrimination and health outcomes among people of color. Perceptions of the cause of discrimination (racial versus other) seem to be important for mental health; however, this relationship has not been fully examined for physical health. Using data from the National Survey of American Life, we find that, among African-Americans, racial discrimination and overall discrimination regardless of attribution are associated with negative health outcomes while non-racial discrimination is not. The results suggest that racial discrimination has a unique adverse effect on physical health for African-Americans that practitioners need to better understand.

Introduction

Discrimination is primarily conceptualized as a form of unfair treatment that operates as a psychosocial stressor for people of color and other materially disadvantaged populations (Landrine & Klonoff, 1996). Two broad categories of discrimination are typically studied. Major lifetime experiences of discrimination encompass singular discrete incidents of unfair treatment in macro areas of society (i.e., the labor market, the criminal justice system, the housing market). Everyday discrimination comprises interpersonal daily hassles and insults such as receiving inferior service and being unfairly followed in stores. Everyday discrimination encompasses chronic psychosocial stressors (Essed, 1991) that are important because they serve as ongoing challenges to the emotional well-being of individuals. Exhaustive reviews of the literature find that perceived major and everyday discrimination have deleterious effects on physical and mental health (Lewis, Cogburn, & Williams, 2015; Williams & Mohammed, 2009, 2013).

Everyday discrimination and health

Research has found higher levels of everyday discrimination among African-Americans than Whites (Ayalon & Gum, 2011; Beatty Moody, Brown, Matthews, & Bromberger, 2014; Luo, Xu, Granberg, & Wentworth, 2012; Turner & Avison, 2003; Williams, Yu, Jackson, & Anderson, 1997). In addition, both African-American adults (Kessler, Mickelson, & Williams, 1999) and African-American adolescents (Seaton, Caldwell, Sellers, & Jackson, 2010) are more likely than their White counterparts to attribute discrimination to racial causes rather than non-racial causes. Data from the Chicago Community Adult Health Study found that 42.9% of Blacks reported racial discrimination, compared to 30.5% of Latinos and 7.8% of Whites. However, Whites were most likely to report non-racial discrimination (55.6% versus 34.8% for Blacks and 27.3% for Latinos) (Hunte & Williams, 2009). Since the gains made in the Civil Rights movement, the nature of racism has largely shifted from overt and blatant forms to invisible and covert forms of racial discrimination (Dovidio & Gaertner, 2000), challenging ideas of a post-racial society that became rampant after the U.S. presidential election of Barack Obama in 2008. For this reason it is imperative to better understand phenomena such as everyday discrimination.

Despite consensus around the negative effects of discrimination, ongoing debates center on whether racial discrimination is an especially pernicious form of unfair treatment for Black Americans, one that is more harmful than other forms of discrimination (Lewis et al., 2015; Williams et al., 2012). Some scholars have suggested that characteristics that are most central to the identity of the self (i.e., ascribed race for African-Americans) are most vulnerable to environmental insults (Thoits, 2013). Therefore, it could be expected that racial discrimination would be especially detrimental to the health of Black Americans.

Some research has explored this idea empirically and those studies reach mixed findings. An analysis of data from the Study of Women's Health Across the Nation (SWAN) found that Black women who attributed discrimination to racial causes had higher levels of cardiovascular reactivity than those who attributed discrimination to non-racial causes, an interaction that was not found among White women (Guyll, Matthews, & Bromberger, 2001). The same data indicated that non-racial discrimination—but not racial discrimination—was associated with coronary artery calcification among African-American women (Lewis et al., 2006).

In this study, we add to the present literature in several critical ways. First, we examine 13 indicators of physical health to acquire a more complete understanding of this issue. Second, in addition to having a physical health problem, we investigate the impact of discrimination on the degree to which a health problem interferes with a person's daily activities. Third, we investigate the relative effects of racial discrimination, non-racial discrimination, and overall discrimination on our indicators of physical health. This is in accordance with recent calls to elucidate potential variation in how discrimination attributions (i.e., racial versus non-racial) affect health outcomes (Lewis et al., 2015). Finally, we use secondary data from a nationally representative sample of more than 3,000 African-Americans who participated in the National Survey of American Life.

Methods

Sample

The National Survey of American Life: Coping With Stress in the 21st Century (NSAL) was collected by the Program for Research on Black Americans at the University of Michigan's Institute for Social Research. The fieldwork for the study was completed by the Institute for Social Research's Survey Research Center, in cooperation with the Program for Research on Black Americans. The NSAL sample has a national multistage probability design which consists of 64 primary sampling units (PSUs). The data collection was conducted from February 2001 to June 2003. A total of 6,082 interviews were conducted with persons ages 18 or older, including 3,570 African-Americans (which is the subsample used for this analysis). The response rate for African-Americans was 70.7%. A more detailed discussion of the NSAL can be found elsewhere (Jackson, Neighbors, Nesse, Trierweiler, & Torres, 2004). The NSAL data collection was approved by the University of Michigan's Institutional Review Board.

Measures

Dependent variables

The present analysis investigated 13 dependent variables, including 11 measures of chronic health and two measures of self-rated health (physical and oral). Each of the health variables is listed in Table 1. Self-rated physical health was measured by respondents' rating of their overall physical health at the present time (1 = poor to 5 = excellent). Self-rated oral health was measured in the same way.

Chronic health problems were measured by respondents' reports of doctor-diagnosed physical health conditions. We assessed total number of problems as well as three overarching categories of chronic health problems: cardiovascular (hypertension, stroke, blood circulation problems, and heart problems or heart attack), respiratory (asthma, chronic lung disease, and tuberculosis), and pain (arthritis or rheumatism, ulcers, very bad headaches or migraines, and serious back problems). These categories are consistent with other research on chronic health conditions among Asian-Americans (Gee, Spencer, Chen, & Takeuchi, 2007).

Table 1. Demographic characteristics of the sample and distribution of study variables, national survey of American life.

	%	N	Mean	SD	Min	Max
Age		3570	42.33	14.50	18	93
Gender						
Male	44.03	1271				
Female	55.97	2299				
Years of Education		3570	12.43	2.23	0	17
Family Income		3570	36832	33068	0	520000
Marital Status						
Married/Cohabit	41.65	1222				
Non-Married	58.35	2340				
Region						
Northeast	15.69	411				
Midwest	18.81	595				
South	56.24	2330				
West	9.25	234				
Employment Status						
Employed	66.83	2334				
Unemployed	10.07	366				
Not in Labor Force	23.10	861				
Any Everyday Discrimination		3527	12.47	8.01	0	50
Everyday Racial Discrimination		3412	8.45	8.85	0	50
Everyday Non-racial Discrimination		3411	3.21	6.36	0	48
Self-Rated Health		3437	3.42	0.95	1	5
Self-Rated Dental Health		3435	3.11	0.99	1	5
# of Cardiovascular Problems		3437	0.50	0.68	0	4
Any Cardiovascular Problems		3435	0.37	0.43	0	1
Interference From Cardiovascular Problems		1306	2.13	1.57	1	12
# of Respiratory Problems		3437	0.16	0.36	0	3
Any Respiratory Problem		3437	0.15	0.32	0	1
Interference From Respiratory Problems		491	1.73	0.96	1	8
# of Pain Problems		3437	0.70	0.80	0	4
Any Pain Problem		3437	0.15	0.32	0	1
Interference From Pain Problems		1681	2.87	1.77	1	12
Total # Chronic Health Problems		3437	1.36	1.31	0	10
Interference From Total # of Chronic Health Problems		2249	3.69	2.96	1	27

Note. Percentages and N are presented for categorical variables. Means and standard deviations are presented for continuous variables. Percentages are weighted and frequencies are unweighted.

We also examined the degree to which chronic health problems interfere with a person's daily life. Respondents were asked, "Currently, how much does this health problem keep you from working or carrying out your daily tasks?" The response categories included a great deal (3), only a little (2), and not at all (1). Responses were summed to create four indexes that measure daily interference from cardiovascular problems, respiratory problems, problems with pain, and problems from all chronic health problems.

Independent variables

The main independent variable is everyday discrimination, which was designed to assess interpersonal forms of routine experiences of discrimination (Williams et al., 1997). In total, there were three measures of everyday discrimination in this analysis, including everyday racial discrimination, everyday non-racial discrimination, and overall discrimination regardless of attribution.

A total of 10 items were used to measure everyday discrimination:

(1) treated with less courtesy;
(2) treated with less respect;
(3) received poor restaurant service;
(4) perceived as not smart;
(5) perceived as dishonest;
(6) perceived as not as good as others;
(7) being feared;
(8) being insulted;
(9) being harassed; and
(10) followed in stores.

Response values for each item included the following: 5 (almost every day), 4 (at least once a week), 3 (a few times a month), 2 (a few times a year), 1 (less than once a year), and 0 (never). Responses were summed with higher scores indicating more discrimination.

Participants who reported experiencing any discrimination were asked to identify the primary reason for such experiences (e.g., race, ethnicity, skin color, gender, sexual orientation, income, age, height, weight). Based on this item, two additional everyday discrimination variables were created: (1) perceived discrimination that was attributed to race and (2) perceived discrimination that was attributed to non-racial reasons.

Several sociodemographic factors (i.e., age, gender, family income, years of education, marital status, region, and employment status) are included as control variables. Age and education are coded in years; household income is coded in dollars. Marital status is coded as married/cohabiting versus not married. Region is coded as four categories (Northeast, North Central, West, and South) and employment status had three categories: employed, unemployed, and not in the labor force.

Analysis strategy

The distribution of basic sociodemographic characteristics, linear regression analyses, and logistic regression analyses were conducted using SAS 9.1.3, which uses the Taylor expansion approximation technique for calculating the complex design-based estimates of variance. All analyses utilize analytic weights. Multivariate logistic regression was used with the dichotomous dependent variables and regression analysis was used with the continuous dependent variables. Odds ratio estimates and 95% confidence intervals are presented for logistic regression analyses, and beta estimates and standard errors are presented for linear regression analyses, with statistical significance determined using the design-corrected F statistic. To obtain results that are generalizable to the African-American population, all statistical analyses accounted for the complex multistage clustered design of the NSAL sample, unequal probabilities of selection, nonresponse, and post-stratification to calculate weighted, nationally representative population estimates and standard errors.

To examine the association of everyday discrimination with chronic health problems across multiple domains, multivariate regression models are presented for presence of a chronic health problem, number of chronic health problems, and interference with daily activities. To explore the relative contributions of discrimination attribution, three models are presented for each dependent variable. The first model investigates the role of everyday racial discrimination, the second model investigates everyday non-racial discrimination, and the final model includes results from analysis of overall discrimination regardless of attribution. All models control for demographic variables. Overall, there are 13 dependent variables and three models are presented for each dependent variable, resulting in a total of 39 multivariate regression models.

Results

Descriptive characteristics of the sample ($N = 3,570$) are presented in Table 1. The average age of the respondents is 42 years (range of 18 through 93) and 44% are male. Respondents had an average of 12.43 years of education and the average family income was $36,832. Around 42% of the respondents are married or living with a partner, 56% resided in the South, and two-thirds of the sample were currently employed.

The multivariate analyses of everyday discrimination on self-rated health and chronic health variables are presented in Table 2. Everyday racial discrimination (row 2 in panels 1 and 2) was significant in 10 of the 13 regression models. Racial discrimination was associated with poorer self-rated physical and oral health, higher odds of all types of health problems, and greater number of health problems within each category as well as total number of chronic health problems. Everyday racial discrimination was also associated with more daily interference from pain problems and from the total number of chronic health problems.

Results for everyday discrimination without attribution were the same (row 1 in panels 1 and 2) with the exception of a significant relationship with interference from cardiovascular problems. Non-racial discrimination was not significant in any of the 13 regressions (row 3 in panels 1 and 2).

Discussion

In this study, we examined the relative associations of everyday racial discrimination, everyday non-racial discrimination, and overall everyday discrimination with

Table 2. Multivariate analysis of overall everyday discrimination, everyday racial discrimination, and everyday non-racial discrimination on selected measures of health problems among African-Americans, national survey of American life.

	Self-Rated Health[a]	Self-Rated Dental Health[a]	# of Cardiovascular Problems[a]	Any Cardiovascular Problems[b]	Interference from Cardiovascular Problems[a]	# of Respiratory Problems[a]
	B(SE)	B(SE)	B(SE)	OR(95% CI)	B(SE)	B(SE)
Overall[c] Everyday Discrimination	-0.01(0.00)	-0.01(0.00)	0.00(0.00)	1.01(1.00–1.02)	0.02(0.01)	0.00(0.00)
p	<0.0001	<0.0001	0.02	0.15	0.003	0.002
$F_{11,24}$	30.10	22.39	50.72	31.59	23.16	4.68
Prob > F	<0.0001	<0.0001	<0.0001	<0.0001	<0.0001	0.0008
N	3403	3401	3403	3401	1287	3403
Everyday Racial Discrimination[c]	-0.01(0.00)	-0.01(0.00)	0.00(0.00)	1.01(1.00–1.02)	0.01(0.01)	0.00(0.00)
p	<0.0001	<0.0001	0.04	0.08	0.09	0.002
$F_{11,24}$	30.58	24.94	52.57	33.14	19.49	4.05
Prob > F	<0.0001	<0.0001	<0.0001	<0.0001	<0.0001	0.002
N	3294	3292	3294	3293	1244	3294
Everyday Non-racial Discrimination[c]	0.00(0.00)	-0.00(0.00)	-0.00(0.00)	0.99(0.98–1.01)	0.01(0.01)	-0.00(0.00)
p	0.76	0.44	0.84	0.28	0.30	0.34
$F_{11,24}$	25.53	24.77	52.62	35.39	15.56	3.92
Prob > F	<0.0001	<0.0001	<0.0001	<0.0001	<0.0001	0.003
N	3293	3291	3293	3292	1243	3293

	Any Respiratory Problems[b]	Interference from Respiratory Problems[a]	# of Pain Problems[a]	Any Pain Problems[b]	Interference from Pain Problems[a]	Total # of Chronic Health Problems[a]	Interference from Total # of Chronic Health Problems[a]
	OR(95% CI)	B(SE)	B(SE)	OR(95% CI)	B(SE)	B(SE)	B(SE)
Overall[c] Everyday Discrimination	1.02(1.01–1.04)	0.00(0.01)	0.01(0.00)	1.02(1.01–1.04)	0.02(0.01)	0.02(0.00)	0.05(0.01)
p	0.001	0.78	<0.0001	0.001	0.003	<0.0001	<0.0001

(Continued)

Table 2. (Continued).

	Any Respiratory Problems[b]	Interference from Respiratory Problems[a]	# of Pain Problems[a]	Any Pain Problems[b]	Interference from Pain Problems[a]	Total # of Chronic Health Problems[a]	Interference from Total # of Chronic Health Problems[a]
	OR(95% CI)	B(SE)	B(SE)	OR(95% CI)	B(SE)	B(SE)	B(SE)
$F_{11,24}$	7.14	5.97	36.93	7.14	20.53	56.36	35.71
Prob > F	<0.0001	0.19	<0.0001	<0.0001	<0.0001	<0.0001	<0.0001
N	3403	487	3403	3403	1662	3403	2222
Everyday Racial Discrimination[c]	1.02(1.01–1.04)	0.00(0.01)	0.01(0.00)	1.02(1.01–1.04)	0.01(0.01)	0.02(0.00)	0.03(0.01)
p	0.001	0.34	<0.0001	0.001	0.04	<0.0001	0.003
$F_{11,24}$	5.97	4.74	40.9	5.97	19.94	82.96	35.01
Prob > F	0.0001	0.0008	<0.0001	0.0001	<0.0001	<0.0001	<0.0001
N	3294	469	3294	3294	1602	3294	2145
Everyday Non-racial Discrimination[c]	0.99(0.97–1.01)	−0.01(0.01)	0.00(0.00)	0.99(0.97–1.01)	0.00(0.01)	0.00(0.00)	0.02(−0.02–0.05)
p	0.33	0.50	0.38	0.33	0.61	0.93	0.31
$F_{11,24}$	5.29	6.96	25.28	5.29	18.51	60.83	29.08
Prob > F	0.0003	<0.0001	<0.0001	0.0003	<0.0001	<0.0001	<0.0001
N	3293	469	3293	3293	1602	3293	2144

Notes. B = regression coefficient; SE = standard error; OR = odds ratio; 95%CI = 95% confidence interval. Significance test of the individual parameter estimates were based on a complex design-corrected *t*-test.
[a] Multivariate regression B (SE) and *p*-values were reported.
[b] Multivariate logistic regression OR (95%CI) and *p*-values were reported.

13 indicators of physical health among African-Americans in the National Survey of American Life. With regard to our primary goal of assessing the relationship between general everyday discrimination and physical health we found that everyday discrimination, regardless of attribution, was associated with poorer health for 11 of 13 measures. These findings are consistent with past literature reviews examining the links between perceived discrimination and hypertension/cardiovascular outcomes (Brondolo, Rieppi, Kelly, & Gerin, 2003; Wyatt et al., 2003). This study also expands on existing literature by finding that not only does discrimination increase the likelihood of having physical health problems, but it is also significantly associated with the extent to which chronic health problems interfere with daily life.

Regarding our secondary aim to distill the relative roles of racial versus non-racial discrimination on physical health outcomes, we found that racial discrimination was associated with poorer health on 12 of 13 physical health outcomes but non-racial discrimination was not significantly associated with any physical health outcomes. These findings are inconsistent with previous studies that have found similar associations between everyday racial and non-racial discrimination with serious psychological distress, generalized anxiety disorder, and major depressive disorder (Kessler et al., 1999). A more recent study found that everyday discrimination—regardless of attribution—was associated with similar levels of stress for Blacks and Whites (Williams et al., 2012). This suggests that the relationship with non-racial everyday discrimination may be different for physical versus mental health outcomes.

At the same time, our findings are consistent with studies highlighting the particularly salient role of racial discrimination (relative to non-racial discrimination) for African-Americans. For example, Chae, Lincoln, and Jackson (2011) found racial discrimination to be more strongly associated with psychological distress than non-racial discrimination among African-Americans; similar results have also been found in a study of generalized anxiety disorder (Soto, Dawson-Andoh, & BeLue, 2011). The unique nature of everyday racial versus non-racial discrimination for African-Americans may be explained by sociological work on the self, which suggests that "[s]tressors that harm or threaten individuals' most cherished self-conceptions should be seen as more threatening, and thus, more predictive of psychological distress or disorder than those affecting less cherished aspects of the self " (Thoits, 2013, p. 361). Thus, the greater impact of everyday racial discrimination in this study may be rooted in the extent to which an African-American's self-identity is tied to race. This study also suggests that stressors related to self-identity may have a greater impact on physical as well as psychological disorders.

It is widely accepted that chronic stressors lead to "wear and tear" on the body, creating dysregulation of the immune and other physiological systems (McEwen & Stellar, 1993). As a recognized psychosocial stressor, everyday discrimination is likely to precipitate the continued release of stress hormones (e.g., cortisol, epinephrine) that may give rise to physical health problems such as those studied here. Moreover, emerging work on vigilance and anticipatory stress supports these findings. This body of work suggests that even the perceived threat of future racial discrimination is associated with higher levels of sleep difficulties (Hicken, Lee, Ailshire, Burgard, & Williams, 2013) and hypertension (Hicken, Lee, Morenoff, House, & Williams, 2013) among Blacks. Future research on these topics is imperative and should continue.

Furthermore, racial discrimination may affect health indirectly by influencing help-seeking behaviors. Experiences of racial discrimination have been associated with delays in seeking medical help and reduced compliance with treatment regimens (Casagrande, Gary, LaVeist, Gaskin, & Cooper, 2007). Some evidence supports the association of discrimination experiences with decreased use of informal support as well (Spencer & Chen, 2004; Spencer, Chen, Gee, Fabian, & Takeuchi, 2010) while other research suggests a more complicated relationship when both informal and professional support are considered (Woodward, 2011; Woodward, Chatters, Taylor, Neighbors, & Jackson, 2010).

There are two important limitations to consider when interpreting these results. First, given the cross-sectional nature of the data, reverse causation is a potential concern. Although limited, studies based on longitudinal data have found that perceived discrimination is associated with self-rated health (Schulz et al., 2006), and even mortality (Barnes et al., 2008). These studies lend support for the idea that perceived discrimination is more likely to cause—rather than be caused by—health problems. In addition, we were unable to explore discrimination that may be attributed to the intersection of multiple social statuses. This is an important direction for future research (Harnois & Ifatunji, 2010).

Implications and conclusions

Despite these limitations this article contributes to the extant literature and has implications for future research as well as service provision. For example, innovative work has explored whether racial identity buffers against the mental health effects of everyday discrimination (Chae et al., 2011) and has identified racial identity as a potential protective factor for the general mental health of Black Americans (Hughes, Kiecolt, & Keith, 2014; Hughes, Kiecolt, Keith, & Demo, 2015). Further exploration of these relationships in relation to both mental and physical health can inform the development of health care and social service interventions that foster and strengthen racial identity.

References

Ayalon, L., & Gum, A. M. (2011). The relationships between major lifetime discrimination, everyday discrimination, and mental health in three racial and ethnic groups of older adults. *Aging & Mental Health*, *15*(5), 587–594. doi:10.1080/13607863.2010.543664

Barnes, L. L., De Leon, C. F. M., Lewis, T. T., Bienias, J. L., Wilson, R. S., & Evans, D. A. (2008). Perceived discrimination and mortality in a population-based study of older adults. *American Journal of Public Health*, 98(7), 1241–1247. doi:10.2105/AJPH.2007.114397

Beatty Moody, D. L., Brown, C., Matthews, K. A., & Bromberger, J. T. (2014). Everyday discrimination prospectively predicts inflammation across 7-years in racially diverse mid-life women: Study of women's health across the nation. *Journal of Social Issues*, 70(2), 298–314. doi:10.1111/josi.12061

Brondolo, E., Rieppi, R., Kelly, K. P., & Gerin, W. (2003). Perceived racism and blood pressure: A review of the literature and conceptual and methodological critique. *Annals of Behavioral Medicine: A Publication of the Society of Behavioral Medicine*, 25(1), 55–65. doi:10.1207/S15324796ABM2501_08

Casagrande, S. S., Gary, T. L., LaVeist, T. A., Gaskin, D. J., & Cooper, L. A. (2007). Perceived discrimination and adherence to medical care in a racially integrated community. *Journal of General Internal Medicine*, 22(3), 389–395. doi:10.1007/s11606-006-0057-4

Chae, D. H., Lincoln, K. D., & Jackson, J. S. (2011). Discrimination, attribution, and racial group identification: Implications for psychological distress among Black Americans in the National Survey of American Life (2001–2003). *The American Journal of Orthopsychiatry*, 81(4), 498–506. doi:10.1111/j.1939-0025.2011.01122.x

Dovidio, J. F., & Gaertner, S. L. (2000). Aversive racism and selection decisions: 1989 and 1999. *Psychological Science*, 11(4), 315–319. doi:10.1111/1467-9280.00262

Essed, P. (1991). *Understanding everyday racism: An interdisciplinary theory* (vol. 2). Newbury Park, CA: SAGE Publications, Inc.

Gee, G. C., Spencer, M. S., Chen, J., & Takeuchi, D. (2007). A nationwide study of discrimination and chronic health conditions among Asian Americans. *American Journal of Public Health*, 97(7), 1275–1282. doi:10.2105/AJPH.2006.091827

Guyll, M., Matthews, K. A., & Bromberger, J. T. (2001). Discrimination and unfair treatment: Relationship to cardiovascular reactivity among African American and European American women. *Health Psychology: Official Journal of the Division of Health Psychology, American Psychological Association*, 20(5), 315–325. doi:10.1037/0278-6133.20.5.315

Harnois, C. E., & Ifatunji, M. (2010). Gendered measures, gendered models: Toward an intersectional analysis of interpersonal racial discrimination. *Ethnic and Racial Studies*, 34(6), 1006–1028. doi:10.1080/01419870.2010.516836

Hicken, M. T., Lee, H., Ailshire, J., Burgard, S. A., & Williams, D. R. (2013). "Every shut eye, ain't sleep": The role of racism-related vigilance in racial/ethnic disparities in sleep difficulty. *Race and Social Problems*, 5(2), 100–112. doi:10.1007/s12552-013-9095-9

Hicken, M. T., Lee, H., Morenoff, J., House, J. S., & Williams, D. R. (2013). Racial/ethnic disparities in hypertension prevalence: Reconsidering the role of chronic stress. *American Journal of Public Health*, 104(1), 117–123. doi:10.2105/AJPH.2013.301395

Hughes, M., Kiecolt, K. J., & Keith, V. M. (2014). How racial identity moderates the impact of financial stress on mental health among African Americans. *Society and Mental Health*, 4(1), 38–54. doi:10.1177/2156869313509635

Hughes, M., Kiecolt, K. J., Keith, V. M., & Demo, D. H. (2015). Racial identity and well-being among African Americans. *Social Psychology Quarterly*, 78(1), 25–48. doi:10.1177/0190272514554043

Hunte, H. E. R., & Williams, D. R. (2009). The association between perceived discrimination and obesity in a population-based multiracial and multiethnic adult sample. *American Journal of Public Health*, 99(7), 1285–1292. doi:10.2105/AJPH.2007.128090

Jackson, J. S., Neighbors, H. W., Nesse, R. M., Trierweiler, S. J., & Torres, M. (2004). Methodological innovations in the National Survey of American Life. *International Journal of Methods in Psychiatric Research*, 13(4), 289–298. doi:10.1002/(ISSN)1557-0657

Kessler, R. C., Mickelson, K. D., & Williams, D. R. (1999). The prevalence, distribution, and mental health correlates of perceived discrimination in the United States. *Journal of Health and Social Behavior, 40*(3), 208–230. doi:10.2307/2676349

Landrine, H., & Klonoff, E. A. (1996). The schedule of racist events: A measure of racial discrimination and a study of its negative physical and mental health consequences. *Journal of Black Psychology, 22*(2), 144–168. doi:10.1177/00957984960222002

Lewis, T. T., Cogburn, C. D., & Williams, D. R. (2015). Self-reported experiences of discrimination and health: Scientific advances, ongoing controversies, and emerging issues. *Annual Review of Clinical Psychology, 11*, 407–440. doi:10.1146/annurev-clinpsy-032814-112728

Lewis, T. T., Everson-Rose, S. A., Powell, L. H., Matthews, K. A., Brown, C., Karavolos, K.,... Wesley, D. (2006). Chronic exposure to everyday discrimination and coronary artery calcification in African-American women: The SWAN heart study. *Psychosomatic Medicine, 68*(3), 362–368. doi:10.1097/01.psy.0000221360.94700.16

Luo, Y., Xu, J., Granberg, E., & Wentworth, W. M. (2012). A longitudinal study of social status, perceived discrimination, and physical and emotional health among older adults. *Research on Aging, 34*(3), 275–301. doi:10.1177/0164027511426151

McEwen, B. S., & Stellar, E. (1993). Stress and the individual: Mechanisms leading to disease. *Archives of Internal Medicine, 153*(18), 2093–2101. doi:10.1001/archinte.1993.00410180039004

Schulz, A. J., Gravlee, C. C., Williams, D. R., Israel, B. A., Mentz, G., & Rowe, Z. (2006). Discrimination, symptoms of depression, and self-rated health among African American women in Detroit: Results from a longitudinal analysis. *American Journal of Public Health, 96*(7), 1265–1270. doi:10.2105/AJPH.2005.064543

Seaton, E. K., Caldwell, C. H., Sellers, R. M., & Jackson, J. S. (2010). Developmental characteristics of African American and Caribbean Black adolescents' attributions regarding discrimination. *Journal of Research on Adolescence, 20*(3), 774–788. doi:10.1111/j.1532-7795.2010.00659.x

Soto, J. A., Dawson-Andoh, N. A., & BeLue, R. (2011). The relationship between perceived discrimination and generalized anxiety disorder among African Americans, Afro Caribbeans, and non-Hispanic Whites. *Journal of Anxiety Disorders, 25*(2), 258–265. doi:10.1016/j.janxdis.2010.09.011

Spencer, M. S., & Chen, J. (2004). Effect of discrimination on mental health service utilization among Chinese Americans. *American Journal of Public Health, 94*(5), 809–814. doi:10.2105/AJPH.94.5.809

Spencer, M. S., Chen, J., Gee, G. C., Fabian, C. G., & Takeuchi, D. T. (2010). Discrimination and mental health-related service use in a national study of Asian Americans. *American Journal of Public Health, 100*(12), 2410–2417. doi:10.2105/AJPH.2009.176321

Thoits, P. A. (2013). Self, identity, stress, and mental health. In C. S. Aneshensel, J. C. Phelan, & A. Bierman (Eds.), *Handbook of the sociology of mental health* (pp. 357–377). New York, NY: Springer. Retrieved from http://link.springer.com/chapter/10.1007/978-94-007-4276-5_18

Turner, R. J., & Avison, W. R. (2003). Status variations in stress exposure: Implications for the interpretation of research on race, socioeconomic status, and gender. *Journal of Health and Social Behavior, 44*(4), 488–505. doi:10.2307/1519795

Williams, D. R., John, D. A., Oyserman, D., Sonnega, J., Mohammed, S. A., & Jackson, J. S. (2012). Research on discrimination and health: An exploratory study of unresolved conceptual and measurement issues. *American Journal of Public Health, 102*(5), 975–978. doi:10.2105/AJPH.2012.300702

Williams, D. R., & Mohammed, S. A. (2009). Discrimination and racial disparities in health: Evidence and needed research. *Journal of Behavioral Medicine, 32*(1), 20–47. doi:10.1007/s10865-008-9185-0

Williams, D. R., & Mohammed, S. A. (2013). Racism and health I: Pathways and scientific evidence. *American Behavioral Scientist, 57*(8), 1152–1173. doi:10.1177/0002764213487340

Williams, D. R., Yu, Y., Jackson, J. S., & Anderson, N. B. (1997). Racial differences in physical and mental health socio-economic status, stress and discrimination. *Journal of Health Psychology, 2*(3), 335–351. doi:10.1177/135910539700200305

Woodward, A. T. (2011). Discrimination and help-seeking: Use of professional services and informal support among African Americans, Black Caribbeans, and non-Hispanic Whites with a mental disorder. *Race and Social Problems, 3*(3), 146–159. doi:10.1007/s12552-011-9049-z

Woodward, A. T., Chatters, L. M., Taylor, R. J., Neighbors, H. W., & Jackson, J. S. (2010). Differences in professional and informal help seeking among older African Americans, Black Caribbeans and non-Hispanic Whites. *Journal of the Society for Social Work and Research, 1*(3), 124–139. doi:10.5243/jsswr.2010.10

Wyatt, S. B., Williams, D. R., Calvin, R., Henderson, F. C., Walker, E. R., & Winters, K. (2003). Racism and cardiovascular disease in African Americans. *The American Journal of the Medical Sciences, 325*(6), 315–331. doi:10.1097/00000441-200306000-00003

Sexual Orientation, Gender, and Gender Identity Microaggressions: Toward an Intersectional Framework for Social Work Research

Paul R. Sterzing, Rachel E. Gartner, Michael R. Woodford, and Colleen M. Fisher

ABSTRACT

Professional ethics compel social workers to address all forms of discrimination and oppression. Microaggressions can contribute to health disparities for marginalized groups; yet, little is known about the frequency, mechanisms, and impact of microaggressions on sexual minorities, cisgender women, and gender minorities—particularly for those with intersecting marginalized identities. This article extends microaggression literature by exploring interrelated constructs of sexual orientation, gender, and gender identity microaggressions, and offering recommendations for future research using an intersectional lens to foster an integrated and complex understanding of microaggressions. Implications of an intersectional microaggression framework for social work education and practice are discussed.

The social work profession strives to eliminate all forms of discrimination and oppression (National Association of Social Workers, 2008). This imperative compels social workers to become more knowledgeable of and skillful at addressing the complexity of contemporary forms of discrimination, such as microaggressions. Little attention has been given to the frequency and health-related consequences of microaggressions for sexual minorities, cisgender women, and gender minorities, particularly for those with intersecting, marginalized identities based on race, ethnicity, ability, religion, and nationality (Nadal et al., 2011; Sue & Capodilupo, 2008). Additional gaps exist regarding the experience of microaggressions for these populations across different developmental periods, identity development stages, and social contexts.

The power of microaggressions rests in their ubiquity, frequency, and ambiguity (Sue, 2010a; Sue et al., 2007; Woodford, Chonody, Kulick, Brennan, & Renn, 2015; Woodford, Kulick, Sinco, & Hong, 2014). Historical, vicarious, and individual-level trauma triggered by the content and imagery of microaggressions may increase their power (Evans-Campbell, 2008)—a profoundly more complex issue when experienced by people with intersecting, marginalized identities. Microaggression content and imagery can cut across a person's identities, triggering traumas associated simultaneously with racism, sexism, heterosexism, transphobia, xenophobia, and ableism. Laverne Cox, a Black transwoman, actress, and advocate, illustrates this in her description of an experience in New York: a Latino cisgender man saw her walking down the street and yelled, "Yo mama, can I holler at you?" A Black cisgender man standing nearby responded, "Yo dude, that's a nigger [man]!" The two cisgender men argued, saying "No man, that's a bitch!" and "No, that's a nigger!" In the end, the Latino cisgender man turned to Laverne Cox and asked, "You ain't a nigger, are you?" (Cox, 2013).

This incident highlights how people with intersecting, marginalized identities may experience microaggressions, as this act simultaneously employs White supremacy, misogyny, and heterosexism. The historical trauma undergirding this microaggression relates to the legacy of slavery and racism that includes the lynching and emasculation (i.e., castration) of Black male bodies (Bush, 1999; Raditlhalo, 2013). Referring to Black men, Laverne Cox explained,

> [they] see my transwoman's body and feel I'm the embodiment of this historic emasculation come to life. So often when I'm called out on the street it's as if I'm a disgrace to the race, because I'm trans. I understand this as trauma. (Cox, 2013)

The cognitive mechanisms that link microaggressions to these historical, vicarious, and individual-level experiences of trauma, however, remain an unexplored area of research.

The existing literature—with notable exceptions (Balsam, Molina, Beadnell, Simoni, & Walters, 2011; Lewis, Mendenhall, Harwood, & Browne Huntt, 2013; Nadal et al., 2015; Nadal, Sriken, Davidoff, Wong, & McLean, 2013)—has little to say about the frequency and impact of microaggressions for people with intersecting, marginalized identities (Nadal, 2013). A major limitation of research that focuses on single-identity forms of microaggressions in isolation is that they typically ignore other systems of power and oppression (e.g., racism, ableism, religious intolerance), resulting in research that primarily reflects a dominant-group (e.g., White, able-bodied, Christian) experience of sexual orientation, gender, and gender identity microaggressions. The impact of microaggressions on individuals with a single marginalized identity (e.g., White, heterosexual, able-bodied, cisgender female) is likely qualitatively different from intersectional microaggressions that target a greater totality of the individual's identities.

Although research on single identity-based microaggressions has identified important themes that uniquely apply to sexual minorities, cisgender women, and gender minorities (Capodilupo et al., 2010; Nadal, Skolnik, & Wong, 2012; Woodford, Howell, Silverschanz, & Yu, 2012; Woodford, Kulick, et al., 2014), a deeper understanding of the impact of intersectional microaggressions is needed for social workers to promote the advancement of health and well-being among oppressed groups. This article aims to advance under-standing of microaggressions by (a) examining microaggression themes related to sexual minorities, cisgender women, and gender minorities, includ-ing theoretical mechanisms explaining their impact on health and well-being, and (b) proposing future directions for social work to address existing research gaps and develop an integrated, theoretically informed, intersec-tional understanding of microaggressions. It concludes with a discussion of the implications of an intersectional microaggression approach for social work education and practice.

Microaggression themes and mechanisms of power

Microaggressions are part of a larger system of oppression that undermines the health and well-being of marginalized groups. They help to maintain cultural imperialism by using often-unintentional insults and invalidations to reinforce dominant-group characteristics as "normal" and superior, while others are conveyed as abnormal and undesirable. Microaggressions may be considered acts of subtle violence in and of themselves, but they also serve as reminders that members of marginalized groups should remain vigilant because of the possibility of unprovoked attack based on their identity (Sue, 2010a). Despite their cumulative, deleterious impact over time, the subtle nature of microaggressions makes them difficult to confront (Sue, 2010b).

Microaggression themes

Researchers have identified microaggression themes that speak to the oppres-sion of sexual minorities, cisgender women, and gender minorities. A theme cutting across these three groups is an endorsement of hetero- and gender-normative culture and behaviors, which includes heteronormative microaggres-sions that tell gay people "not to act so gay in public" (Nadal, Rivera, & Corpus, 2010, p. 227) and gender-normative microaggressions that tell masculine-presenting women "to look and act more feminine"(Capodilupo et al., 2010, p. 204). The use of heterosexist, sexist, and transphobic language, as well as the denial of individual and societal prejudice, are other shared themes across these three groups (Capodilupo et al., 2010; Nadal et al., 2010). Sexual orientation and gender identity microaggressions share four additional themes:

(1) assumptions of sexual pathology and abnormality,
(2) discomfort/disapproval of non-heterosexual and non-cisgender experiences,
(3) assumption of a universal experience, and
(4) exoticization(Nadal et al., 2010).

The literature has also identified and applied certain themes exclusively to cisgender women and gender minorities; however, research is needed to see if they apply to sexual minorities and other marginalized groups, as well. First, Nadal and colleagues (2012) write about the following themes specific to gender identity microaggressions: denial of bodily privacy, familial rejection, and physical threats. Reports of family rejection and experiences of home-lessness among sexual minorities populations compel researchers to undertake further exploration of familial microaggressions as they relate to sexual mino-rities (Rosario, Schrimshaw, & Hunter, 2012). Furthermore, while verbal and street-level harassment may be more prevalent for gender minority individuals, harassment is a common experience in the lives of women (American Association of University Women [AAUW], 2001; Capodilupo et al., 2010) and sexual minorities (Stader & Graca, 2007). Second, Capodilupo and collea-gues (2010) write about microaggression themes specific to cisgender women: objectification, assumption of inferiority, and second-class citizenship. While these themes may have their foundation in women's unique experiences of disenfranchisement and subjugation, sexual and gender minorities may have similar experiences, such as denial of civil rights and protections (i.e., second-class citizenship) and beliefs that gay men cannot play sports (i.e., assumptions of inferiority). These themes compel researchers not only to study microag-gressions in specific populations, but to also examine the underlying dynamics of power and oppression that create settings and contexts conducive to microaggressions.

Microaggressions and health disparities

Minority stress theory posits that minoritized individuals face minority-related stressors in addition to general stressors. These minority stressors are derived from stigma, prejudice, and discrimination, and reflect underlying systems of oppression, such as heterosexism, misogyny, and cisgenderism. Minority stres-sors are considered to be systemic in that they are tied to dominant cultural norms and thus contribute to chronic stress that can lead to increased risk for poor health and well-being among marginalized groups (Meyer, 2003).

Minority stress theory also provides important insights into factors that can strengthen or weaken the relationship between microaggressions and other min-ority stressors (e.g., expectations of rejection, concealment of identity, internalized oppression, other forms of discrimination) and health outcomes, minority-identity characteristics (prominence, valence, and integration), and community-level coping (access to and support from others who share marginalized identities; Meyer, 2003; Meyer, Ouellette, Haile, & McFarlane, 2011). Specifically, the more prominent or central the minority identity is to the individual, the greater potential impact the microaggression can have on well-being. Furthermore, individuals who value their marginalized identity (i.e., positive valence) and have achieved greater integration or synthesis across all their identities (e.g., gender, race, ability, life roles and responsibilities) are theorized to experience less negative health consequences after incidents of microaggressions(Meyer, 2003).

Despite its strengths, minority stress theory does not provide a framework for understanding the complexity and multiplicative impact of microaggressions that simultaneously target multiple marginalized identities (e.g., racial, ethnic, sexual orientation, and gender identity). Intersectionality theory offers important theoretical insights into how to understand and investigate intersectional microaggressions and their impact on health disparities. First, intersectionality theory recognizes that multiple forms of oppression—such as racism, sexism, heterosexism, and ableism—function interdependently to create a "matrix of domination" (Ritzer, 2007, p. 204) that impacts health and well-being (Mann & Kelley, 1997; Nadal et al., 2015). For example, individuals who experience microaggressions based on their racial identities are also at greater risk of being targeted for their other marginalized identities (Yosso, Smith, Ceja, & Solórzano, 2009). However, the construct of intersectional invisibility suggests that individuals with multiple marginalized identities are less likely to experience the same intensity of oppression if they do not conform to the stereotype underlying the microaggression(Purdie-Vaughns & Eibach, 2008). For instance, since a gay identity is stereotypically associated with the imagery of White men, sexual minorities of color could face fewer incidents of microaggression targeting their sexual orientation. This is a rich domain of inquiry calling for future research to uncover the ways in which intersecting identities may function as risk or protective factors to microaggressions and related health outcomes.

Trauma theory also helps explain how this "matrix of domination" leads to the historical, vicarious, and individual-level trauma, bridging the experiences of microaggressions and negative health consequences (Ritzer, 2007, p. 204). As Laverne Cox's story highlighted, historical trauma related to slavery and the emasculation of Black male bodies is passed down across generations within the Black community and appears to play an important role in the microaggression experiences of Black transwomen (e.g., "disgrace to the race"). The content, motivations of perpetrators, and consequences of intersectional microaggressions cannot be fully understood without understanding the historical trauma that may underlie them. Lamble (2008) warns specifically against research that attempts to de-racialize traumatic events that occur to transgender individuals, proposing that this masks the other systems of oppression underlying the microaggression. In addition to historical trauma, vicarious trauma emerges from exposure (e.g., witnessed events, media coverage) to the moments of violence that have targeted sexual minorities, cisgender women, and gender minorities (Noelle, 2002). Microaggressions may also trigger past experiences of identity-motivated rejection that give each incident of microaggression greater weight. Research is needed to explore mechanisms that mediate the connection between microaggressive experiences and psychological distress.

Future directions for social work research on intersectional microaggressions

Existing conceptual frameworks and measurement tools that focus on single-identity microaggressions are unable to capture the multidimensional impact of intersectional microaggressions. Although much can still be learned about single forms of microaggressions, we lay out an agenda to advance the field with an explicit focus on intersectional microaggressions and the developmental factors and social contexts that may influence their content, frequency, and impact.

Developmental factors

Physical development

Microaggression research has focused almost exclusively on adult experiences, largely ignoring the developmental periods of childhood, adolescence, and emerging adulthood. Puberty is a critical period of social, emotional, and peer development, and many marginalized populations may be more at risk during this vulnerable time. Early maturing girls, for example, are more frequently targets of sexual harassment (Hill & Kearl, 2011) and have more negative mental health outcomes and problematic behavioral trajectories than their peers (Mendle, Turkheimer, & Emery, 2007). There are notable racial implications for the influence of early menarche, as Black and Latina girls experience menarche earlier than their White counterparts (Chumlea et al., 2003). Children's developmental capacity to process slights or subtle attacks is of crucial importance to microaggression research, as existing literature suggests that experiences of bullying and harassment increase as children age from middle to high school but may be less impactful for older children (Gruber & Fineran, 2007). As the age of menarche continues to decline in the United States (Anderson & Must, 2005), microaggression research needs to ask critical questions about the experience and impact of microaggressions on developmentally transitioning girls.

Puberty is also a critical time for transgender youths, as the emergence of secondary sex characteristics carry both physical and social burdens (Grossman & D'Augelli, 2006). Literature has explored the role that puberty-suppression hormones can play in improving mental and behavioral health outcomes for transgender youths (de Vries, Steensma, Doreleijers, & Cohen-Kettenis, 2011), but the role and effect of microaggressions during this developmental period has not been assessed. While the peer context is important, adult perceptions, expectations, and treatment of adolescents also changes as they physically develop (Marceau, Ram, & Susman, 2015). More research is needed to understand the frequency and impact of adult-perpetrated microaggressions on adolescent mental health and identity development.

Identity development

Overlapping with physical development is the process of identity development. Consistent with minority stress theory (Meyer, 2003), microaggressions may have a differential impact on health and well-being depending on the centrality of identity, level of internalized oppression, and integration with other identities. For instance, an adolescent engaging in gender identity exploration who holds internalized transphobia is likely to be more negatively affected by incidents of microaggression in comparison to a transman who has synthesized or integrated his gender identity (Singh, Hays, & Watson, 2011). Identity exploration is a vulnerable, transitional stage (Kidwell & Dunham, 1995), potentially increasing the impact of microaggressions that target the particular identity under exploration.

Little is known about the role of identity exploration in health-related outcomes among youths with intersecting, marginalized identities. Research needs to explore the differential impact of microaggressions containing racist, sexist, and heterosexist content for youths who are actively exploring both their racial and transgender identity compared to those who are exploring a single identity. In addition, community-level coping is conceptualized as a protective factor for youths who share a similar marginalized identity (Meyer, 2003), but it is not known whether community-level coping is protective for adolescents with intersecting, marginalized identities, or if that protective influence only emerges in communities where all the marginalized identities align. Research is needed to illuminate interactions among microaggressions, stage of identity development across intersecting identities, and health-related outcomes.

Social contexts

Family

The familial setting is often the first place children are exposed to sexism, heterosexism, and cisgenderism. Microaggressions may primarily serve a gender-policing function in this context, ensuring adherence to heterosexuality and cisgender roles. Research is clear that positive family environments are central to healthy mental and behavioral health outcomes for children, adolescents, and emerging adults (Resnick et al., 1997). Unfortunately, sexual and gender minority youths often experience substantial adversity such as family-level rejection and violence, and subsequent homelessness (Rosario et al., 2012).

No published research has explored the frequency, content, or impact of microaggressions in a familial context. Research examining ambient forms of family-level microaggressions compared to direct forms that specifically target their child's sexual and/or gender identity is critical to understanding this nascent area. An explicit intersectional framework is needed as racial, ethnic, and religious minorities may be more vulnerable to these ambient and direct forms of family-level microaggressions than their dominant-group counterparts. Black sexual and gender minority youths, for example, may experience higher levels of psychological distress due to the anticipation of rejection or losing family support vital to well-being in a racially oppressive society. Research is also needed to identify the content of microaggressions expressed in racial, ethnic, and religious minority families, as historical trauma specific to certain racial or ethnic groups may play an important role in explaining the frequency and impact of intersectional microaggressions.

Education
Educational settings play a pivotal role in shaping the psychosocial development and well-being of minoritized groups. Sexual minorities, cisgender women, and gender minorities face hostility, discrimination, and violence in K–12 and postsecondary educational settings (Woodford, Joslin, & Renn, 2016). While blatant violence still occurs, subtle discrimination, such as pejorative use of "gay," the spreading of sexual rumors, and transphobia, is more common across educational settings (Kosciw, Greytak, Palmer, & Boesen, 2014). Across school settings, studies suggest that interpersonal heterosexism(Birkett, Espelage, & Koenig, 2009; Poteat & Espelage, 2007; Woodford, Han, Craig, Lim, & Matney, 2014) and sexual harassment (Gruber & Fineran, 2007) can contribute to negative psychological outcomes. Recent empirical attention has been given to sexual orientation microaggressions on college campuses (e.g., Woodford, Han, et al., 2014), but more is needed. We especially need research that addresses microaggressions in K–12 systems and that focuses specifically on girls and transgender students. The role of microaggressions in shaping developmental outcomes requires additional study and calls for longitudinal research examining potential effects across developmental periods.

Systems-level interventions are critical for the safety of marginalized students; discrimination is less prevalent in schools with inclusive policies and programs (Chesir-Teran & Hughes, 2009). The effectiveness of programs and policies for reducing racial, gender, sexual orientation, and gender identity microaggressions has yet to be examined. Research on sexual and gender minority discrimination suggests that staff members in elementary and high school systems tend to respond to overt discrimination but ignore microaggressive language (McCabe, Dragowski, & Rubinson, 2013). Finally, given that schools are often hostile spaces for other marginalized groups, such as students of color, it is particularly important that researchers explore the nature, prevalence, and impacts of microaggressions among these various groups (Woodford, Han, et al., 2014; Woodford, Kulick, et al., 2014; Woodford et al., 2015).

Supportive safe spaces

Adolescence is a crucial period for identity development, which corresponds to youths confiding in friends about their sexual orientation and gender identity and seeking out other supportive spaces such as identity-affirming counseling services, girls groups, and queer youth groups. Experiencing microaggressions from one's friends or support network and community may have a differential impact in comparison to those perpetrated by strangers, neighbors, or acquaintances. Balsam and colleagues (2011) created the LGBT People of Color Microaggressions Scale to simultaneously capture sexual and gender minority microaggressions that sexual and gender minorities of color face from other people of color as well as racial microaggressions they may encounter within the sexual and gender minority community. Although it is a critical scale, it does not measure microaggressions perpetuated by sexual and gender minority persons of color who possess a similar constellation of minority identities as the target of the microaggression. For example, the expectation of safety and mutual understanding found in supportive spaces where all marginalized identities align (e.g., Black trans-women support group) may make the experience of gender identity microaggressions (e.g., being told how to enact femininity) particularly acute (Galupo, Henise, & Davis, 2014). This is an important gap and more research is needed to determine the impact of microaggressions perpetrated by friends and those with similar intersecting, marginalized identities.

Implications for social work education and practice

This call for research has important implications for social work education and practice. First, for social workers to effectively address intersectional microaggressions, they require knowledge and facility in critical social work theories such as intersectional theory, feminist theory, queer theory, and critical race theory, which point to the systems of power that are inescapable and interwoven in all interpersonal and environmental exchanges (Abrams & Moio, 2009). Because of the complexity of intersectional microaggressions, these theories provide an investigative lens through which to interrogate microaggressions that occur within classroom settings, clinical encounters, and between professional colleagues. Foundation-level courses for social workers must "center the margins" and prioritize theories and empirical evidence that best address the experiences of people with intersecting, marginalized identities. This emphasis fosters the development of critical consciousness from which social workers can address intersectional microaggressions in direct practice settings and, more importantly, advocate against the inequitable systems of power that undergird these forms of oppression.

To bridge theory and practice divides, we recommend that social work students take coursework and develop skills in anti-oppressive practices such as relational cultural therapy and narrative therapy. Relational cultural therapy emphasizes the therapeutic setting and calls on practitioners to acknowledge the role of historical oppression and contemporary scripts in shaping inauthentic and stratified interactions (Jordan, Walker, & Martling, 2004). By centering on individuals' truths, dynamics of power and oppression, and the complexity of connection, relational cultural therapy positions social work practitioners to both address and combat microaggressions. Narrative therapy also works to challenge dominant discourses that oppress groups with intersecting, marginalized identities, fostering empowerment and respect by creating an anti-oppressive space for exploring one's un-narrated experiences (Freeman, 2011).

While it remains essential for social workers to understand the nature and effects of single-identity-based microaggressions, it is imperative that we examine the complexity of intersectional microaggressions. A multiplicative model is needed that recognizes single microaggressions targeting multiple aspects of an individual's identity may be more impactful. Our call for research will require in-depth, qualitative and novel quantitative methodologies to capture the complexities of intersectional microaggressions. Using non-linear strategies, social work researchers can advance the field by examining the *level* (e.g., relationship between high levels of intersectional microaggressions and depression), *velocity* (e.g., correspondence between rates of intersectional microaggressions and depression rates), and *acceleration* (e.g., relationship between increasing or decreasing microaggression rates and depression rates over time) of microaggressions(Deboeck, Nicholson, Kouros, Little, & Garber, 2015).

References

Abrams, L. S., & Moio, J. A. (2009). Critical race theory and the cultural competence dilemma in social work education. *Journal of Social Work Education, 45*(2), 245–261. doi:10.5175/JSWE.2009.200700109

American Association of University Women, Educational Foundation, & Harris Interactive (Firm). (2001). *Hostile hallways: Bullying, teasing, and sexual harassment in school.* Washington, DC: American Association of University Women Educational Foundation.

Anderson, S. E., & Must, A. (2005). Interpreting the continued decline in the average age at menarche: Results from two nationally representative surveys of U.S. girls studied 10 years apart. *Journal of Pediatrics, 147*(6), 753–760. doi:10.1016/j.jpeds.2005.07.016

Balsam, K. F., Molina, Y., Beadnell, B., Simoni, J., & Walters, K. (2011). Measuring multiple minority stress: The LGBT People of Color Microaggressions Scale. *Cultural Diversity and Ethnic Minority Psychology, 17*(2), 163–174. doi:10.1037/a0023244

Birkett, M., Espelage, D. L., & Koenig, B. (2009). LGB and questioning students in schools: The moderating effects of homophobic bullying and school climate on negative outcomes. *Journal of Youth and Adolescence, 38*(7), 989–1000. doi:10.1007/s10964-008-9389-1

Bush, L. (1999). Am I a man? A literature review engaging the sociohistorical dynamics of Black manhood in the United States. *Western Journal of Black Studies, 23*(1), 49–57.

Capodilupo, C. M., Nadal, K. L., Corman, L., Hamit, S., Lyons, O. B., & Weinberg, A. (2010). The manifestation of gender microaggression. In D. W.Sue (Ed.), *Microaggressions and marginality: Manifestation, dynamics, and impact* (pp. 193–216). Hoboken, NJ: John Wiley & Sons, Inc.

Chesir-Teran, D., & Hughes, D. (2009). Heterosexism in high school and victimization among lesbian, gay, bisexual, and questioning students. *Journal of Youth and Adolescence, 38*(7), 963–975. doi:10.1007/s10964-008-9364-x

Chumlea, W. C., Schubert, C. M., Roche, A. F., Kulin, H. E., Lee, P. A., Himes, J. H., & Sun, S. S. (2003). Age at menarche and racial comparisons in U.S. girls. *Pediatrics, 111*(1), 110–113. doi:10.1542/peds.111.1.110

Cox, L. (2013, December 19). *Bullying and being a trans woman of color* [Video file]. Retrieved from https://www.youtube.com/watch?v=7zwy5PEEa6U&ab_channel=KepplerSpeakers

Deboeck, P. R., Nicholson, J., Kouros, C., Little, T. D., & Garber, J. (2015). Integrating developmental theory and methodology: Using derivatives to articulate change theories, models, and inferences. *Applied Developmental Science, 19*(4), 217–231. doi:10.1080/10888691.2015.1021924

de Vries, A. L. C., Steensma, T. D., Doreleijers, T. A. H., & Cohen-Kettenis, P. T. (2011). Puberty suppression in adolescents with gender identity disorder: A prospective follow-up study. *The Journal of Sexual Medicine, 8*(8), 2276–2283. doi:10.1111/j.1743-6109.2010.01943.x

Evans-Campbell, T. (2008). Historical trauma in American Indian/Native Alaska communities: A multilevel framework for exploring impacts on individuals, families, and communities. *Journal of Interpersonal Violence, 23*(3), 316–338. doi:10.1177/0886260507312290

Freeman, E. (2011). *Narrative approaches in social work practice: A life span, culturally centered, strengths perspective.* Springfield, IL: Charles C. Thomas Publishers, Ltd.

Galupo, M. P., Henise, S. B., & Davis, K. S. (2014). Transgender microaggressions in the context of friendship: Patterns of experience across friends' sexual orientation and gender identity. *Psychology of Sexual Orientation and Gender Diversity, 1*(4), 461–470. doi:10.1037/sgd0000075

Grossman, A. H., & D'Augelli, A. R. (2006). Transgender youth: Invisible and vulnerable. *Journal of Homosexuality, 51*(1), 111–128. doi:10.1300/J082v51n01_06

Gruber, J. E., & Fineran, S. (2007). The impact of bullying and sexual harassment on middle and high school girls. *Violence Against Women, 13*(6), 627–643. doi:10.1177/1077801207301557

Hill, C., & Kearl, H. (2011). *Crossing the line: Sexual harassment at school.* Washington, DC: American Association of University Women.

Jordan, J., Walker, M., & Martling, L. (Eds.). (2004). *The complexity of connection: Writings from the Stone Center's Jean Baker Miller Training Institute* (1st ed.). New York, NY: The Guilford Press.

Kidwell, J. S., & Dunham, R. M. (1995). Adolescent identity exploration: A test of Erikson's theory of transitional crisis. *Adolescence, 30*(120), 785.

Kosciw, J. G., Greytak, E. A., Palmer, N. A., & Boesen, M. J. (2014). *The 2013 National School Climate Survey: The experiences of lesbian, gay, bisexual and transgender youth in our nation's schools.* New York, NY: GLSEN.

Lamble, S. (2008). Retelling racialized violence, remaking White innocence: The politics of interlocking oppressions in transgender day of remembrance. *Sexuality Research & Social Policy*, 5(1), 24–42. doi:10.1525/srsp.2008.5.1.24

Lewis, J. A., Mendenhall, R., Harwood, S. A., & Browne Huntt, M. (2013). Coping with gendered racial microaggressions among Black women college students. *Journal of African American Studies*, 17(1), 51–73. doi:10.1007/s12111-012-9219-0

Mann, S. A., & Kelley, L. R. (1997). Standing at the crossroads of modernist thought: Collins, Smith, and the new feminist epistemologies. *Gender & Society*, 11(4), 391–408. doi:10.1177/089124397011004002

Marceau, K., Ram, N., & Susman, E. J. (2015). Development and lability in the parent-child relationship during adolescence: Associations with pubertal timing and tempo. *Journal of Research on Adolescence*, 25(3), 474–489. doi:10.1111/jora.2015.25.issue-3

McCabe, P. C., Dragowski, E. A., & Rubinson, F. (2013). What is homophobic bias anyway? Defining and recognizing microaggressions and harassment of LGBTQ youth. *Journal of School Violence*, 12(1), 7–26. doi:10.1080/15388220.2012.731664

Mendle, J., Turkheimer, E., & Emery, R. E. (2007). Detrimental psychological outcomes associated with early pubertal timing in adolescent girls. *Developmental Review*, 27(2), 151–171. doi:10.1016/j.dr.2006.11.001

Meyer, I. H. (2003). Prejudice, social stress, and mental health in lesbian, gay, and bisexual populations: Conceptual issues and research evidence. *Psychological Bulletin*, 129(5), 674–697. doi:10.1037/0033-2909.129.5.674

Meyer, I. H., Ouellette, S. C., Haile, R., & McFarlane, T. A. (2011). "We'd be free": Narratives of life without homophobia, racism, or sexism. *Sexuality Research and Social Policy*, 8(3), 204–214. doi:10.1007/s13178-011-0063-0

Nadal, K. L. (2013). *That's so gay! Microaggressions and the lesbian, gay, bisexual, and transgender community* (1st ed.). Washington, DC: American Psychological Association.

Nadal, K. L., Davidoff, K. C., Davis, L. S., Wong, Y., Marshall, D., & McKenzie, V. (2015). A qualitative approach to intersectional microaggressions: Understanding influences of race, ethnicity, gender, sexuality, and religion. *Qualitative Psychology*, 2(2), 147–163. doi:10.1037/qup0000026

Nadal, K. L., Issa, M. A., Leon, J., Meterko, V., Wideman, M., & Wong, Y. (2011). Sexual orientation microaggressions: "Death by a thousand cuts" for lesbian, gay, and bisexual youth. *Journal of LGBT Youth*, 8(3), 234–259. doi:10.1080/19361653.2011.584204

Nadal, K. L., Rivera, D. P., & Corpus, M. J. (2010). Sexual orientation and transgender microaggressions: Implications for mental health and counseling. In D. W.Sue (Ed.), *Microaggressions and marginality: Manifestation, dynamics, and impact* (pp. 217–240). Hoboken, NJ: John Wiley & Sons, Inc.

Nadal, K. L., Skolnik, A., & Wong, Y. (2012). Interpersonal and systemic microaggressions toward transgender people: Implications for counseling. *Journal of LGBT Issues in Counseling*, 6(1), 55–82. doi:10.1080/15538605.2012.648583

Nadal, K. L., Sriken, J., Davidoff, K. C., Wong, Y., & McLean, K. (2013). Microaggressions within families: Experiences of multiracial people. *Family Relations*, 62(1), 190–201. doi:10.1111/fare.2013.62.issue-1

National Association of Social Workers. (2008). *Code of ethics of the National Association of Social Workers*. Retrieved from https://www.socialworkers.org/pubs/code/code.asp

Noelle, M. (2002). The ripple effect of the Matthew Shepard murder impact on the assumptive worlds of members of the targeted group. *American Behavioral Scientist*, 46(1), 27–50. doi:10.1177/0002764202046001004

Poteat, V. P., & Espelage, D. L. (2007). Predicting psychosocial consequences of homophobic victimization in middle school students. *Journal of Early Adolescence, 27*(2), 175–191. doi:10.1177/0272431606294839

Purdie-Vaughns, V., & Eibach, R. P. (2008). Intersectional invisibility: The distinctive advantages and disadvantages of multiple subordinate-group identities. *Sex Roles, 59*(5–6), 377–391. doi:10.1007/s11199-008-9424-4

Raditlhalo, T. S. (2013). "Senses of silence": Historical trauma in *To Every Birth Its Blood*. *Journal of Literary Studies, 29*(3), 99–118. doi:10.1080/02564718.2013.810869

Resnick, M. D., Bearman, P. S., Blum, R. W., Bauman, K. E., Harris, K. M., Jones, J.,... Udry, J. R. (1997). Protecting adolescents from harm: Findings from the National Longitudinal Study on Adolescent Health. *JAMA: The Journal of the American Medical Association, 278* (10), 823–832. doi:10.1001/jama.1997.03550100049038

Ritzer, G. (2007). *Contemporary sociological theory and its classical roots: The basics*. Boston, MA: McGraw-Hill.

Rosario, M., Schrimshaw, E. W., & Hunter, J. (2012). Risk factors for homelessness among lesbian, gay, and bisexual youths: A developmental milestone approach. *Children and Youth Services Review, 34*(1), 186–193. doi:10.1016/j.childyouth.2011.09.016

Singh, A. A., Hays, D. G., & Watson, L. S. (2011). Strength in the face of adversity: Resilience strategies of transgender individuals. *Journal of Counseling & Development, 89*(1), 20–27. doi:10.1002/j.1556-6678.2011.tb00057.x

Stader, D. L., & Graca, T. J. (2007). Student-on-student sexual orientation harassment: Legal protections for sexual minority youth. *The Clearing House: A Journal of Educational Strategies, Issues and Ideas, 80*(3), 117–122. doi:10.3200/TCHS.80.3.117-122

Sue, D. W. (2010a). *Microaggressions in everyday life: Race, gender, and sexual orientation*. Hoboken, NJ: John Wiley & Sons, Inc.

Sue, D. W. (2010b). Microaggressions, marginality, and oppression: An introduction. In D. W.Sue (Ed.), *Microaggressions and marginality: Manifestation, dynamics, and impact* (pp. 3–22). Hoboken, NJ: John Wiley & Sons, Inc.

Sue, D. W., & Capodilupo, C. M. (2008). Racial, gender, and sexual orientation microaggressions: Implications for counseling and psychotherapy. In D. W.Sue (Ed.), *Counseling the culturally diverse* (5th ed., pp. 105–130). New York, NY: Wiley.

Sue, D. W., Capodilupo, C. M., Torino, G. C., Bucceri, J. M., Holder, B. M., Nadal, K. L., & Esquilin, M. (2007). Racial microaggressions in everyday life: Implications for clinical practice. *American Psychologist, 62*(4), 271–286. doi:10.1037/0003-066X.62.4.271

Woodford, M. R., Chonody, J., Kulick, A., Brennan, D. J., & Renn, K. (2015). The LGBQ Microaggressions on Campus Scale: A scale development and validation study. *Journal of Homosexuality, 62*(12), 1660–1687. doi:10.1080/00918369.2015.1078205

Woodford, M. R., Han, Y., Craig, S., Lim, C., & Matney, M. M. (2014). Discrimination and mental health among sexual minority college students: The type and form of discrimination does matter. *Journal of Gay & Lesbian Mental Health, 18*(2), 142–163. doi:10.1080/ 19359705.2013.833882

Woodford, M. R., Howell, M. L., Silverschanz, P., & Yu, L. (2012). "That's so gay!" Examining the covariates of hearing this expression among gay, lesbian, and bisexual college students. *Journal of American College Health, 60*(6), 429–434. doi:10.1080/07448481.2012.673519

Woodford, M. R., Joslin, J., & Renn, K. (2016). Lesbian, gay, bisexual, transgender, and queer students on campus: Fostering inclusion through research, policy and practice. In P. A. Pasque, M. P. Ting, N. Ortega, & J. C. Burkhardt (Eds.), *Transforming understandings of diversity in higher education: Demography, democracy and discourse*. Sterling, VA: Stylus.

Woodford, M. R., Kulick, A., Sinco, B., & Hong, J. (2014). Contemporary heterosexism on campus and psychological distress among Lesbian, gay, bisexual, transgender, and queer students: The mediating role of self-acceptance. *American Journal of Orthopsychiatry, 84* (5), 519–529. doi:10.1037/ort0000015

Yosso, T., Smith, W., Ceja, M., & Solórzano, D. (2009). Critical race theory, racial microaggressions, and campus racial climate for Latina/o undergraduates. *Harvard Educational Review, 79*(4), 659–691. doi:10.17763/haer.79.4.m6867014157m7071

A Mixed-Methods Inquiry Into Trans* Environmental Microaggressions on College Campuses: Experiences and Outcomes

Michael R. Woodford, Jessica Y. Joslin ⓘ, Erich N. Pitcher, and Kristen A. Renn

ABSTRACT

The experiences, including with environmental microaggressions, and well-being of trans* collegians remain an under-researched topic. In this mixed-methods study of a survey sample of 152 trans* collegians, multivariable regression findings suggest that the frequency of experiencing select trans* environmental micro-aggressions (e.g., not having access to comfortable bathrooms as a trans* person) are associated with increased risk for poorer academic outcomes (e.g., developmental challenges) but are not associated with mental health outcomes. Furthermore, inter-views with 18 trans* collegians suggest that students face several systemic microaggressions, including difficulties advancing trans* inclusion. Various reactions, including paths of resistance, were identified. Implications are discussed.

Transgender or trans* students experience interpersonal discrimination, including blatant violence and microaggressions on campus (Rankin, Weber, Blumenfeld, & Frazer, 2010).[1] They also face macro-level environmental microaggressions (Sue, 2010) through institutional policies and practices, and social norms that maintain the male/man and female/woman sex/gender binary (Bilodeau, 2009; McKinney, 2005; Seelman, 2014). Environmental microaggressions are apparent on the systemic level and convey exclusionary messages toward marginalized groups (Sue, 2010). The message that trans* collegians often receive about their most basic needs is that these needs are not an institutional priority.

Genderism, which can be enacted interpersonally and structurally, is a social system undergirded by the belief that there are only two genders and forcibly labels individuals as either men or women (Bilodeau, 2009). Minority stress theory holds that oppression can increase minoritized individuals' risk for negative out-comes (Meyer, 2003). Applied to trans* collegians, this theory suggests that due to their marginalized status on campus, they experience discrimination and stigma, which create stress that can contribute to negative outcomes. These stressors supplement the general stressors of college, and unlike the typical challenges of college, minority stressors are chronic in nature because of the systemic roots in genderism. According to this theory, environmental microaggressions can negatively affect trans* collegians because of the symbolic and sometimes experienced exclusion conveyed through these indignations.

Despite the documented interpersonal and structural discrimination that trans* students experience, little is known about the relationship between trans* collegians' experiences, including encountering macro-level microaggressions, and outcomes. A particular gap exists with respect to quantitative studies. Also, while gender-inclusive restrooms and other trans*-inclusive initiatives are part of the college student affairs "best practices" literature (e.g., Beemyn, Domingue, Pettitt, & Smith, 2005), little is known about their implementation and students' reactions at multiple campuses.

In this mixed-methods study, we address these gaps by using quantitative data to explore the relationship between macro-level microaggressions and psychological distress and academic performance and engagement among trans* collegians. Also, we use qualitative data to describe how such microaggressions, including the sometimes problematic nature of campus initiatives for trans* inclusion, shape trans* students' experiences and well-being. The results provide much-needed evidence to inform interventions tailored to support trans* collegians.

Campus climate and trans* microaggressions

Research suggests that trans* students frequently experience discrimination on campuses, including interpersonal discrimination and systemic barriers to inclusion (Dugan, Kusel, & Simounet, 2012; Rankin et al., 2010). They also tend to fear for their safety, feel uncomfortable with the climate, and see their universities as unresponsive to discriminatory events (Rankin et al., 2010; Seelman, 2014). Researchers assert that the negative treatment trans* students face on campus can result in elevated levels of distress (Effrig, Bieschke, & Locke, 2011; Seelman, 2014) and undermine their academic performance (Rankin et al., 2010). Yet, few researchers empirically examine these claims (McKinney, 2005) and existing quantitative studies either were not conducted with current students (see Seelman, 2016) or did not examine the climate-outcome relationship (see Effrig et al., 2011; Rankin et al., 2010). To support trans* students, within the context of a hostile campus climate marked by persistent and pervasive genderism(Bilodeau, 2009; Nicolazzo, 2015), studies that examine the experiences of current trans* college students are needed (Marine, 2011) to better understand the relationships between campus climate and student success and well-being (Woodford, Joslin, & Renn, 2016; Woodford & Kulick, 2015).

With respect to microaggressions, Nadal, Skolnik, and Wong (2012) conceptualized 12 types of microaggressions that affect trans* people, including systemic and environmental microaggressions, which they concluded are especially harmful. These scholars identified several sub-areas of systemic and environmental microaggressions, including binary gender public restrooms, official identification and forms that specify male/female for sex, and health care systems that are not responsive to trans* individuals. Prior research documented various emotional (e.g., distress, anger), cognitive (e.g., rationalizing perpetrators' behaviors), and behavioral (e.g., avoiding unsafe spaces) responses to microaggressions (Nadal, Davidoff, Davis, & Wong, 2014).

On college campuses, although not described as environmental microaggressions, researchers have identified an array of systemic forms of trans* discrimination, such as sex-segregated bathrooms or housing (Bilodeau, 2009; Seelman, 2014; Seelman et al., 2012). Furthermore, gender-inclusive housing—a recommended best practice—often hinges on whether a student gender-transitions, which ultimately determines how/who is included and excluded from certain campus residential environments (Nicolazzo & Marine, 2015). Reflecting the systemic nature of trans* environmental microaggressions, such physical sites are spaces in which rigid enforcement of the gender binary occurs through hostility and violence (Bilodeau, 2009). These types of macro-level microaggressions can be stressful for students and interfere with their health and academic performance and engagement—all critical outcomes for today's college student (Dugan et al., 2012).

Demonstrating the link between environmental microaggressions and well-being, a recent quantitative study found that among trans* adults who attended college at some point in their lives, environmental microaggressions (lack of gender-inclusive restrooms and housing on campus) experienced during one's college days were positively associated with lifetime suicidality and homelessness (Seelman, 2016). The relationship between these factors among current trans* collegians is unknown, as is the relationship with academic outcomes.

Trans* students can also face marginalization beyond physical spaces, such as difficulties with changing one's name and/or gender on campus records (Seelman, 2013) and being made invisible when completing gendered forms (Seelman, 2014). Barriers can also exist when trying to access trans*-competent health services (McKinney, 2005). Moreover, trans* students can feel marginalized when seeing administrators, staff, faculty, and other students minimize the need to change policies to protect trans* students (McKinney, 2005). Furthermore, a negative campus climate creates a context in which trans* students may not perform as well academically or be as engaged as cisgender students (Dugan et al., 2012).

In this mixed-methods study we answer the following questions:

(1) Quantitatively, what is the relationship between various trans* environmental microaggressions (restrooms, forms, sexual health information,

health care assumptions, and housing) on campus and trans* students' mental health (depression, attempted suicide) and academic performance (grade point average [GPA], academic and intellectual development, developmental challenge) and engagement (satisfaction, social acceptance, affirming attitudes toward trans* people on campus).[2] We hypothesize that trans* exclusion at the environmental level will increase students' risk for poorer mental health and lower academic performance and engagement.

(2) Qualitatively, how do environmental microaggressions shape trans* collegians' experiences and how do they respond to them?

Methods

This concurrent mixed-methods study uses data from the National Study of LGBTQ Student Success (http://www.lgbtqsuccess.net/). The larger study utilized an anonymous online survey and semi-structured interviews to examine the experiences, well-being, and academic success of lesbian, gay, bisexual, transgender, and queer (LGBTQ) collegians. The study received institutional ethics approval.

Quantitative survey component

Procedures
We recruited survey participants through a LGBTQ Midwest college student conference and online LGBTQ student networks. Students who completed the survey at the conference (laptops provided) were given a coupon for a local coffee shop and all participants had the opportunity to enter their names for a random drawing for an iPad. More than 900 students participated in the survey, including 152 trans* students who answered the questions about experiencing microaggressions on campus (i.e., the analytical sample).

Participants
Participants' average age was 23 years ($SD = 2.79$) and 49.3% identified as genderqueer, 31.9% transgender, 15.1% other identity, and 4.6% two-spirit. In terms of sexual orientation, queer was the largest group (34.2%). Most participants were White (77.7%), almost 40% were eligible for Pell grants, and approximately 80% were undergraduate students; juniors were the largest group (23.6%) of all years. Nearly three-fourths attended public institutions, with 38.4% on suburban campuses and 37.7% on urban campuses. Nearly 60% of the participants completed the survey at the conference.

Measures

For multi-item scales, relevant items were reverse-scored and mean scores were calculated. All continuous measures were scored so that higher scores indicate more of the phenomenon of interest. We examined the frequency of experiencing four trans* environmental microaggressions concerning restrooms, forms, sexual health information, and health care assumptions on campus over the past year (0 = never, 1 = very rarely, 2 = rarely, 3 = occasionally, 4 = frequently, 5 = very frequently; see Table 1 for survey items). We also inquired about students' knowledge of gender-inclusive housing policies (yes, no, don't know). The outcome measures are described in Table 1.

Qualitative interview component

Procedures

Sixty LGBTQ students were recruited from conference attendees to be interviewed, 18 of whom identified as trans* (i.e., the analytical sample). Interviews were approximately 60 minutes long. All interviewees received a $25 gift card. The interviews were transcribed and then coded using open coding and the constant comparative method (Charmaz, 2006).

Participants

Gender identities included genderqueer ($N = 5$), transgender ($N = 6$), transgender man ($N = 3$), and others. Sexual orientation included queer ($N = 8$), heterosexual ($N = 3$), asexual ($N = 1$), bisexual ($N = 1$), gay/lesbian ($N = 3$), questioning ($N = 1$), and polysexual ($N = 1$). Most participants ($N = 11$) identified as White and majored in a range of fields, from graphic design to biomedical science. The sample represented 17 different institutions.

Protocol

Interview questions inquired about challenges and successes that students experienced as an LGBTQ college student. Questions specific to microaggressions were not asked. General probes and invitations to elaborate were used.

Results

Quantitative survey component

Encountering gender-binary forms was the most common environmental microaggression reported by survey participants ($M = 3.91$, $SD = 1.62$). Approximately 80% of the participants reported either frequently or very frequently experiencing this microaggression, while about 45% reported experiencing gender-binary sexual health information at these frequency

Table 1. Primary quantitative measures ($N = 152$).

	Variable	Measure/Description		Theoretical Range	M(SD)	N(%)
Environmental Microaggressions	Bathrooms	I did not have access to bathrooms where I felt comfortable as a transgender person.		0–5	2.10 (1.99)	
	Forms	Forms or documentation asked about gender/sex and only included "male" and "female."		0–5	3.91 (1.62)	
	Sexual health information	I received information about sexual health that was limited to cisgender bodies.		0–5	2.76 (1.92)	
	Health care assumptions	A health care worker made inaccurate assumptions about my health needs because they knew or assumed my gender identity.		0–5	1.41 (1.79)	
	Gender-inclusive housing	Does your institution have specific housing policies or spaces for LGBTQ students?	No		–	82 (53.9)
			Yes			45 (29.6)
			Don't know			25 (16.4)[a]
Mental Health	Depression[b]	PHQ-9 measures the severity of depression symptoms in the past two weeks along 9 *DSM-IV* diagnostic criteria (0 = not at all, 3 = nearly every day; Spitzer, Kroenke, William, & Patient Health Questionnaire Primary Care Study Group, 1999).		0–27	9.88 (7.04)	
	Attempted suicide[c]	Attempted suicide in the past year			–	14 (11.7)
Academic Performance	GPA	Self-reported current grade point average.		1–4	3.32 (0.53)	–
	Academic & intellectual development	7-item scale measuring perceived level of development, experiences, and satisfaction with received learning (1 = strongly disagree, 5 = strongly agree; Pascarella & Terenzini, 1980).		1–5	3.73 (0.68)	–
	Developmental challenge	10-item subscale of the Inventory of College Students' Recent Life Experiences scale that addresses challenges of a developmental/academic nature in the past month (1 = not at all part of my life, 4 = very much part of my life; Kohn, Lafreniere, & Gurevich, 1990).		1–4	2.47 (0.58)	–

(Continued)

Table 1. (Continued).

Variable		Measure/Description	Theoretical Range	M(SD)	N(%)
Academic Engagement	Institutional satisfaction	If I had to do it over again, I would choose to attend mycurrent college/university (1 = strongly disagree, 7 = strongly agree; Cortina, Swan, Fitzgerald, & Waldo, 1998).	1–7	5.34(1.87)	–
	Social acceptance	3 items assessing feelings of "fitting in" (1 = strongly disagree, 7 = strongly agree; Cortina et al., 1998).	1–7	4.34(0.78)	–
	Perceived acceptance of trans* people	Item assesses perceptions concerning acceptance of gender-variant/transgender people on their campus (1 = hatred, 6 = celebrated for their unique contributions; adapted from Woodford & Kulick, 2015).	1–6	3.70(1.22)	–

Note. DSM = *Diagnostic and Statistical Manual of Mental Disorders*; PHQ-9 = Patient Health Questionnaire 9.
[a] Don't know was eliminated for analysis purposes; [b] N = 119; [c] N = 120.

levels ($M = 2.76$, $SD = 1.92$). Considerably lower than the other microaggressions, fewer participants (44.8%) reported experiencing inaccurate assumptions about health needs from health care workers more than occasionally ($M = 1.41$, $SD = 1.79$). Accessing restrooms in which respondents did not feel comfortable occurred, on average, rarely ($M = 2.10$, $SD = 1.99$). In terms of housing, 53.9% reported not having inclusive housing policies on their campus (16.4% report don't know).

Results of Pearson's r demonstrated significant correlations between restrooms and developmental challenge ($r = .28$, $p = .001$), social acceptance ($r = -.26$, $p = .001$), and perceived accepting attitudes ($r = -.20$, $p = .02$). Forms were significantly correlated with suicide attempt ($r = -.23$, $p = .01$), academic and intellectual development ($r = -.19$, $p = .02$), and developmental challenge ($r = .18$, $p = .03$). Likewise, health care assumptions and social acceptance were correlated ($r = -.17$, $p = .03$). Also, housing policy was significantly correlated with satisfaction ($r = -.24$, $p = .007$) and social acceptance ($r = -.29$, $p = .001$). No significant correlations were found for sexual health information.

We next conducted multivariable linear regressions (logistic regression for suicide), independently examining each form of environmental microaggression while controlling for age, race, academic year, and conference attendee. Significant associations existed between restrooms and developmental challenge ($\beta = .29$, $p = .001$), social acceptance ($\beta = -.27$, $p = .002$), and perceived affirming attitudes ($\beta = -.16$, $p = .04$). Likewise, significant associations existed between forms and academic and intellectual development ($\beta = -.19$, $p = .03$) and developmental challenge ($\beta = .21$, $p = .02$). The lack of inclusive housing was associated with social acceptance ($\beta = -.25$, $p = .008$) and perceived affirming attitudes ($\beta = -.24$, $p = .006$). No other significant relationships emerged.

Qualitative interview component

While the quantitative data addressed health care, the interviewees only referenced restrooms, forms, and housing. Their narratives reflected experiencing barriers, including when institutions had attempted to address these issues, as well as various reactions to these microaggressions.

Gender-inclusive restrooms

As the quantitative results suggest, not having access to safe restrooms can interfere with trans* students' academic performance and development and engagement. Several students discussed the barriers they faced in terms of availability, as well as locating and accessing gender-inclusive restrooms, when available. For instance, James explained that convincing the administration to get such restrooms was quite a challenge, which reflects the barriers trans* students face having their needs addressed:

> I think it was last year, we're still working on gender-inclusive bathrooms, and it was such a headache. We brought it up, and we were waiting for them [adminis-tration] to talk about it or do something and, of course, nothing happened. It took one of my friends going on a hunger strike for them to actually start talking about it again. Then.... We got back word from the main campus about bathroom codes or some stupid stuff saying that we couldn't do it because we needed a certain number of fixtures [by gender binary] per building and all this bullshit, and it stopped and that was it.

Like James, Toby's efforts to advocate for gender-inclusive bathrooms were similarly stalled by the administration, although apparently support existed: "We [LGBTQ club] got a few gender-neutral restrooms erected. The rest didn't end up getting finished because we wound up in weird conflicts with maintenance over who was paying for the [restroom] signs."

Even when campuses made an effort to make gender-inclusive restrooms available, they were sometimes difficult to find, which represents another trans* microaggression. Maya explained that her campus had added several gender-inclusive restrooms and had made it a policy to include one in every new construction project. Despite these seemingly good-intentioned efforts, these restrooms were sometimes a challenge to locate. In collaboration with her campus' LGBTQ resource center, Maya worked on creating a list of the gender-inclusive restrooms on campus. She described how hard it was to find some of the restrooms when creating the list:

> There's one in the auditorium, and I wanted to figure out specifically what the room number was because it wasn't listed and I wanted to update it [on the list]. So I went to the auditorium and I searched for probably a half an hour. Eventually I found it on the fourth floor, kind of down a hallway from the top of a stairwell.... It's someplace nobody ever goes. It's completely unused.... It was not something anyone was ever likely to find.

The difficulty of accessing inclusive restrooms meant that short breaks in between classes were stressful. As Justin reflected, students would have to choose among getting a snack, chatting with friends, and rushing to use a gender-inclusive restroom: "Use male bathroom on the floor that I have all my classes on, or wander all the way over there, burn five minutes, and not be able to get coffee?"

In addition, even when the restrooms were possible to locate, they may not always be easily accessible: "Yeah, there's one in, like, a different office complex within [a campus] building, and you have to talk to the people at the desk to be able to use it, which for someone who's trying to be discreet about their bathroom use, that's a really uncomfortable situation" (Maya). The requirement of having to obtain access to the facility from a staff person interferes with access for some, and thus is another manifestation of environmental microaggressions.

Gender-binary forms

Even on campuses where there were services available for trans* students, interviewees repeatedly described experiencing frustration with their inability to change their campus paperwork to their chosen name and gender. They also highlighted various behavioral reactions. Kevin explained how seeing his birth name impacted his life on campus:

> The thing that bothers me the most is my lack of ability to change my preferred name on all the university stuff. Every single time I'm e-mailing someone…. They'll all see my birth name and…. It's annoying. I will e-mail professors and tell them. Most are pretty good, although I've had some who… [were not good about it].

Because his birth name was on all campus paperwork, Kevin was forced to repeatedly disclose his trans* status and request that faculty and staff use his chosen name and pronouns. Putting trans* students in this situation can make them vulnerable to interpersonal microaggressions and harassment. Similarly, Justin described the potential consequences of not being able to change campus paperwork: "The records office… automatically [marked] 'M,'… [and] their computer system wanted me to register for Selective Service [mandatory registration for military service]." Categorizing students by their birth name and gender can have implications beyond the classroom.

Gender-binary housing

The challenge of negotiating single-sex male/female residence halls was a consistent concern for our interviewees. When gender-inclusive housing is lacking, students can face increased stressors in various aspects of their lives. For example, Myles explained the potential consequences that being trans* has within housing:

> I can't be out because it's just not supported at all. I work in residence life, so I work in an all-female dorm, and it just wouldn't work out. I can afford to go to [name of college] because I work in residence life, so I get my housing and my meal plan for free, and then I have scholarships. It's just kind of like, if I come out, I lose my job.

He went on to add that having to hide his trans* identity was stressful and he had contemplated transferring to another campus. Myles' experiences and those of other trans* collegians illustrates the additional stress and various concerns that can manifest in one's life due to genderism.

Similarly, a number of other participants spoke about trying to live with unsupportive residential policies. Ky accepted that he needed to live on an all-female floor because the university would not accommodate him:

> I live on a girls' floor now, and I just flaunt my stuff to the bathroom... there's nothing much I can do about it. I'm not going across campus to a restroom that has a shower and it's—I'm not going to do all of that just because they won't accommodate.

Luckily, this living situation was temporary and Ky was excited to move the following year into apartment-style living with a female friend who knows about his transition—and they will have their own bathrooms. Although apartment-style living would afford him more privacy, Ky still was compelled to live with a female student.

As noted, gender-binary forms can lead to trans* students being housed inappropriately, but institutions may not know how to respond when a trans* student discloses their gender identity. Chris explained that from the moment they moved onto campus, they were assigned a roommate according to the gender listed on the university forms, but once Chris' trans* identity was known, the university was uncertain about how to respond:

> You apply for the college; you have to specify your gender [sex] there [male/female], and then they assign you a roommate according to your gender. I put whatever I had to because it's all on my documents.... My roommate didn't come and they put me in a single room, and I was happy [with] it.... I try to make sure that they know that I want a roommate, but they just didn't know... who should they put me with. So... next quarter, they put me with a female who is also asexual, and we are getting along well for now.

Similarly, Maya indicated that when she was transitioning at her campus, the institution did not have a gender-inclusive housing policy (although she noted the institution now has one). At the time, campus officials decided to respond to trans* students' housing needs on a case-by-case basis, most often resulting in trans* students being housed in single rooms. She knew she could not afford a single room so Maya asked to be roomed with another trans* student, but was instead placed with a gay man:

> I mean, he was trans* friendly, I guess.... I think it was a different concept for him.... They put me on a coed floor, so I think all things considered—like, the policies that the school had at the time—they did a pretty good job with that. I still didn't feel totally comfortable.

Although she adapted, she was still forced to be with a male roommate. Similar to other interviewees, this housing situation, a microaggression operationalized through the lack of policy and resources as well as through practice, negated her identity as a trans* woman and caused discomfort that cisgender students do not face.

Discussion

The findings highlight the nature and potential consequences of environmental microaggressions faced by trans* collegians. The quantitative findings illuminate potential relationships between select environmental microaggressions and academic outcomes. The qualitative findings expose some of the nuances surrounding such microaggressions, including how some efforts to address these everyday indignations, such as access to inclusive restrooms, may also reinforce marginalization. Our qualitative findings also capture the lived nature of microaggressions—for example, the difficulties of actually finding gender-inclusive restrooms when they are available—as well as their impact on trans* students and how they respond.

The multivariable regression findings suggest that access to safe restrooms and inclusive forms and housing is associated with students' academic outcomes; higher frequency of not accessing restrooms on campus in which students felt comfortable as trans* people was associated with increased developmental challenge, such as struggling to meet one's own performance standards, doing poorly on graded work, and feeling coursework is too demanding. The frequency of not accessing safe restrooms was also associated with lower engagement in terms of perceptions of social acceptance and the acceptance of trans* people on campus. Moreover, encountering gendered forms also potentially interfered with students' academic performance in terms of lower academic and intellectual developmental and greater developmental challenge. The lack of an inclusive housing policy was associated with lower engagement, namely perceptions of social acceptance and trans* acceptance; housing policy was correlated with institutional satisfaction at the bivariate level. Feeling a sense of belonging on one's campus is a pivotal factor underlying student success (Strayhorn, 2012); yet, few studies have applied this framework to academic outcomes among LGBTQ students. None of the microaggressions were associated with GPA in either level of analysis.

Consistent with minority stress theory, our results suggest that select environmental minority stressors can put trans* students at risk, especially in terms of particular academic outcomes. It is possible that the chronic stress associated with systemic genderism manifested through gendered spaces and forms can disadvantage trans* collegians' academic performance and engagement. However, although much of minority stress research focuses on mental health, in the adjusted models we failed to find relationships between any of the environmental microaggressions and mental health outcomes (a significant correlation was observed between forms and suicide, but failed to maintain significance when control variables were added). The non-statistically significant relationships could reflect our measures, which tap into the very serious mental health problems of depression and behavioral suicide, and the depression measure corresponds to *Diagnostic and Statistical Manual of Mental Disorders* (*DSM*) diagnostic criteria. Measures assessing perceived stress or general well-being might produce different findings. Also, we did not find questions about exposure to assumptions being made about health care needs to be associated with any outcome in the adjusted models, and sexual health information was not significant in either analysis level. Because we did not ask students if they sought out such services on campus, we could not limit these questions to students who used services, which may explain these findings.

The qualitative findings illuminate students' reactions to environmental microaggressions, while highlighting important nuances of trans* students' experiences. Consistent with Nadal and colleagues' (2012) research, we identified various cognitive, emotional, and behavioral reactions to environmental microaggressions. We also noted that trans* collegians may have two simultaneous reactions to environmental microaggressions—like Kevin, who described both an emotional reaction (e.g., annoyance) and a behavioral reaction (e.g., e-mailing professors). Occasionally, two or more environmental microaggressions interact, as was described in Chris' case where ability to access housing was dictated by the gender listed on the housing form.

The interview findings suggest that in addition to making gender-inclusive restrooms available, they must be accessible in terms of location and easy entry. Everyday hassles, such as not being able to access inclusive restrooms, and, when they exist, not being able to easily find them or needing to go through a third party to do so—hassles cisgender students do not face—may interfere with students' performance and engagement on campus (Strayhorn, 2012), which our quantitative results also suggest is the case when trans* students encounter restrooms in which they feel uncomfortable.

The interviewees also reported experiencing challenges when encountering birth sex or legal name on official forms, particularly registration and housing forms and class lists. Although we did not quantitatively explore these specific environmental microaggressions, our multivariable analysis concerning exposure to gender-binary forms and academic development (a primary intended outcome of higher education) support this conclusion. For many interviewees, not being able to list their chosen name or gender on campus records meant that they were often identified by an incorrect name or pronoun, which sometimes created additional stress.

Many of the interviewees actively and creatively responded to the challenges they faced on campus. Maya, for example, helped to develop an app identifying the gender-inclusive restrooms on campus. Similarly, Ky indicated that although he did not want to be placed on a female residence floor, he was able to successfully adapt. Far from simply being subject to campus policies, trans* students were actively engaging with and responding to these policies, often enacting their resilience to adversity (Nicolazzo, 2016) and demonstrating agency through their activism on college campuses (Marine, 2011).

Limitations and future research

Alongside methodological strengths, several limitations exist. The quantitative sample supported the current analysis; however, a larger sample might produce different results and would enable the testing of more complex models, including controlling for interpersonal discrimination, as well as examining potential sub-group differences and the role of intersecting identities. Likewise, more interviewees might shed additional light on the ways that trans* microaggressions are expressed, understood, and addressed, including among sub-groups. The use of convenience sampling limits generalizing the quantitative findings. The data are cross-sectional; thus causation cannot be determined. The use of single-item survey measures limited participant burden; however, they may lack the depth needed to capture complicated phenomenon. In addition to the points raised earlier, future research should build on this study by quantitatively examining other trans* environmental microaggressions, including access to gender-inclusive restrooms and difficulties changing one's name on official forms. Furthermore, studies addressing potential buffers to adversity are needed.

Implications

The results offer several implications for social work and higher education. Efforts are needed to eliminate genderism that is manifested through gendered spaces and other environmental microaggressions. This is especially important to supporting trans* students' academic performance and fostering their engagement on campus. Yet, as suggested by our qualitative findings concerning restrooms, a policy of inclusion alone is insufficient: restrooms and other spaces must be easy to find and access, and in the case of housing, be affordable. Similarly, when name/pronoun-of-choice policies or practices are adopted, they need to be implemented effectively campus-wide. Faculty and others may need training and support in this regard. Helping them understand the importance of such actions is recommended.

Some trans* students may turn to or be referred for academic counseling when they are struggling or are not meeting personal goals. The results suggest that practitioners should assess students' experiences beyond interpersonal mistreatment by examining environmental microaggressions. Eliminating such systemic barriers should be an ultimate goal, but will require considerable time; therefore, it will be important for practitioners to help trans* collegians to develop a positive self-concept in light of the systemic minority stressors they face in their learning environments and to create further opportunities for trans* collegians to resist oppression, including involvement in trans* student groups. It will also be important for counselors to be aware of and refer trans* students to academic supports, when needed. These services must be trans* inclusive and competent. Moreover, practitioner-training programs that seek to increase knowledge about trans* students and the various forms of discrimination they face, including environmental microaggressions, and their strengths are recommended.

Conclusion

Given that institutions of higher education exist to foster students' learning and development, ensuring that trans* college students can thrive in college is an important response to that commitment. Our results suggest that it is essential that environmental microaggressions, namely unsafe and gendered restrooms, as well as gendered forms and housing, be eliminated. We argue, based on the evidence from this study, that environmental microaggressions can increase trans* students' risk for negative outcomes, especially in terms of academic factors. Although, except for the bivariate correlation between gender-binary forms and attempted suicide, our quantitative findings suggested our selected environmental microaggressions are not associated with depression or suicide among trans* students, qualitatively students expressed feelings of stress, frustration, and annoyance in response to these barriers. These reactions over time may lead to more serious concerns. Even when efforts are made by institutions to address environmental microaggressions by providing gender-inclusive spaces, access may be inadequate, which is another microaggression. While trans* individuals make visible pervasive genderism on college campuses, changing restrooms or housing does little to address the systematic overt and covert violent systems that bear down on trans* college students' lives. It is critical that social workers, higher education professionals, and advocates hold institutions responsible for addressing the needs of trans* students.

Notes

1. We use "trans*" to signify an opening up of the category to move beyond simplistic understandings of trans* gender identities and explicitly include identities such as gender nonconforming, genderqueer, and two-spirit (Tompkins, 2014).
2. We use the latter as an outcome given that psychological climate can be critical in shaping student health and development.

Funding

This study was supported by the College of Education, Michigan State University, as well as the National Center for Institutional Diversity and the Curtis Center, both located at the University of Michigan. It was also supported by Wilfrid Laurier University and the Social Sciences and Humanities Council of Canada.

ORCID

Jessica Y. Joslin ⓘ http://orcid.org/0000-0003-1406-5457

References

Beemyn, G., Domingue, A., Pettitt, J., & Smith, T. (2005). Suggested steps to make campuses more trans-inclusive. *Journal of Gay & Lesbian Issues in Education*, *3*(1), 89–94. doi:10.1300/J367v03n01_09

Bilodeau, B. (2009). *Genderism: Transgender students, binary systems and higher education.* Saarbrucken, Germany: VDM Verlag Dr. Müller.

Charmaz, K. (2006). *Constructing grounded theory.* London, UK: Sage.

Cortina, L. M., Swan, S., Fitzgerald, L. F., & Waldo, C. (1998). Sexual harassment and assault: Chilling the climate for women in academia. *Psychology of Women Quarterly*, *22*(3), 419–441. doi:10.1111/pwqu.1998.22.issue-3

Dugan, J. P., Kusel, M. L., & Simounet, D. M. (2012). Transgender college students: An exploratory study of perceptions, engagement, and educational outcomes. *Journal of College Student Development*, *53*(5), 719–736. doi:10.1353/csd.2012.0067

Effrig, J. C., Bieschke, K. J., & Locke, B. D. (2011). Examining victimization and psychological distress in transgender college students. *Journal of College Counseling*, *14*(2), 143–157. doi:10.1002/(ISSN)2161-1882

Kohn, P. M., Lafreniere, K., & Gurevich, M. (1990). The inventory of college students' recent life experiences: A decontaminated hassles scale for a special population. *Journal of Behavioural Medicine*, *13*(6), 619–630. doi:10.1007/BF00844738

Marine, S. (2011). Special issue: Stonewall's legacy: Bisexual, gay, lesbian, and transgender students in higher education. *ASHE-ERIC Higher Education Report*, *37*(4), 1–145.

McKinney, J. S. (2005). On the margins: A study of the experiences of transgender college students. *Journal of Gay & Lesbian Issues in Education*, *3*(1), 63–75. doi:10.1300/J367v03n01_07

Meyer, I. H. (2003). Prejudice, social stress, and mental health in lesbian, gay, and bisexual populations: Conceptual issues and research evidence. *Psychological Bulletin*, *129*(5), 674–697. doi:10.1037/0033-2909.129.5.674

Nadal, K. L., Davidoff, K. C., Davis, L. S., & Wong, Y. (2014). Emotional, behavioral, and cognitive reactions to microaggressions: Transgender perspectives. *Psychology of Sexual Orientation and Gender Diversity*, *1*(1), 72–81. doi:10.1037/sgd0000011

Nadal, K. L., Skolnik, A., & Wong, Y. (2012). Interpersonal and systemic microaggressions toward transgender people: Implications for counseling. *Journal of LGBT Issues in Counseling*, *6*(1), 55–82. doi:10.1080/15538605.2012.648583

Nicolazzo, Z. (2016). *Trans* in college: Transgender students' strategies for navigating campus life and the institutional politics of inclusion.* Sterling, VA: Stylus Publishing.

Nicolazzo, Z., & Marine, S. B. (2015). "It will change if people keep talking": Trans* students in college and university housing. *Journal of College & University Student Housing, 41*(2), 160–177.

Pascarella, E. T., & Terenzini, P. T. (1980). Predicting freshman persistence and voluntary dropout decisions from a theoretical model. *The Journal of Higher Education, 51*(1), 60–75. doi:10.2307/1981125

Rankin, S., Weber, G., Blumenfeld, W., & Frazer, S. (2010). *2010 state of higher education for lesbian, gay, bisexual, and transgender people.* Charlotte, NC: Campus Pride.

Seelman, K. L. (2013). *A mixed methods examination of structural bigenderism and the consequences for transgender and gender variant people* (Doctoral dissertation). Retrieved from ProQuest Dissertations and Theses Database. (UMI No. 3588397).

Seelman, K. L. (2014). Recommendations of transgender students, staff, and faculty in the USA for improving college campuses. *Gender and Education, 26*(6), 618–635. doi:10.1080/09540253.2014.935300

Seelman, K. L. (2016). Transgender adults' access to college bathrooms and housing and the relationship to suicidality. *Journal of Homosexuality, 63,* 1378–1399. Advance online publication. doi:10.1080/00918369.2016.1157998

Seelman, K. L., Walls, N. E., Costello, K., Steffens, K., Inselman, K., Montague-Asp, H., &; Colorado Trans on Campus Coalition. (2012). *Invisibilities, uncertainties, and unexpected surprises: The experiences of transgender and gender non-conforming students, staff, and faculty at universities & colleges in Colorado.* Denver, CO: Authors.

Spitzer, R. L., Kroenke, K., Williams, J. B., & Patient Health Questionnaire Primary Care Study Group. (1999). Validation and utility of a self-report version of PRIME-MD: The PHQ primary care study. *JAMA, 282*(18), 1737–1744. doi:10.1001/jama.282.18.1737

Strayhorn, T. L. (2012). *College students' sense of belonging: A key to educational success for all students.* New York, NY: Routledge.

Sue, D. W. (2010). *Microaggressions in everyday life: Race, gender, and sexual orientation.* Hoboken, NJ: John Wiley & Sons.

Tompkins, A. (2014). Asterisk. *Transgender Studies Quarterly, 1*(1–2), 26–27. doi:10.1215/23289252-2399497

Woodford, M. R., Joslin, J., & Renn, K. (2016). LGBTQ students on campus: Fostering inclusion through research, policy and practice. In, P. A. Pasque, M. P. Ting, N. Ortega, & J. C. Burkhardt (Eds.), *Transforming understandings of diversity in higher education: Demography, democracy and discourse* (pp. 57–80). Sterling, VA: Stylus

Woodford, M. R., & Kulick, A. (2015). Academic and social integration on campus among sexual minority students: The impacts of psychological and experiential campus climate. *American Journal of Community Psychology, 55,* 13–24. doi:10.1007/s10464-014-9683-x

Victimization and Microaggressions Targeting LGBTQ College Students: Gender Identity As a Moderator of Psychological Distress

Kristie L. Seelman ⑩, Michael R. Woodford, and Z Nicolazzo

ABSTRACT
Lesbian, gay, bisexual, transgender, and queer and questioning (LGBTQ) discrimination continues to be common on college campuses. While a number of studies have examined blatant victimization among students, little attention has been given to LGBTQ microaggressions. In this study, we examine both blatant victimization and microaggressions and their association with psychological distress among LGBTQ college students ($N = 497$) and look at whether gender identity moderates these relationships. Both forms of discrimination are associated with lower self-esteem and greater stress and anxiety. Victimization is more negatively associated with self-esteem among trans* students. Our findings emphasize the importance of addressing both blatant and subtle forms of discrimination targeting LGBTQ college students.

Despite the increasing visibility of lesbian, gay, bisexual, transgender, queer and questioning (LGBTQ) people, LGBTQ students frequently experience discrimination and a hostile climate on college campuses (Nicolazzo, 2015; Rankin, Weber, Blumenfeld, & Frazer, 2010; Woodford, Howell, Silverschanz, & Yu, 2012; Woodford, Kulick, Sinco, & Hong, 2014). While a growing number of studies have examined blatant victimization among LGBTQ college students and the connection to student well-being, little attention has been given to microaggressions. In the present study, we examine both blatant victimization and microaggressions and their association with psychological distress among LGBTQ college students and look at whether gender identity moderates these relationships.

Experiences of discrimination impacting LGBTQ college students

Evidence indicates that discrimination is prevalent among the LGBTQ college population at large (Rankin et al., 2010). However, recent studies suggest

Color versions of one or more of the figures in the article can be found online at www.tandfonline.com/wecd.

that rates of discrimination are higher for trans* individuals than cisgender (non-transgender) students (Dugan, Kusel, & Simounet, 2012; Rankin et al., 2010).[1] This implies that harassment and discrimination targeting trans* individuals may be more prevalent and less often challenged by others, aligning with overall patterns within university environments in which cisgender identities are treated as the norm and trans* identities are marginalized (Nicolazzo, 2015; Seelman, 2013). Most research examining topics of LGBTQ discrimination and harassment has focused on blatant behaviors (Nadal, 2013), such as physical and sexual assault or threats of violence (e.g., Effrig, Bieschke, & Locke, 2011). However, the changing nature of discrimination has meant that more subtle forms of discrimination are often more common (Woodford, Han, Craig, Lim, & Matney, 2014).

There is a lack of research about LGBTQ college students' experiences of microaggressions (Woodford, Chonody, Kulick, Brennan, & Renn, 2015). Past studies have documented forms of subtle heterosexist behaviors, including gay jokes and other slurs (Silverschanz, Cortina, Kornik, & Magley, 2008) and the microaggression "that's so gay" (Woodford et al., 2012). While not always labeled as microaggressions, recent work has documented examples of subtle discrimination affecting trans* people in college, such as facing unreasonable barriers to changing one's name or gender on campus records (Seelman, 2013) and witnessing others minimize the need for changing policies to protect trans* people (Case, Kanenberg, Erich, & Tittsworth, 2012).

According to the minority stress model (Meyer, 2003), populations that are socially stigmatized face chronic stress due to prejudice and discrimination, which can put them at risk for poor mental health. This model has been usually applied to sexual minorities, including college students (e.g.,Woodford et al., 2012; Woodford, Kulick, et al., 2014). Several recent studies have used this lens to understand health disparities for trans* individuals (Hendricks & Testa, 2012; Herman, 2013). Effrig and colleagues (2011) applied this model and found trans* students to be at increased risk for psychological distress compared to their cisgender peers; however, they did *not* examine the relationship between discrimination and mental health outcomes.

Although subtle manifestations of LGBTQ discrimination are more prevalent on campuses than blatant forms (Rankin et al., 2010), only recently have scholars investigated the former's relationship with students' health. Emerging research indicates that subtle heterosexism can have a negative impact on sexual minority college students (Silverschanz et al., 2008; Woodford, Han, Craig, Lim, & Matney, 2014; Woodford et al., 2012). In terms of microaggressions, overhearing others use the phrase "that's so gay" as a negative descriptor has been associated with headaches, poor appetite, and feelings of isolation among emerging adult sexual minority students (Woodford et al., 2012). Furthermore, LGBQ microaggressions were associated with greater psychological distress (anxiety and perceived stress) among LGBQ college students (Woodford, Kulick, et al., 2014). In terms of microaggressions targeting trans* individuals, a recent analysis of the National Transgender Discrimination Survey data (using a subsample of participants who ever attended college) found a relationship between being denied access to campus housing or bathrooms—an example of environmental or systemic microaggression—and lifetime suicidality, even after controlling for on-campus victimization by teachers or students (Seelman, 2016a). To the best of our knowledge, researchers have not examined microaggressions specifically among current trans* collegians.

The current study

The present study analyzes the relationship between microaggressions and psychological distress (self-esteem, perceived stress, and anxiety) among LGBTQ students. To shed light on the potential differential impacts of blatant and subtle discrimination, we examine both victimization and microaggressions. Moreover, given that research suggests trans* students experience greater discrimination compared to their cisgender peers, we explore gender identity as a moderator between discrimination and distress.

Specifically, we ask the following: Are experiences of blatant LGBTQ victimization and LGBTQ microaggressions significantly associated with self-esteem, stress, and anxiety among LGBTQ college students? In addition, does gender identity moderate the victimization/microaggression-distress relationship?

Methods

Data were collected among a convenience sample of self-identified LGBTQ college students who participated in an anonymous, Web-based survey ($N = 497$). Participants were recruited via e-mail messages distributed through LGBTQ listservs. To participate, students had to be at least 18 years old, self-identify as LGBTQ, and be current or previous (past-year) college students. Participants provided informed consent. The study received approval from the University of Michigan Institutional Review Board.

Participants

Just under 15% ($N = 72$) of the sample identified as transgender, genderqueer, or another gender-non-conforming identity, while 50% ($N = 244$) were women and 36% ($N = 177$) were men. Almost one-third (29%, $N = 143$) identified as gay, 20% ($N = 97$) as lesbian, 18% ($N = 90$) as queer, 16% ($N = 76$) as bisexual, 11% ($N = 52$) as straight/heterosexual, and 7% as other ($N = 33$).[2] Ages ranged from 18 to 61 years, with a median of 24 years. More than three-fourths (79%, $N = 386$) of the sample were White, and more than half (58%, $N = 289$) were undergraduate students. A small minority (8.4%, $N = 42$) attended schools in Canada. Among participants from the United States, 33 states were represented, with the vast majority of these participants attending schools in the Midwest.

Measures

LGBTQ discrimination on campus

We inquired about the prevalence of LGBTQ discrimination in terms of threats and insults (blatant victimization) as well as LGBQ/trans* microaggressions within the past year (or since coming to campus, if less than one year; 0 = never, 5 = very frequently). Blatant victimization was evaluated using nine items selected and adapted from earlier measures (D'Augelli, 1992; Herek, 1993) to be inclusive of bisexual, queer, and trans* identities (separate questions were used for sexual orientation and for gender identity, with the victimization act content being parallel across the question sets). We dropped five items focused on the most severe physical attacks and threats due to little variance on these items (most had never experienced such attacks). We retained four items for blatant insults (e.g., "Someone verbally insulted me [e.g., 'f'in tranny'] because they knew or assumed I am transgender") and threats (e.g., "Someone threatened to tell others about my sexual orientation").

Given differences between sexual orientation and trans* microaggressions (Nadal, Rivera, & Corpus, 2010), separate scales were used to assess microaggressions on campus based on each identity. Participants who selected man or woman answered the sexual orientation microaggression items, while those who reported a gender identity of transgender, genderqueer, or other were asked to answer the trans* microaggression questions. These scales capture everyday verbal and nonverbal indignations, insults, and invalidations that occur on college campuses. LGBQ microaggressions were documented using a 20-item measure ($\alpha = .91$); sample item "I was told I should act 'less lesbian, gay, bisexual, or queer'" (Woodford et al., 2015). Thirty-four items evaluated trans* microaggressions ($\alpha = .92$); sample item "I was told that I talk about discrimination against transgender or gender queer people too much" (Woodford & Chonody, 2015).

Psychological distress

We assessed self-esteem, perceived stress, and anxiety. An adapted version of the 10-item Rosenberg Self-Esteem Scale was used to measure self-esteem (Rosenberg, 1965). To ensure the measure was accessible and tapped into participants' global self-worth rather than comparative self-concept, we adapted Rosenberg's scale for use among college students by simplifying wording and removing comparisons to others. Self-esteem tends to be unstable in emerging adults (Trzeniewski, Donnellan, & Robins, 2003); hence, participants were instructed to consider items over the past 12 months on a 5-point scale (1 = *never true*, 5 = *almost always true*; α = .91) (Rosenberg, Schooler, Schoenbach, & Rosenberg, 1995). To measure perceived stress, we used the 10-item Perceived Stress Scale (Cohen, Kamarck, & Mermelstein, 1983), which captures the degree to which situations in one's life are considered as stressful during the past month (0 = *never*, 4 = *very often*; α = .90). Anxiety was measured using the Generalized Anxiety Scale (GAD-7) (Spitzer, Kroenke, Williams, & Löwe, 2006), which inquires about symptoms of General Anxiety Disorder within the past two weeks (0 = *not at all*, 3 = *nearly every day*; α = .89).

Sociodemographic variables

Participants reported gender identity, sexual orientation, race, age, student status, and the name of their college (used to determine school location). We assessed gender identity by asking, "How would you describe your current gender identity?" with five options, including "other." This variable was dichotomized (cisgender/trans*) for analysis. Sexual orientation was assessed with, "How would you describe your sexual orientation?" and participants selected from six categories, including "other." Race was originally evaluated using eight categories, which we dichotomized (White/person of color) due to sample size.

Data analysis

We used SPSS, version 22, for all analyses. Univariate outliers were detected on the two interaction terms, so we adjusted the values of outliers to be less extreme, although they remained on the tail end of the distribution (Tabachnick & Fidell, 2007). There were 24 identical multivariate outlier cases across the three models; these cases were significantly more likely to be trans* participants, so we decided to retain these cases, noting that their inclusion may influence models. Several of the independent variables of interest were missing not at random in relation to some of the dependent variables. Tabachnick and Fidell (2007) suggest keeping all cases in such situations due to the bias that can occur when dropping cases that have missing data related to the dependent variables. We therefore chose to use multiple imputation to provide pooled estimates for missing data based on five imputations.

We performed a total of six sequential multiple linear regression models, two for each dependent variable (one including blatant victimization, another including microaggressions). Block 1 included race, gender, and age. Block 2 added the discrimination variable—either victimization or microaggressions.[3] Block 3 included the interaction terms between gender and the discrimination variable.

Results

Descriptive statistics

The mean score for LGBTQ victimization (0.29, for a scale ranging from 0 to 5) suggests that blatant insults and threats typically occurred between "never" and "very rarely," whereas microaggressions occurred about halfway between "very rarely" and "rarely" (mean score of 1.51 on a scale from 0 to 5). For self-esteem, the average score (2.81, on a scale from 1 to 5) was slightly below the scale's midpoint, indicating a moderate degree of self-esteem in the average participant. The mean for perceived stress (1.75, on a scale from 0 to 4) was slightly below the scale's midpoint, suggesting overall appraisals of stress were low. The average score on the anxiety measure (0.87, on a scale from 0 to 3) suggested that symptoms of anxiety occurred slightly less than "several days" during the past two weeks.

Inferential statistics

The results presented here use the pooled data following multiple imputation. However, the Adjusted R^2 values were computed for the original data since these statistics are not produced for pooled results.

Blatant victimization predicting self-esteem

There was a statistically significant difference between trans* and cisgender individuals in Block 1. The results suggest that trans* participants reported an average self-esteem score that was about 0.19 points lower ($p < .05$) than that of cisgender participants. Age was also associated with self-esteem: for each year increase in a student's age, self-esteem was predicted to increase by 0.02 points ($p < .01$). These demographic variables account for about 3% of the variance in self-esteem scores. In Block 2, gender is no longer significant, but age remains significantly associated with self-esteem (B = 0.02, $p < .01$). Experiences of blatant victimization demonstrate a statistically significant negative relationship with self-esteem (B = –0.29, $p < .001$). For every 1-point increase in victimization, self-esteem is predicted to decrease by 0.29 points. This block accounts for 11% of the variance in self-esteem scores.

In Block 3, which accounts for 12% of the variance in self-esteem scores, age remains significantly associated with self-esteem (B = 0.02, $p < .01$). The cross-product interaction term is also statistically significant (gender x victimization B = –0.91, $p < .05$), which suggests that the effect of victimization on self-esteem depends on one's gender identity. The main effect of victimization (B = –0.25, $p < .001$) is the effect among cisgender students, which suggests that victimization has a significant relationship with cisgender students' self-esteem scores so that for each 1-point increase in victimization, self-esteem is predicted to decrease by 0.25 points. The coefficient for the interaction term (B = –0.91, $p < .05$) is the additional effect of victimization on self-esteem among trans* participants, which suggests that with each 1-point increase in victimization, self-esteem is predicted to decrease by 0.91 points. This relationship is also seen in Figure 1. This interpretation of the relationship between victimization and self-esteem by gender identity was also confirmed in post hoc regression models run separately for cisgender and trans* students (results not reported here).

Blatant victimization predicting perceived stress

In Block 1 of the model for perceived stress, only age is significantly associated with perceived stress (B = –0.02, $p < .01$); demographic variables account for 3% of the variance in perceived stress scores. For every 1-year increase in age, stress decreases by 0.02 points. In Block 2, age remains statistically significant (B = –0.02, $p < .01$) and victimization is positively associated with perceived stress (B = 0.23, $p < .001$); for each 1-point increase in the frequency of victimization, one's stress score is predicted to increase by 0.23. This block accounts for 7% of the variance in perceived stress scores. In Block 3, age (B = –0.02, $p < .01$) and victimization (B = 0.20, $p < .01$) remain statistically significant predictors of perceived stress, but the interaction term (gender x victimization) is not significant. This final version of the model accounted for 7% of the variance in perceived stress.

Blatant victimization predicting anxiety

Age is a marginally significant predictor (B = –0.01, $p < .10$) of anxiety in Block 1. The demographic variables account for less than 1% of the variance in student anxiety. In Block 2, victimization is a significant predictor of anxiety (B = 0.23, $p < .001$); this block accounts for 6% of the variance in anxiety. For every 1-point increase in victimization, anxiety is predicted to increase by 0.23 points. Victimization remains statistically significant in

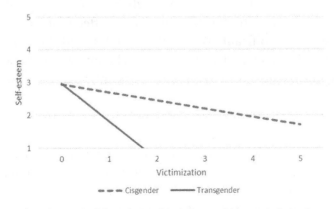

Figure 1. Gender's moderation of the relationship between blatant victimization and self-esteem.

Block 3 (B = 0.21, p < .001), but the interaction term (gender x victimization) is not significant. This block accounts for 6% of the variance in anxiety.

Microaggressions predicting self-esteem

For each of the microaggressions models, the results for Block 1 are identical to those in the victimization models, as only the demographics are entered in the first block. In Block 2 of the microaggressions model predicting self-esteem, gender is no longer significant, but age remains significantly associated with self-esteem (B = 0.02, p < .01). LGBTQ microaggressions are negatively associated with self-esteem (B = –0.16, p < .01). For every 1-point increase in microaggressions, self-esteem is predicted to decrease by 0.16 points. This block accounts for 7% of the variance in self-esteem scores. In Block 3, the main effect of microaggressions remains significant (B = –0.16, p < .01), and the interaction term (gender x microaggressions) does not reach statistical significance.

Microaggressions predicting perceived stress

In Block 2, which accounts for 13% of the variance of perceived stress, age continues to be a statistically significant predictor of stress (B = –0.02, p < .01). Microaggressions are positively related to stress (B = 0.22, p < .001). For every 1-point increase in microaggressions, stress is predicted to increase by 0.22 points. In the final model, age (B = –0.02, p < .01) and microaggressions (B = 0.23, p < .001) remain statistically significant predictors of perceived stress. The interaction term (gender x microaggressions) is not significantly related to perceive stress. The final block accounts for 13% of the variance of perceived stress.

Microaggressions predicting anxiety

In Block 2, microaggressions are positively associated with anxiety (B = 0.20, p < .001): for each point increase in experiences of microaggressions, one's anxiety score is predicted to increase by 0.20. This block accounts for 9% of the variance in anxiety. In Block 3, the main effects of microaggressions remain statistically significant (B = 0.20, p < .001), and the model accounts for 9% of the variance in anxiety symptoms. The interaction between gender and microaggressions is not statistically significantly associated with anxiety.

Discussion

The minority stress model maintains that discrimination can increase LGBTQ students' risk for negative outcomes; however, little is known about the role of microaggressions on students' well-being. When taking the full sample into account, our results suggest that blatant victimization and microaggressions are each independently associated with lower self-esteem and higher levels of perceived stress and anxiety symptoms. Moreover, we found that gender moderated the relationship between victimization and self-esteem such that trans* students had a more strongly negative association between victimization and self-esteem than cisgender students.

Among the full sample, our results support the minority stress framework. At the bivariate level, significant moderate correlations (not reported) were found between each form of discrimination and each outcome in the anticipated direction; the regression models similarly demonstrated that victimization and microaggressions related to greater forms of psychological distress (lower self-esteem; greater perceived stress and anxiety symptoms). These findings are in line with previous research looking at multivariate relationships between victimization and/or microaggressions and well-being (Silverschanz et al., 2008; Woodford et al., 2012; Woodford, Han, et al., 2014; Woodford, Kulick, et al., 2014). The documented significant positive relationships among microaggressions, self-esteem, perceived stress, and anxiety likely reflect the stressors inherent within microaggressions. That is, although often subtle in nature, microaggressions on campus can increase LGBTQ students' risk for these negative outcomes, just as blatant victimization increases such risks.

Looking at the unstandardized beta coefficients for the models (which can be directly compared since microaggressions and victimization were similarly scaled), victimization had the largest coefficient (B = −0.29 before adding the moderation term) in predicting self-esteem compared to either stress or anxiety (B = 0.23 for both). Microaggressions had a higher coefficient for stress (B = 0.22) and anxiety (B = 0.20) and the lowest for self-esteem (B = −0.16). Thus, compared to microaggressions, victimization has a more noticeable relationship with self-esteem, suggesting that blatant insults and threats may have a stronger connection to self-esteem than do microaggressions. Both victimization and microaggressions had similar coefficient results for perceived stress and anxiety symptoms.

The results of the moderation analyses are intriguing. Victimization was significantly negatively associated with self-esteem among cisgender participants, in line with the minority stress model. Furthermore, consistent with this model, victimization was associated with lower self-esteem among trans* students (with a larger coefficient observed compared to that for cisgender students). Experiencing blatant insults and threats may have a particularly impactful presence for trans* students, who, past research has suggested, experience disproportionate victimization on campus (though the present study did not find a statistical difference between trans* and cisgender students in campus victimization). In contrast to self-esteem, an interaction between gender and victimization was not significant for stress and anxiety.

It is possible that, for trans* students, the presence of blatant insults and threats may uniquely connect to self-esteem because such insults and threats are added onto the various other forms of microaggressions and discrimination that a trans* student experiences across all sectors of life. In other words, one's self-esteem, which is likely to remain stable despite the daily indignities of microaggressions, is more likely to be influenced by overt acts of violence, threat, and harm that are part of victimization, thus causing one to have lower assessments of one's self-worth. As noted, the difference between cisgender and trans* students was not found for either stress or anxiety as a function of experiences of victimization. Whereas self-esteem represents a fairly steady overall trait characteristic, both perceived stress and anxiety symptoms can fluctuate much more over shorter spans of time, and our results suggest this can occur similarly for trans* and cisgender students.

Gender did not moderate the relationship between microaggressions and any of the forms of psychological distress. Due to the prevalence of micro-aggressions and other subtle manifestations of discrimination as a more "acceptable" way of expressing prejudice in today's world (Woodford, Han, et al., 2014), LGBTQ students, regardless of gender identity, may regularly feel the impact of microaggressions on their self-esteem, stress, and anxiety such that there is no differentiation in these relationships among these subgroups.

Limitations

The results should be considered in light of the methodological limitations. Given the use of a cross-sectional design, we are unable to determine causation. Although the sample was diverse and large enough for our analysis, it is relatively small, with most participants attending schools in the Midwest portion of the United States. In addition, the number of trans* students ($N = 72$) was a small portion of the sample, and results may be different with a larger sample of trans* individuals. The use of convenience sampling prohibits generalizing the findings. Participants were recruited from online LGBTQ networks; students connected to these networks may be more "out" about their sexuality and/or gender identity, more resilient to discrimination, or possess more personal and social resources than others. Use of a racially diverse sample could help with investigating whether there are racial disparities in experiences of LGBTQ victimization microaggressions.

In addition to exploring the explanatory propositions suggested earlier, we recommend that researchers explore the factors that can foster students' resilience to LGBTQ discrimination. We recommend that the role of campus climate programs and policies be explored, as well as both formal and informal supports available to LGBTQ students. Finally, studies are needed to identify the role of peers and instructors in possibly protecting LGBTQ students from the negative effects of victimization and microaggressions. Research in this direction might identify differential effects of initiatives to protect students from victimization and microaggressions.

Implications

Our findings provide much-needed evidence to inform policy and practice interventions tailored to the needs of LGBTQ college students. Consistent with the *Code of Ethics* (National Association of Social Workers [NASW], 2008), social workers are called to address discrimination both in terms of prevention and treatment. Our results suggest that such efforts need to include both subtle, often minimized, microaggressions, *and* blatant victimization, especially the latter in fostering strong self-esteem among trans* students. Policies and educational programs need to address both aspects of LGBTQ discrimination if an inclusive and safe environment is to be created for LGBTQ students. For example, ally training programs should prepare participants to be able to recognize LGBTQ microaggressions as well as victimization and to effectively intervene in such cases while maintaining personal safety. We believe it will be especially important for student leaders, student affairs staff, and faculty to participate in these programs given that microaggressions can happen anywhere on campus, including residence halls and classrooms.

In clinical settings, our results direct practitioners to inquire about both victimization and microaggressions in order to understand LGBTQ students' well-being. Given that some students may not consider microaggressions to be discrimination, we recommend that practitioners explain the often-subtle nature of contemporary discrimination and give examples. Practitioners may find it beneficial to use the microaggressions scales used in this study to facilitate the assessment process. Social work schools and professional development programs should address microaggressions in their programs (see Keuroghlian, Shtasel, & Bassuk, 2014). Moreover, practitioners need to assess LGBTQ students' coping skills and resilience factors. Furthermore, when lacking, practitioners need to advocate for programs and services that specifically support LGBTQ students.

Notes

1. We use the term *transgender* as an umbrella term incorporating anyone whose self-identified gender identity differs from predominant cultural expectations for their sex assigned at birth. This definition incorporates individuals who choose to biomedically transition from one gender to another (i.e., transsexuals), as well as those who elect not to seek such treatment. The shorter term *trans** is meant to include a range of non-binary gender identities (e.g., genderqueer) as well as those who may not use the term *transgender* for themselves.
2. Some individuals who identified as straight/heterosexual group were trans*. Others, however, were cisgender and reported only heterosexual attraction. When running the multiple linear regression models, we compared final results both with and without this group of 37 cisgender heterosexuals; results were the same either way. Due to the fluid nature of sexuality and gender and the inherent difficult of attaching simple labels to oneself, we chose to retain these respondents in our sample.

3. We originally ran analyses with victimization and microaggressions in the same models; however, these two variables had a moderately strong correlation (.59) that resulted in problems with suppression in the regression models. Therefore, we ran separate regression models for each discrimination variable.

Acknowledgment

We thank the participants, as well as Alex Kulick (PhD student, Department of Sociology, University of California, Santa Barbara), who assisted with the survey and data collection.

Funding

This research was supported by Wilfrid Laurier University and the Social Sciences and Humanities Research Council of Canada. It was also supported by the Curtis Center and the National Institute for Institutional Diversity, both located at the University of Michigan.

ORCID

Kristie L. Seelman ⓘ http://orcid.org/0000-0002-4064-2927

References

Case, K. A., Kanenberg, H., Erich, S., & Tittsworth, J. (2012). Transgender inclusion in university nondiscrimination statements: Challenging gender-conforming privilege through student activism. *Journal of Social Issues, 68*(1), 145–161. doi:10.1111/j.1540-4560.2011.01741.x

Cohen, S., Kamarck, T., & Mermelstein, R. (1983). A global measure of perceived stress. *Journal of Health and Social Behavior, 24,* 385–396. doi:10.2307/2136404

D'Augelli, A. R. (1992). Lesbian and gay male undergraduates' experiences of harassment and fear on campus. *Journal of Interpersonal Violence, 7,* 383–395. doi:10.1177/088626092007003007

Dugan, J. P., Kusel, M. L., & Simounet, D. M. (2012). Transgender college students: An exploratory study of perceptions, engagement, and educational outcomes. *Journal of College Student Development, 53*(5), 719–736. doi:10.1353/csd.2012.0067

Effrig, J. C., Bieschke, K. J., & Locke, B. D. (2011). Examining victimization and psychological distress in transgender college students. *Journal of College Counseling, 14*(2), 143–157. doi:10.1002/j.2161-1882.2011.tb00269.x

Hendricks, M. L., & Testa, R. J. (2012). A conceptual framework for clinical work with transgender and gender nonconforming clients: An adaptation of the minority stress model. *Professional Psychology: Research and Practice, 43*(5), 460–467. doi:10.1037/a0029597

Herek, G. M. (1993). Documenting prejudice against lesbians and gay men on campus: The Yale Sexual Orientation Survey. *Journal of Homosexuality, 25,* 15–30. doi:10.1300/J082v25n04_02

Herman, J. L. (2013). Gendered restrooms and minority stress: The public regulation of gender and its impact on transgender people's lives. *Journal of Public Management & Social Policy, 19*(1), 65–80.

Keuroghlian, A. S., Shtasel, D., & Bassuk, E. L. (2014). Out on the street: A public health and policy agenda for lesbian, gay, bisexual, and transgender youth who are homeless. *American Journal of Orthopsychiatry, 84*(1), 66–72. doi:10.1037/h0098852

Meyer, I. H. (2003). Prejudice, social stress, and mental health in lesbian, gay, and bisexual populations: Conceptual issues and research evidence. *Psychological Bulletin, 129*(5), 674–697. doi:10.1037/0033-2909.129.5.674

Nadal, K. L. (2013). *That's so gay! Microaggressions and the lesbian, gay, bisexual, and transgender community.* Washington, DC: American Psychological Association.

Nadal, K. L., Rivera, D. P., & Corpus, M. J. H. (2010). Sexual orientation and transgender microaggressions: Implications for mental health and counseling. In D. W. Sue (Ed.), *Microaggressions and marginality: Manifestation, dynamics, and impact* (pp. 217–240). Hoboken, NJ: John Wiley & Sons, Inc.

National Association of Social Workers (NASW). (2008). *Code of ethics of the National Association of Social Workers.* Retrieved from http://www.socialworkers.org/pubs/code/code.asp

Nicolazzo, Z. (2015). *"Just go in looking good": The resilience, resistance, and kinship-building of trans* college students* (Doctoral dissertation). Miami University, Oxford, OH. Retrieved from http://www.ohiolink.edu/etd/

Rankin, S., Weber, G., Blumenfeld, W., & Frazer, S. (2010). *2010 State of higher education for lesbian, gay, bisexual & transgender people.* Charlotte, NC: Campus Pride.

Rosenberg, M. (1965). *Society and the adolescent self-image.* Princeton, NJ: Princeton University Press.

Rosenberg, M., Schooler, C., Schoenbach, C., & Rosenberg, F. (1995). Global self-esteem and specific self-esteem: Different concepts, different outcomes. *American Sociological Review, 60*, 141–156. doi:10.2307/2096350

Seelman, K. L. (2013). *A mixed methods examination of structural bigenderism and the consequences for transgender and gender variant people* (Doctoral dissertation). Retrieved from ProQuest Dissertations and Theses Database. (UMI No. 3588397)

Seelman, K. L. (2016a). Transgender adults' access to college bathrooms and housing and the relationship to suicidality. *Journal of Homosexuality, 63*(10), 1378–1399. doi:10.1080/00918369.2016.1157998

Silverschanz, P., Cortina, L. M., Kornik, J., & Magley, V. J. (2008). Slurs, snubs, and queer jokes: Incidence and impact of heterosexist harassment in academia. *Sex Roles, 58*, 179–191. doi:10.1007/s11199-007-9329-7

Spitzer, R. L., Kroenke, K., Williams, J. B., & Löwe, B. (2006). A brief measure for assessing generalized anxiety disorder: The GAD-7. *Archives of Internal Medicine, 166*, 1092–1097. doi:10.1001/archinte.166.10.1092

Tabachnick, B. G., & Fidell, L. S. (2007). *Using multivariate statistics* (5th ed.). Boston, MA: Pearson Education.

Trzesniewski, K. H., Donnellan, M. B., & Robins, R. W. (2003). Stability of self-esteem across the life span. *Journal of Personality and Social Psychology, 84*, 205–220. doi:10.1037/0022-3514.84.1.205

Woodford, M. R., & Chonody, J. (2015, October). Assessing Trans* microaggressions on college campuses: An instrument development and validation study. Paper presented at the 61st Annual Program Meeting of the Council on Social Work Education, Denver, CO.

Woodford, M. R., Chonody, J. M., Kulick, A., Brennan, D. J., & Renn, K. (2015). The LGBQ microaggressions on campus scale: A scale development and validation study. *Journal of Homosexuality, 62*(12), 1660–1687. doi:10.1080/00918369.2015.1078205

Woodford, M. R., Han, Y., Craig, S., Lim, C., & Matney, M. M. (2014). Discrimination and mental health among sexual minority college students: The type and form of discrimination does matter. *Journal of Gay & Lesbian Mental Health, 18*(2), 142–163. doi:10.1080/19359705.2013.833882

Woodford, M. R., Howell, M. L., Silverschanz, P., & Yu, L. (2012). "That's so gay!" Examining the covariates of hearing this expression among gay, lesbian, and bisexual students. *Journal of American College Health, 60*(6), 429–434. doi:10.1080/07448481.2012.673519

Woodford, M. R., Kulick, A., Sinco, B. R., & Hong, J. S. (2014). Contemporary heterosexism on campus and psychological distress among LGBQ students: The mediating role of self-acceptance. *American Journal of Orthopsychiatry*, *84*(5), 519–529. doi:10.1037/ort0000015

"You are a *Besya*": Microaggressions Experienced by Trafficking Survivors Exploited in the Sex Trade

Rita Dhungel

ABSTRACT

This article exposes the prevalence of microaggressions as experienced by female sex-trafficking survivors in their everyday lives. Using a case example from Nepal, this article investigates the under-researched experiences of microaggressions against trafficking survivors and their cumulative effects on their lives. A participatory action research (PAR) process was used with eight trafficking survivors to delineate and explore categories of microaggressive behaviors to them. The results of the study reveal the occurrence of microaggressive behaviors against sex-trafficking survivors, grounded in experiential evidence in personal narratives. Implications for social work education and practices are discussed.

Women survivors of sex trafficking experience a number of challenges in their lives, including social stigma, ostracism from family and community, and unemployment (Cameron & Newman, 2008; Chaulagai, 2009; Chen & Marcovici, 2003; Locke, 2010; McNeill, 2008). Based on the United Nations' trafficking strategies, when the Government of Nepal (GoN) developed the "3P" anti-trafficking strategy, comprising prevention of sex trafficking, protection of those sex trafficked, and prosecution of those doing the trafficking, range of programming from nongovernmental organizations has emerged in the country (Chaulagai, 2009; GoN, 2012; Shakti Samuha, 2013). Despite these efforts, trafficking survivors are still discriminated against and treated differently in multiple ways (Chaulagai, 2009; Sharma, 2014). Not surprisingly, previous studies have identified systemic barriers as the most challenging factors for women survivors of sex trafficking. Systemic barriers such as prolonged criminal legal procedures and feminization of poverty create an oppressive environment and hinder survivors in their attempts to reintegrate into family and community life. What research has not explored is how women experience this oppressive climate on a day-to-day basis in the subtle and nebulous forms of oppression called microaggressions, which can be difficult to describe and define (Sue, Bucceri, Nadal, & Torino, 2007).

A body of literature is beginning to emerge on microaggression as experienced by diverse and overlapping sectors of society. Substantial studies support the presence of specific types of microaggression as experienced by people of color (Constantine, 2007; Hill, Kim, & Williams, 2010; Sue, Bucceri, Lin, Nadal, & Torino, 2007; Sue, Capodilupo, & Holder, 2008; Sue et al., 2007), by women (Capodilupo, Nadal, & Corman, 2010), by people with disabilities (Keller & Galgay, 2010), and by gay, lesbian, bisexual, transgender, and queer (GLBTQ) communities (Nadal et al., 2011; Nadal, Rivera, & Corpus, 2010; Robinson, 2014). Research has also focused on microaggressions based on religion (Nadal, 2008; Nadal, Issa, Griffin, Hamit, & Lyons, 2010) and microaggressions toward international students (Kill & Kim, 2010). This article adds to this emerging literature by focusing on microaggressions experienced by women attempting to reintegrate into their communities following sexual exploitation. It is structured into five sections: (a) methodology of the study; (b) results of the study; (c) impact of microaggressive behaviors; (d) implications to social work research education and practice; and (e) discussion/ conclusion.

Methodology and purpose of the study

OrlandoFals Borda (2001), a founding participatory action research (PAR) theorist, pointed out that PAR was developed to invite community members to participate in research that was aimed toward their benefits. Therefore, PAR was employed to investigate the under-researched and multifaceted experiences of microaggression by trafficked women during the process of their reintegration into their families and society. The purpose of this study was to examine how trafficking survivors perceive the term *reintegration* in the process of their reintegration in the context of Nepal. The study took place in Kathmandu, Nepal, from October 2013 to June 2014.

Participants/Co-researchers

A combination of criterion sampling and maximum variation sampling was used for the recruitment of participants, who are also known as co-researchers. The eight female adult trafficking survivors, ranging from 25 to 40 years of age, who were recruited for this study met the following criteria: (a) They were trafficked for sexual exploitation to brothels in India; (b) they had returned to Nepal from India; and (c) they were currently working and/or living in the shelter of Shakti Samuha, an anti-trafficking agency in Kathmandu, Nepal, formed by trafficking survivors.

Data collection/data creation method

Fals Borda and Rahman (1991) suggested using the term *data creation or generation* instead of the term *data collection* in PAR. Smith, Willms, and

Johnson (1997) suggested that participatory researchers should choose the methods of data collection and analysis that are grounded in the context and issues of community for which the research will be based upon. Therefore, for the purpose of the study, solidarity group meetings and semi-structured interviews were used for data collection/data generation. Solidarity group meetings were used to identify common experiences of reintegration of trafficking survivors and semi-structured individual interviews were employed to gain an in-depth understanding of how survivors experienced oppression in their efforts to reintegrate into their families and communities and how they believe social work practitioners and other members of the community can help them reintegrate into their families and communities.

Through PAR, the researcher and co-researchers were involved in identifying issues in their reintegration, analyzing the problems, and finding ways to address the identified issues collectively (Fals Borda & Rahman, 1991). To elaborate, this study began with engagement with the co-researchers, allowing the researcher to build relationships among the co-researchers. After a few weeks, upon under-standing the values of PAR and roles for co-researchers in the study, the co-researchers were involved in selecting data collection methods and developing agendas for this study, which helped them to get engaged in meaningful dialogues and democratic discussions. Through an action-reflection-action process, the women were not only involved in developing survey questionnaires for peer interviews and the interviews with stakeholders, working in anti-trafficking inter-ventions, but they also administered the interviews and analyzed data.

Data analysis

The process of data analysis began simultaneously with data creation and interpretation suggested by Boakye (2009). All tape-recorded interviews and solidarity group discussions were transcribed in Nepali and then translated into English. In collaboration with the co-researchers, the transcripts were analyzed in the first phase to identify, verify, and clarify themes to ensure they reflected participants' views. The second phase of analysis included detailed reviewing of data from the reflective journal and semi-structured individual interviews. Data were analyzed in such a way that themes and interpretations emerged from the process, addressing the original research question and objectives, as suggested by Grinnell and Unrau (2005)..

The co-researchers were significantly involved in the data analyzing pro-cess through coding and categorizing the data. During the process, the co-researchers subsequent developed themes that will be presented in the fol-lowing section. Overall, data analysis took place in a participatory way at different stages so the women could validate and provide feedback on the themes they identified from the research process.

Results

This section first examines the occurrence of microaggressive behaviors against trafficking survivors, using the typology of microaggressions offered by Sue (2010): microassault, microinsult, and microinvalidation of microaggressions. It then looks at the impact these microaggressions have had on trafficking survivors in their reintegration.

Microassaultive behaviors

In the microaggression taxonomy, microassaults are offenses that closely resemble traditional discrimination used to demean women. The study identified that trafficking survivors experienced microassaults verbally and nonverbally in their everyday lives. An example is when people who are aware of a survivor's past in the sex trade use explicit and intended derogatory remarks to demean the survivors. Survivors reported experiences of microassaults that can be categorized into four taxonomic themes: use of derogatory language; denial of citizenship and treated as other; invisible demonstrations of rejection; and exoticization and sexual objectification.

Use of derogatory language

The trafficked women reported that people who knew their past often use very hurtful and demeaning words against them. The women were often called terms like *besya, randi,* and/or *bhalu* (whores or characterless women who sleep with multiple partners). People would frequently tell them they were "mines and sources" of HIV/AIDS. One of the co-researchers said the following (as translated by me from original Nepalese):

> I can't believe that people are so rude to me. One day while I was on my way to fetch water in my village, I saw a few friends who were going to school and I tried to talk to them. But they said that they don't want to talk to me because "you are bhalu" and I sleep with lots of men. No one except me knows how painful it was.

Similarly, another co-researcher lamented:

> I am not sure if it was their intention but I was frequently called by "besya" (whore) in my own house and village. My own family including husband and relatives utter the word "besya" whenever they are not happy with me, especially when I do not have time and/or am not feeling well to do household chores.

Women reported feeling confused by these terms and were often led to consider the possibility that the sentiments expressed might accurately reflect who they are. The words also forced them to reflect on their past more than they wished to, or when they didn't wish to, and this led them to feel very low and frightened. One of the participants stated,

"When people call me 'besya' I start interrogating myself. Am I really 'besya'? Is this my real identity in this society?"

Denial of citizenship and treated as other

The study found that survivors were often treated as second-class citizens and perceived as other. One co-researcher commented,

> People do not even think that I am also a Nepali and this is my country and I have same rights as they have. While I was searching for a job, I was often told that you can go back to the place and work where you came from. I know what they meant and it was very heartbreaking but there is nothing I can do.

One participant gave an example of how this othering can have legal implications. She reported that she was trafficked at the age of 10 and therefore she had no citizenship certificate at the time of her trafficking since, according to Nepalese law, a person must be 16 years of age to obtain a citizenship. When she returned to Nepal, she went with her father to her own village to apply for citizenship but was turned away. The official told them there was no evidence to prove that she was Nepali as she was never before seen in the village. She further added, "An official asked my father why are you bringing her here and why does she need citizenship now? I know what she did in India and I don't want to support her by granting her a citizenship."

Invisible demonstrations of rejection

The study identified the phenomenon of a false front of acceptance that masks practices and attitudes of rejection. For instance, one survivor shared this story:

> I met a guy in a small gathering and gradually we started liking each other and then dating. He was aware of my past and I was happy that he accepted me as who I am. When his family found this, they were always nice to me when we met, but behind my back they tried to convince him that I was not a good fit. He attempted to ignore them for a while but later he could not leave his family and deserted me. This also made me think critically that no one recognizes me as who I am now and instead everyone views me as a woman who was in brothels. I don't know what my identity is.

Exoticization and objectification

This study heard trafficking survivors talk of being dehumanized and treated as sexualized objects. People would ask women intrusive questions about their sexual history and their physical bodies. For instance, one co-researcher said, "When I was at the court for my case, one of the lawyers asked me to show him my belly to confirm if I was a victim of trafficking. I had no choice not to hear him."

Another survivor shared her experience of being extorted to have sex with the lawyer who was overseeing her case as the only way to have her case resolved in court. The study found that the women were viewed as exoticized objects who were sexually available to anyone who wanted them. One of the participants lamented,

> Perpetrators often ask me to sleep with them and once I refused they said you are a whore and now you are pretending to not be one. I was often told that my body gives an impression to people that I was a sex worker, but I don't know if my body reveals that way.

Microinsultive behaviors

The study identified that trafficking survivors experience microinsultive behaviors in multiple ways. Their experiences are categorized in three themes: assumptions of ignorance and inferiority, assumptions of personal life, and disapproval of religious participation.

Assumptions of ignorance and inferiority

Survivors reported that people assume them to be ignorant and incapable of accomplishments outside of what they imagine the sex trade to be. The co-researchers said they often experienced this demeaning attitude through the small compliments they are paid. One of the participants recalled this instance:

> It was just two days ago when I was conducting master of ceremony at one event that we were sharing our findings of this research, a couple of women congratulated me for the wonderful job I did at the event. The said you look very smart and intelligent but not every survivor is like you; you are so different than other survivors. Despite these, I am still surprised how you got trafficked.

Another co-researcher said,

> When people know I am a survivor they assume that I am HIV positive and often ask me if I am taking medicines. When they find out that I don't have any physical health issues, I am then told wow, you are so lucky then.

Another participant reported, "I was frequently told that I put on makeup very well, and my dressing sense was very modern. But later they would ask me if I learned all these techniques in brothels."

Assumptions of personal life

Study participants reported that people assume survivors will never be accepted back into society or ever able to experience the ordinary joys of marriage and motherhood. One of the co-researchers, for instance, shared that "when people find out that I am married and have a child, they become surprised and ask me with a very different tone, 'Oh! You are married and with whom are you married to?'" Similarly, another woman said that when she told people she has a husband and a daughter, people often tell her, "You are so lucky that someone married you because in most cases people wouldn't even date someone like you."

Disapproval of religious participation

The study found that these women often experience being excluded from traditional religious rituals and activities, whether in their homes or their communities. One co-researcher described it this way:

> You know our culture, it may be religion or not, who knows what it exactly is. Most rituals in our own homes or in communities start and end by blessing and venerating virgin girls. I am not married and as you know culturally it is not even acceptable to have sex before getting married. So, people who don't know my past asked me to participate in their functions but my family and relatives always give me some indications that I should not be attending these rituals. They don't express directly this to me, but always try preventing me from attending these rituals.

Another co-researcher stated,

> I am often asked by my parents and brothers if I am attending religious activities held in communities. Although they know I am going they always ask me the same question over and over again, hoping that I will say no.

Microinvalidation behaviors

This research identified microinvalidation behaviors against trafficking survivors as pervasive, intentional, and delivered in such a way that they are very difficult to report and act against. The women reported their experiences on microinvalidation as categorized into two themes; dismissal of feelings and experiences and assumptions of poor abilities and skills.

Dismissal of feelings and experiences

Survivors reported that their feelings and experiences of microaggressive behaviors against them were not validated and were quite summarily dismissed. Survivors said that when they told someone of their experiences of microaggressions, they were often told they were being too sensitive and/or the person

who conducted the hurtful behavior did not mean to be hurtful. One participant, for instance, said that when she asked people at work to teach her how to
work effectively and efficiently, this was their reply: "I don't know what you
were doing when you were supposed to be in school, and no matter how hard
you work, it doesn't really help you at this age." The woman added,

> When I recognized that it was very inappropriate and disrespectful, I went to my
> manager to complain but instead of supporting me she humiliated me more. I was
> told that this is my reality and wherever I go I will have to face this. She said there
> is no need to take it seriously, as she is sure they didn't mean what they said.

Assumptions of poor abilities and skills

The findings of the study suggest that the women are devalued regardless of
their education and work and lived experiences. For instance, one participant
shared the following:

> When we were going to do interactive sessions in different places through this study,
> we were told we could not represent the agency we work for because they thought we
> did not have good enough knowledge and potential. How sad is it to think that a
> survivor is not capable enough to represent an agency formed by survivors?

Overall, the study indicates the pervasive presence of microaggressions
against trafficking survivors and the various messages of disrespect and
ostracism they convey to recipients, as demonstrated in Table 1. The cumulative impacts of microaggressive behaviors against trafficking survivors are
briefly discussed in the following section.

Cumulative impacts of microaggressive behaviors

The harmful consequences of microaggressions as experienced by women
trafficking survivors, especially in the process of their reintegration into
family and community life, are identified as follows: biological and physical
effects, emotional effects, behavioral effects, and social effects.

Biological and physical effects

The study identified that microaggressive behaviors against trafficking survivors have an adverse impact on their health. For example, one of the co-
researchers highlighted the following:

> My experience on everyday discrimination is not a new phenomenon, as it occurs
> every day. What is new now, I got hypertensions and migraine and more recently I
> am diagnosed with high blood pressure. These types of experiences have interrupted
> my sleeping patterns and I eventually ended up taking anti-depression medicines.

Table 1. Evidence of microaggressive behaviors against trafficked survivors.

Theme	Evidence	Message
1. Microassaults		
Use of derogatory language	You are the source of HIV.	You are polluting our communities.
Denial of citizenship and treated as others	I don't want to support her by granting her a citizenship. You can go back to the place and work where you came from.	You don't belong in our country.
Invisible demonstration of rejection	The parents of my boyfriends were always nice to me when we met, but behind my back they tried to convince him that I was not a good fit.	You are not welcome in our society.
Exoticization and objectification	Perpetrators often asked me to sleep with them and once I refused they said you are a whore and now you are pretending not to be one.	You are a commodity for the public.
2. Microinsults		
Assumptions of ignorance and inferiority	Couple of women congratulated me for the wonderful job I did at the event. They said you look very smart and intelligent and not every survivor is like you.	Trafficked women are not smart and lack intelligence.
Assumptions of personal life	When people find out that I am married and have a child, they become surprised and ask me with a very different tone "Oh! You are married?"	It is unusual for people like you to be loved.
Disapproval of religious participation	I am asked if I am attending religious activities held in communities in a hope that I will say no.	You are not pure enough to attend religious gatherings.
3. Microinvalidations		
Dismissal of feelings and experiences	My supervisor shut me down when I shared how people commented on me and said I was very sensitive.	This is your perception but that is not the reality.
Assumptions of poor abilities and skills	When we were going to do interactive sessions in different places through this study, we were told we could not represent the agency we work for because they thought we did not have good enough knowledge and potential to talk about the agency.	Survivors do not have the potential to hold a professional job or to have a knowledgeable position in the society.

This experience is echoed by another woman, who said,

My head is very heavy all the time, especially immediately after the incident so I am used to this, but what surprises to me. I get a terrible pain on my both legs when I go to bed and it is not going anywhere regardless of the medicine I take. I know this is something that I get from people who treat me very badly.

Emotional/psychological effects

Trafficked women reported feeling distressed and anxious immediately after the incidents. The women further reported an array of emotions and sentiments, ranging from anger, irritation, frustration, fear, and depression to marginalization and hopelessness. For instance, one participant said, "I become very emotional all the time and cry for no reasons. I cry just because I have to hear something about my past on a daily basis which completely diminished my self-confidence and I feel hopeless and always fear." Similarly, another participant reported, "I am diagnosed with severe depressions and I don't feel I am getting better just because the perpetrators' behaviors against us are rigidly engrained in them." The same woman added,

> When people ask me if I learnt everything including makeups, dress-up, and so forth in brothels, obviously it reminds me of the past that I don't even want to recall. I have to live with this trauma every day, which is even more harmful than the situation I was in in the brothels. This makes me feel tired and fatigue all the time.

Behavioral effects

The women identified rudeness and hostility as ways they have responded to the microaggressive behaviors they experience and spoke of these reactions as different to how they behaved before and even during their experience of being trafficked. One co-researcher, for example, reported, "I never think I would be so rude to people including my own daughters and family. I know I frequently behave badly and shout at them for nothing." Another woman echoed this sentiment and added, "I am aware that I express my anger not only to my daughter and husband, but also to teachers and coworkers. Sometimes I even cross the limits and throw dishes and cutleries in the kitchen and leave my home in anger." Another woman alleged,

> When people tell me "you are a besya" and you probably are HIV/AIDS positive so I don't want to be your friend, I just feel hopeless and immediately start acting very differently as if I am drunk. I still remember having a big fight with a bus driver on my way home immediately after I experienced their bad behaviors at work.

Social effects

Isolation and exclusion were identified as social consequences of microaggressive behaviors against trafficked women. Survivors reported that they no longer had any interest in attending social gatherings and participating in any social activities held in their families and communities. In fact, the women were afraid of unpredictable situations in terms of people's behavior toward them. One participant, for example, said, "I like going out but I hesitate to go just because I am frightened if someone treats me badly and demean me publicly. I don't want to be humiliated anymore." Another co-researcher commented, "For me it is beyond being humiliated. I often get my temper so quickly and misbehave with people, who demonstrate dirty behaviors against me." The same woman added,

I often have migraine and feel anxious, which minimized my involvement in community activities. Now no one invites me as they assume parties and community gatherings are not my things, but my reality is completely different but no one knows.

Implications in social work research, education, and practice

In social work practice, there is an urgent need for recognizing microaggressive behaviors against sex-trafficking survivors. In order to increase awareness and help people understand how microaggressions operate, development of anti-microaggressive behavior strategies to educate people about the experiences of trafficked women is fundamental. Furthermore, social workers and agencies working in the areas of human rights and violence against women need to bring the trafficking-survivors community together and provide a "safe space" for them to share their experiences on microaggressions so that survivors have a chance to collectively and individually heal from this element of their experience of sex trafficking and shape collective understanding of how microaggression materializes and operates in their lives.

In addition, research needs to attend to other communities of survivors, such as trafficked survivors exploited for other labor purposes and former child soldiers who may have the similar experiences of microaggressive behaviors against them. Existing research suggests this might be a productive line of inquiry. One study found that traditional gender norms and patriarchal worldviews reinforced judgments against the former child soldiers, especially girls. For instance, people often commented on the tattoos, carvings, and scars that girls received during the war, leading the girls to recall their past life whether they wished to or not (McKay, 2004).

There also needs to be more cross-community research and theory-building. Community-based anti-oppressive practice research would allow oppressed communities to come together in solidarity and develop an anti-discriminatory framework that illuminates microaggressions and intersecting oppressions and points to practice implications.

Even before such research and theory-building gets underway, given the urgency of the situation, the agencies providing services to the communities of survivors must develop programs and services that take the multiple variables of gender, race, ability, and sexual orientation into account. Programs also would benefit from a needs and aspirations analysis to ensure they are responsive to the particular group of survivors with which they are working. This would identify different needs, such as counseling and educational campaigns, and recognize that a one-size-fits-all model will not work.

Discussion/conclusion

This study demonstrates that microaggressions as covert forms of discrimination against trafficked women exploited in sex trade are pervasive, are experienced on a daily basis, and are deeply harmful to survivors in their efforts to reintegrate into their families and communities. Microaggressions are manifested in families from parents, siblings, in-laws, and other relatives, workplaces, and geographical and cultural communities. Overall, in the realm of social work, practitioners and researchers should be conscious of how cycles of microaggressions operate and endure. They should explore possibilities of collaborations among the practitioners and survivors to find ways to prevent these cycles from persisting.

In conclusion, these subtle types of microaggressions function at the individual, community, and policy levels and reinforce multifaceted trauma. In social work, it is imperative for agencies and individual practitioners to use anti-oppressive practice and provide survivors with an opportunity to get involved in the developmental process of identifying and creating mechanisms to confront and reduce the various manifestations of microaggressive behaviors.

References

Boakye, F. (2009). *Women's health and social justice: Understanding the health experiences of northern rural Ghanaian women* (Unpublished doctoral dissertation). University of Calgary, Alberta, Canada.

Cameron, S., & Newman, E. (2008). *Trafficking in human: Social, cultural and political dimensions.* New York, NY: United Nations University Press.

Capodilupo, C. L., Nadal, K. L., & Corman, L. (2010). The manifestations of gender microaggressions. In D. W. Sue (Eds.), *Microaggressions and marginality: Manifestation, dynamics and impact* (pp. 193–213). Hoboken, NJ: John Wiley & Sons, Inc.

Chaulagai, P. (2009). *Trafficking survivors in Nepal: An exploratory study of trafficked women's experiences and perceptions of their reintegration* (Master's thesis). Retrieved from https://bora.uib.no/bitstream/1956/3471/1/58332708.pdf

Chen, C., & Marcovici, K. (2003). *Exploring the status of reintegrated girls: A participatory study, Kaiali, and Kanchanpur, Nepal.* Kathmandu, Nepal: Save the Children US.

Constantine, M. G. (2007). Racial microaggressions against African American clients in cross-racial counselling relationships. *Journal of Counseling Psychology, 54*(1), 1–16. doi:10.1037/0022-0167.54.1.1

Fals Borda, O. (2001). From Cartagena to Ballarat: A report on the joint Fifth World Congress on Action Learning, Action Research, and Process Management and the Ninth World Congress on Participatory Action Research. *Systemic Practice and Action Research, 14*(2), 125–134. doi:10.1023/A:1011399504204

Fals Borda, O., & Rahman, A. (Eds.). (1991). *Action and knowledge: Breaking the monopoly with PAR.* New York, NY: Apex.

GoN. (2012). *A report on anti-trafficking initiatives led by Government of Nepal.* Sighadurbar, Kathmandu, Nepal: GoN.

Grinnell, R. M., Jr., & Unrau, Y. A. (2005). *Social work research and evaluation: Quantitative and qualitative approaches.* New York, NY: Oxford University Press.

Hill, J. S., Kim, S., & Williams, C. D. (2010). The context of racial microaggressions against indigenous peoples: Same old racism or something new? In D. W. Sue (Eds.), *Microaggressions and marginality: Manifestation, dynamics and impact* (pp. 105–122). Hoboken, NJ: John Wiley & Sons, Inc.

Keller, R. M., & Galgay, C. E. (2010). Microaggressive experiences of people with disabilities. In D. W. Sue (Eds.), *Microaggressions and marginality: Manifestation, dynamics and impact* (pp. 241–260). Hoboken, NJ: John, Wiley & Sons, Inc.

Kill, S., & Kim, R. H. (2010). Microaggression experienced by international students attending U.S. institutions of higher education. In D. W. Sue (Eds.), *Microaggressions and marginality: Manifestation, dynamics and impact* (pp. 171–191). Hoboken, NJ: John Wiley & Sons, Inc.

Locke, R. A. (2010). *Rescued, rehabilitated, and returned: Institutional approaches to the rehabilitation of survivors of sex trafficking in India and* Nepal (Master's thesis). Retrieved from ProQuest Dissertations and Theses Database. (UMI No. AAT 1478251.)

McKay, S. (2004). Reconstructing fragile lives: Girls' social reintegration in northern Uganda and Sierra Leone. *Gender & Development, 12*(3), 19–30. doi:10.1080/13552070412331332280

McNeill, L. A. (2008). *The price of a life: Legislating sex work and trafficking in Nepal* (Doctoral dissertation). Retrieved from http://www.angelfire.com/me3/leila3/THESIS_secure.pdf

Nadal, K. L. (2008). Preventing racial, ethnic, gender, sexual minority, disability, and religious microaggressions: Recommendations for promoting positive mental health. *Prevention in Counseling Psychology: Theory, Research, Practice and Training, 2*(1), 22–27.

Nadal, K. L., Issa, M., Griffin, K. E., Hamit, S., & Lyons, O. B. (2010). Religious microaggressions in the United States: Mental health implications for religion minority groups. In D. W. Sue (Eds.), *Microaggressions and marginality: Manifestation, dynamics and impact* (pp. 287–310). Hoboken, NJ: John Wiley & Sons, Inc.

Nadal, K. L., Issa, M., Leon, J., Meterko, V., Wideman, M., & Wong, Y. (2011). Sexual orientation microaggressions: "Death by a thousand cuts" for lesbian, gay, and bisexual youth. *Journal of LGBT Youth, 8*(3), 234–259. doi:10.1080/19361653.2011.584204

Nadal, K. L., Rivera, D. P., & Corpus, M. J. H. (2010). Sexual orientation and transgendered microaggressions: Implicates or mental health and counselling. In D. W.Sue (Eds.), *Microaggressions and marginality: Manifestation, dynamics and impact* (pp. 217–240). Hoboken, NJ: John Wiley & Sons, Inc.

Robinson, J. L. (2014). *Sexual Orientation and Transgender Microaggressions: Implications for Mental Health and Counseling* (Doctoral dissertation). (UMI:1565243.) Retrieved from http://search.proquest.com/docview/1616767777

Shakti Samuha. (2013). *Shakti Samuha annual report 2013*. Kathmandu, Nepal: Shakti Samuha.

Sharma, P. (2014). *Reintegration of victims and survivors of trafficking in Nepal* (Unpublished doctoral dissertation).Wichita State University, Wichita, Kansas.

Smith, S. E., Willms, D. G., & Johnson, N. A. (1997). *Nurtured by knowledge: Learning to do participatory action research*. New York, NY: Apex.

Sue, D. W. (2010). Microaggressions, marginality, and oppression. In D. W. Sue (Ed.), *Microaggressions and marginality: Manifestation, dynamics and impact* (pp. 3–22). Hoboken, NJ: John Wiley & Sons, Inc.

Sue, D. W., Bucceri, J., Lin, A., Nadal, K., & Torino, G. (2007). Racial microaggressions and the Asian American experience. *Cultural Diversity and Ethnic Minority Psychology, 13*(1), 72–81. doi:10.1037/1099-9809.13.1.72

Sue, D. W., Capodilupo, C., & Holder, A. (2008). Racial microaggressions in the life experience of Black Americans. *Professional Psychology: Research and Practice, 39*(3), 2323–2336.

Sue, D. W., Capodilupo, C. M., Torino, G. C., Bucceri, J. M., Holder, A. M. B., Nadal, K. L., & Esquilin, M. (2007). Racial microaggressions in everyday life: Implications for clinical practice. *American Psychologist, 62*(4), 271–286. doi:10.1037/0003-066X.62.4.271

Religious Microaggressions: A Case Study of Muslim Americans

Altaf Husain and Stephenie Howard

ABSTRACT

The increasing population of Muslims in America faces challenges not uncommon to other faith and immigrant communities. One particular challenge is Muslim experiences of various forms of discrimination, prejudice, anti-Muslim bigotry, and microaggressions, especially in post-9/11 America. While microaggressions have been discussed in the social sciences literature, religious microaggressions have not been clearly addressed in the social work literature. This article aims to fill this gap in the literature by examining the connections among racial microaggressions, the racialization of religion, and ultimately religious microaggressions. The article concludes by presenting implications for social work policy, practice, and education in the area of religious microaggressions.

As the population of Muslims in the United States increases, the social work client base is likely to expand to include those individuals who self-identify as Muslim (Husain, 2015). Since the population growth is due to natural births, ongoing immigration, and conversions to the faith, the challenges Muslims face in their daily lives are likely to also require access to various types of health and human services. One particular challenge that has received minimal attention within the social work literature is Muslim experiences of various forms of discrimination, prejudice, anti-Muslim bigotry, and microaggressions. While microaggressions have been discussed in the social sciences literature, religious microaggressions have not been clearly addressed in the social work literature. This article is divided into four major sections and utilizes an interdisciplinary approach to make a unique contribution to the existing literature on religious microaggressions. Following this introduction, an overview is provided of the impact of microaggressions, particularly racial microaggressions, as a preface to a subsequent discussion on the racialization of religion. The next section provides an in-depth examination of religious microaggressions, with a particular focus on the racialization of religion throughout American history. Before the section

Color versions of one or more of the figures in the article can be found online at www.tandfonline.com/WECD.

on final implications for social work, the overall discussion about religious microaggressions is contextualized within the framework of the history and roots of anti-Islamic bigotry in the United States.

The impact of microaggressions

Researchers conceptualize microaggressions as "brief and commonplace daily verbal, behavioral, or environmental indignities, whether intentional or unintentional, that communicate hostile, derogatory, or negative racial slights and insults toward people of color" (Sue et al., 2007, p. 271). The language was originally designed to capture the experiences of people of color; however, its use has been extended for other marginalized and oppressed people to include ethnic, gender, sexual orientation, physical (Sue et al., 2007), and religious minorities (Nadal et al., 2012). To help understand the impact of microaggressions, Sue (2010) presented a process model that traces the immediate impact of microaggression on the victim from the inception of the offense. His process model identifies five distinct phases: the incident, the perception, the reaction, the interpretation, and the consequence. The microaggression flow chart begins with an incident that the client perceived to be "racially motivated" (p. 68). A reaction then follows; the reaction may include rumination over the incident, questioning of his or her perception of the incident, emotionality, a desire to rescue the offender, and/or a sense of empowerment/self-validation. The target may then interpret the meaning of the offense as indicating that he or she does not belong, is abnormal, inferior, untrustworthy, or stereotypical. Over time, the target may demonstrate feelings of powerlessness, invisibility, forced compliance/loss of integrity, or pressure to represent one's group (Sue, 2010). While this model was not designed explicitly as a diagnostic tool, it may be useful in helping clinicians to organize the assessment phase of treatment and to anticipate possible mental health and behavioral outcomes.

Religious microaggression and the racialization of religion

There is evidence of burgeoning interest in religious microaggressions. However, this literature is limited and fragmented. In 2010, Edwards attempted "the first successful expansion of the microaggressions model to a population targeted for their religion, as opposed to their race" (p. 43). He demonstrated that Muslim Americans experience microaggression, which is accompanied by emotional arousal. In 2010, Nadal, Issa, Griffin, Hamit, and Lyons presented a conceptual definition of religious microaggression as follows:"Religious microaggressions can be defined as subtle behavioral and verbal exchanges (both conscious and unconscious) that send denigrating messages to individuals of various religious groups" (p. 297).

These researchers posited that religious minorities have historically been discriminated against and persecuted in America. Their focus was the collective experience of various religious minorities. They contributed a theoretical taxonomy of religious microaggressions to the dialogue. In 2012, Nadal and colleagues empirically evaluated the taxonomy of religious microaggressions among a small sample of Muslim Americans. Their findings supported four of the themes previously proposed and identified two additional themes specific to Muslim Americans:"Endorsing religious stereotypes of Muslims as terrorists, pathologizing the Muslim religion, assuming religious homogeneity, exoticizing Muslim religion, Islamophobic and mocking language, and feelings of being an alien in one's own country" (Nadal et al., 2012, p. 22).

Figure 1 is an example of a microaggression that confirms the idea that Muslim Americans could be made to feel alone, despite being native-born. While the study by Nadal and colleagues (2012) was limited in methodological rigor by a small sample size and purposive sampling techniques, its findings provide support for a differential construct of religious microaggression. This research is also helpful in establishing a conceptual understanding of the lived experiences of religious minorities. Finally, in 2015, Forrest-Bank and Dupper presented at the Society for Social Work and Research conference on religious microaggression in public schools. They explored the qualitative experiences of religious minorities in a public school setting. Their study was the first to explore religious microaggression among children. Their sample population included 50 students from the Jewish, Muslim, Catholic, and Universalist Unitarian faith communities. Their findings indicated that children experience microaggressions in the public school setting at a significant rate (Forrest-Bank & Dupper, 2015). Furthermore, their article on the same topic indicates that teachers were among the perpetrators of religious microaggression(Dupper, Forrest-Bank, & Lowry-Carusillo, 2015). Their findings provide evidence of a need for training among service providers to include schoolteachers and administrators in cultural sensitivity for religious minorities.

Figure 1 is an example of a microaggression that confirms the idea that Muslim Americans could be made to feel alone, despite being native-born. While there have been no studies exploring the mental health impact of religious microaggressions, the implications of more overt forms of Islamophobia have been well-established (Nadal et al., 2010). Experiences of religious discrimination have been linked to lower self-esteem (Moradi & Hasan, 2004) and higher rates of stress in Muslim samples (Rippy & Newman, 2006, 2008). Religious discrimination is also correlated with "paranoia, vigilance, mistrust, and suspicion" that may lead to functional impairment (Rippy & Newman, 2006). Loss of sleep and headaches have also been

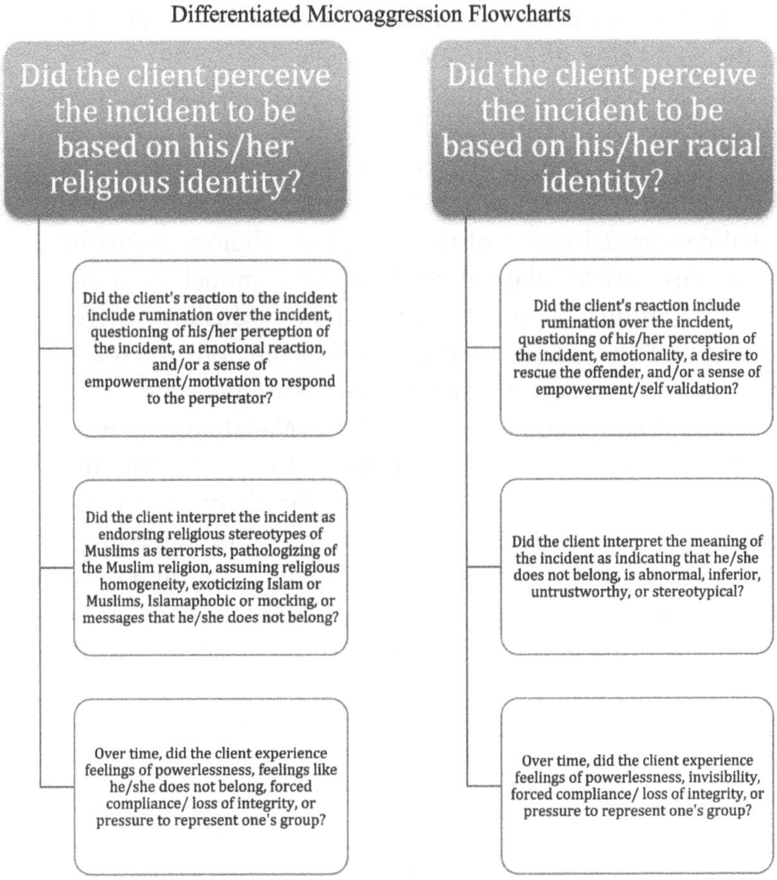

Differentiated Microaggression Flowcharts

Figure 1. In support of a differential conceptualization of the impact of religious microaggression, the authors of this article adapted Sue's process model as a flowchart. The flowcharts in this figure trace the impact of microaggression from the inception of the offense. The flowcharts are intended to help the clinician to structure his or her questions to the client in order to assess the possible impact of the microaggression on the client. The flowcharts are separated by form of microaggression to help identify possible differential outcomes.

associated with religious discrimination (Nadal et al., 2010). However, there have been no studies that have explored the mental health implications of religious microaggression(Nadal et al., 2010). Thus, additional research is needed to determine if the impact of religious microaggressions shares a similar course and symptomatology as that demonstrated in the case of racial microaggressions. In particular, less is known regarding the internalization of Islamophobic messages. While extant studies indicate that forced conformity may have a deleterious impact on targets of microaggression, for Muslims, the loss of religious integrity may be more detrimental than conformity to racial standards, considering the centrality of religion in their lives. However, the long-term effects of distancing oneself from one's racial or ethnic group are not well-documented in the literature. Thus, additional information is needed to understand the impact of acculturation as a result of microaggression on the well-being of Muslim Americans.

Of use in identifying how an individual psychologically copes with experiences of microaggression may be Sue's process model discussed previously (Sue, 2010). However, this model has not been adapted as an assessment tool and is limited in its implications for religious minorities. In support of a differential conceptualization of the impact of religious microaggression, the authors of this article adapted Sue's process model as a flowchart (see Figure 2). The authors desired to illustrate how Muslim Americans psychologically respond and adapt to experiences of religious microaggression.

The religious microaggression flowchart is founded on the taxonomy of religious microaggression as presented by Nadal and colleagues (2012). Similar to Sue's process model, it begins with an incident that the target perceives to be religiously motivated. Next, the client experiences a reaction to the incident that may include rumination over the incident, questioning of his or her perception of the incident, emotionality, and/or a sense of empowerment/motivation to respond to the perpetrator. These reactions are similar to those reflected by the racial microaggression flowchart with the exception of the last item. Edwards indicated that religious microaggressions may elicit anger that can empower the individual to respond to the incident (2010). As such, the religious microaggression flowchart was modified to indicate empowerment/motivation to respond to the perpetrator. The concept of self-validation or the "shifting of fault to the aggressor" was not confirmed in the religious microaggression literature (Sue, 2010, p. 75). Next, the client interprets the incident as falling into one of the themes of religious microaggression as conceptualized and empirically tested by Nadal and colleagues (2012). These themes are religious stereotypes of Muslims as terrorists; pathologizing of the Muslim religion; assumptions of religious homogeneity; exoticizing Islam or Muslims; Islamophobic or mocking language; and

"White American non-Muslim woman: Where you from?

Me: [ ]ville.

Her: I am from there, too.

Me: We should have carpooled into the city together.

Her: [laughs] But I meant... I thought you were an immigrant.

She waits for me to define myself for her. Anyone who is not Native American is an immigrant. But that's not what she means. She wants the name of a country, a box to put me into. I say, "No," and she frowns at my not giving her the critical information. I walk away. She doesn't want to interact with me until she can categorize me. I wonder how many strangers have ever walked up to her and demanded a country in the first minute of the conversation. I want to scream, "Sorry to disappoint you, but I am not your ambassador to The Exotic! I am a Muslim-American woman who wears a headscarf; we are volunteering for a community service project. Made me feel small, annoyed."

Figure 2. Religious microaggression with the theme of assumption of religious homogeneity.

alienation. The cumulative effects of religious microaggressions have not been examined in the literature to the best of the authors' knowledge. However, based on the religious microaggression themes and literature on the impacts of racial microaggressions, feelings of powerlessness, feeling like he or she does not belong, forced compliance/loss of integrity, and pressure to represent one's group may be associated with religious microaggressions. These outcomes are similar to that demonstrated in the case of racial micro-aggression. However, invisibility was removed, as it has not been noted as a theme in the religious microaggression literature. In addition, feeling like he or she does not belong was included to reflect the literature on religious microaggressions(Nadal et al., 2012).

Racialization of religion

The concept of microaggression can be extended to religious minorities by virtue of the historic racialization of religion. In pre-modern America, religious distinction was the basis for discrimination and persecution (Ibrahim, 2008). The roots of religious racialization can be traced back to the concept of Jewish blood (Nirenberg, 2009). The use of religion to demarcate privilege is carried forward in early American history in the race relations between Native Americans and Puritans in 17th-century America, wherein "whiteness emerged... as a common identity across class lines among Europeans, setting the colonial majorities apart from both African slaves and Native Americans" (Joshi, 2006, p. 213). Thus, Christianity served to unite early Americans under a single attribute, but also to identify others as outsiders (see Figure 3). Subsequently, American colonists developed laws explicitly associating Whiteness and Christianity with freedom. As one example, in 1811 in *People v. Ruggles*, the courts codified "the national community as white and Christian" (Ibrahim, 2008, pp. 131–132). This

"'Are you enjoying your vacation to the United States?" I'm 17, in 2008, at the local Walmart. I had been living in the United States since I was about five but people still assume that because I wear a hijab that I'm only here to visit. It made me feel like I would never be a part of the small town that I live in."

Figure 3. Religious microaggression with the theme of alien in own country.

"Chatting light-heartedly with a friend about whether Prince William could marry a Catholic (which she is). I joked that it would be cool if he married a Hindu or a Muslim (which I am). She said, "If he can't marry a Catholic **WHY WOULD HE MARRY A MUSLIM?**" in such a way that made it seem like it would be beyond distasteful and impossible for him to want to marry any Muslim ever. I was just joking around, but her comment made me feel like she'd labeled me and people like me as unlovable, unwanted, and 'beneath' Catholics. I am 20 and it made me feel singled out, hurt."

Figure 4. Religious microaggression with the theme of pathology of the Muslim religion.

ruling subsequently "describes Islam and Muslims as the opposite to Whiteness and Christianity, therefore, as the inferior 'other' that is excluded from the national polity" (Ibrahim, 2008, p. 131; see also Figure 4). In addition, in 1952, the higher courts ruled that one's "espousal of and relationship to Islam" identifies one as non-white (Ibrahim, 2008, p. 132). The racialization of religion was also evident in the violent conversion and persecution of enslaved Black Muslims in early American history, in which enslaved African-Americans were persecuted for practicing Islam (Ibrahim, 2008).

History and roots of anti-Islamic bigotry

Tracing the history of racism, Fredrickson (2002) states explicitly that bigotry rooted in religious difference "long predated the development of scientific racisms and notions of biological difference" (pp. 4–5). The history of Islam in America and the treatment of Muslims demonstrates the intertwining of bigotry rooted in religious difference as well as biological difference vis-à-vis Muslims of Arab origin. To contextualize the current climate of anti-Islamic bigotry and the likelihood of microaggressions directed at Muslims, social workers would benefit from a brief history of the existence of Islam in America and the roots of anti-Islamic bigotry.

Founding to the late 1800s

The current atmosphere of intense anti-Islamic bigotry stands in stark contrast to how Islam and Muslims were dealt with at the founding of the United States, and indeed until the late 1800s. There is no evidence to date pointing to the settlement of free men or women of the Muslim faith during the 1700s, although there is evidence of the existence of enslaved Muslims from West Africa as a part of the Atlantic slave trade (Diouf, 2013). Even so, the Founding Fathers were familiar with Islam as a world religion and the Qur'an was a part of the personal library of former presidents Thomas Jefferson (archived in the Library of Congress) and John Adams. Among the first major powers to recognize the newly founded nation in 1776 was the kingdom of Morocco, and there is ample evidence of American government interactions with the Ottoman Caliphate. Outside of the realm of the remnants of the post-Crusades negative image of Islam, much of the references to the faith are characterized incorrectly as "Muhammadanism," with "Muhammadans" used to reference the adherents of Muhammad, the prophet of Islam. A cursory glance at this period reveals at least a fair treatment of Islam the faith, with concerns about Muslims expressed if at all in the realm of foreign affairs and not in particular about the tenets of the faith. Indeed, at a time when intense bigotry makes at least tacit approval of efforts to exclude Muslims from the public sphere, it seems almost impossible that Benjamin Franklin quite explicitly envisioned not just Muslims but the allowance of a Muslim religious scholar, namely the mufti, in the public sphere: "even if the mufti of Constantinople were to send someone here to preach Islam and teach us about Mohammed, he argued, we should offer a pulpit, we should listen, for we might learn" (Isaacson, 2006, p. 574).

Late 1800s to World War II

The onset of Muslim migration to the United States is connected less with pull events within the United States and more push events, beginning with the disintegration of the Ottoman Empire in the late 1800s. Marvasti and McKinney (2004) note how little was known at the time in the United States about the diverse racial and ethnic backgrounds of Muslims. Whereas the Ottoman Empire stretched well into and beyond lands from which Arabs hailed, U.S. officials nevertheless listed incorrectly immigrants of the Atlantic migration from lands ruled by the Ottoman Empire as "Turkish citizens." Those Muslim immigrants who arrived via the Pacific Ocean suffered a similar fate as far as confusion at the least or outright discrimination at the worst in terms of their treatment. Takaki (1998) notes that Indian immigrants of Hindu, Muslim, and Sikh background arrived into the United States via Angel Island during the late 1800s but the Muslims and Sikhs were lumped into one category and referred to racially as "Hindoos" and even "full-blooded Aryans." In addition, the Muslims suffered a similar fate in terms of discrimination as the other Asian immigrants of the time, ranging from being victims of violence perpetrated by White workers to being referred to as "slaves." Various pieces of legislation were enacted between the late 1800s until after World War II to both deny citizenship to Indians and other non-European peoples and to restrict their migration.

World War II to Iranian Revolution

The end of World War II and the beginning of the end of the bulk colonization and occupation by European powers of mostly Asian and African nations gave rise to not only the drawing and redrawing of national borders but also unparalleled displacement and movement of peoples around the world. Among those on the move and often in search of educational pursuits and the "American dream" were Muslims from mostly South Asia, the Middle East, and North Africa (Haddad, 2004). The arrival of Muslims of Arab origin into the United States was a result of regional instability caused to varying degrees by the 1967 Arab-Israeli war, the onset of civil unrest and ultimately civil war in Lebanon in 1975, and the beginnings in 1978 of the Iranian Revolution (Marvasti & McKinney, 2004). Whereas their Muslim predecessors of the 1800s had blended into American society due to their white skin color and through active efforts at assimilation, the post–World War II Muslim immigrants were not only racially and ethnically diverse but also selected quite actively to retain or at least promote their Islamic identity in the United States. The context of their reception into the United States was marred by conflations in the media and entertainment of all Arabs with Islam. Ibrahim (2008) notes that films especially were responsible for creating an image of Arabs as the "other," dehumanizing not only a people with a great civilization, but also ensuring their second-class status upon arrival into the United States. This vilification of Arabs and Muslims worsened exponentially with the start of the Iranian Revolution and the subsequent hostage crisis.

Iranian Revolution to September 10, 2001

The conflation of Arabs with Muslims, even though a majority of Arabs are not Muslims, continued well after the Iranian Revolution and leading up to and including the first Gulf War and the terrorist attacks of September 11, 2001. Muslims within the United States had received minimal attention prior to the Iranian Revolution. Following the election of President Ronald Reagan and the continuation of the struggle to preserve control of oil supplies from the Middle East, the image of Muslims became associated with the dictatorial regimes of the Middle East, including the now deceased Saddam Hussein of Iraq and Muammar Qaddafi of Libya. American engagement with Islam and Muslims seemed to be confined mostly to foreign interventions, with less contentious framing of Muslim Americans as being responsible for the actions of their coreligionists overseas. Almost coinciding with the fall of Communism, the search for a new global threat ended conveniently with the identification of Islam as the new enemy of civilization. For example, the end of the Russian occupation of Afghanistan was facilitated almost entirely through direct American intervention, including training and arming Afghans and Muslims from around the world who joined the war. Those foreign fighters, called *mujahideen* or "freedom fighters," included Osama bin Laden, and many of them turned their attention to the United States itself as the enemy of Islam. Prior to the terrorist attacks of 2001, bin Laden and his supporters waged unrelenting attacks on the United States and its interests overseas. With every terrorist attack, bin Laden brought upon himself and his followers, including the nations which provided safe havens such as Afghanistan and Sudan, the wrath of the United States (Wedgewood, 1999). As the American armed attacks on bin Laden intensified, the focus publicly shifted from bin Laden as a rogue actor to Islam itself as a religion that was a purveyor of violence. Joshi (2006) asserts that "stereotypes perpetuated by the government and media come [sic] to paint Islam and Muslim as intrinsically—perhaps organically—violent and evil in American public opinion" (p. 218). That public opinion on the most part appeared, at least until the 2001 terrorist attacks, to discern between Muslims overseas and the Muslims of America.

Post-September 11, 2001, to 2015

The post-9/11 anti-Islamic bigotry experienced by Muslims in the United States appears to be just that—a phenomenon spawned by the terrorist attacks that killed more than 3,000 Americans, some of them Muslim Americans. The so-called "war on terror" soon warped into a "war on Islam," with supporters of the latter name conflating terrorism and extremism with Islam itself. It is inconceivable that only the 9/11 terrorist attacks stigmatized Islam as a violent religion and Muslims as innately violent people. Ibrahim (2008) provides critical background as to how the image of Muslims became so vilified, starting in the late 1800s.

> Since 1896, there have been over 900 films made about Arabs portraying them as "brutal, heartless, uncivilized religious fanatics and money-mad cultural 'others' bent on terrorizing civilized Westerners, especially Christians and Jews." Images of Arabs were either implicitly or explicitly conflated with Islam and Muslims, serving not only to dehumanize Arabs but Muslims as well. This conflation of Arabs with Muslims and vice versa prevails even today despite the reality that the majority of Arabs in the United States are Christian and that Arabs are only a minority of the Muslims in the world. (Ibrahim, 2008, p. 137)

Almost as if a sequel to a film was produced, during the period following the 9/11 attacks, there was a seismic shift in the treatment of Muslim Americans, whose existence in the national psyche shifted from loyal Americans to the enemy next door. Whereas people of color including South Asians and Arabs of faiths other than Islam also mistakenly became victims of violence and bigotry, African-Americans who identify as Muslims perhaps suffered the worse fate due to the color of their skin and the choice of their faith. Peek (2011) documented painstakingly the depths of the blaming, marginalization, and traumatization endured by Muslims of diverse backgrounds. And unlike the point being made by Ibrahim (2008) highlighting the scapegoating and stereotyping of Muslims by the film industry intended perhaps for popular consumption without regards to education level, Peek (2011) notes that books were also used in a similar manner. Her research indicates that there were "more than twenty books on the 'Islamic menace' in the one-year period following the 9/11 attacks" (Peek, 2011, p. 6). Although she does not address microaggressions explicitly, Peek (2011) proffers the existence of what she terms "verbal bigotry," noting that such a form of bigotry was likely encouraged by "the rise in anti-immigrant and anti-Muslim rhetoric in the aftermath of the terrorist attacks" (p. 66).

The anti-Islamic bigotry continues to intensify even a decade after the 9/11 attacks but not because of the actions of Muslim Americans. Rather, the 24-hours-a-day, 7-days-a-week news cycle presents as "breaking news" every horrific action of radical and extremist individuals and groups, most of them overseas, and influences the sentiments of average Americans, consuming that news in their living rooms, in doctors' office waiting lounges, airport boarding lounges, and on their smartphones. In 2009, Osama bin Laden was captured and killed and in the years following, there seemed to be relative calm since ostensibly the leader of Al-Qaeda was no more and the "hunt" had concluded. More recently (2014 onwards), the rhetoric in the media and from elected officials has intensified due to the appearance overseas of a barbaric group identifying itself as the "Islamic State." The abhorrent ideology and inhuman actions of this group have been condemned by Muslim American organizations and leaders and prominent Muslims around the world; however, a steady drumbeat persists in the United States, insisting that Muslim Americans do more to curtail the rise of violent extremism. Just as Peek (2011) found in the years after the 9/11 attacks, Muslim Americans continue to experience vulnerability and outright bigotry. In one such incident, a young woman wearing the *hijab* reported "an American white guy" looking at her and spontaneously singing the national anthem loudly. Peek (2011) surmises from the interview that the respondent "was left feeling as though patriotism was being used as a cover for anti-Muslim bigotry" (p. 68). Although not referred to as a microaggression in Peek's book, this incident does reflect the definition of a religious microaggression proffered by Nadal and colleagues (2010), "subtle behavioral and verbal exchanges (both conscious and unconscious) that send denigrating messages" (p. 297), in this case toward Muslim Americans.

Implications for social work policy, practice, and education

The social work literature has more recently highlighted the experiences of Muslim Americans at both the micro and macro levels of direct practice. Emerging literature on microaggressions must take into account the deleterious impact, especially on individuals who self-identify as Muslims. It is imperative to explore some of the implications for social work policy, practice, and education.

Scholars posit that the racialization of Islam as "the inferior other" has created a social divide that paved the way for its re-racialization as the "'fictionalized terrorist enemy'" (Ibrahim, 2008, p. 135). Ibrahim suggests that racialized images of the "terrorist enemy" have created a culture that sanctions "violence and political, economic, and social subordination against Muslim populations both domestically and abroad" (Ibrahim, 2008, p. 135). She asserts that the image of the "terrorist enemy" (see Figure 5) has been evident in U.S. foreign policy since the 1980s (p. 135). Moreover, she

"'Gah! A Muslim with a knife! Terror!'"
After (Canadian) Thanksgiving dinner with friends from my graduate studies program (whom
I used to think of as my family away from home, until this sort of thing kept happening).
Made me feel like **I'll never escape the harm of so-called well-meaning privileged people
who fail to recognize that being ironic about racism can still reproduce it.**"

Figure 5. Religious microaggression with the theme of endorsing religious stereotypes of Muslims as terrorists.

"In the local café with my 6-year-old daughter. A guy comes in and, to the server, makes
cracks about 'Al-Qaeda' and 'terrorists.' Wish I could come up with some scathing-yet-
eloquent reply, when I want to curl up under my hijab and hide. Wish I could shield my
daughter from this. Wish people would believe that this hurts, even though I am White as
well as Muslim."

Figure 6. Religious microaggression with the theme of endorsing religious stereotypes of Muslims as terrorists.

contends that these images (see Figure 6) have penetrated the American consciousness and media (pp. 136–137). As a result, the American public is complacent in anti-terrorism legislation and policies that target and victimize Muslims on the home front and abroad (Ibrahim, 2008; Singh, 2003). Scholars posit that the racialization of Islam is so prevalent that it has given rise to a new collective identity among Arab Americans, indicated as Muslim first—Arab second (Joshi, 2006). Policy practitioners can be vigilant in advocating for fair and just legislation, especially when it targets Muslims explicitly as in the case of policies allowing for profiling and tracking the daily lives of law-abiding citizens, or more implicitly as when policies are categorized as having to do with immigration enforcement but in reality only address immigrants from Muslim-majority countries.

In the context of practice, it is critically important to assess the nature and content of the various sources and forces of socialization as they impact both clients and practitioners. Clients, on the one hand, could increasingly be self-identifying Muslims. On the other hand, clients could also be perpetrators of microaggressions or perhaps even violent actions toward Muslim coworkers or neighbors. To the extent that media and entertainment sources shape our views of religious minorities, social work practitioners will have to exert additional energies to assessing whether or at least to what extent they have internalized the images of Muslims as the "other" on the one hand, and as the "enemy" on the other. Culturally competent practice with Muslim Americans seems to be a logical goal, especially for practitioners whose client base is shifting to include self-identifying Muslims (Husain & Ross-Sheriff, 2011). The racial microaggression literature is useful for identifying strategies for treating clients who present microaggression concerns. Ross-Sheriff offers strategies to reduce "damage done to clients by microaggression" (2012, p. 235). This article is designed for social work practitioners and includes strategies for preventing microaggressions in the helping process. Sue and colleagues review microaggressions and the implications for therapists with a focus "primarily on White therapist-client of color interactions" (2007, p. 271). It is imperative, therefore, that practitioners be prepared to confront their own biases toward Muslims, along with being prepared to assist not only Muslims but other people of color who are not Muslims, such as South Asians and Arabs, but due to the racialization of religion as discussed by Joshi (2006) continue to experience microaggressions intended to be directed at Muslims.

Within the classroom, social work educators have a tremendous opportunity to not only challenge our own preconceptions of Islam and Muslims but to allow safe spaces where students can come to terms with not only their views about Muslims but particularly about how they would feel about taking on a Muslim client. Even if there are no Muslim students in the classroom, it is not impossible that a microaggression could occur toward the Muslim Americans in absentia (e.g., in the case of a student who speaks disparagingly about a particular Muslim individual or about Muslims in general). These microaggressions within the context of the classroom may have implications for the retention of minorities in academia (Ross-Sheriff, 2012). Therefore, it is imperative that religious minorities have opportunities to discourse with those with similar narratives. Mutual aid groups may serve to meet this need for support. Indeed, mutual aid groups have been implicated in the treatment and prevention of negative outcomes for Muslims affected by discrimination (Ali & Bagheri, 2009). As such, it may behoove administrators to implement and support mutual aid groups for Muslim students and faculty. With focused and concerted attention to the needs of Muslim academics, social work educators may help to ameliorate the harmful impact of microaggressions in the lives of Muslim scholars.

References

Ali, S. R., & Bagheri, E. (2009). Practical suggestions to accommodate the needs of Muslim students on campus. *New Directions for Student Services, 125*, 47–54. doi:10.1002/ss.307

Diouf, S. A. (2013). *Servants of Allah: African Muslims enslaved in the Americas.* New York, NY: New York University Press.

Dupper, D. R., Forrest-Bank, S., & Lowry-Carusillo, A. (2015). Experiences of religious minorities in public school settings: Findings from focus groups involving Muslim, Jewish, Catholic, and Unitarian Universalist youths. *Children & Schools, 37*(1), 37–45. doi:10.1093/cs/cdu029

Edwards, R. (2010). *Religious microaggressions towards Muslims in the United States: Group identity and self-esteem as predictors of affective responses* (Doctoral dissertation). Wesleyan University, Middletown, CT. Retrieved from wesscholar.wesleyan.edu

Forrest-Bank, S., & Dupper, D. (2015, January). *Religious microaggression in public schools.* Paper presented at Society for Social Work and Research 19th Annual Conference: The Social and Behavioral Importance of Increased Longevity, New Orleans, LA.

Fredrickson, G. M. (2002). *Racism: A short history.* Princeton, NJ: Princeton University Press.

Haddad, Y. Y. (2004). *Not quite American?: The shaping of Arab and Muslim identity in the United States* (Vol. 26). Waco, TX: Baylor University Press.

Husain, A. (2015). Islamophobia. Retrieved from http://socialwork.oxfordre.com/view/10.1093/acrefore/9780199975839.001.0001/acrefore-9780199975839-e-964

Husain, A., & Ross-Sheriff, F. (2011). Cultural competence with Muslim Americans. In D. Lum (Ed.), *Culturally competent practice: A framework for understanding diverse groups and justice issues* (4th ed., pp. 358–389). Belmont, CA: Brooks/Cole.

Ibrahim, N. (2008). The origins of Muslim racialization in U.S. law. *UCLA Journal of Islamic & Near Eastern Law, 7*(1), 121–155.

Isaacson, W. (2006). Great minds. *Proceedings of the American Philosophical Society, 150*(4), 568–574.

Joshi, K. (2006). The racialization of Hinduism, Islam, and Sikhism in the United States. *Equity & Excellence in Education, 39*(3), 211–226. doi:10.1080/10665680600790327

Marvasti, A. B., & McKinney, K. D. (2004). *Middle Eastern lives in America.* Lanham, MD: Rowman & Littlefield.

Moradi, B., & Hasan, N. T. (2004). Arab American persons' reported experiences of discrimination and mental health: The mediating role of personal control. *Journal of Counseling Psychology, 51*(4), 418–428. doi:10.1037/0022-0167.51.4.418

Nadal, K. L., Griffin, K. E., Hamit, S., Leon, J., Tobio, M., & Rivera, D. P. (2012). Subtle and overt forms of Islamophobia: Microaggressions toward Muslim Americans. *Journal of Muslim Mental Health, 6*(2), 15–37. doi:10.3998/jmmh.10381607.0006.203

Nadal, K. L., Issa, M., Griffin, K. E., Hamit, S., & Lyons, O. B. (2010). Religious microaggressions in the United States. In D. W.Sue (Ed.), *Microaggressions and marginality: Manifestation, dynamics, and impact.* Hoboken, NJ: Wiley & Sons.

Nirenberg, D. (2009). Was there race before modernity? The example of "Jewish" blood in late Medieval Spain. In M. Eliav-Feldon, B. Isaac, & J. Ziegler (Eds.), *The origins of racism in the West* (pp. 232–264). Cambridge, UK: Cambridge University Press.

Peek, L. (2011). *Behind the backlash: Muslim Americans after 9/11.* Philadelphia, PA: Temple University Press.

Rippy, A. E., & Newman, E. (2006). Perceived religious discrimination and its relationship to anxiety and paranoia among Muslim Americans. *Journal of Muslim Mental Health, 1*(1), 5–20. doi:10.1080/15564900600654351

Rippy, A. E., & Newman, E. (2008). Adaptation of a scale of race-related stress for use with Muslim Americans. *Journal of Muslim Mental Health, 3*(1), 53–68. doi:10.1080/15564900802035292

Ross-Sheriff, F. (2012). Microaggression, women, and social work. *Affilia, 27*(3), 233–236. doi:10.1177/0886109912454366

Singh, J. (2003). The racialization of minoritized religious identity: Constructing sacred sites at the intersection of White and Christian supremacy. In J. N. Iwamura & P. Spickard (Eds.), *Revealing the sacred in Asian and Pacific America.* New York, NY: Routledge.

Sue, D. W. (Ed.). (2010). *Microaggressions and marginality: Manifestation, dynamics, and impact.* Hoboken, NJ: John Wiley & Sons.

Sue, D. W., Capodilupo, C. M., Torino, G. C., Bucceri, J. M., Holder, A., Nadal, K. L., & Esquilin, M. (2007). Racial microaggressions in everyday life: Implications for clinical practice. *American Psychologist, 62*(4), 271–286. doi:10.1037/0003-066X.62.4.271

Takaki, R. (1998). *A history of Asian Americans: Strangers from a different shore.* New York, NY: Little, Brown.

Wedgwood, R. (1999). *Responding to terrorism: The strikes against bin Laden.* Retrieved from http://digitalcommons.law.yale.edu/fss_papers/2279

Homeless Microaggressions: Implications for Education, Research, and Practice

Gina C. Torino and Amanda G. Sisselman-Borgia

ABSTRACT

Homeless individuals, often marginalized, are a group not yet explored in the microaggressions literature. However, research indicates that homeless individuals experience discrimination in a variety of contexts by well-meaning providers. This article outlines several microaggressive themes based on the current literature. The themes posited here include the following: Sub-human Status; Invisibility; Aesthetically Unappealing; Criminal Status/Dangerous; Assumption of Mental Illness; Assumption of Substance Abuse; Laziness; and Intellectual Inferiority. The manifestations and messages conveyed within each theme are discussed. Implications for social work education/training, research, and practice based on the themes are delineated.

Introduction

Microaggressions, or subtle forms of discrimination, have recently received attention in many different forums. Studies are showing shifts from more overt forms of discrimination to subtler forms that are often subconscious (Sue, 2010). Microaggressions have the potential to impact many different people psychologically across different settings. The University of California has recently recognized the seriousness of this issue by developing a program to raise awareness on campus and in the workplace. Although the study of microaggressions began with understanding these dynamics within various ethnic groups, the phenomenon exists within and extends to other vulnerable populations as well, such as the mentally ill (Gonzales, Davidoff, Nadal, & Yanos, 2015). The issue of microaggressions has not been examined within the homeless community, although there is a small body of literature documenting some forms of discrimination against homeless men and women in various settings. This article examines literature related to discrimination in homeless individuals and posits that there are microaggressions specific to the homeless population. In addition, it describes how these microaggressions could impact social work education and research. Finally, implications for social work practice are discussed.

Research on the discrimination against homeless individuals

Virtually no literature on the concept of microaggressions toward homeless individuals exists. There is, however, a small body of work that examines the issue of discrimination and stigma toward homeless individuals. Some research done in the 1990s found that the general public had less compassion for homeless people than they did in the 1980s (Link et al., 1995; Phelan, Link, Moore, & Stueve, 1997). Studies have shown that individuals who believe homeless people can change or are responsible for their own fate have less compassion for homeless individuals than those who believe society is at fault for homelessness (Baumgartner, Bauer, & Bui, 2012). A review of several public opinion polls done in the 1980s and early 1990s revealed that the majority of Americans surveyed wanted to help those who were homeless, but that many respondents also believed that the majority of homeless individuals are also addicted to illegal substances (Link et al., 1995). The history of the social welfare system in our country has placed blame on people for being poor and/or homeless.

Because attitudes like this exist, the potential for microaggressions or subtle forms of discrimination against homeless individuals is great. A limited body of studies has found that homeless individuals do in fact feel discriminated against, due to issues associated with their homelessness (Baumgartner et al., 2012; Milburn, Ayala, Rice, Batterham, & Rotheram-Borus, 2006; Shier, Jones, & Graham, 2011; Skosireva et al., 2014; Wen, Hudak, & Hwang, 2007; Zerger et al., 2014). In fact, two studies showed that more individuals reported feeling discrimination in health care settings due to homelessness than ethnicity or race (Skosireva et al., 2014; Wen et al., 2007). One study also found that people were more likely to stigmatize someone or blame them for their circumstances if the person was homeless and poor, rather than housed and poor (Phelan et al., 1997). The literature points to several different circumstances that create opportunities for discrimination and stigmatization toward homeless individuals (Wen et al., 2007; Zerger et al., 2014). Things such as inability to shower and keep clean or wearing odd or dirty clothes make these individuals stand out. The public nature and visibility of the issue and the idea that the individuals are unappealing aesthetically makes them more vulnerable to being stigmatized (Wen et al., 2007; Zerger et al., 2014).

Wen and colleagues (2007) documented the experience in homeless individuals of feeling welcome or unwelcome. Participants described subtle attitudes from health professionals that led them to feel non-human or as if they were an object, and thus unwelcome. Some individuals reacted strongly to these attitudes and reported not wanting to seek further health care services. Zerger and colleagues (2014) discuss the concept of social distance, whereby such subtle attitudes cause homeless individuals to further cut ties with providers and community members. Disinterest from the community and social distancing from homeless individuals can lead to disengagement from services as well.

Furthermore, Shier and colleagues (2011) document that women in their study came upon discrimination in the form of "social exclusion" (p. 371) from employment opportunities, social services, and housing programs. The women in this study reported that there were stereotypes of and biases against homeless individuals that prevented them from breaking through the job market on several occasions. Identification of their address at a shelter or a known shelter telephone number often excluded them from opportunities. Participants also described how feelings and experiences of discrimination, even when subtle, impacted their psychological outlook and behaviors. The women often internalized these experiences, creating additional barriers to moving forward (Shier et al., 2011).

Shame around being homeless and embarrassing appearances has come up in several of the studies conducted on this issue. Homeless individuals interviewed in these studies believe that they are treated differently because of their appearance. Preliminary research in another study showed that the stigma related to mental illness or substance abuse does not necessarily interact with the stigma related to homelessness (i.e., that people discriminated based on homeless status regardless of whether mental health was a factor; Skosireva et al., 2014). The individuals in this study, however, did believe that homeless individuals with mental health histories were more dangerous than those without.

In homeless youths, feelings of discrimination are confounded by identification with an ethnic or sexual minority (Cochran, Stewart, Ginzler, & Cauce, 2002; Milburn et al., 2006; Milburn et al., 2010). Homeless youths who identify as a sexual minority are at an even higher risk for substance abuse and mental health issues than their non-lesbian, gay, bisexual, and transgender (LGBT) counterparts (Cochran et al., 2002). Sexual minority youths who are homeless are more likely to have been abused at home and are also at a higher risk for being victimized after becoming homeless (Cochran et al., 2002). Kidd (2006) found that in homeless youths, feelings of perceived stigma related to homeless status were related to lowered self-esteem, increases in suicidal ideation, and higher likelihood of feeling trapped by one's life circumstances. Milburn and colleagues (2006) found that sexual minority youths reported higher rates of discrimination from family members, but that any contact, including negative discriminatory contact from family members, was associated with the youths finding suitable housing.

Table 1. Homeless microaggression themes.

Theme	Microaggression	Message
Sub-human Status	Being handed food and expected to take it	He/she is like a dog.
Invisibility	Person is overlooked when receiving services in a place of business	He/she does not exist.
Aesthetically Unappealing	Moving away from someone on a bus, subway, in a waiting room, etc., due to unkempt appearance or odor	He/she is disgusting.
Criminal Status/ Dangerous	Locking the car door when passing by a homeless individual	He/she will steal.
Assumption of Mental Illness	Health care worker asking/assuming prior mental health diagnosis	He/she has a mental illness. He/she is crazy.
Assumption of Substance Abuse	Asking a homeless individual, "What is your drug of choice?"	He/she is a drug addict.
Laziness	Telling a homeless individual, "Get a job."	He/she is lazy and does not want to work.
Intellectual Inferiority	Assume that a homeless individual cannot fill out an application due to illiteracy Speaking slowly and loudly to be understood by a homeless individual Assume a homeless individual is "stupid" because she/he is homeless	He/she is stupid.

Based on the review of the literature, the present authors present homeless microaggression themes, which are based on the forms of discrimination faced by homeless individuals (Table 1).

Exploration of homeless microaggressions

The themes presented here reflect forms of microaggressions(Sue et al., 2007). Each theme is accompanied with a dynamic that occurs between the perpetrator and the recipient of the microaggression. This section explores the message of each theme in-depth and discusses the impact these microaggressions can have on homeless individuals.

The first and overarching theme, *Sub-human Status*, represents one where a homeless individual is not treated like a human being but as a lower form of organism, such as an animal. Too often, homeless individuals are treated in ways in which they are not given the same respect as other individuals. For example, a homeless individual may be called derogatory names, be handed some food and expected to take it, and have life decisions made for him or her. In other words, the homeless individual is not human and thus does not deserve the same dignity and respect as others. In a social work setting, clinicians or caseworkers may make major decisions for people (e.g., transition to housing, work, etc.) without consulting the individual. This paternalistic attitude sends the message that people are not capable of performing tasks related to basic survival and that they "need" the social worker to take care of them.

The second theme, *Invisibility*, involves a situation in which one might be overlooked, negated, and/or totally ignored in a variety of settings. For example, if a homeless individual asks someone for the time or directions, he or she might not even be looked at or attended to. Moreover, in a social service setting, a homeless individual may not be "seen" in a waiting room and may have to wait an inordinately long time (two or three hours) before he or she could be seen. The message conveyed in these instances is that one is unimportant and/or does not matter.

The third theme, *Aesthetically Unappealing*, applies to how people treat homeless individuals based on appearance. Because of lack of adequate housing and resources, many homeless individuals do not have frequent opportunities to shower or engage in self-care activities. In addition, individuals may not have the resources to acquire clean clothing and/or launder their clothes. People on the street may hold their noses or step away from homeless individuals due to appearance. The message conveyed is that the person is somehow disgusting and is to be avoided. Social workers in the field may also have physical reactions to appearance and may unconsciously create physical distance while conducting case management work.

It is often presumed that homeless individuals do not have resources and will thus be more likely to steal than others. The fourth theme, *Criminal Status/Dangerous*, presumes that the homeless individual has the intent to commit crime. Similar to the racial microaggression theme presented by Sue and colleagues (put proper ref here), African-American individuals, particularly men, experience instances where one will lock the door in their presence (Sue, 2010). Another example is where one crosses the street and/or clutches a bag tightly while in the presence of African-American individuals. Akin to the experiences of African-Americans, it is being posited that homeless individuals across all racial groups experience similar types of microaggressions. The message conveyed is that the homeless individual is a criminal and is not to be trusted. In social work practice, one may keep "expensive" belongings away from clients and/or unnecessarily lock away items in the presence of homeless individuals.

The fifth theme, *Assumption of Mental Illness*, presumes that the individual has a diagnosable mental illness. Research indicates that 25% to 30% of the homeless population is considered to be mentally ill; clearly, not all homeless people are (Zerger et al., 2014). In social work settings, it may be assumed that the individual seeking services has an existing psychiatric disorder. This message could be conveyed through asking a person, "What is your psychiatric diagnosis?" without conducting an intake assessment.

The next and somewhat related theme is *Assumption of Substance Abuse*. Again, while approximately 40% to 50% of the homeless population has a substance abuse diagnosis, this may not always be true (Zerger et al., 2014). Microaggressions that reflect this theme may be conveyed through a social worker or other health worker asking a person, "What is your drug of choice?" This question assumes that one has a drug of "choice" and that he or she has an addiction.

The sixth theme, *Laziness*, is pervasive in U.S. society. The underlying assumption that the homeless individual is completely responsible for his or her homeless status reflects that Western notion of "rugged individualism" where social context and cultural factors are negated. For example, saying to a homeless person, "Why don't you just get a job?" presumes that they are lazy and do not wish to work. Social workers that aid individuals with job placements may perpetrate microaggressions such as, "Just fill out this application: it is easy" or "Don't you want to work?" when discussing placements with their clients.

The final theme presented here, *Intellectual Inferiority*, assumes that the individual lacks competency in various domains. For example, a social worker may speak to a person using simple language or talk especially loud to be "understood." Also, it may be assumed that a client cannot fill out a health care form or application due to illiteracy or diminished cognitive abilities. These types of microaggressions convey the message that the person is not intelligent and requires assistance.

The implications for the microaggressions presented here are immense. First, any instance where an individual is negated, overlooked, ignored, or presumed to be inferior in any way may lead to a diminished sense of self-worth and lower levels of self-esteem. These psychological consequences could negatively impact any actions that a homeless individual may take to alter their circumstances. Secondly, presuming that one is dangerous or harmful in some way could serve to create a self-fulfilling prophecy. If one is going to assume that I am a criminal, then I might as well become one. Finally, assumption of a mental illness or substance abuse issue could unnecessarily label or track homeless individuals into institutions or services that they may not need. Documenting a potentially wrong or unsubstantiated diagnosis could have implications for future housing or employment acquisition.

Implications for social work education

Training students to guard against the aforementioned homeless microaggressions in social work programs is an important undertaking. One of the major underlying tenets is training social workers to become culturally competent. Briefly, cultural competency focuses on three general areas that include the social worker's awareness, knowledge, and skills (Sue, 2006; Sue, Arredondo, & McDavis, 1992; Sue et al., 1982). Awareness encompasses social workers' self-awareness, which includes clinicians' understanding of cultural beliefs and attitudes about themselves and others (Sue & Sue, 2013;

Sue & Torino, 2005). Knowledge primarily focuses on understanding of clients' beliefs, sociopolitical experiences, worldviews, cultural values, influences, and how all of these guide the clinicians' ability to conceptualize cases and plan treatments for clients. Skills refer to the social workers' ability to effectively use interventions that are sensitive to the clients' contextual and cultural factors, such as the clients' spiritual beliefs and cultural traditions.

With respect to developing cultural competency, scholars agree that the examination of one's own reference groups, including race, gender, class, religion, etc., is fundamental and also challenging (Carter, 2005; Sue & Sue, 2013). It is challenging because many students of social work consider themselves to be "good individuals" impervious to the possession of biases. For example, regarding race, Sue (2005) asserts that White trainees fear that they harbor unconscious biases and prejudices toward people of color. Research on aversive racism and implicit bias supports the contention that all White individuals have internalized racial biases and prejudices (Dovidio, Kawakami, & Gaertner, 2002; Jones, 1997). These implicit biases are extremely resistant to change as they operate unconsciously and manifest in subtle ways (e.g., microaggressions) (Sue, 2010).

Thus, in training social workers to become self-aware of their own thoughts and biases about homeless individuals, training programs need to take into account the various emotional and psychological responses that students might have in developing this self-awareness. In addition, it is important that social work programs provide students with the adequate knowledge and skills needed to work with homeless individuals. Next we discuss some useful teaching strategies that can promote such competence.

It is essential for trainees to develop an intellectual and/or cognitive understanding of, for example, their own social class prior to undertaking an affective exploration of the meaning of social class (Leach, Behrens, & LaFleur, 2002). For example, readings and videos can be focused on some of the homeless microaggression themes presented here (e.g., Invisibility, Assumption of Mental Illness, Assumption of Substance Abuse). Recommended readings include *Handbook of Prejudice, Stereotyping, and Discrimination* (Nelson, 2009); *Poverty in America: A Handbook (3rd ed.)* (Iceland, 2013); and *The American Way of Poverty: How the Other Half Still Lives* (Abramsky, 2014). Videos include *American Refugees: Homelessness in Four Movements* (Wasserman & Clair, 2006); and *The Pursuit of Happyness* (Muccino, 2006).

After any lecture and/or video presentation, it is important for the instructor to facilitate a discussion with the class. Scholars indicate that cognitive understanding of societal discrimination can lead to thoughts about personal classism and personal biases (Sue, 2010). Thus, it is important that as such discussions are facilitated, the instructor attends to emotions brought out in the classroom. It is imperative for the instructor to validate trainees' feelings as they arise and encourage them to further process such emotions in the experiential activities associated with the course.

Experiential learning involves the trainee personally and affectively examining their own reactions, assumptions, beliefs, attitudes, values, standards of normality, prejudices, stereotypes, biases, privileges, and goals (Sue & Sue, 2013). In his Racial-Cultural Counseling Laboratory, Carter (2005) eloquently describes many effective experiential teaching strategies. One well-documented strategy that can assist social workers in coming to terms with social class privilege and biases against homeless individuals is the small-group interview (Carter, 2005). These interviews include prepared questions about such things as stereotypes or personal development with regard to reference groups (Carter, 2005). Examples of interview questions can include the following: What is your earliest recollection about becoming aware of social class? What does being (one's respective social class) mean to you? What do you think others might think about you as a (social class) person? What are some of the biases, prejudices, and stereotypes that you possess about people in lower classes?

Furthermore, experts assert that an autobiography can be especially effective for developing the competencies involving awareness of values, biases, attitudes, and beliefs (Arredondo & Arciniega, 2001). The autobiography is also an opportunity for trainees to document their development by citing recollections from their childhood, and by considering influences from their families, education, and the media with regard to their social class identity and initial experiences with homeless individuals. Within the autobiography, students can be guided to explore the genesis of their assumptions about homeless individuals.

Finally, an approach that can be used in all instructional activities is that of modeling(Ponterotto, 1998). If the instructor and/or small-group facilitator is middle class, it may be helpful to use judicious self-disclosure in admitting to holding biases against homeless individuals as well as the ways in which she or he benefits from class privilege. Also, it would be useful for the instructor to disclose how he or she has committed microaggressions against homeless individuals (e.g., telling a homeless individual to get a job) and how he or she has reflected and grown since recognizing the occurrence of the microaggression.

Implications for research

The ideas put forth in this article regarding microaggressions toward homeless individuals are based upon reviews of the literature and the authors' experiences as clinicians and educators. However, little empirical research has been done to examine discrimination against homeless individuals and no research has been done examining microaggressions toward homeless individuals. Research examining the stigma associated with homelessness demonstrates that people have negative attitudes toward the homeless population, indicating that discrimination and, further, microaggressions are quite plausible.

The research that has been done examining discrimination toward the homeless population must be expanded to include microaggressions. It is imperative that we understand the implications of these subtle acts on those that we serve and work with as social workers. Included in this task is the creation of valid and reliable measurement tools. The literature is not expansive enough on discrimination against the homeless to include tools that have been time tested and validated. Research on microaggressions includes scales developed and validated to measure these acts in various populations. Developing proper assessment tools to measure microaggressions in the homeless community is a logical next step. Furthermore, assessment tools should include items related to the microaggression themes discussed in this article. Information should be gathered on social workers' understanding of the themes and the level to which microaggressions are present in their practice.

Research also needs to include larger and wider samples of homeless individuals from different geographic areas, ethnic groups, and circumstances, including homeless youths, homeless veterans, homeless survivors of domestic violence, homeless post-incarcerated men and women, as well as individuals who are chronically homeless due to the cycle of poverty. Different groups may experience different forms of microaggressions, based on their circumstances, which may or may not impact them differently. It is important to understand these differences, even if they are subtle. It is also important to study and research the impact of homeless microaggressions on these various groups and how it may or may not impede their progress in reintegrating into society. It is also important to examine comparisons between experiences of microaggressions reported by homeless individuals and social workers' own perceptions of their practice. For example, do homeless clients report being treated as if they were "invisible" by social work providers more or less so than the social workers' perceptions of their own behaviors?

In addition to improving sampling and measurement techniques, it will be important to understand how the impact of homelessness microaggressions intersect with other forms of discrimination or microaggressions. For example, it will be important to understand if ethnic and/or gender microaggressions intersect with homeless microaggressions. Understanding the entire picture will provide the opportunity to develop interventions that will effectively assist those who have been impacted, as well as to develop targeted prevention efforts, which include awareness training for the community at large, as well as professionals.

Implications for social work practice

Social work practitioners may be unaware of the ways in which subtle interactions impact their clients, which in turn impacts service delivery. If social workers become more aware of their biases and the ways in which they communicate microaggressions toward homeless individuals, they can work toward a different understanding of the relationship, and the therapeutic alliance. The social work code of ethics puts forth the necessities of self-determination and dignity for the client, and the strengths perspective similarly reminds social workers how important it is to help clients to find their sense of self-worth. When a social worker or service provider acts or reacts with microaggressive behaviors or comments, it will perpetuate a sense of distrust for helping professionals and deny the client an opportunity to find strengths or self-worth. Thus, it is imperative that social workers not only become aware of how they communicate microaggressions that they might be imparting, but also that they find more productive ways of interacting with homeless clients.

Social workers practicing in soup kitchens, homeless shelters, mobile outreach agencies, and hospital settings are among the most likely to work regularly with homeless individuals; however, all social workers will likely come into contact with homeless individuals or families during their practice careers. For example, a school social worker may receive a referral to work with a child and his or her family who have recently become homeless. The social worker must take care not to assume "intellectual inferiority" and place the child in services for children with learning disabilities. Extra care and caution must be taken to engage the clients and families, eliciting strengths and their own perspectives about the needs of the family.

Homeless clients may present for services in a number of settings with a sense of shame or embarrassment about their appearance or lack of cleanliness. It is important that social workers are prepared for this likelihood and find ways to make the client feel comfortable. Social work agencies must work together to find and develop creative strategies to help clients through these difficult times and to provide them with the dignity that they need to work productively with a clinician. Empathy and active listening are essential social work skills for work with this population. Use of these skills and a constant revisiting of what they mean may decrease the risk of microaggressions in a social work setting. For example, in accordance with the "aesthetically unappealing" theme, if a homeless client presents for services and has not showered in days, a social worker may make the assumption that the client is there looking for new clothes. However, the client may have other more pressing issues, and the social worker's subtle assumption or microaggression may make the client feel uncomfortable and shut down. Thus, it is important for the social worker to listen and hear what the client's main concern is before making any assumptions.

Social work supervision is an opportune moment for clinicians who work with homeless individuals to check in with one another about their values and value conflicts, which may create unconscious reactions toward clients, such as the microaggressions discussed in this article. For example, a social worker may be struggling with a homeless client's disinterest in the worker's intervention of offering food leftover from a staff luncheon. In accordance with the theme Sub-human Status, the worker with good intent may assume that the client should take the food, just because they are homeless. The supervisor or supervision group can discuss the potential for microaggression in this intervention and provide the worker with a chance to reflect and handle the issue with the client at the next meeting. This will normalize the practice of discussing these unconscious thoughts, behaviors, and reactions and bring the issue further into consciousness for better practice. Furthermore, supervision can provide a time for social workers to brainstorm different ways of engaging their homeless clients without the use of microaggressions.

The implications for adults, children, and families are vast. Social workers must be prepared to offer support in the most nonjudgmental manner, in order to help the client move past this difficult time. Making assumptions about the individual or family may create a block in the development of a solid therapeutic relationship, making it difficult for the client to trust the social worker. It is important for social workers to assume that all homeless clients have strengths and bring intrinsic worth to the work. Asking questions about a client's or family's abilities, rather than making assumptions, is of utmost importance.

References

Abramsky, S. (2014). *The American way of poverty: How the other half still lives*. New York, NY: Nation Books.

Arredondo, P., & Arciniega, G. M. (2001). Strategies and techniques for counselor training based on the multicultural counseling competencies. *Journal of Multicultural Counseling and Development, 29*, 263–273. doi:10.1002/jmcd.2001.29.issue-4

Baumgartner, B. J., Bauer, L. M., & Bui, K. T. (2012). Reactions to homelessness: Social, cultural, and psychological sources of discrimination. *Psi Chi Journal of Psychological Research, 17*(1), 26–34.

Carter, R. T. (2005). Teaching racial-cultural counseling competence: A racially inclusive model. In R. T.Carter (Ed.), *Handbook of racial-cultural psychology and counseling: Training and practice* (vol. 2, pp. 36–56). Hoboken, NJ: Wiley.

Cochran, B. N., Stewart, A. J., Ginzler, J. A., & Cauce, A. (2002). Challenges faced by homeless sexual minorities: Comparison of gay, lesbian, bisexual, and transgender homeless adolescents with their heterosexual counterparts. *American Journal of Public Health, 92*(5), 773–777. doi:10.2105/AJPH.92.5.773

Dovidio, J. F., Kawakami, K., & Gaertner, S. L. (2002). Implicit and explicit prejudice and interracial interaction. *Journal of Personality and Social Psychology, 82,* 62–68. doi:10.1037/0022-3514.82.1.62

Gonzales, L., Davidoff, K. C., Nadal, K. L., & Yanos, P. T. (2015). Microaggressions experienced by persons with mental illnesses: An exploratory study. *Psychiatric Rehabilitation Journal, 38*(3), 234–241. doi:10.1037/prj0000096

Iceland, J. (2013). *Poverty in America: A handbook.* Berkeley, CA: University of California Press.

Jones, J. M. (1997). *Prejudice and racism.* New York, NY: McGraw-Hill.

Kidd, S. A. (2006). Factors precipitating suicidality among homeless youth: A quantitative follow-up. *Youth & Society, 37*(4), 393–422.

Leach, M. M., Behrens, J. T., & LaFleur, N. K. (2002). White racial identity and white racial consciousness: Similarities, differences, and recommendations. *Journal of Multicultural Counseling and Development, 30*(2), 66–80. doi:10.1002/jmcd.2002.30.issue-2

Link, B. G., Schwartz, S., Moore, R., Phelan, J., Struening, E., & Stueve, A. (1995). Public knowledge, attitudes, and beliefs about homeless people: Evidence for compassion fatigue? *American Journal of Community Psychology, 23*(4), 533–555. doi:10.1007/BF02506967

Milburn, N. G., Ayala, G., Rice, E., Batterham, P., & Rotheram-Borus, M. (2006). Discrimination and exiting homelessness among homeless adolescents. *Cultural Diversity and Ethnic Minority Psychology, 12*(4), 658–672. doi:10.1037/1099-9809.12.4.658

Milburn, N. G., Batterham, P., Ayala, G., Rice, E., Solorio, R., Desmond, K.,... Rotheram-Borus, M. (2010). Discrimination and mental health problems among homeless minority young people. *Public Health Reports, 125,* 61–67.

Muccino, G. (Dir). (2006). *The pursuit of happyness* [Motion picture]. Culver City, CA: Columbia Pictures.

Nelson, T. D. (2009). *Handbook of prejudice, stereotyping, and discrimination.* New York, NY: Psychology Press.

Phelan, J., Link, B. G., Moore, R. E., & Stueve, A. (1997). The stigma of homelessness: The impact of the label "homeless" on attitudes toward poor persons. *Social Psychology Quarterly, 60*(4), 323–337. doi:10.2307/2787093

Ponterotto, J. G. (1998). Charting a course for research in multicultural counseling training. *The Counseling Psychologist, 26*(1), 43–68. doi:10.1177/0011000098261004

Shier, M. L., Jones, M. E., & Graham, J. R. (2011). Sociocultural factors to consider when addressing the vulnerability of social service users: Insights from women experiencing homelessness. *Affilia: Journal of Women and Social Work, 26*(4), 367–381. doi:10.1177/0886109911428262

Skosireva, A., O'Campo, P., Zerger, S., Chambers, C., Gapka, S., & Stergiopoulos, V. (2014). Different faces of discrimination: Perceived discrimination among homeless adults with mental illness in healthcare settings. *BMC Health Services Research 14,* 376–387. doi:10.1186/1472-6963-14-376

Sue, D. W. (2005). Racism and the conspiracy of silence. *The Counseling Psychologist, 33*(1), 100–114. doi:10.1177/0011000004270686

Sue, D. W. (2006). *Addressing racism: Facilitating cultural competence in mental health and educational settings.* Hoboken, NJ: Wiley.

Sue, D. W. (2010). *Microaggressions in everyday life: Race, gender, and sexual orientation.* Hoboken, NJ: John Wiley & Sons.

Sue, D. W., Arredondo, P., & McDavis, R. J. (1992). Multicultural counseling competencies: A call to the profession. *Journal of Counseling and Development, 70,* 477–486. doi:10.1002/j.1556-6676.1992.tb01642.x

Sue, D. W., Bernier, J. E., Duran, A., Feinberg, L., Pedersen, P., Smith, E. J., & Vasquez Nuttall, E. (1982). Position paper: Cross-cultural counseling competencies. *The Counseling Psychologist, 10*, 45–52. doi:10.1177/0011000082102008

Sue, D. W., Capodilupo, C. M., Torino, G. C., Bucceri, J. M., Holder, A. M. B., Nadal, K. L., & Esquilin, M. (2007). Racial microaggressions in everyday life: Implications for clinical practice. *American Psychologist, 62*, 271–286. doi:10.1037/0003-066X.62.4.271

Sue, D. W., & Sue, D. (2013). *Counseling the culturally diverse* (6th ed.). Thousand Oaks, CA: Sage Publications.

Sue, D. W., & Torino, G. C. (2005). Racial-cultural competence: Awareness, knowledge, and skills. In R. T.Carter (Ed.), *Handbook of racial-cultural psychology and counseling: Training and practice* (vol. 2, pp. 3–18). Hoboken, NJ: Wiley.

Wasserman, J., & Clair J. (Directors.)(2010). *American refugees: Homelessness in four movements* [Motion picture]. Bent Rail Foundation.

Wen, C. K., Hudak, P. L., & Hwang, S. W. (2007). Homeless people's perceptions of welcomeness and unwelcomeness in healthcare encounters. *Journal of General Internal Medicine, 22*(7), 1011–1017. doi:10.1007/s11606-007-0183-7

Zerger, S., Bacon, S., Corneau, S., Skosireva, A., McKenzie, K., Gapka, S. O.,... Stergiopoulos, V. (2014). Differential experiences of discrimination among ethnoracially diverse persons experiencing mental illness and homelessness. *BMC Psychiatry, 14*, 353–364. doi:10.1186/s12888-014-0353-1

Microaggressions in social work classrooms: strategies for pedagogical intervention

Hye-Kyung Kang ⓘ and Ann Marie Garran

ABSTRACT

We present an in-depth example from a faculty development and peer consultation seminar to illustrate pedagogical strategies for intervening when microaggressions occur in social work classrooms. We provide a framework for social work educators to conceptualize such microaggressions within the context of larger historical and structural oppression and societal dynamics based on differential power and privilege to foster student learning and professional development. We demonstrate how using a mutual-aid model encourages heightened awareness, reflection, and teaching skill development. It also serves to illuminate how instructors might elucidate, interrupt without alienating, and transform microaggressions in the classroom into a learning opportunity.

Introduction

The social work profession is grounded in the principles of social justice and holds at its core respect for the inherent worth of every individual (NASW, 2008). Growing attention to diversity, anti-oppressive practice, and structural inequality have informed both teaching and practice in social workers' response to marginalized populations (Miller & Garran, 2017). Social workers pursue change with and on behalf of vulnerable and oppressed individuals, groups, and communities to address poverty, discrimination, and other forms of social injustice in an effort to promote human rights, social and political well-being, and social justice (NASW, 2008).

While there is a robust literature on social work's role in eradicating systemic inequality and promoting human rights in this pursuit of social justice (See Baines, 2011; Miller & Garran, 2017; Pinderhughes, 1989; Piven & Cloward, 1971), not much attention is paid in social work to how well instructors are prepared to actually *teach* this content in depth, particularly as it pertains to navigating and facilitating difficult discussions in the classroom (Garran, Kang, & Fraser, 2014). Considering social work's commitment to anti-oppressive practice, it is telling that there is a slowly-growing literature that focuses less on social work's response to marginalized and oppressed clients, and more on the treatment of faculty and students within the academy (See Gutiérrez y Muhs, Niemann, González, & Harris, 2012). This literature speaks to the challenges for students and instructors of color in predominantly white institutions (Sue et al., 2011), or the challenges for sexual minority students and instructors (Nadal et al., 2011). One way that these challenges are manifest is through what is well known in the literature as *microaggressions* (Pierce, 1974; Sue et al., 2011). Microaggressions create an environment that may inhibit academic success of students with marginalized identities by reinforcing stereotype threat (Steele, 2010) and are extremely invalidating to marginalized students (Harwood, Choi, Orozco, Browne Huntt, & Mendenhall, 2015; Woodford, Howell, Kulick, & Silverschanz, 2013).

Social work classes are an effective venue to help students understand the link between individual incidents of microaggression and larger social and historical contexts of oppression. Social work instructors are in an obvious position to teach students about how to recognize and address situations where microaggressions occur, so they can intervene effectively (Sue et al., 2011). We address the issue of microaggressions in social work education in this paper. We offer an in-depth example from a long-running faculty development seminar which among other things, successfully raises awareness of microaggressions and offers pedagogical solutions to combat them (Garran et al., 2014). Implications for social work education and practice are discussed as well.

Microaggressions and social work education

In his work with African Americans, Pierce (1974) described racial microaggressions as: These [racial] assaults to black dignity and black hope are incessant and cumulative. Any single one may be gross. .... These offenses are microaggressions. Almost all black-white racial interactions are characterized by white put-downs, done in automatic, preconscious, or unconscious fashion. These minidisasters accumulate. It is the sum total of multiple microaggressions by whites to blacks that has the pervasive effect to the stability and peace of this world. (p. 515)

The term *microaggressions* is now used more broadly to describe "brief, everyday exchanges that send denigrating messages to certain individuals because of their group membership" (Sue, 2010, p. 24) such as race, ethnicity, gender, class, and sexual orientation. With microaggressions, there is a belief that the world should be a certain way (Sue, Lin, Torino, Capodilupo, & Rivera, 2009); the majority way.

Microaggressions occur in classrooms between students or between instructors and students. Students also experience microaggressions outside of a classroom environment, on- or off-campus. Students with previous experiences of microaggressions often feel profoundly disappointed when they experience them on campus, as they have different expectations for a higher education institution, especially at a social work program (J.L. Miller, personal communication, 5/22/2015). While microaggressions may also manifest in interactions between faculty, administrators and staff (Moore, 2014), in this paper we are particularly concerned with in-class microaggressions because classrooms are a key site of learning and instructors can have a profound impact through attempts at intervention.

Microaggressions that occur in a social work classroom affect more than the individuals directly involved (Solórzano, Ceja, & Yosso, 2000). Some students feel alienated by microaggressions, particularly as the target; other students experience helplessness or guilt that they acted as bystanders (Staub, 2003) and did not intervene on a classmate's behalf. Tension or conflict may inhibit students from speaking or sharing in class (Sue et al., 2009). When microaggressions in the classroom go unnoticed or unaddressed, students feel disconnected from the class and classmates, and often feel angry that the instructor did not intervene. This can diminish the instructor's effectiveness or cause undue classroom tensions.

Microaggressions in the classroom may also leave social work instructors feeling frustrated and ineffectual (Niemann, 2012; Wallace, Moore, Wilson, & Hart, 2012). They may feel disconnected from course material or even from students. Many instructors avoid addressing microaggressions directly in the classroom because students become defensive, 'check out,' or stop listening. Some instructors admit that concerns about teaching evaluations dictate interventions (or lack thereof) when microaggressions occur (Lazos, 2012). But the price of not intervening when microaggressions occur is substantial (Smith, 2004). Failure to intervene results in a hostile, invalidating educational environment for students and one that is consequently difficult for educators navigate. Instructors must find ways to respond because while there is 'perceived' minimal harm (Sue, 2010), over time there is a great effect on the person(s) on the receiving end (Smith, Hung, & Franklin, 2011) – whether students or instructors - and ultimately, on overall campus climate and students' professional development.

Skillful facilitation can transform discussions about microaggressions into valuable teachable moments, regardless of the source of the microaggression (Sue et al., 2009). The compounding factor is that many instructors, newer or seasoned, lack the preparation to adequately deal with microaggressions (Daniel, 2011). Teaching about oppression is recognized to be a difficult task (Adams, Bell, Goodman, & Joshi, 2016; Goodman, 2011); yet, social work instructors often do not receive suitable pedagogical training to do so effectively (Varghese, 2013). Given such a gap in pedagogical training, faculty development seminars provide a valuable resource for social work instructors to gain skills, knowledge, and critical consciousness to navigate contents and process difficult interactions effectively (Garran et al., 2014).

Pedagogy and diversity seminar

Given the need both to develop and support faculty ability to address the challenges of content with a particular focus on power, privilege, and multiple dimensions of oppression including microaggressions, a seminar series entitled *Pedagogy and Diversity* (P&D) began at a social work program in the northeastern United States.[1] P&D is a faculty development seminar that uses a mutual-aid model (Toseland & Rivas, 2011) and offers supportive space for instructors to engage in peer consultation regarding teaching about diversity, social identity, and oppression and how to work with difficult classroom dynamics or intense student or instructor reactions (Garran et al., 2014).

The P&D group meets for two hours a week throughout the semester. Full-time faculty, adjuncts, and doctoral students are invited to attend; all do so voluntarily. Minutes of each meeting are disseminated to the entire teaching community so that others not in attendance may benefit. The composition of the group varies from week to week but generally, there is consistent membership. P&D is co-facilitated by an interracial team of two faculty members who have expertise in teaching about power, privilege, oppression and social location. The seminar has a peer-consultation format though this is also balanced at times with dissemination of didactic information (*e.g.*, social location and microaggressions, transphobia in the social work classroom). Those who participate in P&D benefit from the increased sense of shared experience in teaching complex social justice content. They learn to be more vulnerable about their teaching struggles, build knowledge and skill, raise critical consciousness, and frequently feel more prepared and thoughtful during challenging, highly charged classroom conversations.

One way that P&D is effective in intervening when microaggressions (or other pedagogical challenges) occur in classrooms is that it provides instructors with peers who can draw from their own pedagogical knowledge and skill to problem-solve as a group. It affords one a variety of opinions in terms of naming dynamics at play and possible interventions. It is a powerful faculty development model where attendees can seek counsel on any aspect of teaching, not only when problems arise (Garran et al., 2014). P&D provides participants with real-time support, and with that, the opportunity to discuss issues related to teaching and tangible solutions. Those who attend P&D state that they find it effective because the format affords them the chance to decrease shame, anxiety, and isolation that instructors often feel when seemingly insurmountable challenges in the classroom do occur (J.L. Miller, personal communication, 5/12/2015). Instructors can return to class with some solutions or possibilities of rectifying the situation so that the class might get back 'on track' and relationships might be healed, or at the very least improved.

---

[1]For further details, please see Garran et al. (2014).

Sample consultation session

What follows is a sample vignette to illustrate the process involved in offering an instructor consultation during a Pedagogy and Diversity (P&D) meeting. In this particular P&D session, an instructor requests a consultation from the group. The instructor identifies as white, female, and non-religious; she identifies as lesbian among her instructor peers but is not out to her students. This is week three of the semester. The instructor teaches an advanced practice class where the topic of this week's class was about issues to consider in practice with LGBTQ clients. The class racial demographics are predominantly white, female, with three African American female students, two Asian American female students, and two white male students. One of the Asian female students, Kate, is a Muslim student who wears a hijab.

> About 10 minutes before the end of class, Abby, a white female student, says "No offense, but I am not comfortable having this discussion in front of Kate – I know that Muslims have very strong views about how it is wrong to be queer. As a lesbian, this is politically untenable for me and also makes me feel unsafe, so I can't say what I really feel." Kate responds, "That isn't what I believe – this is unfair and insulting to me as well as to my faith." Some students support Kate, and others support Abby. A different white female student says, "I am glad that this has come up because we are finally being transparent – I am also uncomfortable with the hijab because I feel that it oppresses women." One white male student responds, "Everyone wants to be so politically correct – this is America, you can practice what you like, dress like you want to – it is UN-AMERICAN to harass someone who is practicing her faith." One African American female student (Valerie) quietly remarks that she was in NYC during 9/11 and feels triggered by this conversation.
>
> Before the instructor has a chance to address any comments, the class comes to an end. Afterwards, two groups of students approach her. One group supports Abby and demands that the instructor protect LGBTQ students from potential 'microaggressions by religious fundamentalists' and create a classroom environment that feels safe. The second group urges the instructor to protect religious minorities from ethno-religious scapegoating and microaggressions.

Consultation

Facilitators first ask the instructor what she would like from the consultation. The instructor asks for insights from the group as to the dynamics of what happened, and instructional directions as to what she should do in the next class session. Next, members of the group ask the instructor clarifying questions. These questions serve to help the group to understand the context of the incident: the instructor's reactions at the moment and now, the classroom composition, the type of guidelines for discussion that were in place if any, at what point in the class the incident happened, how often the class meets, and the like.

The instructor answers the clarifying questions. Students had previously discussed their race and gender, and a few students had discussed their sexual orientation; other identities were not discussed. The class had established guidelines on the first day, including respectful interactions, speaking for oneself (*I* statements), not making assumptions, not interrupting or mono-polizing conversations, and equitable participation (known as *step-up and step-back* [Wright, 2015]). The incident happened during the third session near the end of the class session. The instructor stated she felt stunned by the interactions at that moment and also struggled to find to address the inter-actions before class ended. Now she feels terrible that there was no acknowl-edgment or resolution of the issue. She feels torn between requests from two groups of students who approached her, and admits she is irritated and a little embarrassed that this happened at all. Although she is a seasoned instructor, this incident has shaken her confidence about her capacity to manage highly charged classroom discussions. She felt especially bad for Kate, who became a lightning rod, seemingly because of the tangible signs of her religion. As the next step, facilitators ask the group to work in small groups (4–5 people) and theorize what may be going on, including both contextual factors that may be at play and critical interpretations of the students' interactions in terms of group dynamics.

After a small group discussion lasting about 15 minutes, the group mem-bers share their insights with the larger group. Group 1 comments on the microaggressions that seem to target different social identities (sexual orien-tation, race, religious affiliation). They note that the class and the instructor seemed to be placed in a false binary position: to support LGBTQ students or to support visible religious minorities. Further, students may be re-enacting societal dynamics pitting one minority group against another, either for resources or for recognition, ultimately showing a lack of understanding of intersectionality (Jani, Pierce, Ortiz, & Sowbel, 2011).

Group 2 elaborates on points already made. Multiple microaggressions had occurred. First, Kate became equated solely with her religion. Her identity was consolidated and effectively silenced, and some students did not see her humanity beyond her hijab. Second, lack of information and perpetuation of stereotypes reduces a diverse and complex set of beliefs into one problematized discriminatory belief. Even when Kate resists this singu-lar, erroneous depiction of her religion, the assumption persists. Further, the demand that the instructor protects LGBTQ students from 'religious funda-mentalists' conflates everyone who practices Islam with those who are 'fun-damentalists.' This depiction is consistent with media stereotypes in post-9/ 11 politics to the point where the term 'religious fundamentalists' has become synonymous with both Muslims and Islam.

Group 3 points out that as this is the third week of class, the students are not yet a cohesive group and not fully utilizing the class participation guidelines. The incident surfaces some pertinent identities but also normalizes unspoken identities such as sexual orientation and religion of other students. Group 3 posits that the varying identities of people in the room may influence how students respond to the interactions. Students in the classroom who share aspects of their identity with Kate or Abby but have different opinions, may feel silenced by the group dynamics that foreclosed their identities.

Members of Group 4 raise a question around the meaning of 'safe.' This group wondered what each student meant by 'safe' and how they interpreted it n the classroom (Garran & Rasmussen, 2014). For instance, there was concern that Valerie, the African American student who talked about being triggered yet remained quiet, would not have her needs met since she was less vocal. No one had asked her what was triggering; there might be safety concerns for her as well. Such lack of attention or response renders her invisible and could be construed as a microaggression.

The final group, Group 5, raises a question about a possible impact of projection (Rasmussen & Salhani, 2010). Fear and hostility have been projected onto Kate as a symbol of Abby's and other students' misconstrued ideas regarding the religiously-based oppression of LGBTQ people. Group 5 also wonders what identities were projected onto the instructor by both groups of students who asked her for interventions after class.

Following this discussion, facilitators synthesize the themes raised and make connections between the classroom incident and larger societal dynamics involving structural oppression, power, and privilege. The instructor appreciates the scope of considerations by the group. She realizes that what happened was a mix of personalities, identities, and larger societal issues. She wonders how she might have contributed to the dynamic, realizing that she felt her authority had been undermined, resulting in her having withdrawn during the interaction with the students. Perhaps she was reacting, too, to the projective identification of students' feelings of helplessness, which contributed to her lack of response in the moment. The P&D feedback itself illustrates sociocultural and historical sources of microaggressions, how they are internalized as stereotypes and manifest themselves in various interactions.

Facilitators ask the group, "What should the instructor consider doing for her next class session?" One member suggests that she simply move onto her scheduled lesson, noting that perhaps students will have forgotten about the incident. Another member expresses fear of modeling conflict avoidance rather than conflict resolution; students with divergent opinions could feel silenced. Perhaps students would feel intimidated to broach the topic if the instructor does not open up the opportunity. A few members embarrassedly admit that if they were in a similar position, they might choose not to bring it up at all in hopes it would just go away. In light of this discussion, they are reconsidering this option and thinking through what was triggered in them that they would opt for silence and collude with those students who might favor moving on rather than engaging with the difficult dynamic and material.

Someone suggests that the instructor revisit the incident briefly and reemphasize the class participation guidelines. Someone else suggests that the instructor discuss the class participation guidelines in terms of professional behavior. The Code of Ethics 2.01 clearly states that social workers must "treat colleagues with respect and should represent accurately and fairly the qualifications, views, and obligations of colleague" (NASW, 2008, p. 15). One purpose of this practice class is to teach students to identify with the social work profession.

One member emphasizes the importance of social identities implicated in the multiple microaggressions in this incident and suggests that the instructor use a small group activity to explore how our perspectives may be reflective of social location, social identity development, and of one's assumptions about others' social identities (Miller & Garran, 2017). Another member adds that there needs to be a discussion about intersectionality, helping to enhance respect and understanding of one another's social locations and experiences, as is expected of social workers.

Another member adds that it would be important to link what happened in the class with all the complex issues that are unfolding currently in the United States, such as Islamophobia, controversies over marriage equality, increased visibility of transphobia, and heightened awareness of state-sanctioned violence against African Americans. In this way, the instructor can move the focus away from Kate and Abby and contextualize the incident by connecting it to larger societal dynamics, illustrating the reach of microaggressions beyond the personal.

One member suggests that he might choose transparency, taking responsibility for not having responded more effectively in the moment, and discussing how he assumed the role of passive bystander (Staub, 2003), a common response in the microaggressions matrix. He might reflect aloud to the students on his own process — how he continued to think about the incident after class, the consultation with other instructors, and insights gained from the discussion. He hopes that doing this will model for his students' self-reflection, heightened critical consciousness, and the importance of consultation (Goodman, 2011).

Finally, one member states that the instructor can link this incident to practice in terms of rupture and repair (Perlman, 2014). It is important to show students that rupture is often part of relationship building and that repair is possible; in fact, such occurrences may ultimately strengthen relationships. Microaggressions occur in clinical relationships when a clinician inadvertently makes a comment or an assumption based on social identities (Sue et al., 2009). Students benefit from learning that the first step in repair is for the social worker to admit and take responsibility for what happened and address the issue rather than avoid it.

The instructor notes that many of these ideas can enhance student learning (and hers as an instructor). She asks for some specific teaching strategies that she can use to incorporate them. The following strategies were offered by the group:

(1) Adapt a critical incident model (Miller, 2004): a reflective writing exercise (individual, in-class), followed by a pair-share (see Bell, Funk, Joshi, & Valdivia, 2016, p. 167), and then a group-share, of all of their thoughts, feelings and insights about the incident

(2) Incorporate journaling assignments so students can share their reflections privately with the instructor and link their insights to class content (e.g., rupture and repair, therapeutic engagement, social work ethics).

(3) A 'fish-bowl' exercise (see Miller & Garran, 2017, p. 221) that helps students feel heard and provides them an opportunity to be involved in the process differentially

(4) Create a discussion board on an electronic course page (e.g., Moodle™, Blackboard™), moderated by the instructor(s). The instructor can post one or two key questions to which students can respond and see others' responses. Instructors should remind students that class participation guidelines are in effect online. And, the instructor can upload resources such as articles about microaggressions in social work practice and education.

The facilitators express appreciation for the creative ideas offered and add that if the instructor chooses one of the in-class options, it is best to limit the time of the activity. Setting a specific time frame helps establish boundaries for students (Kang & O'Neill, in press), especially in consideration of Kate and Abby, who may feel they are unintentionally or unfairly thrust in the center of attention. The instructor might emphasize that discussions about social identities, oppression, and microaggressions are rarely finished in one session but rather are part of ongoing exploration and conversations (Kang & O'Neill, in press). They also remind the instructor that she can choose to take all or none of the suggestions since she knows her class the best. The instructor states that she is thankful for her colleagues' input and feels more prepared for the next week's session. The P&D session ends with a go-round where instructors are asked to share if they have benefitted from the discussions that day and how.

Discussion

When centered on a vignette such as the one offered above, P&D offers support and tangible solutions to the instructor seeking consultation and also to others in the group that leads to a rich discussion about microaggressions and generates a range of pedagogical options. Participants leave P&D having had the opportunity to discuss their work with peers, and to receive feedback which they can consider incorporating into their teaching, as well as tangible suggestions of how to do so. Instructors also leave P&D feeling heard, which is crucial, particularly in instances when they are questioning their own competency because of an isolated event, or an on-going, troubling class-room dynamic.

Consultation time in P&D can be tense. Disagreements occur: whether it be divergent views on the source of conflict, disagreement about how to move proceed, or strong feelings about how the instructor contributed to the issue in the first place. P&D is a group, and the dynamics can mirror those of differential power and privilege in larger society. Microaggressions certainly occur in such configurations. Often this is the time when the facilitators move to help the group, much in the way that an instructor might intervene during a highly charged classroom discussion. Such facilitation serves to model how instructors might elucidate, interrupt without alienating, and transform micro-aggressions in the classroom into a learning opportunity for everyone. Thus, the facilitators not only illustrate how to problem-solve but also provide a framework for instructors to conceptualize microaggressions within the larger historical and structural contexts of oppression and societal dynamics based on differential power and privilege related to different social locations.

One consideration worth noting is that the consultation with the instructor would vary greatly depending on intersecting social identity factors (e.g., race, gender, age, sexual orientation, religious affiliation, ability status) and position in the academic institution (adjunct, non-tenured, tenured, doctoral student). How might the microaggressions incident in the classroom have affected the instructor and the class dynamics differently with a different identity and positionality factors? For instance, imagine that the instructor's sexual orientation in the con-sultation example was known to the students; maybe Abby would have had an expectation of the instructor that she would be more sympathetic to her view about her lack of 'safety.' Or, imagine a Latino male instruc-tor, new to teaching and put in the same situation he immediately confronts Abby. Abby may accuse him of using his male privilege aggres-sively and his status as a man of color to identify with Kate. Other students may see him as replicating the 'Oppression Olympics' (Miller & Garran, 2017) in that he is being more sensitive or responsive to one issue versus another. He, in turn, could experience this interaction as a microaggression, as instructors of color often experience students challenging their expertise and authority in the classroom (Smith, Hung & Franklin, 2011). There are countless ways that this scenario could play out, but the core issue is that with social identity, social location, and historical and structural inequality, microaggressions are likely to occur and to complicate classroom dynamics. Skilled facilitation and institutional support need to be in place to respond when this happens so that a pedagogically appropriate response can be considered.

Implications for social work education and practice

Microaggressions in classrooms are inevitable when covering most material in a social work curriculum and; they can be gateways to critically reflective learning. Becoming an effective social work instructor takes time, effort, and self-reflection. Much like a 'train the trainer' model (Miller, 2012), P&D helps instructors to become aware of and work through microaggressions. The peer consultation process in P&D also models for instructors what they might want students to learn in preparation for their work as social workers in the field - asking for consultation, receiving input and feedback, connecting microaggression incidents to larger historical and structural oppression, gaining insight through multiple perspectives, and generating effective intervention strategies. The parallel process with classroom teaching is apparent, too, in that it is difficult for some instructors to be vulnerable with peers and bring transparency to their teaching by seeking consultation with P&D. The authors argue that it is indeed an expectation of students in class and in the field that they will share their work for feedback and to further their learning - both their successes and their struggles. Instructors, in turn, model and practice this behavior in class, which helps students learn how to think about and work through microaggressions in the field.

Microaggressions are not avoidable; they are not prevented even with the most carefully crafted classroom discussion guidelines. However, if instructors are trained and supported, microaggressions can be the source of teachable moments, instead of allowing them to go underground or remain unaddressed. The authors offered one way of addressing these incidents that both heightens personal awareness and seeks to situate the microaggressions in larger societal patterns to generate useful pedagogical interventions. With institutional support and a commitment to faculty development, this P&D model can be replicated and adapted in a range of academic institutions to raise critical consciousness and to lessen the isolation, frustration, and invisibility that instructors needlessly experience.

ORCID

Hye-Kyung Kang http://orcid.org/0000-0002-9658-0315

References

Adams, M., Bell, L. A., Goodman, D., &Joshi, K. (Eds). (2016). *Teaching for diversity and social justice* (*3rd* ed.). New York, NY: Routledge.

Baines, D. (Ed.). (2011). *Doing anti-oppressive practice: Social justice social work* (*2nd* ed.). Nova Scotia, Canada: Fernwood.

Bell, L. A., Funk, M. S., Joshi, K. Y., &Valdivia, M. (2016). Racism and white privilege. In M. Adams, L. A.Bell, D. J.Goodman, &K.Joshi (Eds.), *Teaching for diversity and social justice* (*3rd* ed., pp. 133–182). New York, NY: Routledge.

Daniel, C. (2011). Lessons learned: Pedagogical tensions and struggles with instruction on multiculturalism in social work education programs. *Social Work Education, 30*(3), 250–265. doi:10.1080/02615471003789829

Garran, A. M., Kang, H.-K., &Fraser, E. (2014). Pedagogy and diversity: Enrichment and support for social work instructors engaged in social justice education. *Journal of Teaching in Social Work, 34*(5), 564–574. doi:10.1080/08841233.2014.952868

Garran, A. M., &Rasmussen, B. M. (2014). Safety in the Classroom: Reconsidered. *Journal of Teaching in Social Work, 34*(4), 401–412. doi:10.1080/08841233.2014.937517

Goodman, D. J. (2011). *Promoting diversity and social justice* (*2nd* ed.). New York, NY: Routledge.

Gutierrez y Muhs, G., Niemann, Y.F., & Harries, A.P. (Eds.) (2012). *Presumed incompetent: The intersections of race and class for women in academia*. Logan, UT: Utah State University Press..

Harwood, S. A., Choi, S., Orozco, M., Browne Huntt, M., &Mendenhall, R. (2015). *Racial microaggressions at the university of illinois at urbana-champaign: Voices of students of color in the classroom*. Ubana-Champaign, USA: University of Illinois.

Jani, J. S., Pierce, D., Ortiz, L., &Sowbel, L. (2011). Access to intersectionality, content to competence: Deconstructing social work education diversity standards. *Journal of Social Work Education, 47*(2), 283–301. doi:10.5175/JSWE.2011.200900118

Kang, H.-K., &O'Neill, P. (accepted).Constructing critical conversations. *Journal of Social Work Education.*

Lazos, S. R. (2012). Are student teaching evaluations holding back women and minorities? In G.Gutiérrez Y Muhs, Y. F.Niemann, C. G.Gonzalez, &A. P.Harris (Eds.), *Presumed incompetent: The intersections of race and class for women in academia* (pp. 164–185). Boulder, CO: University Press of Colorado.

Miller, J. L. (2004). Critical incident debriefing and social work. *Journal of Social Service Research, 30*(2), 7–25. doi:10.1300/J079v30n02_02

Miller, J. L. (2012). *Psychosocial capacity building in response to disasters*. New York, NY: Columbia.

Miller, J. L., &Garran, A. M. (2017). *Racism in the United States: Implications for the helping professions*. New York, NY: Springer.

Moore, A. W. (2014). The life of a black male scholar: Contesting racial microaggressions in academe. In F. A.Bonner, I. I. F.Tuitt, P. A.Robinson, R. M.Banda, &R. L.Hughes (Eds.), *Black faculty in the academy: Narratives for negotiating identity and achieving career success* (pp. 23–32). New York, NY: Routledge.

National Association of Social Workers (2008). Code of Ethics of the National Association of Social Workers. Retrieved from https://www.socialworkers.org/LinkClick.aspxfileticket= KZmmbz15evc=&portalid=0

Nadal, K. L., Issa, M., Leon, J., Meterko, V., Wideman, M., &Wong, Y. (2011). Sexual orientation microaggressions: "Death by a thousand cuts" for lesbian, gay, and bisexual youth. *Journal of LGBT Youth, 8*(3), 234–259. doi:10.1080/19361653.2011.584204

Niemann, Y. F. (2012). Lessons from the experiences of women of color working in academia. In G.Gutiérrez Y Muhs, Y. F.Niemann, C. G.Gonzalez, &A. P.Harris (Eds.), *Presumed incompetent: The intersections of race and class for women in academia* (pp. 446–499). Boulder, CO: University Press of Colorado.

Perlman, F. T. (2014). Psychoanalytic psychotherapy with adults. In J. R.Brandell (Ed.), *Essentials of clinical social work* (pp. 221–276). Thousand Oaks, CA: Sage.

Pierce, C. (1974). Psychiatric problems of the black minority. In S.Arieti (Ed.), *American handbook of psychiatry* (pp. 512–523). New York, NY: Basic Books.

Pinderhughes, E. (1989). *Understanding race, ethnicity, and power.* New York, NY: Simon and Schuster.

Piven, F. F., &Cloward, R. A. (1971). *Regulating the poor.* New York, NY: Pantheon Books.

Rasmussen, B., &Salhani, D. (2010). A contemporary Kleinian contribution to understanding racism. *Social Service Review, 84*(3), 491–513. doi:10.1086/656401

Smith, D. (2004). Black faculty coping with racial battle fatigue: The campus racial climate in a post-civil rights era. In D.Cleveland (Ed.), *A long way to go: Conversations about race by African American faculty and graduate students* (171–192). New York, NY: Peter Lang.

Smith, W. A., Hung, M., &Franklin, J. D. (2011). Racial battle fatigue and the miseducation of black men: Racial microaggressions, societal problems, and environmental stress. *Journal of Negro Education, 80*(1), 63–82.

Solórzano, D., Ceja, M., &Yosso, T. (2000). Critical race theory, racial microaggressions, and campus racial climate: The experiences of African American college students. *Journal of Negro Education, 69* (1/2), 60–73.

Staub, E. (2003). Notes on cultures of violence, cultures of caring and peace, and the fulfillment of basic human need. *Political Psychology, 24*(1), 1–21. doi:10.1111/0162-895X.00314

Steele, C. M. (2010). *Whistling vivaldi and other clues to how stereotypes affect us.* New York, NY: W. W. Norton & Company.

Sue, D. W., Lin, A. I., Torino, G. C., Capodilupo, C. M., &Rivera, D. P. (2009). Racial microaggressions and difficult dialogues on race in the classroom. *Cultural Diversity and Ethnic Minority Psychology, 15*(2), 183–190. doi:10.1037/a0014191

Sue, D. W. (2010). Microaggressions in everyday life: Race, gender, and sexual orientation. Hoboken, NJ: John Wiley.

Sue, D. W., Rivera, D. P., Watkins, N. L., Kim, R. H., Kim, S., &Williams, C. D. (2011). Racial dialogues: Challenges faculty of color face in the classroom. *Cultural Diversity and Ethnic Minority Psychology, 17*(3), 331–340. doi:10.1037/a0024190

Toseland, R., &Rivas, R. (2011). *An introduction to group work practice (7th ed.).* Boston, MA: Prentice Hall.

Varghese, R. (2013). *Transformation in action: Approaches to incorporating race and racism in social work practice and curriculum* (Open Access Dissertations, Paper 736). Retrieved from http://scholarworks.umass.edu/open_access_dissertations/736/

Wallace, S. L., Moore, S. E., Wilson, L. L., &Hart, B. G. (2012). African American women in the academy. InG.Gutiérrezy Muhs, Y. F.Niemann, C. G.Gonzalez, &A. P.Harris (Eds.), *Presumed incompetent: The intersections of race and class for women in academia* (pp. 421--438). Boulder, CO: University Press of Colorado.

Woodford, M. R., Howell, M. L., Kulick, A., &Silverschanz, P. (2013). "That's so gay": Heterosexual male undergraduates and the perpetuation of sexual orientation microaggressions on campus. *Journal of Interpersonal Violence, 28*(2), 416–435. doi:10.1177/0886260512454719

Wright, D. E. (2015). *Active learning: Social justice education and participatory action research.* New York, NY: Routledge.

The impacts of processing the use of derogatory language in a social work classroom

Laurie A. Walker, Deborah K Davis, and Melissa Lopez

ABSTRACT

Classroom content focused on diversity often includes dialogue and student use of derogatory language, as well as opportunities for self-reflection, modeling, collaboration, and continuous development. This article is a critical reflection by a White teacher, a White student, and a student with Mexican American heritage on a critical incident involving student use of racially derogatory language in a story. The experiences are framed with Mezirow's accidental disorienting dilemmas and a decolonizing teaching pedagogy, which create an opportunity for transformative learning.

The approach resulted in a strong process and storytelling orientation for the class and a deeper appreciation for the power of language.

Many Master of Social Work (MSW) students believe they are well informed on the topics of multiculturalism and therefore are unaware or resistant to taking a learning posture in diversity and oppression focused classes. The course curriculum, structure, pedagogy, and a responsive approach to critical incidents may provide key tools for a social justice focused approach to diversity courses that take into account the importance of relationships in resisting prejudice, discrimination, and the use of derogatory language. In this article, a White teacher and student and a student with Mexican American heritage reflect on: (a) their initial approach to a diversity and oppression course; (b) debriefing a critical incident using derogatory language; (c) their race, power, and privilege; as well (d) their key learning over a year after the course.

The experiences are framed with Mezirow's (2000) accidental disorienting dilemmas, which create an opportunity for transformative learning. Mezirow (2000) identified ten stages that begin with an experience that causes an awareness of the need to engage in a self-examining learning process that occurs in the context of both dialogue and new actions resulting in new skills, roles, confidence, and perspective. The stages of transformative learning include:

> a disorienting dilemma; self-examination with feelings of fear, anger, guilt or shame; a critical assessment of assumptions; recognition that one's discontent and the process of transformation are shared; exploration of options for new roles, relationships and action; planning a course of action; acquiring knowledge and skills for implementing one's plans; provisional trying of new roles; building competence and self-confidence in new roles and relationships; a reintegration into one's life on the basis of conditions dictated by one's new perspective." (Mezirow, 2000, p. 22)

Those experiencing power and privilege and those experiencing oppression in the situation, can utilize the transformative learning steps as a structured process as a group and as individuals.

The classroom context and the instructor's race, power, and privilege

I chose to teach a diversity-focused course for the first time, as a White Assistant Professor that relocated to the southwest, because I wanted to use my power and privilege to advocate for social justice for populations experiencing various forms of oppression. The state-level policies and practices where I resettled outspokenly focused on limiting the rights of people who were undocumented immigrants, women, and/or Lesbian Gay Bisexual and Transgender. I spent the summer before my first semester of teaching familiarizing myself with the existing curriculum, local politics and issues, and articulating my own pedagogical approach to the course given my White outsider identity in a school with a large portion of students of color.

Established curriculum

The department's approach to the curriculum included the use of the Marsiglia and Kulis (2009) culturally grounded continuum. The continuum assumes that individuals range from being unaware of a population and/or resistant to working with them to contemplating/becoming aware, sensitive, culturally competent, and culturally grounded in working with specific populations. The goals of the curriculum included helping students identify the geneses of oppression (including migration, colonization, and annexation of land), consequences of oppression, as well as a process of establishing power, wellness, and liberation (Marsiglia & Kulis, 2009; Prilleltensky, 2008; Young, 2000). The approach assumed that students need to develop knowledge, attitudes, and behaviors that enable them to become change agents in collaboration with their clients through engagement as cultural learners, in dialogue across multiple boundaries, in order to work with heterogeneous populations and unique individuals (Marsiglia & Kulis, 2009). Course assignments were structured around learning inquiry teams that place students in small groups to write and present on topics of their choice, which provide a consistent set of relationships to engage in a transformative learning process (Marsiglia & Kulis, 2009; Mezirow, 2000). Each team dialogued to practice giving critical professional feedback on student presentations because supervision, peer consultation, and trainings are a means for social workers to stay current on diversity content (Smith et al., 2006).

Developing a relational and decolonizing approach as a White instructor

As I tuned in to the experiences of students in the southwest, I recalled a brief yet profound experience with an Indigenous student from the southwest who informed me that my approach to a policy course was from a "White perspective." My focus on existing social problems and policies as defined by those in political power did not acknowledge that Indigenous populations in the United States who are often familiar with and navigate the dominant culture policies, as well as additional laws, policies, and procedures that are specific to their Indigenous Nation. She helped me understand the power I have to set the frame of the course content as an instructor of the dominant culture in the United States that unintentionally forefronts the privileged perspectives of a settler colonial person (Tuck & Yang, 2012). As a result, I tried to reimagine a different classroom climate for the students in my new role settling in to a new region with only a vague awareness of the local Indigenous perspectives (Marsiglia & Kulis, 2009; Tuck & Yang, 2012). I took a relational approach given the mix of White students and students of color in order to engage the students with each other, myself, and the course content and create engagement in a learning process that did not center settler/dominant culture ways of knowing (Allan, Benjamin, Sakamoto, & Gutiérrez, 2011; hooks, 1994; Mezirow, 2000; Palmer, 2000; Tuck & Yang, 2012).

I incorporated decolonizing teaching methodologies focused on knowledge sharing and creation in a context that forefronts Indigenous ways of knowing such as story circles (Allan et al., 2011; Fire, 2006; Gorski, 2007; Tuhiwai Smith, 2008). Story circles are a means of experiential learning that start where students are and develops their ability to: (a) problematize Eurocentric ways of knowing; (b) acknowledge colonization, domination, physical and psychological warfare, and genocide; (c) seek to reconcile histories in a manner that balances physical, mental, emotional, and spiritual perspectives; and (d) transform future social work practice to be emancipating and empowering (Allan et al., 2011; Fire, 2006; Gorski, 2007; Tuck & Yang, 2012). I wrestled with whether or not it was appropriate for me as a White instructor to lead decolonizing activities, but decided to try starting the course with a story circle given that both national social work conference sessions and my local doctoral education included decolonizing techniques taught by Indigenous instructors to multicultural groups (Allan et al., 2011; Tuck & Yang, 2012; Tuhiwai Smith, 2008). I made commitments to myself to differentiate between decolonizing engagement methods (Allan et al., 2011; Tuhiwai Smith, 2008), cultural appropriation (Tuck & Yang, 2012), culturally grounded practice (Marsiglia & Kulis, 2009), and debates regarding whether leaders need to be insiders of the cultural engagement techniques.

Engaging the students with a decolonizing pedagogy and a co-learning approach

The first day of class I was transparent about the decolonizing approach, as I acknowledged that the classroom was built on what was once Indigenous Mexican land and named a specific sacred place to a local Indigenous Nation that was visible from the campus (Tuck & Yang, 2012). We sat in a circle, where I explained the sacredness and ground rules of story circles (such as speaking one at a time in the order that we sat in, not taking notes, not drawing, and not using technology) (Allan et al., 2011). I modeled sharing my own ancestry (including my ancestors involvement in slave trade and my own culpability), my reasons for working as a social work professor in the present, and my future career goals (Tuck & Yang, 2012). Students were able to both voice and listen to aspects of each other's identities as a starting point for co-learning, which helped ground the students in the diversity of the classroom (such as various ages, ethnicities, religions, and those that were adopted).

I role modeled familiarizing myself with the local Indigenous populations and regional history as a co-learner that acknowledged: (a) resistance to colonization and the annexation of Indigenous land; (b) the resulting modes of control (such as secured borders); and (c) structural strategies of colonization (such as surveillance and criminalization) (Tuck & Yang, 2012). I sought out mentoring via peer consultation, read and watched videos (fiction, nonfiction, academic, and local organizational sources), learned about local events and groups, and developed relationships with students of various identities within and outside the classroom.

A student with Mexican-American heritage's perspective on the diversity course

I entered the diversity and oppression course in my first year as a MSW student feeling confused about my own ethnicity and cultural experience. I am the child of a White mother from Wisconsin and a Mexican father who immigrated to the United States at the age of 17. I was caught off guard and felt vulnerable when I was asked to share my cultural experience on the first day of class because I felt an uncomfortable balance with my identities. I introduced myself to the class as someone of Mexican-American heritage with various cultural influences and throughout the class I established a more solid understanding of my own personal experience. The course allowed me to build on my prior undergraduate coursework focused on the US-Mexico Border, Mexican-American Studies, and policy. We were challenged in every class to put theory into practice in engaged-conversation that held each other accountable, which included the discussion of why the use of derogatory language was inappropriate in social work professional contexts. I developed a greater cultural sensitivity from these learning experiences.

A White student's perspective on the diversity course

I am an older student, twice divorced, a mother of two, a strong feminist, and a White Southerner that struggles with the South's legacy of racism. I have worked throughout my life to be aware of and eradicate my unconscious biases, as a lifelong advocate for social justice, equity, and opportunity. I never wished to be a part of dance of the South where,

> We learned the dance that cripples the human spirit, step by step by step, we who were White and we who were colored, day by day, hour by hour, year by year until the movements were reflexes and made for the rest of our lives without thinking. (Smith, 1994, p. 96)

I grew up with divisions of race, social class as an indicator of worth, and negative attitudes toward ethnicities that are different from my own, which were difficult to recognize as instilled reflexes. I tried to ingrain in myself a new choreography that aligns with my outspoken nature, which included 25 years of volunteering, political action, and protest and a newfound commitment to developing clinical skills that enable me to respond to socioeconomic and cultural differences with respect and mindfulness. As a result, I entered the course confident that I was aware, knowledgeable, and sensitive to issues regarding diversity and oppression and how to address them (Marsiglia & Kulis, 2009). Yet, participating in the class reminded me that: (a) we can never grow complacent about our cultural competence; (b) that a moment of mindlessness has the potential to damage relationships and others' feelings of safety both personally and professionally; and (c) cultural humility is a lifelong process that challenges hubris and encourages ongoing deeper self-examination (Tervalon & Murray-Garcia, 1998). Cultural humility is a relational openness, as a means of naming our own biases, welcoming feedback, and resetting our trajectory when our actions and words do not match our stated intentions (Tervalon & Murray-Garcia, 1998).

Critical reflection of a disorienting dilemma before the next class

A white student's perspective

I embrace the storytelling tradition of my Southern heritage as a means of communicating, connecting with others, and relating what is being taught in a class with what I have experienced. However, my choice to repeat a specific racial slur used by my ex-husband, who was Latino, as an example of intragroup racism in a multicultural classroom became an exercise in disconnection, privilege, and pride. I felt a twinge when I stated the derogatory word and an urge to pull the word back, but it was already out. I did not think about it again until my professor asked to speak with me in her office. She noted that the use of the slur, quoted or not, may have had an impact on other students. She asked me to consider the safety of other students and how that feeling of safety may have been diminished by my use of the word. She told me she planned to send out an email to my classmates and discuss the issue in class.

I initially tried to defend myself with my "credentials" as a non-racist person. I felt shame and embarrassment because my actions were not in keeping with my stated beliefs. I found the next few days difficult as I experienced a compulsion to defend myself; however, no rational explanation excused the impact of my behavior. I decided to take responsibility for how my use of a derogatory word might have caused pain for others. My professor sent an email to the class that stated during the upcoming class, "we will start by discussing the use of derogatory terms in professional social work settings and resisting and dismantling prejudice and discrimination in our daily lives." After several drafts and feedback from my professor, I also sent an email to the class stating,

> Yesterday in class I quoted a word my ex-husband used to degrade or disparage Latinos/Latinas. What I realized is that it does not matter that I was quoting and outraged, the word has the same negative impact as if I were saying it directly and supporting its use. I could have easily stated that he used a derogatory word without using the word itself, and would have done so had I taken a moment for thought and consideration before speaking. I am deeply sorry and promise to take more care in the future. I am very open to discussion if any of you feel the need to talk this out with me either here via email, personally, or in class about how you felt about my language, and will do my best to both make amends and integrate feedback.

The other students' responses to the email varied: (a) some thanked me; (b) one expressed concern that we would not be able to openly discuss racist comments; (c) none of the Mexican Americans responded perhaps because they felt unsafe or the apology was insufficient; and (d) one White male student downplayed the incident, expressed annoyance at political correctness, and stated that I was being too hard on myself. I am grateful he was the embodiment of that internal voice that wanted to avoid shame by excusing, which helped me articulate why my word use was not "okay" and was not something I believe or wish to represent.

A student with Mexican-American heritage's perspective

The day that another student used the derogatory word in class I was upset by the content of the story she shared and shocked by hearing the derogatory word. The word she used was not a word I heard spoken often and it brought back memories of discrimination my family has experienced. I was not upset with her, but rather with the story she shared, and the history of the derogatory word. I initially processed the incident with my sister, who helped me to articulate why the derogatory word upset me. The other student and I had our internship together twice a week and we had become very close. I struggled with how to respond to the incident given our relationship and the upcoming class discussion. I am sure we discussed the incident outside of class, although I do not remember the exchanges, but I know my urge was to avoid causing her further shame.

A teacher's perspective

I spent quite a bit of time thinking about: (a) the use of derogatory language in the classroom; (b) my own prior experiences with similar incidents as a student that required naming our discontent, ongoing dialogue, and an emphasis on personal and collective healing; and (c) my role in leading the student and the classroom through this disorienting dilemma (Mezirow, 2000; Tuck & Yang, 2012). I was aware of my own fear-based response (wide eyes, heart beating faster, knots in stomach, and likely blushing) and scanned the room to see student responses (Mezirow, 2000). I felt a mix of guilt, shame, and physical symptoms that unsettled my own "innocence" for not responding more proactively (Mezirow, 2000; Tuck & Yang, 2012).

In an effort to both alleviate my unsettled feelings and live up to my intent to use my privilege to work for social justice for populations experiencing oppression, I critically assessed: (a) my own assumptions about social work professionals' use of derogatory language; (b) my choice of teaching methods beginning with a story circle rather than clearly established ground rules; and (c) my own power as the instructor and my responsibility to create a safe classroom environment particularly for the Mexican-American students that were the largest minority group enrolled in a university situated on land that was Mexico 150 years ago (Mezirow, 2000; National Association of Social Workers, 2008). I feared that the incident caused harm to relationships with students of color and contributed to racial tensions under my authority as an instructor, rather than developing social workers as allies on issues faced by Latinos/Latinas in our local community.

I consulted with colleagues and spent the week checking in with students in the class to explore my, "options for new roles, relationships, and actions" (Mezirow, 2000, p. 22). At the time, I saw my role with the student that used the derogatory language as mainly focused on making sure she was both taking care of herself, reflecting on the incident, and "unsettling her inno-cence" as a descendent of White settlers that repeated a derogatory word used to describe the Indigenous populations of the region (Tuck & Yang, 2012, p. 10). I also sought to take responsibility and use my power and privilege in a manner that did not focus on relieving our guilt as settlers, but rather focused on taking responsibility to act in a manner that acknowledged and sought to address issues of power and privilege in daily interactions (Tuck & Yang, 2012). I revisited my teaching pedagogy to inform my knowl-edge and skills in developing a course of action in the next class session (Mezirow, 2000). I committed to: (a) assert ground rules rooted in the NASW Code of Ethics that forefronts the importance of human relation-ships, working toward social justice, and encourages the use of professional, inclusive, specific, and accurate language; (b) name the role of othering language in establishing settler colonial sovereignty; and (c) name an expec-tation for cultural humility and resisting racial coding (biased comments or jokes that set the boundaries and direction of power) (NASW, 2008; Palmer, 2000; Sleeter, 1994; Stewart, 2007; Tervalon & Murray-Garcia, 1998; Tuck & Yang, 2012). I recommitted to relational processes with students over email and spent time talking in the hallway at school or during office hours, as a means of role modeling working through feelings of fear, anger, guilt, pain, and shame by talking through tensions when crossing cultural boundaries (Mezirow, 2000). Students of color challenged me to focus on similar current events and the nonresponse of a nearby university, which informed my planning for the next class session and gave me a means of establishing a safe space to practice new roles in these relationships (Mezirow, 2000).

Responding to the disorienting dilemma within the classroom

A teacher's perspective

The classroom felt tense and required a more directive leadership including a lecture that gave me the chance to practice a new role in the classroom that sought to, "reduce the harm that White supremacy has had on White people, and the deep harm it has caused non-White people over generations" (Jacobs, 2009, p. 21; Mezirow, 2000; Tuck & Yang, 2012). I reminded students that social workers will regularly engage in cross-cultural relationships and will experience tension, embarrassment, and other forms of discomfort, yet they can choose to be open, adaptable, trusting, and accepting in any given moment, in order to develop and maintain relationships. I used local currents events in print and video forms in an effort to: (a) indirectly illustrate less personal examples of derogatory/discriminatory words and actions; (b) various public responses that ranged from unaware to resistant, contemplation, sensitivity, and competence; (c) examples of local responses to discrimination against people of Mexican descent to teach students about hot anger (expressing emotion and intensity which may result in alienation and broken relationships) and cold anger (calm and collected actions that function from a grounded place that seeks to create a socially just outcome) (Rogers, 1990); (d) began a classroom dialogue that did not single out the White student that used the derogatory language in class the previous week; and (e) had students reflect individually regarding where they grew up, personal and professional identities, the populations they work with, and current/historical events (Marsiglia & Kulis, 2009). Student responses varied from unawareness and resistance to contemplation, sensitivity, and perhaps cultural humility (Marsiglia & Kulis, 2009; Tervalon & Murray-Garcia, 1998). Regrettably, the approach centered two White perspectives and did not create a decolonizing pedagogical space for students experiencing marginalization, which may have felt more chaotic but might have created more space for a dialogue that centered and gave voice to the wisdom and strength of various perspectives (Mezirow, 2000; Tuck & Yang, 2012).

The reasons the initial story with the derogatory word was shared in the classroom were complex and required years of ongoing dialogue to understand. Regardless, the story did not connect with other students and the impact of repeating the derogatory word in a room of people that have heard those terms used to disparage themselves, their families, and their classmates centered the power and perspectives of the settler/colonizer in our classroom space (Tuck & Yang, 2012). The othering language normalized the experience of the permanent settler and described Mexican Americans as a foreign contagion rather than acknowledging that the land was Mexico prior to annexation and migration by US settlers (Tuck & Yang, 2012). The storyteller strived to describe how racial bias occurs even within groups toward subgroups yet the message was lost in translation because the story did not take into account: (a) her privilege as a White person; (b) the race of the person she was making an example of; (c) the geographic location of the classroom; (d) the current sociopolitical climate in the state that was anti-immigrant; and (e) a sociopolitical climate that not only fore-fronted White/settler colonial perspectives as innocent, but also prohibited teaching history from Mexican American and Indigenous perspectives in local schools via state law (Tuck & Yang, 2012).

A White student's perspective

I do not have a clear memory of the classroom discussion because I was concerned I had done damage that an apology could not heal, I was very nervous, my adrenaline was flowing, and I was frustrated by the responses that claimed the right to say derogatory words. I remember sensing my own inadequacy in explaining that my language conjured prior experiences with racism and abuse. I told a fictional story that illustrated my mistake that reached my classmates,

> Imagine there is a man standing outside screaming racial slurs at the top of his lungs and I hear him, as I am coming to class. No one else here has heard him. Just me. Then I come to class and quote every word he said. I have essentially brought that man into this room and let him strike all of you. It does not matter that I am quoting. I am enabling the damage.

Students nodded along during my story and those who seemed to be fighting the most at least looked thoughtful. A classmate that was an older Latina woman in my class small group, who often shared her experiences of oppression while growing up in the southwest, thanked me for sharing my experiences and extending kindness and forgiveness to me, which reassured me. I learned that safe space is something to honor because it is valuable and fragile since: (a) one moment of thoughtlessness and cultural ignorance is all it takes to damage relationships; (b) an activist's resume, past actions, or present beliefs can quickly become meaningless without thoughtful and vulnerable consideration of one's words and actions; and (c) that working through relationships that have been harmed takes an ongoing mindful and humble awareness that is responsive to feedback, self-confrontation, and vigilance against insensitivity. I now recognize that I am much lower on the culturally grounded continuum than I first thought and I do my best to recognize when I am overestimating how much I know. I do not need to share stories of my own outrage to connect with others, rather I need to be self-aware of my own privilege and power particularly in my social work practice including clients who may be hesitant to share their feelings with me given the power imbalance. The following quote from Nouwen, McNeill, & Morrison (1983) summarizes my new posture to diversity and oppression content:

> No to racial injustice means a call to look our own bigotry straight in the eye, and no to world hunger calls upon us to recognize our own lack of poverty. No to war requires us to come to terms with our own violence and aggression, and no to oppression and torture forces us to deal directly with our own insensitivities. And so all our no's become challenges to purify our own hearts. In this sense, confrontation always includes self-confrontation. (p. 123–124)

We are not on a continuum, but rather part of a dynamic learning process of self-examination and humility moving by fits and starts – forward and back (Tervalon & Murray-Garcia, 1998).

A student with Mexican-American heritage's perspective

My participation in the class was a lesson in graciously engaging a range of responses to cultural insensitivity by directly addressing and increasing a sense of accountability in holding ourselves as social workers to an inclusive ethical standard. The debriefing helped me: (a) process my own discomfort with the story; (b) understand the negative impact of derogatory words; and (c) look at my own spoken derogatory words. I was struck by the defensive and joking responses of some of my classmates, as I went through an often uncomfortable and internal process of exploring my own cultural experience, applying course content that was not necessarily verbalized by anyone during the course, and developing my own sense of cultural groundedness and humility (Tervalon & Murray-Garcia, 1998). In retrospect, I would have liked to more directly address the source of White student defensiveness and sense of being unfairly burdened with guilt or attacked, as a means of relieving some of the tension. Much of the content in this class was new to me and made me uncomfortable at times, but I was grateful for the opportunity to explore my own cultural experience and improve my cultural groundedness and humility (Marsiglia & Kulis, 2009; Tervalon & Murray-Garcia, 1998). As a student who was not as comfortable speaking in class, I found it difficult to challenge louder voices that dominated, whether those voices were White students or other Mexican Americans presenting their experiences as concrete and not acknowledging a range of experiences within any given ethnicity. I appreciate my classmate's willingness to engage in discussion, yet my advice to her is to consider her words and her stories carefully, particularly in restating a derogatory word that most others would not speak out loud.

Key learning

We believe debriefing the use of derogatory language in the classroom led to building a group process that worked toward building understanding, connection, and healing for all involved (Prilleltensky, 2008). The relational and decolonizing teaching pedagogy resulted in creating space that allowed for a strong process and storytelling orientation for the course (Palmer, 2000; Tuck & Yang, 2012). As a result, the majority of students identified the power of language as one of the key things they learned in the course during the final story circle (Marsiglia & Kulis, 2009; Sleeter, 1994; Stewart, 2007). We learned how to engage in a transformative learning process that enabled individuals and the group to reflect and act in a manner that develops the skills needed to: (a) challenge derogatory language and other forms of discrimination; (b) name our power and privilege, (c) disrupt microaggressions in social work education and practice; and (d) role model cultural humility via a learning posture that relationally engages tense accidental disorienting dilemmas (Marsiglia & Kulis, 2009; Mezirow, 2000; Prilleltensky, 2008; Tervalon & Murray-Garcia, 1998). As helpers we have more power and should model cultural humility to create the sorts of changes that we hope to see in our relationships, classrooms, and society (Prilleltensky, 2008; Tervalon & Murray-Garcia, 1998).

References

Allan, B., Benjamin, A., Sakamoto, I., & Gutiérrez, L. (2011, October). *Decolonizing the social work classroom: Looking at the past, in the present, for the future panel.* Panel Discussion at the Annual Program Meeting of the Council on Social Work Education, Atlanta, Georgia.

Fire, A. (2006). Recommendations to enhance the educational experience of aboriginal social work students. *Critical Social Work, 7*(2).

Gorski, P. (2007). Good intentions are not enough: A decolonizing intercultural education. *Intercultural Education, 19*(6), 515–525. doi:10.1080/14675980802568319

hooks, B. (1994). *Teaching to transgress: Education as the practice to freedom.* London: Routledge.

Jacobs, A. (2009). *Undoing the harm of white supremacy.* Masters Thesis, The Gallatin School, New York University.

Marsiglia, F. F., & Kulis, S. (2009). *Diversity, Oppression & Change: Culturally Grounded Social Work.* Chicago, IL: Lyceum Books.

Mezirow, J. (2000). *Learning as transformation: Critical perspectives on a theory in progress.* San Francisco, CA: Jossey-Bass.

National Association of Social Workers. (2008). *Code of ethics: Guide to the everyday professional conduct of social workers.* Washington, DC: National Association of Social Workers.

Nouwen, H., Mcneill, D. P., & Morrison, D. A. (1983). *Compassion: A reflection on Christian life.* New York, NY: Doubleday.

Palmer, P. (2000). *Let your life speak: Listening for the voice of vocation.* Danvers, MA: John Wiley & Sons, Inc.

Prilleltensky, I. (2008). The role of power in wellness, oppression, and liberation: The promise of psychopolitical validity. *Journal of Community Psychology, 36*(2), 116–136. doi:10.1002/(ISSN)1520-6629

Rogers, M. B. (1990). The first revolution is internal. In: *Cold anger: A story of faith and power politics* (pp. 55–64). Denton, TX: University of North Texas Press.

Sleeter, M. C. (1994). White racism. *Multicultural Education, 1*(4), 5–8, 39

Smith, C. A., Gantt, A., Cohen-Callow, A., Cornelius, L. J., Dia, D. A., Harrington, D., & Bliss, D. L. (2006). Staying current in a changing profession: Evaluating perceived change resulting from continuing professional education. *Journal of Social Work Education, 42*, 465–482. doi:10.5175/JSWE.2006.042310002

Smith, L. (1994). *Killers of the dream.* New York, NY: W.W. Norton. (Originally published 1949).

Stewart, J. (2007). *Teaching resistance: An exercise in critical pedagogy.* Retrieved October 19, 2012, from radical pedagogy.icaap.org/content/issue9_1/stewart.html

Tervalon, M., & Murray-Garcia, J. (1998). Cultural humility versus cultural competence: A critical distinction in defining physician training outcomes in multicultural education. *Journal of Health Care for the Poor and Underserved*, 9(2), 117–125. doi:10.1353/hpu.2010.0233

Tuck, E., & Yang, K. W. (2012). Decolonization is not a metaphor. *Decoloniztion: Indigineity, Education, & Society*, 1(1), 1–40.

Tuhiwai Smith, L. (2008). *Decolonizing Methodologies: Research and Indigenous People.* New York: Zed Books.

Young, I. M. (2000). Five faces of oppression. In: M. Adams (ed), *Readings for diversity and social justice.* New York, NY: Routledge.

Microaggressions: Intervening in three acts

Amie Thurber and Robin DiAngelo

ABSTRACT
The deleterious effects of microaggressions on members of marginalized groups are well documented. Less clear are the practice skills needed to intervene when microaggressions take place, particularly in ways that maintain strong relationships with students, colleagues, and/or clients. Furthermore, too often discussions of responses to microaggressions are restricted to the position of bystander, ignoring the ways that human service providers may also perpetrate or be targets of injustice. Using vignettes from our practice experience, we provide guiding principles for constructive microaggression intervention from three key social locations: perpetrator, witness, and target.

Robin is in town for a visit. We meet for dinner, then walk to the local ice cream shop. The sign at the entrance proudly lists the shops' signature flavor: Trailer Trash. It stops Robin cold. As I look at my friend, who has shared and written openly about the physical and psychological pain of being raised without enough money for food, dental care, and shoes that fit, she says, "Huh. So that's what they think poor people are – human garbage."

From an ice cream shop to an master of social work (MSW) classroom, microaggressions occur everywhere, all the time. These seemingly small, ostensibly singular acts of oppression permeate the lives of people of color and other marginalized groups. Ample testimony and empirical research make evident the ways that microaggressions compile and compound to have deleterious physical and mental health effects and to create hostile climates for members of oppressed groups (Sue et al., 2007). In an era when educators and employers alike are increasingly concerned with recruiting and retaining a diverse cohort and creating equitable conditions within our schools, communities, and institutions, it is widely recognized that human service professionals must be able to recognize microaggressions (Constantine, 2007; Sue et al., 2007). Less clear are the practice skills needed to intervene in these settings, particularly in ways that maintain strong relationships with students, colleagues, and/or clients. Even as our collective analysis of the causes and consequences of systemic inequalities becomes more complex, many people remain dissatisfied with their capacity to interrupt oppression in their everyday lives. In seeking to help answer that need, we also hope to complicate the question.

In our experience as educators and practitioners, we (Amie and Robin) often witness microaggressions and must determine if, when, and how to respond effectively. As white people occupying these same roles, we also *perpetuate* microaggressions, which require a different set of skills related to critical reflexivity, accountability, and restorative action. Further, as women, a person raised poor (Robin) and a Jewish person (Amie), we are both at times *targets* of microaggressions. In these moments, we depend on yet another set of practices related to centering, discernment, and reclaiming voice. In the pages that follow, we present considerations for responding to microaggressions in three acts, addressing these three distinct social positions. In each case we introduce a vignette, drawn from our practice experience of being witness to, perpetrating and being the target of microaggression. We then offer core principles for responding in each type pf scenario. Intentionally broad, these principles serve to illuminate possibilities rather than proscribe specific responses. We then return to the vignette for each act, exploring how we applied these principles in a single, highly contextual, moment. Though the three vignettes are presented as singular examples, they are not anomalies. We selected stories that embody patterns we have experienced repeatedly working in diverse regions and practice contexts in the United States. Through the following dialectic process – moving between depth and breadth, between abstract and concrete – we hope to nuance human services professionals' understanding of our responsibilities to students, clients, one another and ourselves in the face of microaggressions.

Act 1: Witness

My colleague Mary, an African American woman, and I are co-leading an anti-racism workshop for a mixed-race group. Mary is leading the section on internalized racial oppression. She prefaces by noting that it is a very sensitive to discuss internalized racism in the presence of white people, and asks the white participants to just listen. As she begins sharing some of the ways that people of color are impacted by racism, a white woman repeatedly interrupts to question her. Finally, in response to an example Mary provides of how people of color experience internalized racism, the white woman states, "I think it's more complex than that."

These are familiar moments for most of us. We are sitting in a meeting, attending a conference, or teaching a class and somebody says something we find deeply problematic. We feel compelled to respond in some way, but are not sure what we should do. As a witness to microaggressions, there is no one right way to answer the questions of if, when, and how to respond, though there are some principles that may help us to discern our next steps.

Rather than ask what will be gained by intervening, ask what will I lose by not acting

Some people decide whether or not to respond to microaggressions based on their assessment of whether or not their intervention will make a difference. Unfortunately, you cannot fully know in advance the impact of your actions. Given the hopelessness many people feel in the face of systemic oppression, you will likely underestimate your ability to effect positive change. But acting in solidarity is in itself an intervention, even if you do it poorly or do not see immediate results.

Speaking up, and the risk-taking that involves, can be empowering for witnesses to microaggressions. In situations in which you fear there may be repercussions because someone is present who holds more power in the specific context – a supervisor, for example – a different kind of courage is needed: the courage to elevate the decision to take righteous action above the *possibility* of backlash. Ultimately, this is a personal and ethical decision: Do I protect myself and collude with systemic oppression, or do I engage in liberatory practice and accept the risks that may go with it? Most often, all that is at risk is a moment of discomfort (and with practice, even this can dissipate over time). There is much more to lose by not acting: integrity; alignment of your values with your behaviors; the trust of those targeted by the microaggression, passive collusion with oppression and; peace of mind.

Clarify your goals

Discerning how and when to act is often determined by who you want to influence. Do you want to shift the understandings and/or actions of those perpetuating harm? Are you seeking to provide support to, stand in solidarity with, or protect those targeted? Are you concerned with raising the consciousness of and/or mobilizing other bystanders? Depending on who you want to reach, you may determine that immediate action is needed, or that additional time is needed to craft a strategic response. However, the stakes surrounding when to act and who to influence change when people are directly and immediately harmed by a microaggression. In these instances, inaction may signal agreement with the hurtful beliefs and behaviors, and an immediate intervention may be necessary to disrupt this collusion.

Ground your actions in care

Once you have decided if and when to act, you are left with determining how. What exactly do you say? If only we could offer a flow chart of possible responses to microaggressions: *If the perpetrator is your supervisor, then...; if there are members of the target group in the room, then...* but in reality, every situation is unique and there are a multitude of possible responses. Even the most skillful response can be met with resistance, causing unintended negative consequences; there are no guaranteed right moves. That said, the Social Work Code of Ethics is instructive, requiring us to "treat each person in a caring and respectful fashion," to promote "socially responsible self-determination," and enhance other's "capacity and opportunity to change" (NASW, 2008). In the context of responding to microaggressions, this means that we care not only for those who may be harmed by hurtful comments or actions, but that we care for those who perpetrate harm. To be clear, caring for those who enact microaggressions does not entail excusing harmful behavior, privileging the sensitivities of the oppressors over the pain of the oppressed, or colluding with dominant group fragility (DiAngelo, 2012). To privilege the temporary feelings of discomfort the perpetrator may experience over ethical intervention on behalf of the marginalized is not an act of care, it is an act of collusion. Authentic acts of care serve to support human development by providing opportunities for critical self-reflection and reparation of relationships, even though they are uncomfortable. Indeed, dominant group discomfort – when engendered by interruption of the status quo – is necessary for socially just transformation.

It is often presumed that the most sensitive way to respond when someone perpetuates a microaggression is to "call them in" rather than "call them out." Calling out is associated with shaming someone into re-evaluating their actions, while calling in is associated with *inviting* someone to reevaluate their actions (DiAngelo & Sensoy, 2014). Calling in is based on the recognition that people are more likely to change when they do not feel defensive, and thus may be more willing to reevaluate when they are addressed one-on-one rather than publicly via social media or other forms of critique. We contend that the framing of the intervention is often more important than whether the intervention takes place in the public or private sphere. A private conversation is not guaranteed to be more caring than a public one, and a public intervention is not necessarily without care. Further, as discussed above, changing the thinking of the individual perpetrating a microaggression is only one possible goal for the intervention. A public harm often calls for a public response. Whether done privately or publicly, approaching an intervention with compassion increases the likelihood that the intervention may foster growth in the aggressor. Equally important, a compassionate response engenders humility. Recognizing someone else's microaggression today offers no assurance you will not be perpetuating a microaggression tomorrow. Returning to the vignette that opens Act 1, we provide one example of how we applied these three principles in context.

"I think it's more complex than that." *As Mary's white co-trainer, I was painfully aware that there had been no interruptions or questions during my earlier facilitation. Further, given that Mary had specifically asked white people to just listen, I felt unsettled by the continued questions from this white* *woman. Her behavior invalidated Mary's presentation, conveying that she knew Mary's reality better than Mary herself. In claiming that internalized racial oppression was "more complex" than Mary – who actually experienced it – described, the white participant ultimately reinforced the racist premise that African Americans are not as intelligent as whites.*

I did not want to take over and "rescue" Mary by assuming she needed my intervention, as that would risk reinforcing the same problematic dynamics already at play. Yet to sit back as a white woman and leave Mary to deal with this aggression on her own was not acceptable. I decided to check in with Mary. I leaned in and quietly asked her if she would like me to intervene. She said yes. I spoke up, saying, "I would like to pause for a teachable moment here." I then laid out what was racially problematic about the participant's engagement. The room erupted, with half the group defending my intervention and the other half claiming by naming the dynamics in the room I was mistreating the white participant. I quickly checked back in with Mary on next steps, and she suggested that we break the participants into racial affinity groups to diffuse the tension and allow each group to discuss the racial dynamics in the room. Although I wish I could say that the white woman received my intervention well, she did not. She withdrew in anger. However, it was a powerful lesson for the rest of the group. The people of color were reassured that I would not be complicit in Mary's invalidation through silence, and white participants were able to see a white person take a constructive stand in the face of microaggressions while not undermining the leadership of a person of color. While it was anxiety-producing to speak up and to bear the back-lash of white fragility, it was critical for me personally and as a model for other white people to break with white solidarity and step into the risk of conflict in service of racial justice.

Act 2: Perpetrator

I was co-leading a training for a racially diverse group of human service professionals about racial disparities in the child welfare system. In sharing an example of the racism tribal communities endure, I recalled an incident in which white adults and their children hurled the epithet, "praire-n...," at indigenous youth participating in a cultural event. My use of that term – in full – had an impact on the African American people in the room that I did not see or understand. I continued with the workshop; they could not.

Most of us occupy at least one dominant social location, by virtue of our professional status, age, ability, race, gender identity, sexual orientation, class, or other social identity. We are socialized into these power relations without our choice, and they shape how we understand the world, ourselves, and others. It is inevitable, often despite our best intentions, that where we occupy positions of dominance, we will act in ways that perpetuate oppression.

Look into rather than away from our oppressive patterns

Social workers have a responsibility to attune to our interactions within and across group lines, to notice how we are responding to others and how others respond to us (Taylor, 2013). We can train ourselves to become more aware of our internal frameworks, which include implicit biases and assumptions, as well as our external behaviors – the ways we act from these frameworks. While it is our obligation to be self-reflective, as people socialized into color-blind ideologies and thus trained to *not see* oppression, it is inevitable that we will have blind spots (Bonilla Silva, 2014). Further, because mainstream society teaches us that people who engage in oppressive acts are immoral, we often respond to the suggestion that we have acted in ways that are hurtful with defensiveness and denial. However, because most microaggressions are unaware and unintentional, it is imperative that we openly receive and honestly consider this feedback whenever it is offered. We can assume that racism, sexism, and classism are always operating in every social setting, whether it is visible to us or not. Given this, the question is not, *did oppression occur*, but rather *how is it occurring in this specific context* (DiAngelo, 2016)?

Accountability is a process, not a procedure

There is not a single action one takes to "be accountable" for one's actions and move on. Rather, accountability requires a long-term commitment to assuming responsibility for the consequences of our actions, regardless of our intentions. We are accountable to those immediately affected as well as those with whom we will have future contact. We are also accountable to ourselves and our profession, and to the alignment of our professed values with our actual behaviors. The process of accountability begins with an initial assessment of the impact of our actions. Results of our microaggressions may include causing others pain, contributing to oppressive messages and representations, damaging group functioning, weakening community trust, tarnishing our credibility, and jeopardizing our personal and professional relationships. It is often essential to seek consultation from someone who can help us process our own feelings (such as confusion, shame, and grief) and assist us in thinking through the consequences of our actions and possibilities for reparation.

Seek restorative action

When we learn that we have acted in ways that cause others harm, it is often appropriate to meet with persons directly affected by our actions. In so doing we can acknowledge our conduct, articulate how we plan to change our behavior, invite them to share the impact of our actions, and ask if there is anything they need to say or hear in order to continue our work together.

Microaggressions that occur in a group setting often require restorative action within the group as a whole (though additional one-on-one work may also be needed). In an organizational context, microaggressions can be an indicator that institutional responses are needed, such as improved staff training or revisions to outdated protocols.

The purpose of restorative action is to ameliorate oppression, not to ask for forgiveness or reassurance. Trust is rebuilt over time, and we should not press people in order to relieve our own impatience and/or anxiety. There is always a risk that we may not be able to repair the relationship with a person or group, but we certainly can't move forward in a constructive way without first taking responsibility for our behavior. More often than not, we have found that people targeted by microaggressions respond to authentic attempts at restorative action with appreciation, generosity, and a desire to move collective work forward. We return to the vignette opening Act 2 to illustrate these principles in practice.

I continued with the workshop; they could not

Looking back, it is painful to remember the arrogance and ignorance I now realize that I exhibited in that training. It only came to my attention at the end of the day, when a white woman approached me and said, "We have a problem. A number of the African American people are upset about what you said." *Although not a novice educator at the time, I was stunningly unaware I had done anything problematic. Oblivious, I asked her what I had said.* "The n-word." *I glanced toward my co-facilitator, an African American woman, and noticed she was intently listening to a group of African American participants who were obviously distressed. Clearly, we did have a problem.*

My co-facilitator and I spent the next several hours talking through what happened and formulating a plan for our last day with the group. Much of this time was spent with her generously investing in my continued education. As I listened to my colleague, my awareness of my own internalized dominance deepened. I had believed that I had the authority to use the hurtful language as a teaching tool because my intention was clearly good – I was advancing dialogue about racism. As my understanding of the impact of my language grew, I ached for the suffering I had caused, burned with the humiliation of not having known better, and was furious at myself for letting down my co-facilitator, a woman I deeply admire. I had compromised my credibility, and my actions reflected poorly on her and the work we were leading together. Nonetheless, by the end of the day we had a plan.

The next morning my colleague opened the session. "When we lead this work, inevitably someone – a participant, a co-trainer, or yourself – will do or say something that is unintentionally hurtful to someone else; someone will make a mistake. Part of what we want to model today is how to clean up those mistakes. Amie made a mistake yesterday. I'm going to invite her to say something to the group, and then invite you to share what it was like for you to have this happen in yesterday's session." *I then addressed the group. I acknowledged the harm I had caused, apologized for my behavior, and made a commitment that I would never make the same mistake again. My colleague then invited participants to share their reflections. Several African American participants thanked her for creating the space to share, reflecting that it had been incredibly hard to hear me use that word. One woman said, "I know what you were trying to do, but once I heard that word I couldn't hear anything else all day." One man said that if I could make that mistake, then clearly I did not belong in this field. Several younger African American participants said my use of the word – given the context – didn't bother them, and one of the few indigenous women in the room shared, "That word didn't bother me; I've heard it my whole life."*

When there were no more hands raised, I thanked everyone for sharing their perspectives, acknowledged the range of impacts, and apologized again for the pain I had caused. We then continued with the training. As we closed out that afternoon, we asked for highlights from the three-day session. One older African American woman spoke up, "My highlight of the three days was this morning. It's not uncommon that white people make mistakes. It is uncommon that they apologize. Thank you."

Act 3: Target

I am a participant in a week-long training designed to help educators make pedagogical connections between the Jewish holocaust and the genocide of indigenous North American tribes. Asked to share what drew us to the course, I speak of my Jewish heritage. When the introductions reach the other side of the room, a white, Protestant-identified woman shares that she was motivated to attend by her pain over the continued injustice in the world, including that perpetrated by the state of Israel. She swivels her head toward me, points her finger at me accusingly, and says, "You and I will have to have a talk."

Our multiple social locations become more or less salient in any given context. In the previous vignette my (Amie) racial dominance was most salient. This time, my Jewish identity was at the forefront of my experience. Responding to microaggressions when you are the target poses distinct challenges.

Your first responsibility is to yourself

Whether seemingly indirect and impersonal, or specific and targeted, experiencing microaggressions can be deeply disorienting. You may immediately feel pulled *out of* your body, unmoored, adrift, numb or shut down. You may immediately be pulled *into* your body, aware of little else beyond the pumping of your blood and the beating of your heart. You may feel fear or anger, pain, or shock. Because they are so common and so often denied, you may not even notice the offense at all. When we, as human service professionals, find ourselves targeted with microaggressions, it is critical to notice and affirm what we are feeling, and take time to re-center. You don't have to – and often are unable to – respond in the moment. Re-centering practices might include physical activity, a cultural and/spiritual ritual, talking it through with others who share your identity or an understanding ally, journaling, or quiet reflection. Centering reconnects us to the internal and external resources available to help address the harm we have experienced.

Consider possibilities for action

Our initial reactions to microaggressions often come before we have time to reflect and center. In the absence of such time, we simply do our best – we are sometimes thoughtful, sometimes reactive, and sometimes avoidant. Yet regardless of how you respond in the moment, there are almost always follow-up opportunities. Considering these possibilities requires discernment, beginning with identifying what you hope to achieve. You may have short-term objectives related to follow-up with a specific person or group, or longer-term changes related to policy or broader social change efforts. Once you have identified your goals, you can evaluate possible strategies for moving forward. It is critical to weigh possible risks and benefits to your own and others' well-being, security, and safety. Talking with a trusted friend or colleague can provide useful clarity and perspective, although ultimately it is up to each of us to decide for ourselves how to respond.

Reclaim your voice

When targeted by microaggressions, you may feel an internal responsibility to speak out on your own behalf or an obligation to speak on behalf of others who share your identity. You may also receive external pressure to respond from colleagues or supervisors. Yet targets of oppression do not *owe* a response to anyone. You always have the choice to respond, and given the risks of confronting microaggressions that may be perpetrated by people with social and/or institutional power over us, you may choose not to respond at all. To *not respond* directly when you are the victim is not the same as not responding when you are a witness or perpetrator; because of the difference in power positions, it is one of several *valid and strategic choices* in service of your mental health.

Should you choose to act, you can reclaim our voice in powerful ways: speaking up to the aggressor, enlisting allies, going to an affinity group for support, or starting a campaign or other political action. You can also use silence as an act of resistance to oppressive interactions, refusing to educate others about the impacts of their behavior and refraining from opening yourself up to further attack. We return now to the opening vignette to illustrate how these principles shaped one response to being the target of a microaggression.

"You and I will have to have a talk." *I had been listening intently to this stranger's introduction, and was shocked to suddenly find her remarks directed at me, and with such apparent hostility. The room was full of seasoned educators and our facilitators were highly skilled. Yet after a brief pause, the next person began their introduction as if nothing had happened. Had something happened? I looked around for a reassuring glance from someone; no one met my eyes. I felt my face flush and my throat constrict. I wrote down her words so I wouldn't forget. Through the rest of the day I struggled to remain present, stewing in shock, anger, pain, confusion, isolation, disappointment, and surprise by my surprise. I was clearly unprepared for this experience.*

The day included time for reflective writing, which I used to process my initial reactions. By the end of the day, though still disappointed that no one in the room had intervened, I felt compelled to speak up. I approached the woman and asked if she had a minute to talk. She did. "So," *I began,* "It sounds like you have some strong feelings about Israel." *She took the invitation to recount her concerns about the treatment of Palestinians, speaking with both passion and the fierceness of someone waiting to be challenged. I listened, thanked her for sharing, and reflected,* "It also sounds like you made some decisions about where you thought I stood on Israel." *After an awkward moment of silence followed by some incomplete references to the couple of Jewish people she once knew, she softened:* "You're right. I did make an assumption – I don't know what you think." *I suggested that if she wanted to know what I thought, she could ask. She agreed and we moved forward.*

Conclusion

Microaggressions cause harm, damaging people's sense of humanity as well as our social relationships. After just a few hours or weeks of studying oppression, many the people we work with grow impatient and want us to *just tell them what to do* when they see a microaggression. This is a lifelong journey without a quick fix. The desire for easy answers may be driven by a deep discomfort with *not knowing*, a sense of desperation and feelings of powerlessness. While these feelings are understandable, the drive to skip over the hard work of critical analysis and self-reflection must be resisted. Even if there were a recipe for interrupting microaggressions, handing human service providers a list of quick-fix behaviors before people fully understand the issues risks making behavior more problematic, rather than less.

Instead of a recipe for action, we offered a set of guiding principles for responding to microaggressions from the positions of witness, perpetrator, or target. Yet even this is an oversimplification. Each of us is embedded in complex socio-political power relations, and embody multiple and intersecting identities. We may find ourselves as witness, perpetrator and target of microaggressions in a single day, or even in a single interaction. Developing the skills, perspectives, and capacity to repair the harm caused by microaggressions requires us to challenge our socialization in new and often uncomfortable ways. While we do not suggest this process is easy, we can testify that taking the risk to respond to microaggressions offers a powerful opportunity to restore humanity and repair relationships in the face of oppression. We don't have it have it all figured out before we act. The deepest learning often comes from our mistakes. We may not get it right by everybody, but what is most important is that we step into the struggle for justice. Doing so is the most exciting, powerful, intellectually stimulating and emotionally fulfilling journey we have ever undertaken.

Acknowledgments

We are grateful to the many friends and colleagues who have invested in our development and informed our thinking with regard to responding to microaggressions, in particular Deborah Terry-Hays. We also wish to thank Ryan Tolleson Knee and Lia Saroyan for their contributions to earlier versions of this manuscript.

References

Bonilla-Silva, E. (2014). *Racism without racists: Color-blind racism and the persistence of racial inequality in America*. Plymouth, UK: Rowman & Littlefield Publishers.

Constantine, M. (2007). Racial microaggressions against African American clients in cross-racial counseling relationships. *Journal of Counseling Psychology, 54*(1), 1–16. doi:10.1037/0022-0167.54.1.1

DiAngelo, R. (2012). White fragility. *International Journal of Critical Pedagogy, 3*(3), 54–70.

DiAngelo, R. (2016). *What does it mean to be white?: Developing white racial literacy* (2nd ed.). New York, NY: Peter Lang.

DiAngelo, R., & Sensoy, O. (2014). Calling In: Strategies for cultivating humility and critical thinking in antiracism education. *Journal of Understanding and Dismantling Privilege, 4*(2), 192–203.

National Association of Social Workers. (2008). *NASW code of ethics*. Washington, DC: NASW.

Sue, D. W., Capodilupo, C. M., Torino, G. C., Bucceri, J. M., Holder, A. M. B., Nadal, K. L., & Esquilin, M. (2007). Racial microaggressions in everyday life: Implications for clinical practice. *American Psychologist, 62*(4), 271–286. doi:10.1037/0003-066X.62.4.271

Taylor, C. (2013). Critically reflexive practice. In: M. Gray, & S. A. Webb (Eds.), *The new politics of social work* (pp. 79–98). New York, NY: Palgrave Macmillan.

Teaching racial microaggressions: implications of critical race hypos for social work praxis

Lindsay Pérez Huber and Daniel G. Solorzano

ABSTRACT

This article provides a conceptual understanding of racial microaggressions from a critical race theoretical (CRT) perspective, as relevant to the field of Social Work. To do this, we utilize *Critical Race Hypos*, hypothetical pedagogical tools developed from existing literature on racial microaggressions, and meant to engage critical dialogue on everyday racism in the lives of People of Color. We explain the pedagogical utility of *Critical Race Hypos* for engaging discussions about racial microaggressions in social work training. This article provides three Critical Race Hypos that focus on common questions about racial microaggressions set within the context of a social work graduate program classroom. The article concludes with implications of these hypos for social work theory and practice.

We are critical race theorists in education who have been engaged in research on racial microaggressions for almost two decades. What drew us to this research was the powerful way racial microaggressions affords People of Color to name the everyday, incessant, and cumulative forms of racism they experience. These often subtle forms of racism can be wrongly perceived as insignificant and frequently dismissed (Solorzano, 1998). As a conceptual framework, racial microaggressions names and validates the racism that targets People of Color in everyday life.

As we will show in this article, racial microaggressions can also serve as an effective pedagogical framework to teach race and racism. We offer this article as a response to the need to have meaningful discussions about race and racism in social work training. This article provides a brief overview of the theoretical position we take, critical race theory (CRT) in Education that has led to our theorizing of racial microaggressions. We then present three Critical Race Hypos as pedagogical tools to explore racial microaggressions. We argue that these hypos can engage effective discussions on everyday racism in social work classrooms and beyond. We conclude with reflections and implications of these pedagogical tools.

Color versions of one or more of the figures in the article can be found online at www.tandfonline.com/WECD.

Critical race theory and social work

CRT originated in the 1980s from the work of lawyers, activists, and legal scholars as a new strategy for dealing with the emergence of a post-Civil Rights racial structure in the United States. CRT in the Law challenged the dominant discourse on race and racism by examining how legal doctrine is used to subordinate and marginalize certain racial and ethnic groups. In the mid-1990s CRT moved to the field of Education (Ladson-Billings & Tate, 1995; Solorzano, 1997). Solorzano (1997) defined CRT in Education as the work of scholars and practitioners who are attempting to develop an explanatory framework that accounts for the role of race and racism in Education, and that works toward identifying and challenging racism as part of a larger goal of identifying and challenging all forms of subordination. Solorzano posited five tenets that form the basic perspectives, research methods, and pedagogy of a CRT in Education that we believe can be adapted for use in social work.[1] A CRT perspective includes the following: (1) the centrality of race and racism and intersectionality with other forms of subordination, (2) the challenge to dominant ideologies that frame Communities of Color as deficient, (3) the centrality of experiential knowledge of Communities of Color, (4) the interdisciplinary perspectives necessary to understand the complexities of oppression and resistance, and (5) the commitment to social justice.

In this article, we argue that each of these five tenets are not new in and of themselves, but, collectively, they represent a challenge to existing modes of scholarship (see Razack & Jeffery, 2002). We define a CRT in Social Work as a set of basic perspectives, methods, and pedagogy that seeks to identify, analyze, and transform those structural, cultural, and interpersonal aspects of society that maintain the racial, gender, and class subordination of Communities of Color (i.e., racism and white supremacy). Indeed, CRT in Social Work is critical and different from other frameworks because (1) it challenges the traditional paradigms, texts, and separate discourses on race, gender, and class by showing how they intersect to impact the everyday lives of Communities of Color, (2) it helps focus on the racialized, gendered, and classed experiences of Communities of Color, (3) it offers a liberatory or transformative solution to racial, gender, and class oppression, and (4) it utilizes the interdisciplinary knowledge base of Education, Law, Ethnic Studies, Woman's Studies, History, Social Work, Psychology, and Sociology to better understand experiences of Communities of Color. It should be noted that CRT in Social Work is not static, and we should use (and extend) as many of the five tenets as possible to examine the everyday experiences of Communities of Color.[2] CRT in Social Work can also be used to understand the experiences of Students and Faculty of Color in social work classrooms, as well as the experiences of Clients of Color in their respective communities.

CRT provides important tools for theorizing and teaching race and racism generally, and in social work in particular. One underdeveloped Critical Race tool in the Social Work literature is racial microaggressions (see Ross-Sheriff, 2012; Wright, 2013).

Racial microaggressions

Racial microaggression is a concept grounded in more than four decades of research. It began with the work of Harvard University professor Dr. Chester Pierce, who initially coined the term in 1970 (Pierce, 1970). Racial microaggressions are those manifestations of racism that People of Color encounter in their everyday public and private lives. Specifically, racial microaggressions are one form of systemic racism that (a) are verbal and non-verbal assaults directed toward People of Color, often carried out automatically or unconsciously; (b) are based on a Person of Color's race, gender, class, sexuality, language, immigration status, phenotype, accent, or surname; and (c) are cumulative—taking a physiological, psychological, and academic toll on those targeted by them. Racial microaggressions are particularly significant for social workers, whose professional goals include supporting and improving the well-being of others.[3]

Critical race hypos

In the late 1990s, Yamamoto (1997) posed the challenge to Critical Race scholars to connect CRT with everyday experiences of People of Color. We argue that racial microaggressions are not only conceptually relevant to Critical Race research but also to pedagogy. Microaggressions can help build a bridge between theory and practice—engaging in Critical Race Praxis (Yamamoto, 1997). It provides a conceptual tool for People of Color to "name their pain," as an anti-oppressive strategy necessary in the process of liberation (Freire, 1970). Thus, in the Freirean sense, the naming of the construct of microaggressions becomes a critical pedagogical tool that enables People of Color to name the racism encountered in their everyday lives in order to confront and challenge it. It is precisely this connection between theory and lived experience where we see racial microaggressions as a form of Critical Race Praxis. In the following section, we employ microaggressions as praxis, connecting the conceptual framework we provide earlier with the everyday experiences of People of Color. In line with Critical Race Praxis, we provide critical race "hypotheticals" or "hypos." Critical Race Hypos build on Bell's (1999) "racial hypos" that utilized the traditional pedagogical practices of case law hypotheticals to engage law-school students in the "contradictions and dilemmas faced by those attempting to apply legal rules to the many forms of racial discrimination" that exist in US society (p.316).[4] Similar to Bell, we use the pedagogical tool of Critical Race Hypos to show the ways racism emerges in the everyday experiences of People of Color, through racial microaggressions. We use the term *Critical Race Hypos*, because we believe this pedagogical tool can be useful for discussions that extend beyond race, to other social locations and intersectional positionalities that are significant in the lives and experiences of People of Color.

Similar to Bell's (1999) use of "racial hypos," these Critical Race Hypos are not fictional, but based on scholarly research. Unlike Bell's use of racial hypos, the Critical Race Hypos provided here include a response.[5] However, there are many responses possible for these hypos. We have crafted responses grounded in research, teaching, and personal experiences with microaggressions. We hope this section prompts readers to consider how these hypos can be used in their own classrooms within social work and beyond to prompt discussions, reflections, and responses to race, racism, and racial microaggressions.

These Critical Race Hypos are based on three common questions about racial microaggressions. Each hypo has been constructed to address each of these questions, which include the following: (1) What are racial microaggressions? (2) Why the focus on the target and not the perpetrator in the analysis of racial microaggressions?, and (3) Can People of Color perpetrate microaggressions against other People of Color? Before presenting these hypos we set up the "hypothetical" scene for the reader to understand the context of "Critical Race Hypo no. 1" and those that follow.

The scene

The hypothetical scene where our hypos take place are in Dr. Cynthia Lara's graduate course, "Social Work Macro Practice: Oppression and Social Justice." This class is offered as a required course for the masters in social work program at Saint Michaels University. In this hypo, Dr. Lara is engaged in a presentation with her class to better understand the conceptual framework of racial microaggressions. This presentation has several objectives for Professor Lara. She hopes the presentation and discussion will allow the class to engage in a critical dialogue about everyday racism and its effects on People of Color. In addition, she hopes it will allow students to see the connection of everyday racism with larger systems of oppression, and how an understanding of racial microaggressions is useful for social work professionals interested in the well-being of Communities of Color. Her 30 students are mostly white, and from middle-class and upper-middle class backgrounds. There are four Students of Color in the class, including Anna and Nadia, two Latina women, Kevin, an African-American male student, and Tasha, an African-American female—all from working-class backgrounds. Saint Michaels University is located in the Southern California area, and as such, the graduate students in her program will most likely pursue their careers as social workers in the diverse communities of greater Los Angeles. Dr. Lara has prepared a multi-media PowerPoint presentation that includes definitions of racism and models to understand racial microaggressions. The class has also been assigned a reading to help facilitate discussion. She begins the class in Critical Race Hypo no. 1.

Critical Race Hypo no. 1: What are racial microaggressions?

Dr. Lara begins:

> Let's take out our readings for today. In preparation for our class discussion, you have read about racial microaggressions (Pérez Huber & Solorzano, 2015a). Let's begin with an understanding of what racial microaggressions look like in the experiences of People of Color. I'd like to share with you a media clip from a television show some of you may know. This clip is from *Saturday Night Live*, and it features a skit with African-American actress and performer, Queen Latifah. The skit is a parody of an Excedrin commercial, where Queen Latifah plays "Linda," and discusses what it's like to be one of the only African American women in her workplace. The skit is called "Excedrin for Racial Tension Headaches." I am providing you with the transcript as well.

Dr. Lara hands out the printed transcript of the skit to each student and plays the media clip. She asks students to follow through the transcript as the clip plays (Fey, Steele, and McCarthy-Miller, October 2004).

> [Queen Latifah on screen, close-up on face]
>
> Queen Latifah: Do I get stress headaches at work? Yes, definitely. From the moment I get in, it's "Denise, we need this," "Denise we need that." Which is stressful, because my name is Linda. Denise is the other black woman that works here. By 10 a.m., someone in the copy room makes a joke about Kobe Bryant, and everyone looks at me to make sure it's okay. And I smile like it's okay, but, really, my head and neck are starting to throb. Then, I spend the rest of the afternoon training my interns and answering their questions, like, "Yes, black people use shampoo," and "No, I don't know any good reggae clubs around here,' and 'Yes, Condoleezza Rice is very articulate, why do you sound so surprised?" And, "No, I can't tell you where to buy weed!"
>
> [audience laughter, holds up product]
>
> And that's when I reach for Excedrin. New Excedrin for Racial Tension Headaches. Excedrin R.T. works fast. Taking me from "Oh no you didn't!" to "I wish a mother [bleep] would!
>
> [narrator off screen]
>
> Excedrin…for Racial Tension Headaches. Fast relief for hundreds of years of nagging pain.
>
> [audience laughter]

The class laughed following the clip. Dr. Lara follows up, "In this short clip, the character of Linda takes us through several examples of racial microaggressions. Yes, it's funny, but this is more than comedy. What are the microaggressions we saw?"

Response to Critical Race Hypo no. 1

Dr. Lara projected a figure for the class on the screen (Figure 1). "I'd like to use this model from the reading to help us" (see Pérez Huber & Solorzano, 2015a).

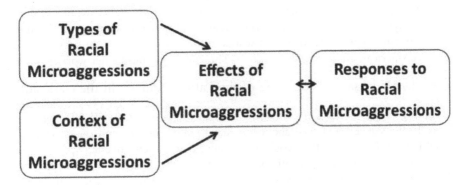

Figure 1. Types, context, effects, and responses to racial microaggressions.

Dr. Lara referred students to the model and began, "In your readings, Pérez Huber and Solorzano provide this model to help explain how People of Color experience microaggressions. According to the model, there are types, contexts, effects and responses to racial microaggressions."

Dr. Lara continued to explain each of these elements.

The "types" describes how one is targeted by this form of everyday racism. This can be according to one's race/ethnicity, their class status, gender, language, sexuality, immigration status, phenotype, accents or surname. The "context" describes where and how the microaggression occurs. For example, the context can be in a classroom, a store, the doctor's office, a client's home, in the workplace, or on the street.

She pauses and points to the word, "effects." She continued:

Now, there are also effects that microaggressions have on People of Color who are consistently targeted by them. Examples of effects could be self-doubt, anger, stress, poor academic performance and poor health outcomes. Finally, the model describes the responses People of Color have to them. These responses can be denying they exist, or self-policing (i.e., not going to certain restaurants or stores). However, responses can often challenge incidents of racial microaggressions, such as creating counterspaces where one can heal from the daily barrage of this everyday racism (Ek, Cerecer, Alanis, and Rodriguez, 2010).

Dr. Lara poses the question to the class, "So how would we use this model to analyze the experiences of Queen Latifah's character in the skit?"

A white male student, Martin, quickly responds. He answers, "Well, when I first saw this, I just thought it was funny. I don't think her co-workers meant to insult her, they were probably joking." Dr. Lara says, "Ok, but as I mentioned earlier, these were more than just racial jokes. Tell us what was happening?" (Solorzano, 1998). She looks around the room to show that she does not expect the response to come from Martin alone. Martin remains silent, but Emily, a white female student in the class responds:

> Well, the type of microaggression is a racial microaggression, right? She mentioned the stereotypic comments her co-workers make and how they confuse her for the other African American woman that works in the office, which insinuates that all African American women look the same. The context would be her workplace.

"Ok," Dr. Lara says. Nadia, one of the Latina students in the class, adds:

> According to the model there are also effects and responses to racial microaggressions. In the skit, Linda talked about how her head "throbbed" and she develops a racial tension headache—this would be an effect. At the end of the clip, she also shows how she responds to the microaggression by taking Excedrin R.T. and gaining the strength to challenge this racism in the comments she makes right at the end.

Dr. Lara responds:

> Exactly. I agree with your analysis, Nadia. You and Emily have explained that the model seems to be an effective tool in allowing us to understand the types, context, effects, and responses to the racial microaggressions Queen Latifah's character experiences. These microaggressions can be subtle acts, such as pronouncing a name wrong, or being called upon as the "spokesperson" for one's racial group (Kohli & Solorzano, 2012).

Linda also alludes to other microaggressions she experienced, such as criminalization, when she said her coworkers assume she knows where to buy drugs (Smith, Allen, Danley, 2007). Nadia replies, "So in this one-minute skit, Linda takes us through the model of racial microaggressions, telling us how she experiences types, context, effects, and responses." Martin interrupts, "Ok, but I don't understand how this is useful for *us*. We're in social work." There is a silence.

Dr. Lara refrains from responding, hoping a student will. Kenneth, the only African-American male student says:

> I do. I can see how this is really useful for those of us who will work in Communities of Color. The model allows me to name experiences I go through almost everyday; that my family and friends experience everyday as African Americans. Some of those same comments have been directed to me, by other students in this program.

Kenneth pauses for an uncomfortable silence. "I have lived those effects in the model, I have felt the sting of microaggressions when they happen, and the burden they cause over time" (Yosso, Smith, Ceja, & Solorzano, 2009). He continues, "But it is also useful for me as a future social worker in the field. When I work with other People of Color, this model also provides a *name for their pain*, it validates their experiences, rather than dismissing them (Freire, 1970). Understanding the unique challenges Communities of

Color face in their well-being, is our responsibility as social workers (see Woody & Green, 2001). How effective we are in our professions depends on our ability to help our clients navigate these challenges."

Critical Race Hypo no. 2: Why the focus on the "target" of microaggressions?

Dr. Lara nodded her head and responded, "Kenneth, that's an important point, and this is precisely the purpose of these models—to be used as tools for those of us working in the field with diverse populations." Meredith, a white female student in the class raises her hand. Dr. Lara nods, signaling her to contribute to the discussion. Meredith comments, "I see how microaggressions are useful, but we have been only talking about how People of Color experience them. Isn't it also important to understand how people might engage this everyday racism, but not know they are microaggressing?" Martin quickly adds:

> Right, I agree. I was a psychology major in undergrad, and we used a term that seems similar to microaggressions, implicit bias. Implicit bias is a concept developed in psychology to understand how people can automatically or unconsciously act in discriminatory ways, although they don't intend to do so (Greenwald & Krieger, 2006). There's even a test that was developed to reveal your hidden biases.[6]

Martin continues, "Don't you think this concept is much more useful for social workers? I think it helps us, as social workers, understand the hidden biases we might have when we are working in diverse communities."

Response to racial microaggressions Hypo no. 2

Dr. Lara responded, "Yes, this is a question I get often." Dr. Lara advances the PowerPoint to another model (see Figure 2). "I think this model can help

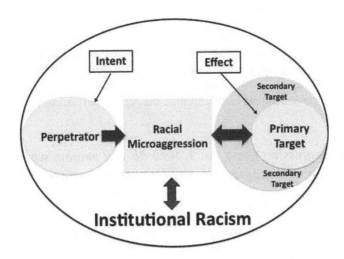

Figure 2. Targets and perpetrators of racial microaggressions.

us. What you seem to be asking is about the perpetrator and the target of microaggressions."

Dr. Lara points to the term, "institutional racism" and begins to explain:

This model positions racial microaggressions within a system of institutional racism. According to Pérez Huber and Solorzano (2015a), institutional racism can be understood as formal or informal structural mechanisms, such as policies and processes that systematically subordinate, marginalize, and exclude People of Color that mediate experiences with racial microaggressions. Now, this model is important because it illustrates that microaggressions are much more than interpersonal exchanges—they exist because of the ideology and structures that perpetuate and reproduce racism.

Dr. Lara looks to Martin and continues, "Martin, let me get to your question with this figure. Yes, implicit bias is similar in that it also seeks to understand the unconscious or automatic ways a perpetrator might enact a microaggression" (Greenwald & Krieger, 2006). She continued:

In this model, there is a perpetrator of the microaggression, someone or something that enacts racism. There is also a target of the microaggression, who it was directed toward. When a racial microaggression occurs, the primary target is the Person of Color the microaggression was directed to. However, there can also be secondary targets impacted, even though they did not directly experience it.

Dr. Lara points to the term "intent" in the model. "So, implicit bias is concerned with the intent of the perpetrator. Now, I am a Critical Race Theorist, so I am more concerned with the effects of microaggressions on People of Color " [pointing to the model]. Tasha chimed in, "this is the third CRT tenet, the centrality of experiential knowledge." Professor Lara continued, "Exactly, Tasha. I focus on the target and not the perpetrator because using a CRT lens means that my research focus is on the lived experiences of People of Color, and understanding how racism mediates *their* daily lives." Anna's face lit up. She added:

Racial microaggressions then, make a lot of sense for our profession. If we are committed to supporting the well-being of others, we *should* be more concerned about the ways everyday racism impacts People of Color, rather than understanding whether a perpetrator was intentional or not. In many ways, racial microaggressions are the enactment of the implicit bias of the perpetrator.

Racial microaggression Hypo no. 3: How do you explain when People of Color engage in microaggressive acts against each other?

Anna transitioned the discussion with a question:

Dr. Lara, I see how these frameworks can be used to understand microaggressions. But I'm thinking about the experiences we have within our own communities, with other People of Color who may engage microaggressions. For example, I grew up in Boyle Heights, an area of Los Angeles that is almost exclusively Latina/o. Growing up, some of the most painful forms of discrimination I have experienced were being teased for having an accent, or having a darker skin tone. However, many of the perpetrators were other Latinas/os. How do we explain when People of Color engage in microaggressive acts against each other?

Martin adds, "I'm also curious about this. Are only whites considered perpetrators? That's what the model suggests to me (see Figure 2). I agree with Anna. Perpetrators can't exclusively be white people."

Response to racial microaggressions Hypo no. 3

Dr. Lara paused to see if one of the students had a response. Kenneth interjected, "Well, let's revisit our definitions of racism, Dr. Lara." Dr. Lara went back through the PowerPoint presentation and projected a slide with the definition of racism. Kenneth began to read it out loud (see Figure 3):

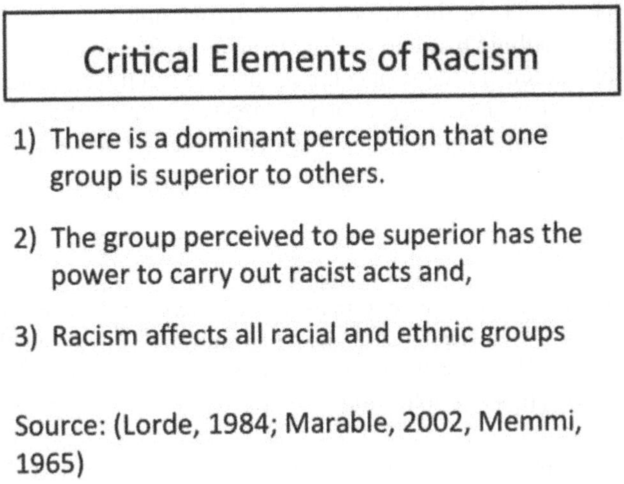

Critical Elements of Racism

1) There is a dominant perception that one group is superior to others.

2) The group perceived to be superior has the power to carry out racist acts and,

3) Racism affects all racial and ethnic groups

Source: (Lorde, 1984; Marable, 2002, Memmi, 1965)

Figure 3. Critical elements of racism.

According to Audre Lorde, Manning Marable, and Albert Memmi, there are three critical elements of racism: (1) there is a dominant perception that one group is superior to others, (2) the group perceived to be "superior" has the power to carry out racist acts and, (3) racism affects all racial and ethnic groups (Lorde, 1984; Marable, 2002; Memmi, 1965; Solorzano, Ceja, & Yosso, 2000).

Anna responded, "So, going back to the concept of racial microaggressions, I can see how they are carried out because of a perceived superiority of whites. But going back to my question, don't People of Color also internalize these perceptions?" Kenneth responded:

Well, I think the answer to that question is, yes. People of Color do internalize perceptions of white superiority. Malcolm X (see Worth and Pearl, 1972) explained this in a speech in the early 1960s and he began with a similar question, "Who taught you to hate yourself?" In this speech, he cautioned African Americans of the ways we can internalize white superiority through various forms of media. But I think we need to return to your initial questions, Anna and Martin—Can People of Color engage in racial microaggressions? According to this definition they can't.

Martin interjects, "Now, I'm sorry, but I don't buy that. Anna said:

I don't think I agree with that either. I've been in plenty of discussions with other Latinas/os who feel they are superior to, for example, other Latina/o immigrants. I have another example—my younger brother has been *consistently* harassed by police growing up in my community. But many of these officers are other Latinos. How could that not be racism?

Kenneth responded:

I know these can be very painful experiences. I've seen this in my community as well. However, I don't see this as racism. I think we understand racism to be an abhorrent act, something that creates deep pain, anguish, and anger. When we see or hear acts of "racism" in our own communities, we feel those emotions. In fact, I would say, that sometimes these experiences are even more hurtful when acted out by other People of Color, other people [Kenneth makes air quotes with his fingers] "like us."

He adds:

But those emotions do not equate to racism. We have to understand that racism is not only a perceived superiority, but that the "superior" group has the power to carry out racist acts. Historically, People of Color in the U.S. have never possessed that power (Pérez Huber & Solorzano, 2015b).

The class fell silent for a few moments. Anna responded, "I think I see your point with the definition. Microaggressions occur because of the structures of institutional racism that remain in place, like the model we saw earlier" (see Figure 2). Kenneth responded:

I would argue, yes. The underlying racist ideologies that uphold these structures provide the justification for those structures to exist. So, the power to create and maintain those structures is key. While some People of Color may have internalized those ideologies, historically, we have never possessed the power to create the institutions where resources are unequally distributed.

Kenneth continued, "But we can contribute to maintaining these structures by perpetuating racism within our own communities, with other Communities of Color, and maybe by acting on behalf of white interests as in the case of the Latino police officer." Dr. Lara interjected, "I think I have a model that can help explain. Dr. Lara advanced another slide in her PowerPoint presentation" (Figure 4).

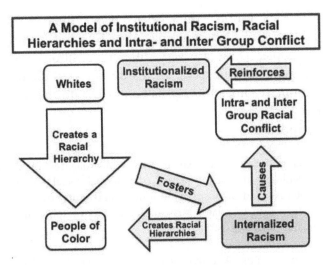

Figure 4. A model of institutional racism, racial hierarchies, and intra- and inter-group conflict. For an earlier version of this model, see Kohli and Solorzano (2011).

"I think about this question as well Anna, and I've developed this model to help make sense of the racial conflict that occurs within and between Communities of Color. Let me walk us through this model and see if it can help us."

Dr. Lara began:

The model begins with institutionalized racism. Institutionalized racism creates a racial hierarchy that places whites above People of Color, as illustrated on the left side of this model. That hierarchy fosters internalized racism in the right corner of the model. When People of Color internalize this racism, there are consequences. Internalized racism can reinforce and recreate racial hierarchies within and between People of Color and cause intra- and inter group racial conflict. Intra-group meaning the conflict that arises within racial groups, such as Anna's example of her brother with other Latina/o police officers. Inter-group conflict occurs between different racial groups. These conflicts reinforce a cycle of institutionalized racism where whites and whiteness are perceived to be superior.

Dr. Lara paused for a response. Anna comments:

So, to go back to our question about whether People of Color can engage in microaggressions, this model tells us that a better way to describe these experiences are intra- and inter-group racial conflict that emerges from the very structures and practices of institutional racism. But something else comes up for me when I see this model. When we talk about the (re)production of racial hierarchies, what we are really talking about is white supremacy. Dr. Lara, I think it's important to name these racist ideologies. It is the beliefs and ideologies of white supremacy that create racial hierarchies that are reinforced by institutional racism—.

Martin abruptly interrupts, "Wait, so now I'm supposed to believe that white supremacy is to blame for microaggressions? So, does that make me a white supremacist? I can't agree with that." Martin's voice was raised. Dr.

Lara responded, "No, I don't think that's what Anna is saying. She is identifying the ideological underpinnings of racism, not blaming any particular group of people. These are very different positions." Martin looked confused. Anna was quiet (silenced). Dr. Lara redirected the discussion, "I'd like to return to our readings to help us here. How do the readings explain these ideologies?"

Kenneth responded:

Yes, Pérez Huber and Solorzano, explain that a macroaggression is "the set of beliefs and/or ideologies that justify actual or potential social arrangements that legitimate the interests and/or positions of a dominant group over non-dominant groups, that in turn lead to related structures and acts of subordination" (Pérez Huber & Solorzano, 2015a, p. 303).

Dr. Lara responds, "Yes. According to these researchers, the term macroaggression would explain those ideologies. For me, this term is important because it helps us get to, what Judge Robert Carter called the "disease," rather than the "symptoms" of racism. Let me show you what I mean." Dr. Lara advances the PowerPoint presentation to a new slide. "In reflecting on his work as an NAACP attorney in the landmark *Brown v. Board of Education* decision in 1954, Judge Carter (1988) said this" (Professor Lara reads from the PowerPoint slide):

The NAACP lawyers erred. The lawyers did not understand then how effective white power could be in preventing full implementation of the law; nor did it realize at the time that the basic barrier to full equality for blacks was not racial segregation, *a symptom*, but white supremacy, *the disease*. (Carter, 1988, p. 1095, emphasis ours)

Anna hesitantly responds:

Carter urges us to position our discussions of racism and racial microaggressions as "symptoms" of a larger "disease," white supremacy. Understanding racial microaggressions in this way, does allow me to see how People of Color cannot engage in racial microaggressions in the same ways as whites. Communities of Color have never been the beneficiaries of white supremacy and therefore, never possessed the institutional power white supremacy provides.[7]

Anna paused. "I think I understand...but that is so depressing. Where is the hope in this discussion?" The class fell silent once more. Dr. Lara noticed the clock, the class had already ran over time. She had to end the class, but promised to continue this conversation in the next meeting, asking the students to think about Anna's question on hope. Dr. Lara left feeling like the discussion needed some closure, but realized how difficult these conversations can be. It was a start, at least. When Dr. Lara returned home that night, she checked her email one final time before going to bed and saw she received an email from Anna.

Although she felt physically and mentally exhausted by the discussion she had in class that night, she opened the email. It read,

Dear Dr. Lara,

I know we said we would continue our conversations about racial microaggressions next week, but I felt like the class ended on somewhat of a "hopeless" note, and I don't want to wait until next week to address this. As I was on the commute back home tonight, I realized that this conversation was not at all hopeless. Dr. Lara, I think I really understand the frameworks you have presented tonight. As I reflected on these models, the Saturday Night Live skit and the class discussion, I realized racial micro-aggressions takes on a much deeper meaning for me in terms of social work praxis. This concept has given me a way to name the racist experiences I encounter almost everyday, and to connect those experiences to a larger system of institutional racism rooted in white supremacy. Intuitively, I have known that I am treated differently because I am Latina. Over time, these experiences have impacted how I think about my own potential and possibilities. However, these models help me explain and validate those experiences. They give me a "name" to place on all of those painful experiences I've had. Dr. Lara, your models provide me with strategies to respond to microaggressions and have a language for them. They also provide a way to create an "arsenal of responses"[8]— concepts and frameworks to use when I need to explain how racism emerges in very real ways in the lives of People of Color. This work tells me that these are not only my experiences. I will have a name and a language for the experiences of my clients in the field. This goes beyond my practice as a social worker. These frameworks provide a pedagogy; perhaps they can be apart of what Freire calls a "pedagogy of hope."[9] They provide a means to (re)claim the humanity of People of Color whose histories and life experiences are erased by the denial of racism. Now I know I'm not crazy![10] These frameworks are tools that provide me hope.

Muchísimas gracias Dra. Lara,[11]

Anna

Conclusion: reflections on pedagogical strategies

We presented these Critical Race Hypos to illustrate the pedagogical and theoretical implications of racial microaggressions in the social work classroom. Within these hypothetical discussions, we also provided peda-gogical strategies useful for engaging critical dialogue. For example, Dr. Lara prompted discussion through questions (Hypo no. 1). She would intentionally pause and refrain from responding to allow students to contribute their thoughts. Dr. Lara would also look around the room when a question is posed to show students she didn't expect any one person in particular to respond (Hypo no. 1). She used visual models (as illustrated in the figures throughout the hypos) to prompt discussion. Finally, Dr. Lara redirected the discussion to return to the focus of the dialogue (when Martin becomes upset in Hypo no. 3).

We also provided responses to the hypotheticals that illustrate possibilities for the outcomes of these conversations, while recognizing that there are many other possible responses to these Critical Race Hypos. In addition, these hypos highlight that these conversations are difficult, uncomfortable, and rarely, does everyone involved agree. As you read these hypos, we hope they resonated with past discussions you may have had in your classrooms, with colleagues, in community spaces, and with family that may provide some ideas about how to engage discussions of everyday racism—how to engage a Critical Race Praxis. This praxis serves multiple purposes. It makes theory engaging and relevant to the everyday experiences of People of Color, and provides tools that enable People of Color to "name" their experiences. Naming oppression allows for processes of confrontation, resistance and dismantling of racism to occur, which in turn leads to liberation (Freire, 1970).

These Critical Race Hypos interrogated race and racism with the concept of racial microaggressions. However, the hypos could also be used to examine other intersections, such as gender and patriarchy.[12] We offer these critical race hypos as a tool to engage discussions about a range of positionalities, including race, gender, class, and others. Further, the hypos prompted discussions of everyday experiences and larger systems of oppression that mediate them. Making these structural and interpersonal relationships is critical for engaging meaningful dialogue on race, racism, and systems of oppression.

We conclude this article, acknowledging that there is much work to be done. We hope that the models, Critical Race Hypos, and pedagogical strategies provided here will be useful for future research and practice within and outside of academia for social workers, educators, and activists. We hope that readers will take these "tools" to build and develop other frameworks and strategies that help understand and analyze the ways systemic oppression emerges in everyday experiences within the field of Social Work and beyond. We hope this work does, in turn, provide a pathway toward liberation. We hope that Anna's reflections on the framework for racial microaggressions do indeed lead to a reclaiming of humanity for People of Color. We conclude, as did Anna, with hope.

Notes

1. For a more detailed description of these tenets, see Solorzano (1997). We also believe that social work has and will adopt additional tenets specific to the field (see Razack & Jeffery, 2002).
2. For over a decade, the field of Social Work has engaged with CRT in the training of social workers to better serve diverse communities by interrogating, critiquing, and extending the concepts of cultural competence, cultural sensitivity, multiculturalism, diversity, racial disparities, and racial inequalities. See, for example, the work Kolivoski, Weaver, and Constance-Huggins (2014) and Quinn and Grumbach (2015) who discuss some of these developments in social work scholarship.
3. For a "Code of Ethics of the National Association of Social Workers," see National Association of Social Workers (2008).

4. Bell (2008a, 2008b) also acknowledged the influence of Paulo Freire on his pedagogical strategies used in law classrooms, such as the racial hypos described here.

5. Derrick Bell's use of racial hypos in the classroom did not include responses. Rather, the responses to and questions about Bell's hypos were prompted by his law students. In our critical race hypos, we provide responses and imbed questions that commonly emerge in discussions about race, racism, and racial microaggressions to better illustrate the pedagogical implications of the hypo. We also call for additional responses beyond the ones we propose.

6. See Project Implicit, available at http://www.projectimplicit.net/index.html.

7. We intentionally state that "Communities of Color" (non-white racial groups) have never benefitted from white supremacy. Thus, we do not claim that individual People of Color have never benefitted from white supremacy. Manning Marable (2002) uses the term "race traitors" to describe individual People of Color who have used their positions of power to undermine the conditions of Communities of Color and thwart progress toward racial justice.

8. We use the term "arsenal of responses" based upon the ongoing discussions that have taken place for over 20 years in Dr. Solorzano's graduate student seminar, *Research Apprenticeship Course* (RAC) in the Graduate School of Education and Information Studies at UCLA. In these discussions, generations of young scholars have theorized an "arsenal" of strategies to counter and challenge racism in research, teaching, and everyday interactions.

9. See Freire (1970).

10. See Gildersleeve et al., (2011).

11. Thank you so much Dr. Lara.

12. Critical Race Hypos could also be used to examine other types of microaggressions, including gender microaggressions, racist nativist microaggressions, and sexual orientation microaggressions.

References

Bell, D. (1999). The power of narrative. *Legal Studies Forum, 23*(3), 315–348.

Bell, D. (2008a). *Race, racism, and American law* (6th ed.). New York, USA: Wolters Kluwer.

Bell, D. (2008b). *Race, racism, and American law. Teachers manual* (6th ed.). New York, USA: Wolters Kluwer.

Carter, R. (1988). The NAACP's legal strategy against segregated education. *Michigan Law Review, 86*(6), 1083–1095. doi:10.2307/1289155

Ek, L. D., Cerecer, P. D. Q., Alanís, I., & Rodríguez, M. A. (2010). "I don't belong here": Chicanas/Latinas at a Hispanic Serving Institution creating community through *muxerista* mentoring. *Equity & Excellence in Education, 43*(4), 539–553. doi:10.1080/10665684.2010.510069

Fey, T., Steele, A., (Writers) & McCarthy-Miller, B., (Director). (2004, October). Saturday night live, episode 567 [television series episode], In L. Michaels (Producer), *Saturday night live*. New York, USA: CBS.

Freire, P. (1970). *Pedagogy of the oppressed*. New York, USA: Continuum.

Gildersleeve, R., Croom, N., & Vasquez, P. (2011). 'Am I going crazy?!': A critical race analysis of doctoral education. *Equity & Excellence in Education, 44*(1), 93–114. doi:10.1080/10665684.2011.539472

Greenwald, A. G., & Krieger, L. H. (2006). Implicit bias: Scientific foundations. *California Law Review, 94*(4), 945–967. doi:10.2307/20439056

Kohli, R., & Solorzano, D. (2011). Black and brown high school student activism. In L. Urrieta, & A. Revilla (Eds.), *Marching students: Chicana/o Identity and the politics of education 1968 and the present* (pp. 131–147). Reno, NV: University of Nevada Press.

Kohli, R., & Solorzano, D. (2012). Teachers, please learn our names!: Racial microaggressions and the k-12 classroom. *Race, Ethnicity, and Education, 15*(4), 441–462. doi:10.1080/13613324.2012.674026

Kolivoski, K., Weaver, A., & Constance-Huggins, M. (2014). Critical race theory: Opportunities for application in social work practice and policy. *Families in Society: the Journal of Contemporary Social Services, 95*(4), 269–276. doi:10.1606/1044-3894.2014.95.36

Ladson-Billings, G., & Tate, W. (1995). Toward a critical race theory of education. *Teachers College Record, 97*(1), 47–68.

Lorde, A. (1984). *Sister outsider: Essays and speeches.* Berkeley, CA: Crossing Press.

Marable, M. (2002). *The great wells of democracy: The meaning of race in American life.* New York, USA: BasicCivitas.

Memmi, A. (1965). *The Colonizer and the colonized.* Boston, MA: Beacon Press.

National Association of Social Workers (NASW). (2008). *Code of ethics of the national association of social workers.* Washington, DC: National Association of Social Workers.

Pérez Huber, L. (2011). Discourses of racist nativism in California public education: English dominance as racist nativist microaggressions. *Educational Studies, 47*(4), 379–401. doi:10.1080/00131946.2011.589301

Pérez Huber, L., & Solorzano, D. G. (2015a). Racial microaggressions as a tool for critical race research. *Race Ethnicity and Education, 18*(3), 297–320. doi:10.1080/13613324.2014.994173

Pérez Huber, L., & Solorzano, D. G. (2015b). Visualizing everyday racism critical race theory, visual microaggressions, and the historical image of Mexican banditry. *Qualitative Inquiry, 21*(3), 223–238. doi:10.1177/1077800414562899

Pierce, C. (1970). Offensive mechanisms. In F. Barbour (Ed.), *The Black seventies* (pp. 265–282). Boston, MA: Porter Sargent.

Quinn, C. R., & Grumbach, G. (2015). Critical race theory and the limits of relational theory in social work with women. *Journal of Ethnic & Cultural Diversity in Social Work, 24*(3), 202–218. doi:10.1080/15313204.2015.1062673

Razack, N., & Jeffery, D. (2002). Critical race discourse and tenets for social work. *Canadian Social Work Review, 19*(2), 257–271.

Ross-Sheriff, F. (2012). Microaggression, women, and social work. *Journal of Women and Social Work, 27*(3), 233–236. doi:10.1177/0886109912454366

Smith, W., Allen, W., & Danley, L. (2007). 'Assume the position ... you fit the description.' Psychosocial experiences and racial battle fatigue among African American male college students. *American Behavioral Scientist, 51*(4), 551–578. doi:10.1177/0002764207307742

Solorzano, D. (1997). Images and words that wound: Critical race theory, racial stereotyping, and teacher education. *Teacher Education Quarterly, 24*(3), 5–19.

Solorzano, D. (1998). Critical race theory, race and gender microaggressions, and the experiences of Chicana and Chicano scholars. *Qualitative Studies in Education, 11*(1), 121–136. doi:10.1080/095183998236926

Solorzano, D., Ceja, M., & Yosso, T. (2000). Critical race theory, racial microaggressions and campus racial climate: The experiences of African American college students. *Journal of Negro Education, 69*(1/2), 60–73.

Sue, D. (2010). *Microaggressions in everyday life: Race, gender, and sexual orientation.* Hoboken, NJ: John Wiley & Sons, Inc.

Woody, D. J., & Green, R. (2001). The influence of race/ethnicity and gender on psychological and social well-being. *Journal of Ethnic and Cultural Diversity in Social Work, 9*(3–4), 151–166. doi:10.1300/J051v09n03_08

Worth, M., (Producer), & Pearl, A., (Director). (1972). *Malcom X: His own story as it really happened [Motion Picture]*. USA: Warner Brothers.

Wright, P. (2013). Implications of microaggressions in social work. *Academic Exchange Quarterly, 17*(2), 45–50.

Yamamoto, E. (1997). Critical Race Praxis: Race theory and political lawyering practice in post-civil rights America. *Michigan Law Review, 95*(4), 821–900. doi:10.2307/1290048

Yosso, T. J., Smith, W. A., Ceja, M., & Solorzano, D. G. (2009). Critical race theory, racial microaggressions, and campus racial climate for Latina/o undergraduates. *Harvard Educational Review, 79*(4), 659–691. doi:10.17763/haer.79.4.m6867014157m707l

Examining racial microaggressions as a tool for transforming social work education: the case for critical race pedagogy

Susan Nakaoka and Larry Ortiz

ABSTRACT

This conceptual article utilizes the *testimonios* of two professors of color to describe racial microaggressions as one manifestation of how the university privileges those most in line with the dominant cultural narrative. Providing an epistemological disconnect for those that are "othered," the structure of the academy needs examination and in some cases, dismantling, in order to provide a truly emancipatory environment for faculty and students. Using microaggressions as the tool to expose these macro failings, critical race pedagogy is proposed as a step toward liberatory social work education.

Introduction

A growing movement has exposed the hostile campus racial climate often experienced by professors and students of color. *Presumed Incompetent*, called the "must-have manual for women of color in the academy," is a compilation of narratives that showcase the experiences of female professors of color (Carodine, 2014, p. 286). A facebook page for the book has over 15,400 followers and showcases events that impact race, class, and gender in the academy. In another social media campaign, an attempt to confront microaggressions on campus, the hash tag "#ilooklikeaprofessor" has garnered attention as professors of color, especially women and non-gender conforming, post their pictures to expand the definition of people's perception past the vision of professor as older White males with blazers and elbow patches (Pritchard, Koh, & Moravec, 2015).

At elite institutions, the presence of students of color has enhanced significance, and young scholars are pushing back. In the "I, too, am Harvard" campaign African American students launched a YouTube video and produced a play about the microaggressions that they face on a daily basis in the esteemed institution (Butler, 2014). At UCLA, a slew of separate incidents that includes offenses against African American, Asian American, and

Mexican American students have led to a campus initiative, naming legal scholar Jerry Kang as their first Vice Chancellor for Equity, Diversity, and Inclusion (Hampton, 2015).

For faculty and students of color, microaggressions are the common occurrence that reminds them that, despite their academic achievement, they do not belong in academia. Although microaggressions are often considered unintentional, minor offenses, the cumulative impact of them over time can have a harmful impact for those experiencing them (Solórzano, Ceja, & Yosso, 2000; Sue, Rivera, Watkins, Kim, R., Kim, S., & Williams, 2011). Solórzano et al. (2000) define microaggressions as "subtle insults (verbal, nonverbal, and/or visual) directed at people of color, often automatically or unconsciously" (p. 60). Miller and Garran (2007) equate microaggressions to a "…1000 papercuts instead of one deep wound (p. 97)."

We advocate examination of microaggressions in the larger context of the social structures in which they occur. In other words, what are the institutional and systemic forces that through their very existence, their assumptive premises permit a university environment to be hostile for people of color? How can we address the master narrative so that academia can become the democratic spaces that they are meant to be? We believe this is done best by looking simultaneously at the micro side (downstream) of microaggressions and the structural side (upstream), particularly the narrative upon which these social exchanges are formulated.

Drawing upon our combined experiences of over 40 years in social work education, this paper situates our personal and professional experiences with microaggressions and micro invalidations within the discipline. Social work education's commitment to diversity is extensive as seen through its prominent place in accreditation standards spanning 50 years (Jani, Pierce, Ortiz, & Sowbel, 2011). With this kind of external accrediting expectation, the authors maintain social work is ideally situated to both innovate and model anti-racist and anti-oppressive structures and practice.

The macro in microaggressions

Perry (2005) talks about the architecture of race, in that racism and oppression are conjured in meta-narratives that legitimize mechanisms that privilege Whites over people of color. Following this logic, microaggressions, although encountered at an interactional level, are really rooted in the violence of structural marginalization. Solórzano and Huber (2014) suggest that microaggressions can be used as a tool to dissect the macro-societal forces that perpetuate inequality. They go on to define *macroaggression* as:

The set of beliefs and/or ideologies that justify actual or potential social arrangements that legitimate the interests and/or positions of a dominant group over non-dominant groups, that in turn lead to related structures and acts of subordination (p.7).

By examining a historical and contemporary example of racial microaggressions, Solórzano and Huber (2014) identify and disentangle the structural and ideological issues that are tied to each. We utilize this technique by identifying microaggressions in the university setting as a tool to elucidate the macro themes within the dominant culture of the institution that prevent individuals of color from success while privileging Whites.

Macroaggressions and the diverse university

African American and Latino students are found to experience consistent microaggressions that reflect cumulative impacts on mental health (usually in the form of anxiety and increased stress) and academic performance (bias in assigning grades and in some cases student attrition). (Solórzano et al., 2000; Vakalahi, Sermon, Richardson, Dillard, & Moncrief, 2014; Yosso, Smith, Ceja, & Solórzano, 2009).

Although the social work student body consists of a relatively high percentage of African Americans (15.4% of graduates in 2014), a recent study shows that African American female MSW students remain isolated from faculty, other students, and the curriculum (Vakalahi, et al., 2014). When examining Latino/as and Asian Americans, issues of diversity are more complex.

Latinos and Asian Americans are not entering social work programs in numbers commensurate with the population. The number of Latina/o graduates from MSW programs remains consistent over the last three years in the range of 9% (CSWE, 2016; CSWE, 2015; CSWE, 2014). Meanwhile, the Latina/o share of the US population has inched above 17%. This may be related to few efforts to intentionally recruit Latinos, and Latinos not feeling social work is a profession whereby they can make a difference (Roccio, Baek, & Ortiz, 2015).

Asian Americans and Pacific Islander MSW graduation numbers are also underrepresented and stagnant. The number of Asian American graduates remains constant at 3%, Pacific Islanders at .3% despite the growth of Asian Americans in the overall US population to 5.6% in 2010 (CSWE, 2015). If statistics for Asian Americans and Pacific Islanders were disaggregated, there would likely be clearer patterns of concern for certain groups, such as Southeast Asian students and Pacific Islanders. The experiences of Latino/as and Asian Americans and Pacific Islanders in social work education have not been addressed in the literature on microaggressions.

The experiences of faculty within predominantly White institutions have been recently highlighted in the literature, and emerging themes include: "presumed incompetence," excessive scrutiny, and micro invalidations (Douglas, 2012; Kupenda, 2012; Orelus, 2013; Sue et al., 2011; Wilson, 2012). Although some of this intersectional literature discusses the experiences of Latino and Asian American professors or students (Arriola, 2012; Lugo-Lugo, 2012; Solórzano, 1988; Võ, 2012), the majority of the work focuses on the African American experience. For example, the aforementioned anthology only includes one article on the Asian American experience, and each of the articles speak to one group only, and there are none that describe the experience of biracial or multiracial academics. This rather singular focus points to what Delgado and Stefancic (2012) refer to as the Black/White binary, meaning that racial and cultural discussions in the United States are dominated rather myopically and exclude other racial and ethnic groups and those that identify as biracial or multiracial. Thus, co-examining the narratives of a Latino male professor and an Asian American female professor, both of mixed background, is instructive to the discussion on microaggressions.

Methodology: *Testimonio* with CRT influence

We chose *testimonio* as our approach to incorporate self-reflexivity into our critical reflection of social work education from our experiences throughout our academic careers (as graduate students and as faculty). First, culturally, *testimonio* is appropriate given our cultural heritage and context. As a second-generation Mexican American male and a third-generation Japanese American/Chicana female, this method feels consistent with our values and epistemology. The importance of oral tradition in our culture is aligned with the use of the retelling of microaggressions as a tool to understanding larger societal forces. Second, *testimonio* allows for reflection and resistance. Huber (2010a) describes *testimonio* as flowing from Chicana feminist epistemology and describes it as "a process of 'collective memory,' transcending a single experience and connected to a larger group struggle" (p. 83). Told from within the US context, *testimonios* are also counter-stories, which are resistant narratives told from a non-majoritarian perspective that deconstruct the deficit-centered stories that are the norm (Delgado Bernal, 2002; Solórzano & Yosso, 2002). Third, *testimonio* is appropriate for our field, since reflexivity and self-critique are central to social work practice and education.

Testimonio can be process as much as it is method and is described as "a verbal journey of a witness who speaks to reveal the racial, classed, gendered, and nativist injustices they have suffered as a means of healing, empowerment, and advocacy for a more humane present and future" (Huber, 2010b,

p. 851). Often linked with CRT, *testimonio* as a method is described as a qualitative approach that elicits reflexive thinking from the subjects (Flores & Garcia, 2009; Huber, 2010a; Huber, 2009; Urrieta & Villenas, 2013).

In this article, we employ *testimonio* as a process. From 2006 to 2013, we were colleagues within a medium-sized state university that was a majority students of color campus. Our ongoing connection is rooted in our deep need for camaraderie in the face of the consistent difficulties we face within the context of the academy. The *testimonios* provided below represent our running dialogue as we recount our lived experiences as students and faculty of color. Targeted discussions and interviews with each other during the summer and fall of 2015 provide the content for the narrative provided below.

Critical race theory and social work education

Social work education has a long and rather circuitous history with diversity and social justice. Jani et al. (2011) suggest the role of diversity within social work education has evolved over time. It was not until EPAS 2008 and 2015 that the social justice issue emerged forcefully both as a premise but also as a competence and related expected practice behaviors. Within the social work literature, CRT has emerged as a mechanism that can propel discussions of multiculturalism forward toward a model of transformational change and social justice (Abrams & Moio, 2009; Ortiz & Jani, 2010).

Education literature provides a significant contribution to the CRT literature on pedagogy that defines CRT as "a strategy to foreground and account for the role of race and racism in education and works toward the elimination of racism as part of a larger goal of opposing or eliminating other forms of subordination based on gender, class, sexual orientation, language and national origin" (Solórzano & Yosso, 2002, p. 24). The remedy we suggest is a curriculum that targets the dominant narrative and structural marginalization that follows. Lynn, Jennings, and Hughes (2013) establish critical race pedagogy as an "explicitly liberatory pedagogy" in which they outline four key elements: the endemic nature of racism, recognition of the understanding of the power dynamics inherent in American society (including the culture of who is in power), the importance of examining self through reflexivity, and the practice of advocating for justice and equity in education as a precursor to justice and equity in society (p. 620).

The authors propose to look at the means by which the privileging of knowledge is structured in social work education. There are two ways in which the privileging of knowledge takes place in higher education. One, structurally through the governance process, which includes the determination of who is worthy to study at the university and who is worthy to teach, what is considered good — or — truthful knowledge. This is translated into a governance structure that values/privileges one narrative over another. Two, what is taught in the curriculum. Except in isolated situations, curriculums are founded on dominant culture "ways of knowing," that is, EBP — and while evidence practice is always valued — what is really meant here refers to the method the evidence was obtained, which almost always follows methods founded on positivistic science, randomized controlled trials, specifically. Persons drawing upon knowledge schemes not conforming to the narrative are relegated to "other" status, both individually and as a member of a group. This social position leaves them vulnerable to microaggressions and micro invalidations, specifically regarding the worthiness of their fit in academe.

The authors

As part of the context for the *testimonio* to follow, the authors have constructed a short autobiographical narrative of their educational journey.

Larry Ortiz is a second-generation Latino whose father was an unauthorized migrant farm laborer and mother descended from a Dutch immigrant family. Growing up in west Michigan, Ortiz encountered intense discrimination and faced daily assaults on his character by the majority culture while enduring suspicion from the Latino community as a "halfer." Ortiz learned a tremendous amount from his parents about doing good, justice, respecting and engaging diverse persons. The family was a "settled working class" using a term advanced by Bettie (2014) meaning they owned a house, a small plot of land that allowed his father a "truck farm" to sell vegetables in the streets of their nearby town to supplement the meager wages from his factory job. His mother worked at home and in the field caring for the family to help meet its economic needs. Ortiz attended public schools and headed for the ministry until his position on the Vietnam War and his questions in doctrine classes caused administrators to ask him to leave school. Eventually, Ortiz found the social work profession, and he finished his undergraduate degree and completed his MSW program before earning a doctorate in sociology. With his ex-wife, Ortiz raised two sons, both young adults, one an immigration attorney and the other librarian and artist.

Susan Nakaoka is a Sansei, a third-generation Japanese American, who was born and raised in East Los Angeles and a surrounding suburb. Her grandparents were farm laborers and small business owners. Her parents were born in the World War II concentration camps in which Japanese and Japanese Americans were forcibly imprisoned. Her parents were her working class heroes that provided her with a stable home and supported her education above all other family needs. Nakaoka attended public schools throughout her academic career and was the first in her family to obtain a graduate degree. Her master's degrees in Asian American Studies and Social Welfare as well as her doctorate in Urban Planning are all from one major public research university. As a single parent, Nakaoka has raised a multiracial son (Mexican American and Japanese American) who is currently attending a four-year public university. Having the physical appearance of a multiracial individual, Nakaoka has experienced microaggressions throughout her life that focus on race, gender, and the negation of her belonging to a specific ethnic community.

Testimonio

The accounts listed below illustrate themes inherent in the dominant narrative that creates a hostile environment for faculty and students of color in MSW programs. These themes also have broader implications outside of the university, as they mediate the institutions and structures of the everyday lives of people of color. The *testimonios* have implications for three areas of social work curriculum: 1. "Othering" students and faculty — Who belongs? What support exists for those from varied backgrounds? 2. Knowledge production — what types of knowledge are respected, who is qualified to teach and how is narrative and varied epistemologies valued? And 3. The explicit curriculum — how are persons and communities of color represented so that their mere presence does not elicit micro assaults and micro invalidations? Are their stories present? Is their history valued?

The help

> Ortiz: As a newly hired social work professor at a small, parochial Hispanic Serving Institution with a totally White administration, I attended the first convocation marching in full regalia with the other faculty. Afterward, I returned my rental robe in the "staging room" and was walking out of the door to go home when I was approached by the President of the university's board, a White woman, who handed me her regalia. Shocked, I stopped in my tracks and without thinking did not take her robe and instead pointed in the direction of where the regalia was being collected and stated: "you can hang it up over there – that is where I hung mine."

> Nakaoka: As a MSW student, I was introduced to a senior level faculty of my department. When the faculty member learned of my Japanese heritage, he became excited, bowed to me and said something in Japanese. When I responded that I was third generation Japanese American and thus did not understand Japanese, the faculty member proceeded to inform me about his travels and research in Japan. From that point forward, when the faculty member saw me in the hallway, he would bow and say "konichiwa."

These microaggressions clearly served to underscore the trespassing of persons of color in the institution. In both cases, the offender found their encounters with the authors counter to their idea of who should be present in the university. In Ortiz's case, the microaggression was based on the Board President's essentialist assumption that Mexicans at the university were the "help." Perhaps given the social context of the transaction, it was an understandable assumption given the social conditions of south Texas. Hence, the dominant cultural narrative led to an offensive exchange. In Nakaoka's case, it served to "other" her as a MSW student. Immediately, she became the "Japanese" student, and not known to the senior faculty as anything else. By placing her in this essentialist box, she was not allowed any other identities — such as a macro social worker, a social work student with over 8 years of practice experience, or a graduate student who was a working single parent who was excelling in a program that was meant for full-time, traditional students. By ascribing the racialized identity to Nakaoka, her ability to become known for something else in the mind of the senior faculty member was obscured. In fact, her identity became a Japanese female that was supposed to bow back to the White male in the hallway.

Keepers of knowledge

Ortiz: At the same university a newly minted Latina doctorate that had just been hired as an Assistant Professor walked into my office frustrated and laughing. She disclosed that a White student had just met her in the hallway and "complemented" her on the teaching she was receiving in her Research class, stating how the Latina faculty member presented the material so clearly and how much the she (student) was learning. After a long pause the student went on to exclaim: "...wow I have never had a Latina professor before."

Nakaoka: Soon after receiving my doctorate, I taught a summer class that included content on race and oppression. As the weeks went by, the one White male student in the class became more uncomfortable with the content. Halfway through the class, the student became visibly agitated when presented with a video and literature regarding the social construction of race. Because his wife's medical doctor had asked about her "race" during her prenatal exam the student insisted there were biological determinants of race and challenged me throughout my lecture. After class, the student wrote me an email that stated: "Do you really believe our medical doctor is that naïve regarding biology and a social worker with a racial agenda has more advanced biological knowledge? You are not the first teacher to get so extremely defensive about protecting CRT. You also appear just about as white as the other white teachers who preach against white privilege, abhor meritocracy and issue assignments for a grade, bemoan capitalism and request we pay our $1000 tuition." Because his wife was from Japan, he felt he had added legitimacy – he could not be racist because his wife and unborn son were ethnically Japanese.

These microaggressions are based on essentialist assumptions and easily attributable to "ordinary" racism in Delgado & Stefanic's (2012) terms. The student in Dr. Ortiz' situation in all reality probably never did have a Latina instructor, and in her assumptive world, this professor was "worth writing home about" letting everyone know there are Latina exceptions out there. Clearly, this exchange was offensive and in some ways hurtful to the Latina professor. The student in Nakaoka's case questioned her credentials and attacked her standing due to her newly achieved status as a Ph.D. His assault on her racial identity was based in his inability to believe that scholars of color could present information that could be accurate (in this case, material on the social construction of race). The fact that Nakaoka subscribed to these ideas yet appeared White to the student, meant that she was "over compensating" and trying to fit in with the students of color. It was not conceivable that the information being presented was valid. The master narrative on Latinas and Asian American females made this exchange permissible and acceptable. In this case, both the student and the narrative need to be challenged.

Lowered expectations

Ortiz: In one of my roles as director of a newly conceptualized MSW program in accreditation candidacy, serving a largely minority student body in the southwest, I was strongly committed to students completing a thesis as a graduation requirement. Four reasons guided my thinking: (a) the university had a reputation as less than academically challenging and requiring such a rigorous assignment would serve as a counter narrative to the university's reputation; (b) the largely diverse student body had lived experiences valuable to advancing knowledge and the questions they were interested in pursuing were founded on questions only they could ask; (c) the completion of such a work, no matter how arduous, would ultimately be empowering to these students, many of whom were first generation immigrants and English learners; and, (d) these students learning experiences reinforce the EPAS of research to practice and practice to research, thus adding to the knowledge base of promising practices with diverse populations. Despite a complete and total absence of support from the administration on this issue, I raised funds to provide mentoring and learning support for students who struggled with their research and writing. However, White faculty, and only they, bitterly complained year after year about the thesis. They constantly undermined the endeavor through disrupting faculty meetings with their agenda and going so far as filing a bogus grievance (ultimately denied) with the union stating the thesis was an excessive workload issue (even though they received load credit for the assignment). Finally, one day one of the dissenting White faculty members walked into my office and pleaded the case by stating"...[Y]ou know Larry, our students are simply not capable of completing this type of work. We need to accept that and provide them with something more in line with what they can handle." The faculty person went on to present an alternative assignment which was similar to what I had used in my beginning undergraduate research methods classes.

Nakaoka: In the company of two White female professors, I spoke about the lack of social work scholars who focus on a critical race perspective. One of the faculty, who is younger than me, suggested that there were scholars on the East coast that did "race work." As if I was not present in the room, the other faculty member commented to the first one, "well, if you don't go to conferences, then how would you know that?" implying that I do not attend national conferences and thus would not know the leading scholars in the field. The first faculty member nodded sympathetically. The assumptions made by these two White women were faulty, since I

*have been invited and accepted to present at more national, peer-reviewed confer-
ences than the first faculty member, but there was an assumption that I was less
accomplished than my younger colleague.*

These micro invalidations are based in part on the master narrative often
owned by White liberals. The part that is designed to placate the "poor and
marginalized" by lowering standards and expectations believing they are not
capable of achieving what is expected of the White and privileged. The
deleterious impact of this is that the marginalized are further set back having
been subject to lower standards, and the privileged position of the white
liberals remains intact.

These types of microaggressions were designed to reinforce the gentry role
of Whites in the academy, which is to question and gate-keep the academy
from intruders who are not up to par. This intrusive micro invalidation
encountered on a personal level can be directly linked to: (a) the social
construction in the master narrative that gives ownership of academe to
White European males, and in cases in which there are only women present,
White European females; (b) the lack of institutional structures to protect
persons at "lower ranks" from indignities such as this one designed to
marginalize the faculty and doctoral students of color into "othered" roles
in the academy; and (c) the culture of fear that often prevails among non-
tenured faculty and doctoral students, especially those persons of color. This
fear is rooted, at best, in a belief that the university is not *our* world, and, at
worst, I (person of color) am presumed incompetent therefore I need to stay
quiet (silencing their voice).

Discussion

The meaning and impact of the microaggressions described above reflect the
element of the power dynamics of the culture of the academy. Lynn et al.
(2013) describe this as their second tenet in critical race pedagogy and
explain, "This culture of power often divides communities of color from well-
meaning whites who wish to support those who they consider to be less
fortunate" (p. 619). They go on to note that in the field of education,
"acknowledging and understanding one's privileged place in the culture of
power can be difficult given the quest for egalitarianism professed by many
professionals in the field of education" (p. 619). As we have shown, social
work education also struggles with the constant negotiation of power within
the culture of MSW programs.

The three themes mentioned earlier (othering students and faculty, knowledge production, and the explicit curriculum) are places to start integrating
critical race pedagogy. Educating social workers on the meta-narratives that
direct their micro interactions could occur through an explicit curriculum

that utilizes critical race pedagogy by: 1. Recognizing the historical and contemporary meta-narratives that perpetuate racism; 2. Deconstructing these narratives by analyzing history, critiquing neo-liberalism and the current political economy; 3. Recognizing that social workers' bias is inevitable due to the impact of these meta-narratives on their realities; 4. Emphasizing reflexivity and self-critique as a way to mitigate bias; and 5. Developing social work practice models that are strength based rather than those that use a deficit approach or those that pathologize communities of color in order to work toward equity in the classroom as a precursor to justice and equity in society.

Impacting the systemic/macro issues through implicit curriculum is more nuanced. Increased diversity in faculty and student body is only the first step. Recognizing divergent epistemologies, insurgent histories of social work, and de-colonizing methodologies are additional steps that can add value to the academy and validate the work of faculty and students of color.

Conclusion and recommendations

By highlighting the voices of social work professors and students of color, this article has proposed that social work education must be centered on deconstructing the dominant narrative that sustains the system of racial oppression and White supremacy that perpetuates inequality and (permit) the social interactions experienced as microaggressions and invalidations. To reduce the prevalence and impact of microaggressions on students and the communities in which they serve, MSW students must be educated about and learn to dismantle structural forms of racism.

Through critical race pedagogy, social work educators can begin to deconstruct the systems that perpetuate microaggressions by disentangling the multiple levels at which they originate. Although not the only answer, a social work curriculum that centers on these ideas can uncover the prevalence of microaggressions as markers of inequality faced by students and the communities they serve. For instance, at a public university on the west coast, there is a master of social work program that is based on a CRT framework — all of the courses include a CRT perspective. Other programs include elective or required courses on CRT or other frames such as "anti-oppression" or "anti-racist." Such an approach works toward dismantling the dominant narrative that permeates social work education by exposing racism as endemic to US society, examining the culture of power, promoting reflexivity and self-critique, while working toward social justice.

References

Abrams, L. S., & Moio, J. A. (2009). Critical race theory and the cultural competence dilemma in social work education. *Journal of Social Work Education, 45* (2), 245–261. doi:10.5175/JSWE.2009.200700109

Arriola, E. R. (2012). 'No Hay Mal Que por Bien No Venga': A journey to healing as a latina lesbian law professor. *Gutiérrez Y Muhs Et Al*, 372–392.

Bernal, D. D. (2002). Critical race theory, Latino critical theory, and critical raced-gendered epistemologies: Recognizing students of color as holders and creators of knowledge. *Qualitative Inquiry, 8* (1), 105–126. doi:10.1177/107780040200800107

Bettie, J. (2014). *Women without class: Girls, race, and identity.* Oakland, CA: University of California Press.

Butler, B. (2014, March 5). 'I, too, am harvard': Black students show they belong. *Washington Post.* Retrieved from https://www.washingtonpost.com/blogs/she-the-people/wp/2014/03/05/i-too-am-harvard-black-students-show-they-belong/

Carodine, M. D. (2014). Presumed incompetent too: A review of the new must-have manual for women of color in the academy. *Indiana Journal of Law and Social Equality, 2* (2), 3.

Council on Social Work Education (2014). 2013 Annual Statistics on Social Work Education in the United States. https://www.cswe.org/getattachment/3ea00923-9d60-436d-be4a-9014b78478cc/2013-Statistics-on-Social-Work-Education-in-the-Un.aspx

Council on Social Work Education (2015). Annual Statistics on Social Work Education in the United States - 2014. https://www.cswe.org/CMSPages/GetFile.aspx?guid=5e8fc9fa-9299-4b54-acc6-0e6583323f1a

Council on Social Work Education (2016). Annual Statistics on Social Work Education in the United States. 2015. https://www.cswe.org/getattachment/992f629c-57cf-4a74-8201-1db7a6fa4667/2015-Statistics-on-Social-Work-Education.aspx

Delgado, R., & Stefancic, J. (2012). *Critical race theory: An introduction.* New York, NY: NYU Press.

Douglas, D. D. (2012). Black/out: The white face of multiculturalism and the violence of the Canadian academic imperial project. In G. Gutierrez Y Muhs, Y. Flores Niemann, C. Gonzalex, & A. Harris (Eds.), *Presumed incompetent: The intersections of race and class for women in academia* (pp. 50–64).

Flores, J., & Garcia, S. (2009). Latina testimonios: A reflexive, critical analysis of a 'Latina space' at a predominantly White campus. *Race Ethnicity and Education, 12* (2), 155–172. doi:10.1080/13613320902995434

Hampton, P. (2015, March 31). Law professor named UCLA's first vice chancellor for equity, diversity and inclusion. *UCLA Newsroom: University News.* Retrieved from http://newsroom.ucla.edu/releases/law-professor-named-uclas-first-vice-chancellor-for-equity-diversity-and-inclusion

Huber, L. P. (2009). Disrupting apartheid of knowledge: Testimonio as methodology in Latina/o critical race research in education. *International Journal of Qualitative Studies in Education, 22* (6), 639–654. doi:10.1080/09518390903333863

Huber, L. P. (2010a). Using Latina/o critical race theory (LatCrit) and racist nativism to explore intersectionality in the educational experiences of undocumented Chicana college students. *The Journal of Educational Foundations, 24* (1/2), 77.

Huber, L. P. (2010b). Beautifully powerful: A LatCrit reflection on coming to an epistemological consciousness and the power of testimonio. *American University Journal of Gender, Social Policy & the Law I, 18*, 839.

Huber, L. P. Solorzano, D. G. (2014). Racial microagressions as a tool for critical race research. *Race Ethnicity and Education, 18* (3), 297–320. Retrieved from http://www.tandfonline.com/doi/abs/10.1080/13613324.2014.994173

Jani, J. S., Pierce, D., Ortiz, L., & Sowbel, L. (2011). Access to intersectionality, content to competence: Deconstructing social work education diversity standards. *Journal of Social Work Education, 47* (2), 283–301. doi:10.5175/JSWE.2011.200900118

Kupenda, A. M. (2012). Facing down the spooks (essay). In G. Gutierrez Y Muhs, Y. Flores Niemann, & G. Carmen (Eds.), *Presumed incompetent: The intersections of race and class for women in academia.*

Lugo-Lugo, C. (2012). A prostitute, a servant and a customer service representative: A Latina in academia. *Presumed Incompetence: The Intersections of Race and Class for Women in Academia,* 40–49.

Lynn, M., Jennings, M. E., & Hughes, S. (2013). Critical race pedagogy 2.0: Lessons from Derrick Bell. *Race Ethnicity and Education, 16* (4), 603–628. doi:10.1080/13613324.2013.817776

Miller, J., & Garran, A. M. (2007). The web of institutional racism. *Smith College Studies In Social Work (Haworth), 77* (1), 33–67. doi:10.1300/J497v77n01_03

Orelus, P. W. (2013). The institutional cost of being a faculty of color: A critical personal reflection. *Current Issues in Education, 16,* 2.

Ortiz, L., & Jani, J. (2010). Critical race theory: A transformational model for teaching diversity. *Journal of Social Work Education, 46* (2), 175–193. doi:10.5175/JSWE.2010.200900070

Perry, I. (2005). Of Desi, J. Lo and color matters: Law, critical race theory the architecture of race. *Cleveland State Law Review, 52,* 139.

Pritchard, S., Koh, A., & Moravec, M. (2015, August 10). We Look like Professors, Too. *Inside Higher Ed.* Retrieved from https://www.insidehighered.com/views/2015/08/10/essay-explains-new-hashtag-campaign-draw-attention-diversity-professors-and-their

Roccio, B., & Ortiz (2015,October 15–18) *Latinos in social work education: A call for action.* Presentation made Council on Social Work Education 61st Annual Program Meeting, Denver, CO.

Sermon, V. H., Richardson, M., Dillard, A., & Moncrief, A. (2014). Do you see me? The complex experiences of women of color MSW students. *Intercultural Education, 25* (5), 418–427. doi:10.1080/14675986.2014.967973

Solórzano, D., Ceja, M., & Yosso, T. (2000). Critical race theory, racial microaggressions, and campus racial climate: The experiences of African American college students. *Journal of Negro Education,* 60–73.

Solórzano, D. G. (1988). Critical race theory, race and gender microaggressions, and the experience of Chicana and Chicano scholars. *International Journal of Qualitative Studies in Education, 11* (1), 121–136. doi:10.1080/095183998236926

Solórzano, D. G., & Yosso, T. J. (2002). Critical race methodology: Counter-storytelling as an analytical framework for education research. *Qualitative Inquiry, 8* (1), 23–44. doi:10.1177/107780040200800103

Sue, D. W., Rivera, D. P., Watkins, N. L., Kim, R. H., Kim, S., & Williams, C. D. (2011). Racial dialogues: Challenges faculty of color face in the classroom. *Cultural Diversity and Ethnic Minority Psychology, 17* (3), 331. doi:10.1037/a0024190

Urrieta, L., Jr, & Villenas, S. A. (2013). The legacy of Derrick Bell and Latino/a education: A critical race testimonio. *Race Ethnicity and Education, 16* (4), 514–535. doi:10.1080/13613324.2013.817771

Võ, L. T. (2012). Navigating the academic terrain: The racial and gender politics of elusive belonging. *Presumed Incompetent: The Intersections of Race and Class for Women in Academia*, 93–109.

Wilson, S. (2012). They forgot mammy had a brain. *Presumed Incompetent: the Intersections of Race and Class for Women in Academia*, 65–77.

Yosso, T., Smith, W., Ceja, M., & Solórzano, D. (2009). Critical race theory, racial microaggressions, and campus racial climate for Latina/o undergraduates. *Harvard Educational Review*, 79(4), 659–691. doi:10.17763/haer.79.4.m6867014157m7071

Addressing microaggressions and acts of oppression within online classrooms by utilizing principles of transformative learning and liberatory education

Amelia Ortega, Malwina Andruczyk, and Matthea Marquart

ABSTRACT

Social work education is experiencing growth and challenge as many universities and colleges begin to offer distance education options for both BSW and MSW students. While work on creative solutions to microaggressions and acts of oppression in the physical classroom is available, work on addressing these issues in online classrooms is still yet to emerge. Through an application of transformative learning theory and principles of liberatory education to a case study, we hope to contribute to an emerging dialogue around best practices in addressing microaggressions and acts of oppression in online learning environments.

Introduction

Social work education has been moving online in recent years, with 78 schools offering online degrees as of March 2017, according to the (Council on Social Work Education, n.d.). While there are many benefits to online education, including increased access to education for rural students and students in need of flexible schedules due to work and family responsibilities, unique challenges regarding marginalization within online settings are emerging.

The hostile behavior of people who post online comments has been well documented. This can be attributed to factors including distance from the person to whom the comments are directed and the ease of committing acts of aggression in writing versus in speech (Wolchover, 2012). This is relevant for online education because online instruction frequently includes written elements such as asynchronous discussion boards and synchronous typed chat areas during live class sessions. As one student stated: "I just felt that students feel more comfortable making comments that are offensive to other students when they're online" (Ortega, Marquart, & Andruczyk, 2015, p. 23).

Verduin and Clarke define distance learning as "any formal approach to learning in which the majority of the instruction occurs while educator and learner are at a distance from one another" (as cited in Abels, 2005, p. 23). Distance education provides opportunities for critical pedagogical decisions and approaches to student engagement, learning, and development of class-room culture. Using the principles of transformative learning (Mezirow, 1978) and liberatory education (Freire, 1985; Hooks, 1994), this article provides a framework for acknowledging the social locations and identities that emerge within online classroom spaces, as well as strategies for addressing experiences and incidences of microaggressions within online courses. We have grounded this writing in our shared histories as feminist educators and a social justice pedagogy utilizing collaborative teaching teams. Along with this is our shared belief in the classroom as a transformational space.

As social workers and educators, much of our collective investment in standards of practice is derived from our core social work ethic "1.05 Cultural Competence and Social Diversity" (National Association of Social Workers, 2008) that states in part:

> "Social workers should obtain education about and seek to understand the nature of social diversity and oppression with respect to race, ethnicity, national origin, color, sex, sexual orientation, gender identity or expression, age, marital status, political belief, religion, immigration status, and mental or physical disability" (Social Workers' Ethical Responsibilities to Clients section, para. 5).

This article discusses theoretical frameworks for addressing overt and covert marginalization in an online classroom, offers a case study of how our instructional team responded to an incident involving a microaggression committed by an online student, and provides suggestions for how lessons from our experience might be applied in other online classrooms.

Key terms and definitions

In setting the tone for our case study, we want to review some relevant terms for our work with the identities and social locations present in an online classroom.

Affinity groups

Affinity groups are composed of participants who gather based on a parti-cular social identity to engage in dialogue (Douglas, 2008; Tauriac, Kim, Lambe Sariñana, Tawa, & Kahn, 2013). They are meetings that can occur once or on an ongoing basis. When the topic is racism, affinity groups may form around the racial identities of participants. Participants may choose to meet based on the shared identity of being People of Color, Multiracial, Black, Latinx (we intentionally use this spelling of the term in order to be gender inclusive), White, and so on. The goal of affinity groups is to provide a space in which group members can speak freely and have their personal experiences validated while also creating a space that will support positive and productive dialogue across groups in the future. This process may look different when the affinity group focuses on a marginalized identity than when the affinity group focuses on a privileged identity. Again, using race as the example, white affinity groups are a space to promote antiracist belief and dismantle consciously or unconsciously held racist beliefs and values, with a core goal being that in a conversation across racial groups, white people do not invalidate the lived experiences of people of color (Michael & Conger, 2009).

Racial identity development

A great deal of work has been done on racial identity development since the 1970s, including People of Color racial identity (Helms, 1995), Black racial identity (Cross, 1971, 1978, 1991; Helms, 1990), AsianAmerican racial identity (Kim, 1981, 2012), White racial identity (Helms, 1990; 1997; Ponterotto, Utsey, & Pedersen, 2006), and Biracial identity (Poston, 1990), and more recently work on Latinx racial identity is also emerging, particularly in relation to health and the U.S. Census (Amaro & Zambrana, 2000; Borrell, 2005). Most racial identity development models define commonly occurring stages in one's racial identity. Initial stages consist of unawareness of or unquestioning acceptance of one's social location based on race. Following this are stages consisting of discovery and conflict based on the reality of racism and beliefs about race that have been internalized by the individual and those around them. Final stages consist of redefining one's racial identity. As racial identity development theories have evolved, theorists and educators have also begun to address the seemingly linear nature of racial identity development and suggest a more flexible view. Stages may be experienced in a different order, reexperienced, and borrowing from Tatum, can be pictured as movement on a spiral staircase (Helms, 1997; Tatum, 1992). Racial identity development theory can be a helpful tool in the classroom, as it provides a process-oriented framework that supports the idea that the instructional team and students in the classroom may all play a role in encouraging positive development for one another.

Microaggressions

"Racial microaggressions are brief and commonplace daily verbal, behavioral, or environmental indignities, whether intentional or unintentional, that communicate hostile, derogatory, or negative racial slights and insults toward people of color. Perpetrators of microaggressions are often unaware that they engage in such communications when they interact with racial/ethnic minorities. Microaggressions seem to appear in three forms: microassault, microinsult, and microinvalidation. Almost all interracial encounters are prone to microaggressions" (Sue et al., 2007 p. 271).

This definition stresses the importance of acknowledging how frequently racial microaggressions occur. This is done with the goal of confronting and ending racial microaggressions, not one of merely accepting this as a fact. Racial microaggressions have been shown to negatively impact mental and physical health outcomes for people of color (Sue et al., 2007); work has also been done on the negative psychosocial impacts of committing microaggressions for white people (Spanierman, Poteat, Beer, & Armstrong, 2006). Given this information, we as an instructional team see the benefits of addressing racial microaggressions for everyone involved.

Selected literature review

Social work education brings students together to study the theory and practice around many topics related to forms of oppression, such as racism, classism, and sexism, among many others. It is natural for dialogue, discussion, and debate to occur around these topics in a learning environment among students and instructional staff that are in various places in their own analyses of each form of oppression. Literature focusing on microaggressions and acts of oppression in the classroom is emerging from educators from within the social work field and related fields like psychology and education. However, this literature is still usually limited to experiences within the physical classroom.

In their reflection on their experiences as professors, Dunn, Dotson, Ford, and Roberts describe the steps they take to confront acts of oppression within the classroom as well as prevent them (2014). Their approach includes attention to their use of self. For example, Dunn writes about being a White professor teaching about racism and the importance of locating herself and her racial identity in her teaching. In her work on the application of racial identity development theory in the classroom, Tatum shares lessons she has learned through her many years of experience of working with students of color and White students in a classroom where race is the topic (1992). Tatum utilizes racial identity development theory as a core framework in her classroom, which helps her and her students strive to be compassionate with each other through understanding that each person is in a process. Tatum shares activities to help students reflect and feel heard, as well as be accountable to each other. Work on the positive impacts of racial affinity groups on intergroup dialogue in educational settings has ranged from work with high school students to graduate school students (Michael & Conger, 2009; Tauriac et al., 2013). In a study on racial microaggressions and difficult dialogues on race, Sue, Lin, Torino, Capodilupo, and Rivera focus on racial microaggressions in classrooms and the role of educators in addressing them (Sue, Lin, Torino, Capodilupo, & Rivera, 2009). Sue and his colleagues found that without direct and meaningful facilitation from educators, many students of color experienced dialogues on race following microaggressions to be invalidating through unspoken reinforcement of racist worldviews. This aligns with our assessment that incidents of racial microaggressions in any classroom space, and particularly online classrooms, should be prepared for and responded to in a meaningful way.

Theoretical framework

Creating classroom culture

Professors and classroom leaders operate as the gatekeepers to learning process, holding open or closed the doors to dialogue and collective learning. In residential classroom settings, race, gender, ethnicity, class, and many other identities are visible in the space at all times. While faculty may promote self reflexive dialogue, as Hooks (1994) says:

> Even though students enter the "democratic" classroom believing they have the right to "free speech," most students are not comfortable exercising this right to "free speech." Most students are not comfortable exercising this right–especially if it means they must give voice to thoughts, ideas, feelings that go against the grain, that are unpopular (p. 179).

While we recognize the many ways in which identity and social locations define and influence residential classroom "norms", we are asking the questions: How are these norms created within online classrooms? What role do online course instructors have in shaping online classroom culture? Distance learning is facilitated through the use of instructional technology; we suggest that this use must at all times be intentional. We suggest that creating an online classroom culture that promotes challenging dialogue and maintains core values of antioppressive pedagogy is a new challenge for distance learning educators.

Transformative learning

The principles of transformative learning provide a platform from which to develop a unique perspective on the learning needs of students and create strategies to engage students in conversations about social positionality/social location. For the purposes of this article, we are defining social location as the intersectional identities (race, class, gender, sexuality, geographic, etc.) that are experienced and formed through interpersonal, structural and internalized views of self. A useful question to begin your process of thinking through a transformative learning lens may be: "What social locations do I hold that inform my teaching?"

Transformative Learning, first described by Jack Mezirow in the 1970s, is now a greatly utilized framework for adult education. Cooper (n.d.) describes his work:

> Three common themes characterized Mezirow's theory of the mechanism of transformational learning in the classroom. These were experience, critical reflection, and rational discourse. The students' life experiences provided a starting point for transformational learning (Mezirow, 1991). Mezirow considered critical reflection to be the distinguishing characteristic of adult learning, and saw it as the vehicle by which one questions the validity of his/her worldview. He identified rational discourse as a catalyst for transformation, as it induced the various participants to explore the depth and meaning of their various worldviews, and articulate those ideas to their instructor and classmates. (Theories of Transformational Learning section, para. 7).

As instructors, we consider our primary objective for course design to be driven by the opportunity to create dialogue, promote rational discussion, and explore worldview. While transformative learning principles ideally support a cohesive and growth-oriented process of articulation of these views, opening dialogue primarily through video and written contribution additionally opens opportunity to enact violence through these technologies. If the "idea of a fundamental change in perspective or frame of reference (King, 2002) is at the heart of transformative learning" (as cited in Cooper, n. d.), an experience of a group or individual microaggression or act of violence then becomes an opportunity to promote change in perspective. This change can be promoted through critical use of technology, through direct naming and acknowledgment of the act and engaging all students as key stakeholders in the transforming the conditions of the classroom.

From theory to application

The authors of this article were members of the instructional team for an online course being piloted at a social work school located within a large, urban university in the northeast of the United States; we were the instructor, teaching assistant (TA), and online instructional support person. Students were in their first semester of a residential master's program and had the option of taking our online course in lieu of taking the same course in person. The course was consisted of asynchronous work completed independently by students in the learning management system Canvas, and mandatory synchronous weekly live virtual class sessions hosted on the web conferencing platform Adobe Connect. Students participated in the weekly classes via the following tools: webcam, microphone, polls, status icons, virtual breakout rooms, and live typed chat. Instruction during classes was conducted on webcam and mic, with slides and media. To build community, the instructional team logged in early before each class to play music and chat with students, and everyone in the course was featured in a weekly participant spotlight once during the semester, including the members of the instructional team.

Special considerations that made the online classroom different from an in-person classroom included the inability to read body language, the ability of students to hold private typed chat side conversations without the knowledge of the instructional team, the nature of an online classroom that allows for simultaneous activity such as simultaneous instructor lecture and student typed chat, and the permanence of class recordings and archives of publicly typed chat conversations.

During one live virtual class session, some students used language in the typed chat conversation that was experienced as racially microaggressive by other students in the class, which led to an argumentative discussion in the typed chat. Please see Appendix A for a decision tree for applying strategies from this incident to online classrooms. In our course, one of the TA's roles during live class sessions was to curate the typed chat area, so she was able to note the situation right away and bring it to the instructor's attention. The instructor and TA verbally acknowledged the chat room dialogue and requested that students pause their use of chat in order to focus on the class content. Instructors made clear that this discussion would be continued later with a focus on building skills for intentional dialoguing. Directly after class, the instructional team met to debrief and plan a response. Next, the instructor and TA sent an announcement to the class with the assignment to complete two additional readings and post on a newly created discussion forum, titled "Reflections on Discussing Culture and Identity in Online Classroom Spaces." The readings were "Racial Microaggressions in Everyday Life: Implications for Clinical Practice" by Sue, Capodilupo, Torino, Bucceri, Holder, Nadal, and Esquilin and "European American (White) Racial Identity Development" by Ponterotto, Utsey, and Pedersen.

In the discussion forum, students were asked to respond to the following four questions prior to the next class session. The discussion forum was intentionally set up so that students were able to read and comment on their peers' posts only after posting their own responses first:

(1) How did it feel to read the chat room discussion? What was the experience like for you?
(2) Reflecting on last week's class, were you active in this chat discussion? Were you able to say what you wanted to? Did you leave class with additional thoughts that you would like to contribute here?
(3) What have other conversations around identity, race, culture, oppression, and colonization been like for you at our school? How was this discussion similar or different?

(4) And lastly…. what can you contribute that might change the experience of this conversation for yourself?

During the week before the next class session, the instructor contacted the school's Advising Office and the school's online program associate director to apprise them of the situation, the instructional team met to debrief further and to plan the upcoming class session, the instructor met one on one with the students who committed the microaggression, and the instructor met with the students who had strongest reactions to the microaggression. During the following class session, the instructor gave a brief lecture on the topic of dialogue and discussion, and then the instructor and TA divided the class into two affinity groups, a White affinity group and a "People of the Global Majority" affinity group. The term "People of the Global Majority" was used to provide a contrast to disempowering terms commonly used to describe People of Color such as "minority," wherein simply shifting from a national perspective to a global perspective helps us to recognize that most people in the world are not of European descent.

The affinity groups met in separate virtual breakout rooms to talk using mics, with the groups facilitated by a member of the instructional team based on instructor affinity with the racial identities. After the affinity based discussions, instructors facilitated a cross-racial dialogue on camera. All students were encouraged to take a turn coming onto camera and mic to share a critical question about an experience of racial identity. Questions were drawn from personal narratives of marginalization and observations about stereotyping; questions were also centered around the experiences of specific identity groups. These questions were then engaged by peers, who each chose to come onto camera to respond. Students openly remarked during the class and emailed instructors after class that this was a unique experience that increased their understanding of critical use of self in the classroom.

As educators we maintain an objective of developing students' skills for self-reflection and self-awareness. While many forms of intersectional microaggressions are enacted in everyday life, we have observed racial microaggressions in a variety of online engagements and unique classroom spaces. Specific experiences can be best understood through the lens provided by Sue et al. (2007), we can understand classroom-based experiences and common microaggressions as incidences of colorblindness, minimization of racial-cultural issues, stereotypic assumptions, and dysfunctional helping. Colorblindness, or the act of "not seeing color," has emerged in online learning spaces that do not contain on-camera presence. Stereotypic assumptions of identity based on perception of individual names, approaches to engagement in dialogue and language choice often emerge in discussion forums where students are unable to view each other face to face. Statements such as "everyone is equal in this class" and "this is obviously a safe space" connote identity blind approaches to building relationship and can be experienced in fact as marginalizing and silencing. Additionally, online courses are often geographically diverse as we draw from an increasingly broader national and international community of students. Geographically diverse classrooms provide a unique space for students who may not have previously engaged with people outside of their homogenous communities and who may not have previously had to confront their racial assumptions of who constitutes "other." Lastly, dysfunctional helping and patronizing microaggressions may surface in spaces where students perceive specific racialized "others" to not have access to resources both academic and non-academic. We have experienced students developing tools and resources for specific students without examining the message and patronizing impact this may have on peer relationships. Since online classrooms may rely on students' expression of thought and process in written form, the propensity for enactments of privilege and use of assumptive language is increased. Recognition of the forms racial microaggressions can take, particularly in online classrooms, is crucial to formulating an effective response.

Responding to the microaggression in our online classroom required a great deal of time and energy, especially as the situation was a first for the school's nascent online program and there were no formal policies in place specific to online verbal or written comportment. Therefore, we offer our experience as a discussion starter for other schools or instructors who may be looking for situations to anticipate and prepare for when moving to online courses. As one student said (as cited in Ortega et al., 2015):

> "I believe this form of oppression [microaggression] is more likely to occur via online course format for several reasons. It is obviously linked to the 'hide behind the screen' tactic; the person doing the oppressing finds it easier to type inappropriate things since they are hidden from view. For the oppressor, there is a heightened sense of boldness in typing something they would not particularly say to the oppressed. They can counter an opinion without seeing the hurt or anger they are causing to another person (sans webcam)" (p. 21).

We offer some of our lessons learned, with the hope that they may benefit other online instructors. We have learned to consistently read all student written contributions frequently to alleviate lapse in time and response to microaggressive statements. Employing an anti-racist pedagogy to online learning requires that we be prepared for *when* a microaggression occurs, not *if*. When an opportunity to address a microaggression is brought to your attention by students working to understand your own blind spots and stay open to feedback and collaborative response is helpful. We believe that collaborating whenever possible is a best practice for online instruction; seeing collaboration as something that will take you further rather than longer is a challenge for all educators. Collaborative classroom presence increases the likelihood that incidents will be addressed, built upon and managed from a student-centered, growth-oriented approach. If you teach alone, locate another voice to support your framework, you may wish to draw on TedTalks, consult a colleague or include contemporary writing from current and relevant blogs to support your intervention. Lastly, work to keep all students involved, including students who are responsible for the microaggression. We have found that holding the group accountable for support, "calling in" all parties involved and using technology (e.g., webcam, chat curators, student facilitators) to facilitate classroom community and connection between peers impacts the group's capacity for resiliency and growth during and after a critical incident.

Conclusion

This critical incident produced a structured set of strategies aimed at student engagement and also shifted our attention globally to language choice and pedagogical decisions. Post incident, we paid fresh attention to the language of both assignment descriptions and instructions. We also encouraged students to prewrite their discussion forum responses and to self-reflectively read their work prior to posting publicly. As educators, our preparation for student posting shifted to include more detailed instruction on professional writing, use of voice, communication of values, and awareness of social location. Our feedback to student work also shifted, and we placed new value on providing feedback that even in a discussion forum post, students needed to use citations, seek current academic publications to support their perspectives, and develop their rationale for arguments. As Dweck (2007) writes, "Growth-minded teachers tell students the truth and then give them the tools to close the gap" (p. 199). We observed that many students entering as first year social workers were comfortable voicing their own perspectives, but however, they required additional support, instruction, and resourcing to hone their written communication of these viewpoints.

This critical incident resulted in our building a closer relationship with the oncampus Writing Center, transparency regarding the areas of need for online instructors within our institution and illumination of the silos between administrative offices for addressing student comportment. Lastly, while the course centered historically marginalized voices, we paced the introduction of terminology related to social justice, social identity, and historical experience with additional time for question and answer and application of new language within the class final projects.

We are interested in further research on the ways in which transformative learning principles impact the collaborative relationships between coteaching faculty and selfreflection regarding pedagogical risk taking. We also believe that further research on racial microaggressions in online classrooms will be vital to developing a more critical lens toward distance learning and online community. We encourage educators and educational researchers to join this dialogue about the contemporary challenges of distance learning and uses of technology in mediating experiences of microaggressions.

Disclosure statement

No potential conflict of interest was reported by the authors.

References

Abels, P. (2005). *Distance education in social work: Planning, teaching, and learning.* New York, NY: Springer Publishing Company.

Amaro, H., & Zambrana, R. E. (2000). Criollo, mestizo, mulato, LatiNegro, indígena, white, or black? The US Hispanic/Latino population and multiple responses in the 2000 census. *American Journal of Public Health, 90* (11), 1724. doi:10.2105/AJPH.90.11.1724

Borrell, L. N. (2005). Racial identity among Hispanics: Implications for health and wellbeing. *American Journal of Public Health, 95* (3), 379–381. doi:10.2105/AJPH.2004.058172

Cooper, S. (n.d.). Theories of Learning in Educational Psychology. *Quilts, Persian Cats, Old Violins & Other Fascinating Stuff.* Retrieved from http://www.lifecirclesinc.com/Learningtheories/humanist/mezirow.html

Council on Social Work Education. (n.d.). *Online and Distance Education.* Retrieved from http://www.cswe.org/Accreditation/Information/OnlineandDistanceEducation.aspx

Cross, W. E. (1971). The Negro to Black conversion experience: Toward a psychology of Black liberation. Black World, 20, 13–27.

Cross, W. E. (1978). The Thomas and Cross models of psychological Nigrescence: A literature review. Journal of Black Psychology, 4, 13–31.

Cross, W. E. (1991). Shades of Black: Diversity in African American identity. Philadelphia: Temple University Press.

Douglas, P. H. (2008). Affinity groups: Catalyst for inclusive organizations. *Employment Relations Today, 34* (4), 11–18. doi:10.1002/ert.20171

Dunn, A. H., Dotson, E. K., Ford, J. C., & Roberts, M. A. (2014). "You Won't Believe What They Said in Class Today": Professors' reflections on student resistance in multicultural education courses. *Multicultural Perspectives, 16* (2), 93–98. doi:10.1080/15210960.2014.899779

Dweck, C. S. (2006). Mindset: The new psychology of success. New York: Random House.

Freire, P. (1985). *The politics of education: Culture, power, and liberation.* Hadley, MA: Greenwood Publishing Group.

Helms, J. E. (1990). *Black and White racial identity: Theory, research, and practice.* Westport, CT: Greenwood Press.

Helms, J. E. (1995). An update of Helm's White and people of color racial identity models. In Versions were presented at the Psychology and Societal Transformation Conference, U Western Cape, South Africa, Jan 1994, and at a workshop entitled "Helm's Racial Identity Theory," Annual Multicultural Winter Roundtable, Teachers Coll–Columbia U, Sage Publications, Inc., New York, Feb 1994.

Helms, J. E. (1997). *Implications of Behrens (1997) for the validity of the White Racial Identity Attitude Scale.* Thousand Oaks, CA: SAGE Publications.

Hooks, B. (1994). *Teaching to transgress.* New York, NY: Routledge.

Kim, J. (1981). *Processes of Asian American identity development: A study of Japanese American women's perceptions of their struggle to achieve positive identities as Americans of Asian ancestry.* Available from Proquest. AAI8118010. http://scholarworks.umass.edu/dissertations/AAI8118010

King, J. (2012). Asian American racial identity development theory. In C. Wijeyesinghe & B. W Jackson (Eds.), New perspectives on racial identity development: a theoretical and practical anthology (2nd ed.) (pp.138–160). New York, NY: NYU Press.

Mezirow, J. (1978). Perspective transformation. Adult Education, 28 (2), 100–109.

Mezirow, Jack. (1991). Transformative Dimensions of Adult Learning. San Francisco: Jossey-Bass.

Michael, A., & Conger, M. C. (2009). Becoming an antiracist white ally: How a white affinity group can help. Perspectives on Urban Education, 6 (1), 56–60.

National Association of Social Workers. (2008). Code of Ethics. Retrieved from https://www.socialworkers.org/pubs/code/code.asp

Ortega, A., Marquart, M., & Andruczyk, M. (2015). Addressing acts of oppression within online classrooms: Best Practices and Collaborative Solutions. [PDF document]. Workshop presented at the Social Work Distance Education Conference, Indianapolis, April 16, 2015. doi.10.7916/D8PK0F9H

Ponterotto, J. G., Utsey, S., & Pedersen, P. (2006). European American (White) racial identity development. Mental health, and prejudice. In O. U. JG Ponterotto, & P. B. Pedersen Eds., Preventing Prejudice: A Guide for Counselors, Educators, and Parents (2nd). Thousand Oaks, CA: SAGE Publications. Retrieved from http://www. sagepub. com/upmdata/11558_Chapter_5. pdf iconBook

Poston, W. S. C. (1990). The biracial identity development model: A needed addition. Journal of Counseling and Development, 69(2), 152.

Spanierman, L. B., Poteat, V. P., Beer, A. M., & Armstrong, P. I. (2006). Psychosocial costs of racism to whites: Exploring patterns through cluster analysis. Journal of Counseling Psychology, 53 (4), 434. doi:10.1037/0022-0167.53.4.434

Sue, D. W., Capodilupo, C. M., Torino, G. C., Bucceri, J. M., Holder, A., Nadal, K. L., & Esquilin, M. (2007). Racial microaggressions in everyday life: Implications for clinical practice. American Psychologist, 62 (4), 271. doi:10.1037/0003-066X.62.4.271

Sue, D. W., Lin, A. I., Torino, G. C., Capodilupo, C. M., & Rivera, D. P. (2009). Racial microaggressions and difficult dialogues on race in the classroom. Cultural Diversity and Ethnic Minority Psychology, 15 (2), 183. doi:10.1037/a0014191

Tatum, B. (1992). Talking about race, learning about racism: The application of racial identity development theory in the classroom. Harvard Educational Review, 62 (1), 1–25. doi:10.17763/haer.62.1.146k5v980r703023

Tauriac, J. J., Kim, G. S., Lambe Sariñana, S., Tawa, J., & Kahn, V. D. (2013). Utilizing affinity groups to enhance intergroup dialogue workshops for racially and ethnically diverse students. The Journal for Specialists in Group Work, 38 (3), 241–260. doi:10.1080/01933922.2013.800176

Wolchover, N. (2012, July 25). Why is everyone on the internet so angry? Scientific American, Retrieved from http://www.scientificamerican.com/article/whyiseveryoneontheinternetsoangry/

Appendix A: Decision Tree

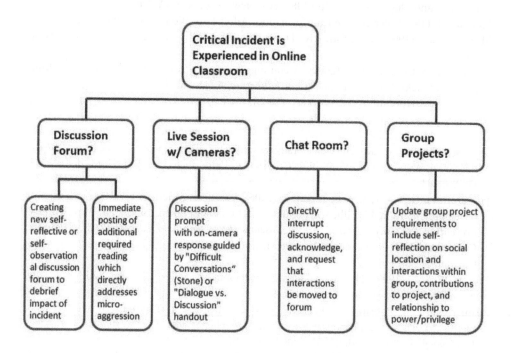

Multiracial Microaggressions: Implications for Social Work Education and Practice

Babe Kawaii-Bogue, Sreten Franovic, and Andrew Jolivette

ABSTRACT

Racism scholars have made intentional efforts to produce research for the development of educational strategies to address racial microaggressions. Similarly, the counseling profession has made a conscious effort to create multicultural guidelines and standards that can assist in the prevention of racial discrimination in therapeutic practice. However, no educational strategies or counseling standards have been created to address monoracism in social work education or practice settings. The authors propose education and practice recommendations to advance social workers multicultural training. To that end, this article focuses on (1) presenting the multi-faceted array of racial microaggressions faced by Multiracial populations, (2) documenting racial microaggressions faced by Multiracial students in social work education and practice settings, and (3) proposing considerations for the inclusion of Multiracial populations in social work education and practice efforts.

The population of Multiracial Americans is increasing three times faster than the general population (Pew, 2015). By 2050, Multiracial Americans are projected to be 20% of the United States population (Jones & Bullock, 2012). Prior to the 2000 Census, Multiracial Americans were unable to report their racial identities as two or more races, such that they were forced to either select only one racial category or select multiple racial categories. Between the 2000 and the 2010 Census, the percentage of people reporting two or more races increased by 32%, while the population reporting one race, increased by only 9% (Pew, 2015). The term *Multiracial* is used to classify populations with heritages consisting of two or more racial or ethnic groups (e.g., black/white, Asian/Latino, Native American/black/white) (Root, 1995). The opposite term, *monoracial*, refers to the second racial grouping of individuals, who have heritages of only one racial or ethnic group.

Monoracism has been defined by scholars as "a social system of psychological inequality where individuals who do not fit monoracial categories may be oppressed on systemic and inter-personal levels because of underlying assumptions and beliefs in singular, discrete racial categories" (Johnston & Nadal, 2010, p. 123). Monoracism is a form of racial discrimination targeting Multiracial populations and is perpetrated by monoracial populations (e.g., a monoracial teacher asks an Asian/white student to join either a person of color group or a white racial group for a discussion on racism). In this instance, the teacher is operating from a monoracist perspective, assuming that all people identify with only one racial group or that Multiracial people identify only with their minority racial group [i.e., hypodescent]) or their white racial group.

Multiracial microaggressions are the "daily verbal, behavioral, or environmental indignities, whether intentional or unintentional, enacted by monoracial persons that communicate hostile, derogatory, or negative slights toward Multiracial individuals or groups" (Johnston & Nadal, 2010, p. 126). Johnston and Nadal (2010) performed two studies to create the only known taxonomies that identify Multiracial populations' experiences with racial microaggressions. The authors of these two studies found that Multiracial populations' experiences with racial microaggressions are different from the microaggressive experiences documented for monoracial populations.

The following taxonomical microaggressions will first be described broadly and then grounded in examples of a Multiracial recipient encountering the microaggression. The documented Multiracial microaggression taxonomies are as follows: (1) *Exclusion or Isolation*, which occurs when a Multiracial person is made to feel excluded or isolated based on their mixed racial heritage, (2) *Exoticization and Objectification* transpires when a Multiracial person is made to feel dehumanized or treated like an object, (3) *Pathologizing of Identity and Experiences* occurs when a Multiracial person's identity or experiences are viewed as psychologically abnormal, (4) *Assumption of a Monoracial or Mistaken Identity* arises when a Multiracial person is assumed to be monoracial or mistaken as a different racial group than which they identify, (5) *Denial of Multiracial Reality* occurs when a Multiracial person's experiences are invalidated by monoracial people, and (6) *Microaggressions Based on Stereotypes* refers to experiences where Multiracial people are stereotyped based on their monoracial phenotypes (Johnston & Nadal, 2010).

Multiracial microaggressions in social work education

Case example

With a better understanding of the racial microaggressions faced by Multiracial Americans, we will now examine the social work education literature and consider the Multiracial microaggressions likely to arise in social work education settings. An extensive review of the literature revealed a dearth of documentation on the microaggressive experiences of mixed race people in social work education settings. However, one article in the literature depicted a clear example of a detailed Multiracial microaggressive experience in a social work education setting. In the article, a white social work professor discusses a race talk with a mixed race student (Staller, 2014). In the article, the professor documents her encounter with the mixed race student in a closed-door conversation. According to the article, the mixed race student attempted to engage her professor to discuss her experiences of racial microaggressions in the professor's classroom. The mixed race student raised concerns about the professor's usage of the terms, "alien" and "negro" in their social work class. In the meeting, the student sought to ask the professor to refrain from using the words further in course discussions. The professor reported how she committed Multiracial microaggressions in the classroom and how she "silenced" the mixed race student from having a fruitful race talk in their private meeting.

In this case, one Multiracial microaggression the professor commits is the *Assumption of a Monoracial or Mistaken Identity*. To explain, the professor describes her perceptions of the encounter and writes that the mixed race social work student "identifies as an African American. I use the words 'self-identified' because – had I been asked to describe her race – I would have said, 'white.' Perhaps, if pushed harder, I would have described her as 'ethnic looking.'" The professor concludes that she "didn't see who [the student] was" (Staller, 2014, p. 170). One consideration regarding *assuming a monoracial or mistaken identity* is for instructors and students alike, not to assume students identify with their perceived race(s). In the case example with the professor above, the Multiracial African American student addressed the professor's usage of the term "negro" in the social work classroom, and the professor assumed the student was white. If the classroom had no other African American students present (apart from the mixed race student in the scenario), the white professor and other students in the classroom might not have been as cautious of their potentially microaggressive language toward African Americans.

The racial composition of a social setting (e.g. a social work classroom) can dictate the degree of microaggressive experiences for a mixed race person. To explain, mixed race people are subjected to racial microaggressions just by way of oftentimes not appearing to be one or more of their racial identities. Thus, unknown to the perpetrators, mixed race individuals can witness the constant belittlement of their racial minority group(s). Whereas, if a mixed race person phenotypically appeared solely as a member of their minority racial group(s), they might not be subjected to as many microaggressions due to a mistaken identity.

The article written by the white social work professor in this case study is also an example of what could be perceived as a misuse of power and privilege by a white professor. Specifically, the white professor used her power to define the reality of the racial encounter and used her power as a journal editor to publish their private race conversation in her journal without the student's knowledge or permission. Race scholars have discussed this characteristic of racial dialogues by purporting that white professors have "greater authority and power... to define racial reality" (Sue, 2013, p. 665). Scholars have also documented that race talks "between members of different racial and ethnic groups...[can] involve an unequal status relationship of power and privilege among participants" (Sue, 2013, p. 665). The professor confessed in the article, stating:

> I got defensive...[and] delivered my defense as a barrage of arguments hurled at my student. As I asserted my power, my privilege, my authority, and my unfettered sense of 'rightness,' I silenced her. My best attempts at repairing the damage, failed. Her cultural experiences as an African American woman, had been denied a fair hearing (Staller, 2014, p. 171).

The "defensive[ness]" discussed by the professor is a commonly reported occurrence for white participants who engage in race talks. The white participants' defensiveness and shutting down of race talks is believed to stem from a fear of 1) appearing racist, 2) recognizing their own racism, 3) confronting white privilege, or 4) taking responsibility to eliminate racism (Sue, 2013).

Further considerations for multiracial inclusivity

Another Multiracial microaggression that can arise for mixed race students is the commonly reported experience of *racial isolation or exclusion* (Johnston & Nadal, 2010).

For instance, mixed race people's experiences are often excluded from instructional materials, even in courses discussing issues about race. Thus, Multiracial students can feel easily excluded from conversations pertaining to race. Just as monoracial people of color have been forced to adapt to a Eurocentric society and an overexposure to a Eurocentric curriculum, Multiracial people are accustomed to living in a monoracial culture and are accustomed to being taught an exclusively monoracial curriculum. With that said, efforts to diversify and decolonize educational material is still on the horizon for schools of social work, and within that effort, it is crucial to begin to assess and address a potentially monoracist curriculum. Another way in which monoracism can present itself in an educational setting is through the deliberate or unintentional racial dichotomization of students (i.e., students of color vs. white students). When students are divided into racial groups for course activities, it is important to understand the effects of racial dichotomization on mixed race people. Allowing mixed race students to choose their own way of identifying racially (or respecting their choice to not identify racially), as well as creating space for them to process their experiences (i.e. creating a mixed race group or "border racial identity group" for an intergroup racial dialogue) is critical to the inclusion of mixed race students in a social work course.

Furthermore, when discussing the topic of race, it is vital to examine areas of the curriculum that can potentially exclude mixed race perspectives. Inclusivity efforts are imperative to integrating mixed race experiences in course curriculums and validating students of mixed race heritages in social work course discussions. Again, we encourage intentional curriculum planning to create spaces for diverse experiences to be voiced, moving towards the inclusion of mixed race students in racial dialogues. A simple inclusive question an instructor can pose during a class discussion about race could be, "Might anyone who holds another racial identification wish to add to this racial discussion?" Another simple yet overlooked way to address monoracism in the classroom is to include mixed race authors on course reading lists and discuss the importance of their unique racial insights and perspectives on race relations and across the social work discipline.

Benefits of multiracial inclusivity

From examining previous literature on Multiracial microaggressions, we know that Multiracial populations have several unique experiences that are important for social work educators to consider. Scholars have noted that Multiracial populations are subjected to racial microaggression experiences from their own family members (Nadal, Sriken, Davidoff, Wong, & McLean, 2013) and their own racial communities (Gaskin, 1999). Because of these unique racial experiences, a mixed race student might bring a heightened racial sensitivity to the classroom. For instance, mixed race students might be able to quickly identify racial microaggressions in educational settings. It is important to consider whether a mixed race student can offer unique insights into race discussions, especially since people of color are more open to discussing racial topics in the classroom than their white counterparts (Sue, 2013). If a mixed race student is willing to engage in a racial dialogue with students or professors, it is imperative to acknowledge that the mixed student might bring a rare racial insight to the dialogue. In order to foster productive race talks in social work classrooms, it is essential to obtain feedback from students with multiple racial/ethnic backgrounds.

Consider the following questions when evaluating Multiracial inclusivity in your social work classroom and education setting: (a) What assumptions am I making about students' knowledge and experiences based on their phenotypes? (b) How can I create a classroom environment to ensure that Multiracial students feel more included in race talks? (c) How do my Multiracial students prefer to be identified racially (e.g., mixed race, Multiracial, biracial, African American)? (d) How might a Multiracial student's perspective add to a class discussion on racism? (e) How can I incorporate Multiracial perspectives in my course curriculum to combat monoracism and work toward the inclusion of Multiracial students in my course?

Multiracial microaggressions in social work practice

In an effort to maintain cultural humility in working with racial groups, social workers must first recognize the social stressors facing a particular racial group, and then understand how that racial group copes with these unique stressors. Therefore, this section focuses on Multiracial microaggressions that can arise in social work practice. Furthermore, we consider how a social worker can address these microaggressions in practice settings. Finally, we will draw upon recent Multiracial discrimination coping research to suggest focal areas for addressing microaggression experiences through strength's based practice with Multiracial populations.

The existing literature on clinical practice with Multiracial populations has focused heavily on racial identity processes (see Edwards & Pedrotti, 2008; McDowell et al., 2005, Rockquemore, Brunsma, & Delgado, 2009) and has historically viewed Multiracial populations through a pathology-based lens (e.g., Gibbs, 1987). A number of the documented Multiracial microaggressions consist of racial slights directed towards the racial identities of mixed race people. Contextually, Multiracial populations occupy a unique social position, because they can assume three or more racial perspectives: two or more monoracial viewpoints and a Multiracial viewpoint. Thus, working with this population will require cultural sensitivity in working with clients potentially carrying several racial perspectives.

Racial identity

The first topic area that might arise when working with Multiracial populations is *racial identity*. It is important to keep in mind that racial socialization processes and racial perspectives are different than an individual's held racial identity. For instance, two Multiracial siblings with the same biological parents and social upbringings might hold different racial identities. Researchers have found that Multiracial clients can embrace various racial identities: (a) a singular monoracial identity, (b) multiple monoracial identities, (c) a Multiracial identity, (d) an extraracial identity, and (e) a situational identity (Renn, 2008). Scholars have also revealed that women are more likely to identify as Multiracial than men (Pew, 2015). Thus, it is more common in siblings from mixed race heritages to see a brother identify as monoracial and a sister identify as Multiracial. Moreover, Multiracial Americans are arguably the most racially and ethnically diverse group in the United States. As a result, racial identities among this population will vary tremendously depending on a client's racial socialization process, their familial racial composition, their community's racial demographics (their community of origin demographics and their present community demographics), and the client's generational status.[1]

Given differences in generational status, gender, and racial socialization processes among mixed race people, it is important not to assume Multiracial clients identify racially with their parents or their siblings, or even that a client holds a racial identity. Additionally, Multiracial Americans have often reported experiences with others denying their racial identities (Johnston & Nadal, 2010; Nadal et al., 2013). Therefore, it is important to be aware of and respect the ways in which clients choose to identify themselves, if they choose to identify racially. Asking clients if and how they choose to identify can validate individuals who have potentially encountered resistance to choosing their own racial identities.

Exclusion/isolation

The denial of mixed race people's racial identities can lead to their feelings of racial exclusion and isolation. The exclusion of Multiracial people from monoracial groups and communities has been identified in the literature as a common Multiracial microaggression (Root, 1990). Psychotherapy services might serve as one of the only spaces where Multiracial people can gain racial affirmation and acceptance. Interestingly, Multiracial populations are the highest consumers of psychotherapeutic services, utilizing services at a higher rate than any other racial/ethnic group, including monoracial white populations (Harris, Edlund, & Larson, 2005). We propose that this elevated usage of therapy services is due in part to a scarcity of communities and spaces for Multiracial populations to process their unique racialized experiences. That is, that not having a validating racial experience or "racial home" might account for the comparably high percentage of Multiracial clients using psychotherapeutic services.

---

[1]Generational status is an important consideration for understanding the sociopolitical context and racial socialization conditions in which a Multiracial individual was raised. Specifically, generational status can be determined based on the length of time between the repeal of anti-miscegenation laws (i.e. year 1957) and a person's birth year. Closer to the time period of anti-miscegenation laws, society was less accepting of interracial relationships and Multiracial people, such that individuals were less likely to identify as Multiracial.

Conclusion

Multiracial populations are often denied racial identities, they are excluded and isolated from monoracial spaces, and as a result, the population is often left out of conversations about race. The facilitation of more discussions about Multiracial experiences may benefit both a client and an educational community. The majority of the practice recommendations presented in this article focus on the types of Multiracial microaggressions and why they might present with Multiracial clients in social work practice settings. We refer to the plethora of previous literature providing guidance on how to engage this population in social work practice settings (see Fong, Spickard, & Ewalt, 1995; Jackson & Samuels, 2011; Jackson, Wolven, & Aguilera, 2013; Jackson, 2016; Johnston & Nadal, 2010; McDowell et al., 2005). For example, Johnston and Nadal (2010) applied their aforementioned Multiracial microaggression taxonomy to include practice recommendations for addressing each micro-aggressive taxonomy in clinical therapeutic settings (see Johnston & Nadal, 2010).

Finally, the focus on language usage is critical to the inclusion of Multiracial communities in education settings and for the personal growth of Multiracial clients in practice settings. It is our belief that monoracism is rooted in the dehumanizing language used to refer to Multiracial populations (e.g., *half* racial group, *part* racial group, racial group %). We urge social work educators and practitioners to begin to dismantle monoracism by using "whole-person" language choices (e.g., Multiracial black, instead of *half* black) and by acknowledging Multiracial people's rights to self-identify, even if this includes their preference for using terms such as, "half-Asian." Through an awareness of Multiracial microaggressions, the reshaping of language, and efforts towards the inclusivity of Multiracial populations in education and practice settings, social workers will become more equipped to empower one of the fastest growing racial groups in the United States.

References

Edwards, L. M., & Pedrotti, J. T. (2008). A content and methodological review of articles concerning multiracial issues in six major counseling journals. *Journal of Counseling Psychology, 55*(3), 411–418. doi:10.1037/0022-0167.55.3.411

Fong, R., Spickard, P. R., & Ewalt, P. L. (1995). Editorial: A multiracial reality: Issues for social work. *Social Work, 40*(6), 725–728.

Gaskins, P. (1999). *What are you? Voices of mixed-race young people.* New York, NY: Holt.

Gibbs, J. T. (1987). Identity and marginality: Issues in the treatment of biracial adolescents. *American Journal of Orthopsychiatry, 57*(2), 265–278. doi:10.1111/j.1939-0025.1987.tb03537.x

Harris, K. M., Edlund, M. J., & Larson, S. (2005). Racial and ethnic differences in the mental health problems and use of mental health care. *Medical Care, 43*(8), 775–784. doi:10.1097/01.mlr.0000170405.66264.23

Jackson, K. F. (2016). Culturally competent social work practice with biracial/multiracial persons. In: D. W. Sue (ed), *Multicultural social work practice: A competency-based approach to diversity and social justice*. New Jersey, USA: John Wiley & Sons, Inc.

Jackson, K. F., & Samuels, G. M. (2011). Multiracial competence in social work: Recommendations for culturally attuned work with Multiracial people. *Social Work, 56*(3), 235–245. doi:10.1093/sw/56.3.235

Jackson, K. F., Wolven, T., & Aguilera, K. (2013). Mixed resilience: A study of multiethnic Mexican American stress and coping in Arizona. *Family Relations, 62*(1), 212–225. doi:10.1111/fare.2013.62.issue-1

Johnston, M. P., & Nadal, K. L. (2010). Multiracial microaggressions: Exposing monoracism in everyday life and practice. In: D. W. Sue (Ed.), *Microaggressions and marginality: Manifestation, dynamics, and impact* (pp. 123–144). New Jersey, USA: John Wiley & Sons Inc.

Jones, J. M., Lynch, P. D., Tenglund, A. A., & Gaertner, S. L. (2001). Toward a diversity hypothesis: Multidimensional effects of intergroup contact. *Applied and Preventive Psychology, 9*(1), 53–62. doi:10.1016/S0962-1849(05)80037-X

Jones, N. A., & Bullock, J., (2012). The two or more races population: 2010. 2010 Census Brief Series. Washington, DC: U.S. Census Bureau. Available from: https://www.census.gov/prod/cen2010/briefs/c2010br-13.pdf

McDowell, T., Ingoglia, L., Serizawa, T., Holland, C., Dashiell, W., & Stevens, C. (2015). Breaking the mold: Multiracial awareness in family therapy. *Journal of Marital and Family Therapy, 31*, 399–411.

Nadal, K. L., Sriken, J., Davidoff, K. C., Wong, Y., & McLean, K. (2013). Microaggressions within families: Experiences of multiracial people. *Family Relations, 62*(1), 190–201. doi:10.1111/fare.2013.62.issue-1

Pew Research Center. (2015). *Multiracial in America: Proud, diverse and growing in numbers*. Washington, D.C: The Pew Research Center. Available from: http://www.pewsocialtrends.org/files/2015/06/2015-06-11_multiracial-in-america_final-updated.pdf and the citation recommendation is on the bottom of the first page.

Renn, K. A. (2008). Research on biracial and Multiracial identity development: Overview and synthesis. *New Directions for Student Services, 2008*, 13–21. doi:10.1002/ss.v2008:123

Rockquemore, K. A., Brunsma, D. L., & Delgado, D. J. (2009). Racing to theory or retheorizing race? Understanding the struggle to build a Multiracial identity theory. *Journal of Social Issues, 65*(1), 13–34. doi:10.1111/josi.2009.65.issue-1

Root, M. P. P. (1990). Resolving "other" status: Identity development of biracial individuals. *Women and Therapy, 9*(1–2), 185–205. doi:10.1300/J015v09n01_11

Root, M. P. P. (1995). *The multiracial experience: Racial borders as the new frontier*. Thousand Oaks, CA: Sage.

Staller, K. M. (2014). Difficult conversations: Talking with rather than talking at. *Qualitative Social Work, 13*(2), 167–175. doi:10.1177/1473325014521335

Sue, D. W. (2013). Race talk: The psychology of racial dialogues. *American Psychologist, 68*(8), 663–672. doi:10.1037/a0033681

Sue, D. W., Arredondo, P., & McDavis, R. J. (1992). Multicultural competencies/standards: A call to the profession. *Journal of Counseling & Development, 70*, 477–486. doi:10.1002/j.1556-6676.1992.tb01642.x

Sue, D. W., Capodilupo, C. M., Torino, G. C., Bucceri, J. M., Holder, A., Nadal, K. L., & Esquilin, M. (2007). Racial microaggressions in everyday life: Implications for clinical practice. *American Psychologist, 62*(4), 271–286. doi:10.1037/0003-066X.62.4.271

Racial microaggressions in social work education: Black students' encounters in a predominantly White institution

Leslie D. Hollingsworth, Desmond U. Patton, Phylicia C. Allen, and Kimson E. Johnson

ABSTRACT

Research findings have substantiated encounters with racial microaggressions by Black students in predominantly White institutions. Yet no studies focus on students in social work programs. This is important since racial microaggressions can affect students' academic, social, and emotional experiences, as well as career preparation of counseling students. In this study we examined encounters reported by 10 Black Master of Social Work students. We present an in-depth case example as support for the emergence of a *Racial Microaggressions Interaction Framework*, demonstrating how students define racial microaggressions and the socioemotional continuum along which they proceed following encounters. Implications are discussed for teaching from a culturally relevant competence perspective.

In writing for the *Encyclopedia of Social Work*, Rodgers (August 2015) describes racism as "pervasive, endemic, and historically rooted in systemic assumptions inherent in superiority based on race." While overt expressions have become less prevalent, subtle expressions are more frequent. Racial microaggressions constitute one form. Originally introduced by Pierce (1970), racial microaggressions were conceptualized by Sue et al. (2007) as "brief and commonplace daily verbal, behavioral, or environmental indignities, whether intentional or unintentional, that communicate hostile, derogatory, or negative racial slights and insults toward people of color" (p. 271). The current study arose from complaints of Black students in one Master of Social Work program about experiences with racial microaggressions. Two Black faculty members and a Black alumna used focus groups to examine students' experiences—how they defined racial microaggressions and how they processed the experience. We situate our findings within racial microaggressions literature, extending current knowledge to illuminate perceptions of Black social work students.

Literature review

Drawing on efforts to differentiate racial microaggressions from traditional racism, Sue and colleagues (2007) created a taxonomy of racial microaggressions. Microassaults are "verbal or non-verbal attacks ... intended to hurt" (p. 274). Microinsults "convey rudeness and insensitivity and demean a person's racial heritage or identity" (p. 274). Microinvalidations "exclude, negate, or nullify the thoughts, feelings or reality of a person of color." Racial microaggressions were further categorized into eight original themes. These researchers categorized racial microaggressions into distinct themes: (1) perceived as an "alien in one's own land;" (2) intelligence assigned on the basis of race; (3) color blindness or denial of reality of race; (4) assumption of criminal status on the basis of race; (5) denial of personal racism; (6) denial race plays a part in life successes; (7) pathologizing cultural values/communication styles; (8) ascribing second-class status on the basis of race; and (9) environmental microaggressions at systemic or environmental levels (p. 276). A subsequent focus group study of Black Americans (Sue, Nadal, Capodilupo, Torino, & Rivera, 2008), reduced these themes to six and identified two new ones—assumption of inferior status and assumed universality of the Black experience. The "invisibility to the perpetrator and others of the perpetrator's race" (p. 275) gives rise to dilemmas, for recipients, regarding whether or how to respond (Sue et al., 2007, pp. 277–279).

Black students' experiences with microaggressions and discrimination

Building on the Sue et al. (2007) conceptualization, Wong, Derthick, David, Saw, and Okazaki (2013) identified 60 published scholarly papers and 13 dissertations on racial microaggressions. Of the 36 conducted in a university context, 18 involved Black Americans as have a number of subsequent studies. Solorzano, Ceja, and Yosso (2000) noted that racial microaggressions exist in both academic and social spaces in the collegiate environment of African American college students and negatively affect campus racial climates. Racial microaggressions occurred in campus-academic, -social, and -public spaces. Smith, Allen, and Danley (2007) identified anti-Black male stereotyping and marginality at four major universities—experiences that led to hyper-surveillance and control.

Constantine and Sue (2007) identified seven microaggression themes in a focus-group study of 10 self-identified Black counseling and clinical psychology doctoral supervisees. Torres, Driscoll, and Burrow (2010) noted three categories of racial microaggression experiences among 97 African American doctoral students and graduates: assumption of criminality/second-class citizen, underestimation of personal ability, and cultural/racial isolation. Underestimation of personal ability was associated with greater perceived stress at 1-year follow-up which was, in turn, related to greater depressive symptoms. Robinson (2012) identified microinsults and micro-inequities as the primary types of microaggressions experienced by African American women and Latina doctoral students in counselor education programs. These experiences affected emotional, academic, and career, as well as interpersonal/social, physical, psychological, personal, and spiritual components of wellness. Blume, Lovato, Thyken, and Denny (2012) found ethnic minority college students in a predominantly White institution reported significantly more microaggressions than their European American counterparts, with self-efficacy and microaggressions significantly associated with anxiety and with binge drinking. Nadal, Wong, Griffin, Davidoff, & Shriken (2014) show that racial microaggressions negatively predict lower self-esteem. Finally, there is evidence of an intersection between race, gender, and class in the experiences of Black students in higher education environments (Morales, 2014).

Research questions

Of the 18 university-associated studies of racial microaggressions reviewed by Wong et al. (2013) and other studies involving Black students, none focused on graduate students in social work programs.[1] Hence, we explored perceptions of Black students in a graduate school of social work, using focus groups to produce qualitative data (Kruger, 1988). Our overarching questions were: How did Black students define racial microaggressions?. How did they perceive occurrences of racial microaggressions in the various domains of their graduate education?

Method

Participant characteristics

Participants self-identified as Black, African American, or Afro-Caribbean. (Students with these self-identifications comprised 11% of the 649 students enrolled in the school.) Of the four participants in the second focus group, three were MSW research assistants (RAs) who had helped recruit and facilitate the first focus group. The majority were in their second year of the 2-year program; three were in their first term. Three attended a Historically Black College or University as undergraduates. Eight were women. No other demographics were collected.

---

[1]Since undergraduate majors were not specified, it is possible that some African American undergraduates represented in the 18 studies were social work majors.

Sampling procedures

Because we were interested in the nature of racial microaggressions experienced by Black graduate students, we limited our sample to that population, following the concept of "theoretical sampling" (Corbin & Strauss, 2008, p. 144). Ten Black MSW students volunteered for two focus groups—six in the first group, four in the second. Students were recruited via meetings of the Association of Black Social Work Students, e-mail, and word-of-mouth.

Research design

Focus groups constituted the design around which our study was conceptualized. Kruger (1988) notes "the focus group presents a natural environment where participants are influencing and influenced by others" (p. 30). Accordingly, "the researcher serves the function of moderating, listening, observing, and eventually analyzing, using an inductive process" (p 30).

Data collection

Using the university's Institutional Review Board procedure, participants signed informed consent forms that explained the purpose, content, and process of the study, including videotaping. Data collection occurred on two separate days during fall 2014. Focus groups were held in a private conference room of the school. A structured protocol directed the interviews, ensuring that all participants received the same questions and followed the same procedure. Included were the study's historical background, it's purpose, and its potential usefulness. Questions included participants' definition of racial microaggressions and anonymous examples of racial microaggressions encountered, observed or perceived in different parts of the school (peer/classroom/or field instruction interactions), university, or broader community. Participants also gave suggestions for managing racial microaggressions presented in printed vignettes.

Data analysis and results

Consistent with recommendations of Krueger (1988) and Corbin and Strauss (2008), we began with open coding of transcribed data from the first focus group, coding for major evident categories. We then coded data from the second group, applying codes from the first, then identifying additional codes. To ensure trustworthiness, two research team members coded the data independently and then collaborated in arriving at final codes and categories. From open coding we identified seven categories of information on racial microaggressions: *definition(s), examples, responses, effect* (immediate), *impact* (broader, longer term), *suggested corrections,* and *risk or protective factors as context.*

Definitions

"Something that is unbeknownst." *I've understood racial microaggressions as something that is unbeknownst to the person that's sort of delivering the microaggression.*

"Passively saying things that are offensive." *Anytime I think of something being like a micro ...so it's something that may not occur where we're just walking up to people and we're calling people out of their name...; rather, we're sort of passively saying things that are offensive and not sort of giving a care once you say it.*

"Just straight up aggression." *So I would call the majority of the micro-aggressions that I felt, macroaggressions—just straight-up aggression—and you didn't want to direct it at me, so you wanted to keep it general. And we patty-cake around the term racism.*

Examples, responses, effects, and impact

These categories emerged from analysis of transcripts containing participants' perceived encounters with racial microaggressions within class, field instruction, social interactions, university, and broader community domains. From these we arrived at the meanings of each category and used these to develop the codebook. From analysis of stated or implied meanings, we identified a "core phenomenon" (Corbin & Strauss, 1990, p. 14) of conceptual interest and essential to the process being studied. That core phenomenon was an observed or experienced encounter with a perceived racial microaggression. We then engaged in axial coding (Corbin & Strauss, 1990, p.13), returning to the data and identifying categories around the core phenomenon. Here we observed one additional category—thoughts or interpretation, and a pattern in the relationship of the other four to the core phenomenon. Corbin and Strauss (1990) refer to this as an "axial coding paradigm" (p. 13). Below we provide one case example that depicts this paradigm.

"[Race] is not an expression. This is who I am."

Jasmine is in her first semester of the MSW program after having attended this same university as an undergraduate. She described an experience in which a student in a class she was in made a comparison between race and what she perceived as self-selected expression.

So, I was sitting in one of my classes the other day and someone was giving information about their internship. And so this White [student] was saying that [the student] was experiencing issues in [their] internship because [they] went for this orientation and they were telling [the student] "Well for this job you have to cover up your tattoos." *And so [the student] said they felt really uncomfortable because that's a form of expression*: "Why should I have to cover up my tattoos to get this job?" *And [the student] was like,* "You know, that's just as if someone goes and tries to apply for this job, and they're African American and they turn them down because they're African American. This is my tattoo. This is who I am." [Encounter/core phenomenon] *and I was frustrated.* [Feeling] *that's like comparing oranges and apples. This (race)—it's not an expression; it's who I am. I can't cover it up and go into a job and get the job.* [Thought or interpretation] *so afterwards—I didn't really address it right then* [Intent] *because I was frustrated. So, I took the professor to the side, and was telling [the professor]* [Response] "I feel a certain kind of way because this is not a form of expression. This is who I am." *You know?* "A tattoo is equivalent to somebody sagging their pants." *And if you go into a work environment, of course that's not professional. Right? And so [the professor] was just like,* "Well how do you think we should deal with this?" *And I'm like:* "Can you confront it in the classroom?" *And the professor was like,* "Well I think you should probably talk to [the student] one-on-one" *and stuff like that.* [Encounter] *and, it was just kind of something that goes back to me. Like,* "Here! You deal with the issue." [Thought or interpretation] *and it's like,* "God! God, I'm tired of dealing with this issue!" [Feeling] *you know?* "You guys talk about cultural competence and you have no awareness...." [Impact] *so yeah. That's one (example).*

In observing the pattern or sequence of interactions that occurred in the above case example and in similar cases emerging from the transcripts, we identified what we labeled a "Racial Microaggressions Interaction Framework." This framework depicts the process a Black graduate social work student may progress through in encountering a racial microaggression:

Phase 1. The student encounters a particular interaction.

Phase 2. The student interprets the encounter as a racial microaggression.

Phase 3. The student experiences certain feelings or emotions associated with the encounter.

Phase 4. The student develops an intent to address the perceived racial microaggression.

Phase 5. The student responds according to her or his intent.

Phase 6. (Depending on how the response is met), the student thinks further about the long erterm impact—in Jasmine's case hopelessness about the cultural competence of faculty.

Risk and protective factors

Through our analysis of transcript data, we identified factors that potentially affect outcomes of students' encounters – both risk factors and protective factors. The instructor's response to Jasmine's request created a risk of further frustration and hopelessness. However, the focus group moderator thought to ask what response Jasmine would have preferred:

Moderator: *So in that case, how would you have wanted [the instructor] to confront the issue?*

Jasmine: *I would have wanted [the instructor] to confront it; not "Yeah! OK. That's right!" But ...to actually confront it. Like, if I was in the classroom with another professor who's African American—a specific professor that I—I love [that professor]; [that professor] is real cool. [That professor] would have said, "No! That's not right." And, I think it's because [the second professor] is African American and knows how we're feeling whereas this White professor—I don't think that [that professor] was aware of how the people in the classroom were feeling—well the African Americans particularly. And so, I just feel like we talk about cultural competence in this classroom and, yet, they are not really aware.*

Discussion

Given research confirming Black students' experiencing of racial microaggressions in academic settings, we proceeded from the assumption that social work students would not be immune from such experiences. We examined the question of how social work students defined racial microaggressions and what encounters with racial microaggressions in academic and surrounding domains were consistent with their definitions. Their responses, exemplified in the case example of Jasmine, led us to observe a sequence or pattern of interactions surrounding a social work student's encounter with a perceived racial microaggression. We labeled this phenomenon a *Racial Microaggressions Interaction Framework*, made up of six phases. The six phases do not always occur consecutively. For example, a feeling may seem to occur before the thought or interpretation. This may mean the feeling is so intense that the student isn't aware of having interpreted the event in a way that precipitated the feeling. Multiple encounters can occur within the same interaction or a response may be experienced as another racial microaggression.

In keeping with considerations of the external validity of the *Racial Microaggressions Interaction Framework*, the first author noted its similarity to Miller, Miller, Nunnally, and Wackman's (1991) use of the"awareness Wheel" as devised by Miller, Nunally, and Wackman (1975). This phenomenon, which had to do with relational conflicts, had five dimensions—sensing, thinking, feeling, wanting, and doing. It was used to help persons experiencing adverse relational interactions with understanding the source of a conflict. The idea was that understanding could provide the groundwork for problem-solving and change. One individual sensed (perceived) a problematic response on the part of the other, thought about or interpreted it, experienced certain feelings, developed a desire or "wanting" (intention) to address the problematic behavior, and responded (by doing or acting). Similar to our experience, Miller et al. observed that the recipient's response could constitute another problematic behavior, leading to an unsuccessful outcome and an exacerbation of the problem.

After identifying our *Racial Microaggressions Interaction Framework*, we discovered that Sue, Capodilupo, and Holder (2008) had described a similar phenomenon. From their focus groups with 13 self-identified Black/African American graduate students in a school of education, five domains were identified in participants' descriptions of racial microaggression encounters: incident, perception, reaction, interpretation, and consequence. As was the case in our findings, these researchers note the domains did not necessarily occur in sequential order.

The fact that these studies identified a phenomenon similar to that of our *Framework* supports the external validity of our work. However, it also means our findings are not unique.

Implications for teaching in social work

Miller, Miller, Nunnally, and Wackman (1991) suggest that the interactional patterns they identified can be used to change problematic relational processes. They encourage teaching couples to recognize the problematic sequence, to interrupt the process, and to communicate about it in a way that prevents an escalation of conflict. These processes are very important in managing difficult communication dialogues. However, a power imbalance can place Black students in predominantly White social work programs at a disadvantage in affecting outcomes. (See Sue, Capodilupo, Nadal, & Torino, 2008). Counseling psychology research on such effects in supervisor-supervisee relationships and outcomes, can be useful (Constantine & Sue, 2007).

Sue, Lin, Torino, Capodilupo, and Rivera (2009) encourage the use of knowledge about racial microaggressions and the different domains in which they are experienced to facilitate difficult dialogues in the classroom. They suggest strategies such as "legitimizing the discussion on race, validating feelings of the participants in class, willingness to accept a different racial reality from students of color, comfort in addressing race and racism, and using a direct approach in managing the discussion" (p.188). These suggestions coincide with what we labeled "protective factors." Unhelpful instructor strategies described by Sue et al. participants included "taking a passive approach, disengaging, or simply ignoring the dialogue" (p. 188).

The social work profession emphasizes cultural competence. We call attention to Jasmine's request that social work faculty be "culturally aware of what Black people are going through" and "of how Black people are feeling." Hollingsworth and Phillips (2016) provide one example of a graduate social work course designed to strengthen awareness of the history, culture, and practice of Black (African-descent) people from an affirmative perspective. References cited within the article may direct faculty members to other helpful resources.

Benefits and limitations

This study contributes to the production of knowledge of the nature and depth of racial microaggressions that occurred within one graduate social work program, as experienced by Black students. Implications for teaching have been proposed. Recruiting an all-Black focus group sample facilitated by Black peers may have increased the participants' candor. An entirely Black research team may have helped with designing the study and identifying themes and perspectives. The careful and thorough training of the moderators allowed the process to move smoothly. A possible limitation is the small sample. Participants may not have represented all possible experiences and perspectives. Research assistants who also participated in the second focus group may have brought a different perspective that otherwise may not have been introduced. This must be balanced by their desire to have their voices heard.

Conclusion

Our study demonstrates that a school of social work may not be immune from what has been described as a subtle and often invisible form of racism. The knowledge presented here suggests that non-Black social work students or faculty, through a lack of cultural knowledge and awareness, can contribute to an oppressive experience for Black students; that Black students, while struggling with the untoward effects of racially oppressive experiences, are often simultaneously struggling to correct them and improve outcomes in the process; that left unresolved, racial microaggressions contradict the mission and core values of the profession; that racial microaggressions detract from, rather than support the well-being of Black students; that allowing such an environment to persist ultimately fails to properly educate students for culturally competent social work practice; and finally, that the development of cultural competence is a complex and culturally individual process.

Note

1. Since undergraduate majors were not specified, it is possible that some African American undergraduates represented in the 18 studies were social work majors.

Funding

This work was supported by the Office of the Provost and Executive Vice President for Academic Affairs [TLTC Quick Wins Proposal QW#78].

References

Blume, A. W., Lovato, L. V., Thyken, B. N., & Denny, N. (2012). The relationship of microaggressions with alcohol use and anxiety among ethnic minority college students in a historically White institution. *Cultural Diversity and Ethnic Minority Psychology, 18*(1), 45–54.

Constantine, M. G., & Sue, D. W. (2007). Perceptions of racial microaggressions among Black supervisees in cross-racial dyads. *Journal of Counseling Psychology, 54*(2), 142.

Corbin, J., & Strauss, A. (1990). Grounded theory research: Procedures, canons, and evaluative criteria. *Qualitative Sociology, 13*(1), 3–21.

Corbin, J., & Strauss, A. (2008). *Basics of qualitative research* (3rd ed.). Thousand Oaks, CA: Sage.

Hollingsworth, L. D., & Phillips, F. B. (2016, December 15). Afrocentricity and social work education. *Journal of Human Behavior in the Social Work Environment*. Retrieved from http://www.tandfonline.com/eprint/vGCYqRyg4r43ecQmJHnK/full

Krueger, R. A. (1988). *Focus groups: A practical guide for applied research*. Newbury Park, CA: Sage Publications.

Miller, S., Nunally, E. W., &Wackman, D. B. & (1975). *Alive & Aware*: Improving Communication in Relationships. Minneapolis, MN: Interpersonal Communication Programs, Inc.

Miller, S., Miller, P., Nunnally, E. W., & Wackman, D. D. (1991). *Talking and listening together*. Couple communication one/Edition 1. Littleton, CO: Interpersonal Programs.

Morales, E. M. (2014). Intersectional impact: Black students and race, gender, and class microaggressions in higher education. *Race, Gender, and Class, 21*(3-4), 48–66.

Nadal, K. L., Wong, Y., Griffin, K. E., Davidoff, K., & Sriken, J. (2014). The adverse impact of racial microaggressions on college students' self-esteem. *Journal of College Student Development, 55*(5), 461–474.

Pierce, C. (1970). Offensive mechanisms. In: F. Barbour (Ed.), *The Black seventies* (pp. 265--282). Massachusetts, USA: Porter Sargent.

Robinson, D. M. (2012) The Perceived Relationship between Wellness and Microaggressions in African American and Latina American Female Doctoral Students in Counselor Education Programs (Doctoral dissertation).Dissertation, Georgia State University, 2012.) Retrieved from http://scholarworks.gsu.edu/cps_diss/68

Rodgers, S. T. (2015, August). Racism. *Encyclopedia of Social Work*, doi:10.1093/acrefore/9780199975839.013.1009

Smith, W. A., Allen, W. R., & Danley, L. L. (2007). Assume the position... you fit the description: Psychosocial experiences and racial battle fatigue among African American male college students. *American Behavioral Scientist, 55*(4), 551–578.

Solorzano, D., Ceja, M., & Yosso, T. (2000). Critical race theory, racial microaggressions and campus racial climate: The experiences of African American college students. *The Journal of Negro Education, 69,* 60–73.

Sue, D. W., Capodilupo, C. M., & Holder, A. M. B. (2008). Racial microaggressions in the life experience of Black Americans. *Professional Psychology: Research and Practice, 89*(3), 329–336.

Sue, D. W., Capodilupo, C. M., Nadal, K. L., & Torino, G. C. (2008). Racial microaggressions and the power to define reality. *American Psychologist, 63*(4), 277–279.

Sue, D. W., Capodilupo, C. M., Torino, G. C., Bucceri, J. M., Holder, A. M. B., Nadal, K. L., & Esquilin, M. (2007). Racial microaggressions in everyday life: Implications for clinical practice. *American Psychologist, 62*(4), 271–286.

Sue, D. W., Lin, A. I., Torino, G. C., Capodilupo, C. M., & Rivera, D. P. (2009). Racial microaggressions and difficult dialogues on race in the classroom. *Cultural Diversity and Ethnic Minority Psychology, 15*(2), 183–190.

Sue, D. W., Nadal, K. L., Capodilupo, A. I. L., Torino, G. C., & Rivera, D. P. (2008). Racial microaggressions against Black Americans: Implications for counseling. *Journal of Counseling & Development, 86,* 330–338.

Torres, L., Driscoll, M. W., & Burrow, A. L. (2010). Racial microaggressions and psychological functioning among highly achieving African Americans: A mixed-methods approach. *Journal of Social and Clinical Psychology, 29*(1), 1074–1099.

Wong, G., Derthick, A. O., David, E. J. R., Saw, A., & Okazaki, S. (2013). The what, the why, and the how: A review of racial microaggressions research in psychology. *Race and Social Problems, 6,* 181–200.

Index